Deleuze, Guattari, and the Problem of Transdisciplinarity

Also available at Bloomsbury

Deleuze and Guattari: Selected Writings, Kenneth Surin
Deleuze and Becoming, Samantha Bankston
Musical Encounters with Deleuze and Guattari, ed. by Pirkko Moisala, Taru Leppänen, Milla Tiainen, and Hanna Väätäinen
Bloomsbury's *Deleuze Encounters* series
Space after Deleuze, Arun Saldanha
Feminist Theory after Deleuze, Hannah Stark
Bloomsbury's *Schizoanalytic Applications* series
Deleuze and the Schizoanalysis of Feminism, ed. by Cheri Carr and Janae Sholtz
Deleuze and the Schizoanalysis of Religion, ed. by F. LeRon Shults and Lindsay Powell-Jones

Deleuze, Guattari, and the Problem of Transdisciplinarity

Edited by Guillaume Collett

BLOOMSBURY ACADEMIC
LONDON • NEW YORK • OXFORD • NEW DELHI • SYDNEY

BLOOMSBURY ACADEMIC
Bloomsbury Publishing Plc
50 Bedford Square, London, WC1B 3DP, UK
1385 Broadway, New York, NY 10018, USA
29 Earlsfort Terrace, Dublin 2, Ireland

BLOOMSBURY, BLOOMSBURY ACADEMIC and the Diana logo are
trademarks of Bloomsbury Publishing Plc

First published in Great Britain 2020
Paperback edition published 2021

Copyright © Guillaume Collett and Contributors, 2020

Guillaume Collett has asserted his right under the Copyright, Designs and Patents
Act, 1988, to be identified as Editor of this work.

For legal purposes the Acknowledgments on p. ix constitute
an extension of this copyright page.

Cover image © Jitendra Singh / Getty Images

All rights reserved. No part of this publication may be reproduced or transmitted
in any form or by any means, electronic or mechanical, including photocopying,
recording, or any information storage or retrieval system, without prior
permission in writing from the publishers.

Bloomsbury Publishing Plc does not have any control over, or responsibility for, any
third-party websites referred to or in this book. All internet addresses given in
this book were correct at the time of going to press. The author and publisher
regret any inconvenience caused if addresses have changed or sites have
ceased to exist, but can accept no responsibility for any such changes.

A catalogue record for this book is available from the British Library.

A catalog record for this book is available from the Library of Congress.

ISBN:	HB:	978-1-3500-7155-1
	PB:	978-1-3502-5954-6
	ePDF:	978-1-3500-7156-8
	eBook:	978-1-3500-7157-5

Typeset by Integra Software Services Pvt. Ltd.

To find out more about our authors and books visit www.bloomsbury.com
and sign up for our newsletters.

Contents

Contributors	vi
Acknowledgments	ix

	Introduction: Philosophy, Disciplinarity, and Transdisciplinarity in Deleuze and Guattari *Guillaume Collett*	1
1	Philosophy and History of Philosophy: Deleuze as a Trainee Guard of Philosophy's Epistemological Borders *Giuseppe Bianco*	15
2	Guattari, Transdisciplinarity, and the Experimental Transformation of Research *Andrew Goffey*	35
3	The Semiotics of De-Modeling: Peirce and Guattari on the Diagram *Guillaume Collett* and *Chryssa Sdrolia*	47
4	Bachelard and Deleuze on and with Experimental Science, Experimental Philosophy, and Experimental Music *Iain Campbell*	73
5	Diagrammatic Transdisciplinarity: Thought outside Discipline *Kamini Vellodi*	105
6	Hermeticism instead of Hermeneutics: The History of Philosophy Conceived of as Mannerist Portraiture *Sjoerd van Tuinen*	132
7	*Try Again. Fail Again. Fail Better*: The Role of Literature in Deleuze's Transcendental Empiricism *Emma Ingala*	160
8	*Deleuze, Practical Philosophy*: The Trans/disciplinary Basis of the Deleuzian Conception of Immanence *Guillaume Collett*	182
9	Architectonics without Foundations *Edward Willatt*	214
10	Independence, Alliance, and Echo: Deleuze on the Relationship between Philosophy, Science, and Art *Gavin Rae*	237

Index	262

Contributors

Giuseppe Bianco is a postdoctoral researcher at the Universidade de São Paulo. His more recent books include *Après Bergson. Portrait de groupe avec philosophe* (Presses universitaires de France, 2015) and *Georges Politzer, le concret et sa signification: psychologie, philosophie et politique* (Hermann, 2016).

Iain Campbell is an Edinburgh-based independent researcher and educator. He has written on topics across philosophy, music, sound studies, and art theory for publications including *Parallax, Sound Studies,* and *Deleuze Studies*. He received a PhD from the Centre for Research in Modern European Philosophy, Kingston University London, in 2016, with a thesis exploring experimental practices of music and philosophy in John Cage and Gilles Deleuze. He has lectured in philosophy, politics, and art at the University of Brighton and is on the editorial board of *Eventual Aesthetics*.

Guillaume Collett is a research fellow in the Centre for Critical Thought at the University of Kent. He works on twentieth-century French philosophy, psychoanalytic theory, and contemporary political thought. He is the author of *The Psychoanalysis of Sense: Deleuze and the Lacanian School* (Edinburgh University Press, 2016) and coedits the journal *La Deleuziana*.

Andrew Goffey is Associate Professor and Director of the Centre for Critical Theory at the University of Nottingham. He is the author (with Matthew Fuller) of *Evil Media* (MIT Press, 2012) and the editor (with Éric Alliez) of *The Guattari Effect* (Bloomsbury, 2011) and (with Roland Faber) *The Allure of Things* (Bloomsbury, 2014). He is also the translator of numerous works in the fields of philosophy and critical theory, including *In Catastrophic Times, The Virgin Mary and the Neutrino* and *Capitalist Sorcery* by Isabelle Stengers, *Powers of Time* by David Lapoujade, and *Schizoanalytic Cartographies* and *Lines of Flight* by Félix Guattari.

Emma Ingala is Senior Lecturer in the Department of Logic and Theoretical Philosophy and Vice-Dean of Academic Organization in the Faculty of Philosophy at the Universidad Complutense de Madrid (UCM), Spain. She specializes in post-structuralist thought, political anthropology, feminism, and psychoanalysis. She is the principal investigator for the international research project "Critical Thinking and Literary and Artistic Digital Representations of the Crisis in Europe and the Mediterranean," a member of the research group "Metaphysics, Critique, and Politics" and the Institute for Feminist Research at UCM, and coeditor of the journal *LOGOS*. Her recent publications include coediting (with Gavin Rae) the volumes *Subjectivity and the Political: Contemporary Perspectives* (Routledge, 2018) and *The Meanings of Violence: From Critical Theory to Biopolitics* (Routledge, 2019).

Gavin Rae is Conex Marie Skłodowska-Curie Experienced Research Fellow at the Universidad Carlos III de Madrid, Spain, where he is the principal investigator for the research project "Sovereignty and Law: Between Ethics and Politics." He specializes in post-Kantian philosophy with particular emphasis on ethics, sociopolitical philosophy, and theories of subjectivity. He is the author of *Realizing Freedom: Hegel, Sartre, and the Alienation of Human Being* (Palgrave Macmillan, 2011), *Ontology in Heidegger and Deleuze* (Palgrave Macmillan, 2014), *The Problem of Political Foundations in Carl Schmitt and Emmanuel Levinas* (Palgrave Macmillan, 2016); and the coeditor (with Emma Ingala) of *Subjectivity and the Political: Contemporary Perspectives* (Routledge, 2018) and *The Meanings of Violence: From Biopolitics to Critical Theory* (Routledge, 2019).

Chryssa Sdrolia is Research Associate in the School of Social, Historical & Literary Studies at the University of Portsmouth. She has coedited the volume "Deleuze and Philosophical Practice" for *Deleuze Studies* (2013) and has written on Charles S. Peirce's semiotics, post-structuralism, and pragmatism.

Sjoerd van Tuinen is Associate Professor of Philosophy at Erasmus University Rotterdam. He is the editor of several books, including *Peter Sloterdijk. Ein Profil* (Fink Verlag, 2006), *Deleuze and the Fold. A Critical Reader* (Palgrave Macmillan, 2010), *Speculative Art Histories* (Edinburgh University Press, 2017), and *Art History after Deleuze and Guattari* (Leuven UP, 2017). Van Tuinen is currently finalizing his monograph on Deleuze and mannerism called *Matter, Manner, Idea*.

Kamini Vellodi is Lecturer in Contemporary Art Theory and Practice at Edinburgh College of Art, University of Edinburgh. She is the author of *Tintoretto's Difference. Deleuze, Diagrammatics and Art History* (Bloomsbury, 2018) and a number of articles on continental philosophy of art, the philosophy of art history, and sixteenth-century visual art. She is Series Editor of *Refractions. At the Borders of Art History and Philosophy* (Edinburgh University Press), and an editorial board member of the journal *Art History*.

Edward Willatt is the author of *Kant, Deleuze and Architectonics* (Bloomsbury, 2010) and coeditor (with Matt Lee) of *Thinking between Deleuze and Kant* (Bloomsbury, 2009). He works on the concept of architectonics in the history of philosophy and in relation to contemporary debates concerning interdisciplinarity and transdisciplinarity.

Acknowledgments

This book emerges (belatedly) from a conference co-organized with Masayoshi Kosugi on "Deleuze, Philosophy, Transdisciplinarity," held at Goldsmiths, University of London, in February 2012, and co-organized by the University of Kent with help from the AHRC. This subsequently led to a 2013 issue of *Deleuze Studies* on "Deleuze and Philosophical Practice," coedited with Kosugi and Chryssa Sdrolia. The approach taken by this volume stems from these two research efforts and so thanks are due first of all to Masayoshi and Chryssa, who were both central to the shaping of this research project and who provided much camaraderie in the process, as well as to Marjorie Gracieuse, Craig Lundy, Daniela Voss, Iain MacKenzie, Les Back, Jean-Claude Dumoncel, Patrice Maniglier, Éric Alliez, Sjoerd van Tuinen, and Ian Buchanan, who offered helpful suggestions and advice, discussion, textual commentary, institutional support, and drafts of unpublished work. At Bloomsbury, particular thanks are due to Liza Thompson and Frankie Mace, as well as to the three anonymous book proposal reviewers for their valuable input. Last but not least, I would like to thank the volume's contributors for their enthusiasm, skill, and patience throughout the course of this project. The authors threw themselves into the task of wrestling with the problems posed by our initial call for papers and by the subsequent evolution of the project in turn developing analyses exceeding the initial problematic. And additional gratitude is owed to Martine, John and Seb Collett, and Krista Bonello Rutter Giappone for their encouragement and support particularly during the final stages of the editing process.

Introduction

Philosophy, Disciplinarity, and Transdisciplinarity in Deleuze and Guattari

Guillaume Collett

It might surprise even seasoned readers of Deleuze and Guattari to find the following statement in the blurb written by them for the French edition of *What Is Philosophy?* (1991): "Philosophy is not interdisciplinary."[1] Rather, as they explain, philosophy is a "whole" discipline with an irreducible content and methods, and if it does engage with other disciplines it is by means of lines of "resonance" or as they put it in the text, "interference" (Deleuze and Guattari 1994: 216–17). However, rather than constituting a late betrayal of an earlier position, as is sometimes argued—such as the one found in their 1980 text *A Thousand Plateaus*, notorious for the vast array of disciplines it draws on and for its high degree of cross-disciplinary experimentation—this late position, at least for Deleuze, can be shown to stem from his earliest writings on philosophy.[2] This long-term coexistence of two seemingly antagonistic perspectives coinhabiting Deleuze and Guattari's writings necessitates closer scrutiny and examination, and this provides one of the key starting points for the present volume. Moreover, this volume will demonstrate in different ways that adopting a strong disciplinary stance regarding philosophy far from prohibits the development of a theory of cross- or trans-disciplinary articulation. Indeed, it calls for it. This volume shows in varying ways that affirming some kind of disciplinary irreducibility provides disciplines with a deeper grounding in their outside, or in their other, than if they are considered able to unproblematically coexist on the same "inter-disciplinary" or "multi-disciplinary" plane, comprised of self-identical disciplines *only then* opening on to one another (through interrelationality or through multiplication, respectively). In short, this volume argues by and large that it is *because* disciplines are irreducible to one another and unable to directly communicate that their differences are not flattened out but able to cut across and creatively nourish disciplinarity from within.

The benefits of bringing the problem of transdisciplinarity to the fore when considering the work of Deleuze and Guattari are at least twofold. Firstly, it enables us to better appreciate the nature of their "philosophy." Insufficient attention has been paid to the clear evidence that Deleuze's philosophical problematic cannot be reduced to the positing of disciplinary objects internal to philosophical intentionality—such as subjects, objects, substances, monads, Forms, and so on[3]—but rather that it superposes itself onto a transdisciplinary problematic spanning the disciplines, from which it then extracts, nevertheless, a specifically philosophical content relative to the disciplinary milieu surveyed. To put it rather schematically, if philosophy for Deleuze is ultimately a "virtual" philosophy (Alliez 2004: 85), it is thus ontologically incomplete or only half-finished, produced as the conceptual counter-actualization of extra-philosophical domains. Given that being for Deleuze is historically contingent becoming—understood as a counter-actualization *of the present* (not only a *counter-actualization* of the present)—his ontology necessitates that being be contingent on the extra-philosophical and worldly. Be that as it may, even as contingent in this way, philosophy nonetheless does not representationally model itself on the actual but rather conceptually expresses an irreducibly philosophical object (a virtual or incorporeal event), which it extracts from the actual. Deleuze signals this, for instance, in the 1994 preface to the American edition of *Difference and Repetition*, writing that he needed to draw on extra-philosophical domains to formulate his key concept of "*different/ciation*" (Deleuze 2007: 302). But this concept is nonetheless irreducibly philosophical insofar as it expresses a conceptual event (understood in *What Is Philosophy?* as the remit of specifically philosophical activity), namely pure difference.[4]

The history of philosophy is saturated with philosophies looking outside themselves to complete their autonomous practices. Yet few philosophies are as "philosophically" minimalistic or ontologically incomplete as Deleuze and Guattari's and thus as radically immanent to their nonphilosophical outside (which is not to say identical to it). Co-articulating these two halves—for Deleuze and Guattari, the actual and the virtual or history and becoming—requires a delicate (trans)disciplinary balance so as to neither, on the one hand, overdetermine philosophical activity with the fixed possibilities materially undergirding counter-actualization, nor, on the other hand, dis-anchor ontology from the world. Focusing on this intertwining of the virtual and the worldly helps, for one, offset the (often Badiou-inspired) critique that Deleuze and Guattari's ontology remains ultimately transcendent, preestablished, and/or disengaged from worldly concerns. Rather, ontological incompleteness shifts the focus to the practice conditioning philosophy's access to being. What is this practice? Deleuze noted in a 1990 interview that his and Guattari's political philosophy hinges most fundamentally on an analysis of the history of capitalism's structural mutations (Deleuze and Negri 1995: 171). If their philosophy is to be seen as a philosophy (in excess) of the present (and thus of capitalism) this would suggest that, in their work, political economy provides the basis for a kind of transdisciplinary and transmutational pivot between history and becoming.[5] Alternatively, we could point to an aesthetic—or, as Guattari would later put it, "ethico-aesthetic"—practice of the lived contingent on (if creatively outstripping) its concrete milieus, given the inseparability of collective thought and action from sensory territorial signs plugged into the real (the point of transmutation). In short, an emphasis on the essential incompleteness of Deleuze and Guattari's ontology allows a greater emphasis to be rightly placed on history (and geography), practice and contingency or the concrete, and on problematizing or experimental and creative processes, all of which gather the nonphilosophical into the heart of the philosophical.

Secondly, as well as inviting a multifaceted reappraisal of their ontology, reframing Deleuze and Guattari's work through the notion of transdisciplinarity can provide resources to critique and methodologically refine the often-unquestioned appropriation of their work by inter-, multi-, and trans-disciplinary research. When Guattari explicitly engages the problematic of transdisciplinarity in a 1991 article, writing that "transdisciplinarity must become transversality" (Guattari 2015), he provides us with the definitive key to understanding his equally theoretical and practical approach to transdisciplinary relations—namely, through the notion of transversality, which is to say by means of a concrete analysis of the mutually informing relations between institutions and collective thought and action. However, as Andrew Goffey points out in his contribution to the volume, Guattari's theoretico-practical constructs are more often than not decontextualized and reified as preformed concepts unproblematically applied across a myriad of disciplines. The same goes for much of Deleuze and Guattari's joint work, and Deleuze's solo writings. In short, while their work has been thoroughly incorporated into the theoretical humanities and social sciences, less attention has been paid to the methodological specifics of this process. This is not to claim, of course, that their work is simply "not interdisciplinary," as they provocatively write, but rather that more attention must be paid to exactly *how* their work is to be engaged across disciplines, precisely because this kind of engagement *precedes* the very ontology and philosophical conceptuality being supposedly imported (if not determining it unidirectionally).

Furthermore, Deleuze and Guattari's work provides the means to critically address the very presuppositions and limitations of extant cross-disciplinary research practices themselves—presuppositions and limitations, which surely find their way to varying degrees into the cross-disciplinary appropriation of Deleuze and Guattari's own work today—and moreover to find more dynamic alternatives to them. Turning to mainstream transdisciplinarity, this less than fifty-year-old framework consolidated itself during the 1990s into an approach designed to find practical, policy-oriented solutions to "life-world" societal problems afflicting advanced globalized societies, from climate change to implementing continuous learning and development programs.[6] Responding to the growing interconnectedness and complexity of the contemporary world, the general idea behind this strain of transdisciplinarity became that disciplines must reorient their focus away from their disciplinary objects (without necessarily negating their irreducibility) to transdisciplinary problems ultimately spanning the globe (see Maniglier, forthcoming). However, as Osborne (2015) notes, while in some respects constituting an advance on the uses typically made of disciplinary knowledge (and, we can add, despite sharing with Deleuze a theoretical investment in the notion of problem), this mainstream approach to transdisciplinarity has become so "straightjacketed" by policy as to now be indistinguishable from it and thus from today's "corporate-managerial" hegemony (16).[7]

Deleuze and Guattari's work can be critically mobilized to show how, as with the social and human sciences during the mid-twentieth century,[8] and structuralism during the 1950s–1960s, contemporary transdisciplinarity amounts to yet another example of a "rival" or pretender to philosophy, seeking to lay transdisciplinary foundations immanent to the fields of knowledge but ultimately re-disciplinarizing and refounding itself on a transcendent element (here, capital, and in the previous cases, "man" or the "social," and the "signifier"), which takes precedence over the specificities of the disciplines it ordinates (1994: 10). Arguably, Deleuze and Guattari are not concerned with preserving philosophy's singular, "unrivaled" status merely for the sake of disciplinary integrity but rather to keep philosophical critique alive—particularly in a radically immanentist (as well as anticapitalist and nonhuman) form—and founding a genuine transdisciplinarity is part and parcel of this approach. It is interesting to note that for a text primarily concerned with establishing disciplinary irreducibility, *What*

Is Philosophy?'s year of publication (1991) contextualizes it within the formative years of transdisciplinarity's consolidation and policy-oriented direction, which is to say during the early, idealistic, "post-ideological" years of "globalization," in the wake of the fall of the USSR. Highlighting this conjuncture makes the political dimension of their position that "Philosophy is not interdisciplinary" more readily apparent, philosophy functioning, we could say, to counter-actualize the collaborative spirit of the times: globalist transnationalism centered on a corporatist "free-market" consensus, combined with expanded social and technological bases for global "communication." Indeed, in an influential text from this period, Gibbons et al. (1994) couch contemporary transdisciplinarity in terms of "the expansion of the market for knowledge and the increased marketability of science" (46), in relation to which we can also situate the later exponential growth of the highly marketable and global Deleuze studies industry.

In this light, capital could be considered as functioning as a kind of "rhizome" or vector of transdisciplinarity and indeed can be seen as semiotically-materially undergirding the kind of knowledge-production Deleuze and Guattari's own *Capitalism and Schizophrenia* project would earlier develop (as an ontology of the capitalist present) as a means both to concentrate its historical conditions and also to critically and creatively rework them so as to form an alternative model of transdisciplinary inquiry. Guattari hints at this in an interview from 1972, commenting on the inadequacy of psychoanalysis and political science considered as independent disciplines (as well as ethnology and linguistics), when attempting to account for the irruption of May '68 in France (Deleuze, Guattari et al. 2004: 235-36). This is an event that Guattari himself would later argue attested to the historically unprecedented socio-psychic penetration of capital during the postwar years (society and psyche as a factory) (Guattari and Negri 1990), which by insinuating itself into every pore of society and psyche during this period would also reorient their relations to one another in terms of this common element.[9] Guattari adds that "the point of calling into question the division of the various disciplines […] is not the dissolution of these sciences. The point is to refit these sciences so they better measure up to their object of inquiry" (Deleuze, Guattari et al. 2004: 236).

*

Using the lens of a complex trans/disciplinarity, this volume aims to reframe Deleuze and Guattari's work in order to help clarify the workings of their thought and its trans/disciplinary basis, as well as its contribution to questions of transdisciplinarity more generally, in philosophy and beyond. Although a range of disciplines and disciplinary relations are engaged in this volume, it is this reframing itself and its many facets that are of central concern, rather than drawing up an exhaustive typology of every one of the many disciplinary articulations that their work treats.

Turning now to the volume's content, Giuseppe Bianco's chapter "Philosophy and History of Philosophy: Deleuze as a Trainee Guard of Philosophy's Epistemological Borders" opens the volume with an account of the genesis of Deleuze's "exceptionalist" position in the history of philosophy during the 1950s. According to this position, philosophy as a discipline is considered epistemologically irreducible to psychological, historical, or social factors. Yet, in reconstructing in detail these very influences on Deleuze's early philosophical apprenticeship, Bianco thereby questions two of Deleuze and Guattari's key claims in *What Is Philosophy?*: philosophy's epistemological irreducibility to the extra-philosophical and the suggestion opening the book that the question "what is philosophy?" "can perhaps be posed only late in life" (Deleuze and Guattari 1994: 1). Bianco begins with an overview of the French intellectual scene in the immediate aftermath of the Second World War, showing how history of philosophy in France sought to preserve the identity of its genre when faced with attempts by the historical and social sciences to dethrone philosophy as "synthesis of the totality of knowledge." This would culminate in the works of two of Deleuze's teachers during this period, Ferdinand Alquié and Martial Gueroult, who both considered philosophy to be—as Alquié puts it—independent from "material or social causes." Moreover, Bianco shows that from Alquié, Deleuze would derive an understanding of philosophical systems according to which the "existential dimension of philosophizing" is nonetheless essential to their genesis, a position Gueroult rejected emphasizing instead a system's synchronic logic as irreducible framework for solving contingent problems. Bianco argues that Deleuze attempted to form during this period an unstable synthesis of both teachers' epistemological positions, which would extend to Deleuze's works from the 1960s, and that despite some discrepancies in their approach, both teachers ultimately provided Deleuze with a strong conception of philosophy's disciplinary irreducibility.

The next two chapters provide a counterbalance to this position by shifting to Guattari's engagement with the problematic of transdisciplinarity. Andrew Goffey's "Guattari, Transdisciplinarity, and the Experimental Transformation of Research" singles out Guattari's practice of research as key to understanding his relation to questions of transdisciplinarity. What this practice amounts to above all, Goffey argues, is a viewpoint on knowledge production bypassing theory/practice distinctions on both sides, which Goffey shows was informed above all by Guattari's formative engagement with institutional psychoanalysis. On the one hand, this viewpoint enabled Guattari to develop a machinic and transversal critique of theory, particularly its structuralist variant, on the basis that he considered thought as the epiphenomenon of institutional and collective practices of enunciation. On the other hand, this led Guattari to disregard practice in itself as foundational, at least when considered as discretely separate from theory (for instance as the empirical verification of a hypothesis), given the pragmatic creativity inherent to collective and institutional modes of thought. This approach firmly renders Guattari's research practice as experimental in the nonscientific sense. Goffey explains how this in turn underpins Guattari's later engagement with the framework of transdisciplinary research, particularly emphasizing his 1991 article "Transdisciplinarity Must Become Transversality." If this framework shared Guattari's concern with using theory to effectuate practical change, Guattari nonetheless sought to push further its blurring of the theory/practice distinction (via his work on transversality) so as to denaturalize its ontology and reorient it along ecosophical lines, ultimately to serve a more politically radical project. Goffey thereby demonstrates that it is precisely this transversal practice of research—understood properly as institutionally embedded and collective thought and action—that risks being lost in the secondary literature, not least literature on transdisciplinarity, as long as we mistake Guattari's constructs for contextually fixed and preestablished concepts.

In "The Semiotics of De-Modeling: Peirce and Guattari on the Diagram," Guillaume Collett and Chryssa Sdrolia turn to the notion of diagram, initially derived from the semiotician Charles Sanders Peirce, to further explore both Guattari's and Peirce's pragmatic critiques of the concept or, more specifically in this chapter, the model. Collett and Sdrolia argue that both Peirce and Guattari, if in differing ways and to serve different ends, converge on a critique of the notion of model, if the latter is taken to mean a theoretical framework severed from the contextual conditions of its production. Collett and Sdrolia focus on structural linguistics as one of the key models threatening immanence in Peirce's and Guattari's respective fields of investigation: semiotics and psychoanalysis. In the case of Peirce, his discovery of a process of semiosis at work in any domain (to the extent that the world is constantly speaking in its own signs) and contextually immanent to that domain is contrasted with Saussure's conception of signification according to which structure transcends its applications. In the case of Guattari, it is shown how his development of an alternative—semiotic and not structuralist—psychoanalysis to the one established by the Lacanian school again centers on the latter's overreliance on a broadly Saussurian model of language, which for Guattari compromises the Lacanian school's ability to conceive of the immanent workings of the unconscious. In both cases, the notion of diagram—developed by Peirce and reinvented by Guattari—is shown to function as a machine for de-modeling structures, thereby taking on a transdisciplinary function as long as this function is itself not considered in terms of a model separate from its contextual applications, which is to say from questions of practice, process, experimentation, and creation.

Iain Campbell's chapter, "Bachelard and Deleuze on and with Experimental Science, Experimental Philosophy, and Experimental Music," extends Goffey's concern with the notion of the experimental in Guattari, and in its relation to questions of transdisciplinarity, by using this notion to engage the works of not only Deleuze but also Gaston Bachelard and John Cage. Distinguishing the "experimental" (open-ended contexts productive of the new) from the "experiment" (controlled environments for testing predefined hypotheses), yet maintaining the echo of the one in the other, Campbell puts forward the experiment/al as a candidate for a genuinely transdisciplinary research method, which is to say one "establishing the reciprocal meeting of divergent disciplinary systems," eschewing both meta-disciplinarity and relativism. Firstly, in the fields of philosophy and science, this allows us to reconsider any perceived opposition between Bachelard's (*experiment*al) philosophy of science and Deleuze's (experiment*al*) history of philosophy. Bachelard offsets the "scientistic foreclosure" of the experimental by making the experiment hinge on historical and transcendental "problems," which Campbell considers particularly influential for the Deleuze of the 1960s and beyond. Turning to music, Campbell argues that likewise, any neat separation between an American "experimental" tradition and a European avant-garde more concerned with the "careful management of the parameters of sound," including through the use of sound technologies, is problematized by the work of Cage. Drawing on the insights of this case study, Campbell suggests that in separating out philosophy, science, and art, Deleuze and Guattari's *What Is Philosophy?* should not be considered as simply turning its back on the transdisciplinarity of the Deleuzian experiment/al but rather as defending science's capacity for creativity. Campbell considers this necessary to resist the experiment/al's subsumption under a technocratic model of transdisciplinarity serving the neoliberal state, proposing instead a more progressive approach to technological innovation and to practice more generally.

Kamini Vellodi's chapter, "Diagrammatic Transdisciplinarity: Thought outside Discipline," begins with a historical overview of the emergence of disciplines and of disciplinary relations, covering the differences between inter-, multi-, and trans-disciplinarity. While it is often considered that the "most politically and theoretically adventurous and engaged practice, occurs at the borders of disciplines," it is necessary to further stipulate that such "border work" can only retain its radical potential so long as it does not in turn stabilize as an institutionalized norm. Thus, what is no less crucial than the exterior frontier of a discipline is its internal "zone of turbulence" disrupting a discipline's normalization from within. It is this approach that Vellodi argues is at work in Deleuzo-Guattarian transdisciplinarity, which centers on an attempt to wrest thought away from disciplinarity as such, rather than merely to range across or between disciplines. Vellodi shows how this conception of transdisciplinarity emerged from Guattari's work on transversality and on the diagram, as well as how the diagram would take center stage in Deleuze and Guattari's joint work and Deleuze's later solo work. The diagram is shown to function by articulating signs that are material, productive, and asignifying, putting thought in contact with its disruptive and creative outside, and with the outside of disciplinarity as such, through a practice that "overcomes disciplinary autonomy." This outside is further explicated in terms of pure, nonfigurative sensation, considered as thought's transdisciplinary and transcendental genetic element. For Vellodi, this means that "all thought is artistic" and that art is not confined to its disciplinary localization, despite being defined by Deleuze and Guattari at times as the discipline that thinks through sensation. Transdisciplinarity in Deleuze and Guattari is thus considered as a means of responding to "real encounters" manifested through sensation, which both disrupt disciplinary regulation and challenge the contemporary mainstream understanding of transdisciplinarity.

The next two chapters continue to explore art's role in mediating between thought and its experiential outside, but with more specific regard to philosophy in particular. In "Hermeticism instead of Hermeneutics: The History of Philosophy Conceived of as Mannerist Portraiture," Sjoerd van Tuinen examines how Deleuze's solo work in the history of philosophy can be understood in terms of a "transmedial transfer" of particularly mannerist procedures from the arts to philosophy. Van Tuinen argues that Deleuze's expressionist (and antirepresentationalist) approach to reading other philosophers and thinkers—according to which a productive difference is introduced within this process exceeding the identificatory fixity of the author-function—employs a specifically mannerist set of devices to achieve this. A number of key mannerist devices are singled out as serving this purpose in Deleuze's work, stretching across literature, music, painting, theater, and cinema. Collectively, for van Tuinen, they amount to a methodology that can be termed a "mannerist art of portraiture." A mannerist, which is to say an expressive and thus immanent, method of thinking, reading, and writing allows the becomings of the "indeterminate and heterogenetic forces" or matters of expression worked with to not be curtailed in the name of fidelity to the "original" but determinately and creatively drawn out. Van Tuinen thus shows that mannerism provides an immanent Deleuzian methodology, which can be considered in a way as itself rooted in art, despite immanence being seemingly determined as solely philosophical in *What Is Philosophy?*. Indeed, van Tuinen proposes that the distinction established in the latter text between philosophical concepts and the "plane" of immanence on which their expressivity is inscribed is necessary precisely because concepts' coherence is not itself conceptual but "material and practical," which is to say "nonphilosophical" and in a way aesthetic.

In "*Try Again. Fail Again. Fail Better*: The Role of Literature in Deleuze's Transcendental Empiricism," Emma Ingala homes further in on the essential, or internally constitutive, relation between philosophy and its aesthetic, nonphilosophical outside, focusing specifically on the role played by literature in this regard in the pre-Guattarian Deleuze of the 1960s. Ingala argues that the walls conceptual, which is to say philosophical, thought runs up against attest not to its failure but to its success. In reaching a genuine paradox or conceptual impasse, thought reaches not only its discursive and conceptual limit but also its point of greatest ontological insight, its point of (non-)access ("failing better") to what in Deleuze's early ontology is a play of difference and repetition always exceeding the movement of the concept. The chapter frames this discussion both in terms of Deleuze's identification of a transcendental-empirical domain of real, and not merely possible, experience (that of pure difference), and secondly through the Platonic aporia. In both cases, it is shown that Deleuze and Plato have had to turn to literature and myth, respectively, at key points in the elaboration of their philosophies in order to effectuate a final conversion to being or to thought's outside. Moreover, Ingala shows that Kant himself ventured into this nonphilosophical terrain internal to philosophy, his recounted nightmares bearing witness to an unruly, uncategorizable world he unconsciously perceived. Deleuze will reverse yet recuperate all these insights by prioritizing failure's movement of differentiation away from (and thus toward) success over its neat partition. Ingala argues that, with respect to this, literature's "power of fiction" is considered to be the fact that it "will not be taken for a dogmatic affirmation, [it] will not stabilize the object into a conceptual identity," thereby expressing a real experience.

The next chapter shifts from a consideration of philosophy's aesthetic outside to a concern with philosophy's political, and more generally practical outside, further engaging points raised by van Tuinen regarding the "practical coherence" of concepts in Deleuze. In *"Deleuze, Practical Philosophy*: The Trans/disciplinary Basis of the Deleuzian Conception of Immanence," Guillaume Collett provides a reading of Deleuze's conception of philosophical immanence emphasizing its basis in Spinoza's practical philosophy. Collett begins by addressing what a specifically philosophical conception of immanence amounts to, for Deleuze, showing how immanence implicates philosophy in extra-philosophical processes, but also how this immanence is nonetheless contingent on a constructive practice, be it philosophical or otherwise. It is then shown how such an approach stems in Deleuze's work from his 1960s engagement with Spinoza. Collett argues that Deleuze's "expressionist" reinvention of Spinozist metaphysics should be understood in terms of an attempt to develop a new conception of immanence that is "immanent" to its contingent construction by a practice of the concept. This is examined through an analysis of Deleuze's reading of Spinoza's three kinds of knowledge. In the final section, it is suggested that if Deleuze's "expressionist" model of specifically philosophical, which is to say conceptual, immanence was later critiqued by Deleuze and Guattari, who sought in *Capitalism and Schizophrenia* to account for thought and action through a transdisciplinary approach they termed "diagrammatic," one can identify a final late stage in their political philosophy in which philosophical disciplinarity (what Bianco refers to in his chapter as its "exceptionalism") is repoliticized to counter the diagram's embeddedness in relations of power. Collett claims that if the sociopolitical diagram provides the transdisciplinary hinge between disciplines and their outsides (namely chaos), philosophy's practical and political function, for Deleuze, consists in counter-actualizing this diagram.

The final two chapters put forward models through which to assess the strengths and weaknesses of Deleuzo-Guattarian transdisciplinarity. Edward Willatt's chapter, "Architectonics without Foundations," shows how in extending and reformulating architectonics, understood as the "attempt to provide the foundation and hierarchical organization of the disciplines of knowledge," Deleuze and Guattari transform architectonics into a genuinely transdisciplinary framework, which is to say a nonhierarchical one (un-)founded on chaos itself. Willatt begins with an analysis of the architectonic found in Kant's work, showing how it sets out "principles which must govern [disciplines'] relations with matter," founding disciplines on a transdisciplinary a priori framework. While, for Willatt, Deleuze and Guattari's work shares with Kant the ambition of "setting out the principles of a method that fully realizes what is important in our encounters with the world," a method they will term rhizomatics, their approach also differs significantly. In particular, the rhizome rejects any supplementary dimension that would orientate it from without, enabling it to be immanent to its object. Turning to *What Is Philosophy?*, Willatt demonstrates how Deleuze and Guattari will seek to (un-)found the disciplines on chaos, extending the method of the rhizome through "geophilosophy" understood as a deterritorialized rootlessness. What this method allows for is a de-hierarchization of the disciplines, given that each disciplinary grouping studied (philosophy, sciences, arts) distinguishes itself from chaos through irreducible means. The rhizome (now called the "Thought-brain") spans the disciplines to the extent that each of these disciplinary groupings manifests an irreducible immanence to its object, and relative degrees of openness to the chaos un-founding them, preventing both a return to a supplementary meta-disciplinary dimension and the privileging of one discipline over another less well-founded one.

The final chapter, Gavin Rae's "Independence, Alliance, and Echo: Deleuze on the Relationship between Philosophy, Science, and Art," provides a critical reading of the epistemological and ontological basis of Deleuzo-Guattarian transdisciplinarity. If Bianco shows how Deleuze's apprenticeship in philosophy appears to contradict his own claim that philosophy is irreducible to extra-philosophical influence, Rae considers Deleuze's 1960s ontology to potentially clash with his and Guattari's later argument that philosophy, science, and art must be epistemologically distinguished as irreducible disciplines. Rae contends that if, according to Deleuze's *Difference and Repetition*, difference is ontologically prior to its relata, and to thought, then any separation between disciplines appears to be, at best, secondary to or derived from a philosophical ontology and, at worst, absolute (barring the possibility of transdisciplinary encounter), both of which would appear to annul the possibility that Deleuze and Guattari's approach is genuinely transdisciplinary. Although Rae leaves open the question of whether or not this constitutes a genuine problem for Deleuzo-Guattarian transdisciplinarity, he affirms that framing the debate in such a way draws attention to a key and under-acknowledged tension. After providing an overview of Deleuze and Guattari's understanding of philosophical, scientific, and artistic activity, as presented in *What Is Philosophy?*, Rae points out that this above-mentioned tension manifests itself in the three modes of transdisciplinary interference Deleuze develops, and particularly in the difference between "extrinsic" (alliance) and "intrinsic" (echo) interference. These are discussed through comparisons with Karen Barad's distinction between "inter-action" and "intra-action," and Sartre's opposition between pre-reflective and reflective consciousness. For Rae, intrinsic interference would potentially provide the most fruitful model of transdisciplinarity because it "overcomes [disciplines'] difference in kind," such that "the content of the various disciplines infiltrates and shapes the content of the others," epistemologically dovetailing with Deleuze's differential ontology.

This volume does not arrive at an overall consensus regarding Deleuzo-Guattarian transdisciplinarity, but several shared themes and congruent perspectives present themselves as well as a few points of disagreement. Hopefully, this will provide some building blocks and open avenues for future research, as well as offering some critical resources for engaging today's mainstream transdisciplinary research framework.

Notes

1. The blurb is reproduced here: http://www.leseditionsdeminuit.fr/livre-Qu_est_ce_que_la_philosophie__-2024-1-1-0-1.html (last accessed July 08, 2018).
2. See for instance Deleuze's 1967 comment regarding the "specificity of philosophy" (in Deleuze et al. 2004: 106).
3. See Ferdinand Alquié's intervention in Deleuze et al. 2004: 105–06.
4. We see this in the definition of "problematic Ideas"—the "structuralist" (see Maniglier, forthcoming), transdisciplinary basis of *Difference and Repetition*, developed in its fourth chapter—as "structure-event-sense" complexes (Deleuze 2004: 240).
5. Pace Badiou (2009), this seems to give politics a precise and fundamental role within Deleuze and Guattari's oeuvre, despite not appearing as a standalone discipline alongside philosophy, science, and art in *What Is Philosophy?*
6. See Osborne 2015: 10.
7. For further discussion of these themes, particularly in connection to twentieth-century French philosophy, see P. Osborne, S. Sandford, and É. Alliez, eds, 2015, and issues 165 and 167 of *Radical Philosophy* collected as "From Structure to Rhizome: Transdisciplinarity in French Thought" (2011), accessible here: https://www.radicalphilosophyarchive.com/category/dossiers/165-from-structure-to-rhizome-transdisciplinarity-in-french-thought (last accessed August 21, 2018).
8. See Bianco in this volume.
9. It is perhaps no coincidence that structuralism also flourished during precisely this period.

Bibliography

Alliez, É. (2004), *The Signature of the World: What Is Deleuze and Guattari's Philosophy?*, trans. E. Ross Albert and A. Toscano, London: Continuum.

Badiou, A. (2009), "Existe-t-il quelque chose comme une politique deleuzienne?," *Cités*, 4 (40): 15–20.

Deleuze, G. ([1968] 2004), *Difference and Repetition*, trans. P. Patton, London: Continuum.

Deleuze, G. ([1994] 2007), "Preface to the American Edition of *Difference and Repetition*," in G. Deleuze, *Two Regimes of Madness: Texts and Interviews, 1975–1995*, trans. A. Hodges and M. Taormina, 300–03, New York: Semiotext(e).

Deleuze, G., and Guattari, F. ([1991] 1994), *What Is Philosophy?*, trans. G. Birchill and H. Tomlinson, London: Verso.

Deleuze, G., Guattari, F. et al. ([1972] 2004), "Capitalism and Schizophrenia," in G. Deleuze, *Desert Islands and Other Texts, 1953–1974*, trans. M. Taormina, 232–41, London: Semiotext(e).

Deleuze, G., and Negri, A. ([1990] 1995), "Control and Becoming," in G. Deleuze, *Negotiations, 1972–1990*, trans. M. Joughin, 169–76, London: Columbia University Press.

Deleuze, G. et al. ([1967] 2004), "The Method of Dramatization," in G. Deleuze, *Desert Islands and Other Texts, 1953–1974*, trans. M. Taormina, 94–116, London: Semiotext(e).

Gibbons, M., Limoges C., Nowotny H. et al. (1994), *The New Production of Knowledge: The Dynamics of Science and Research in Contemporary Societies*, London: SAGE.

Guattari, F. ([1991] 2015), "Transdisciplinarity Must Become Transversality," trans. A. Goffey, *Theory, Culture & Society*, 32 (5–6): 131–37.

Guattari, F., and Negri, A. ([1985] 1990), *Communists Like Us: New Spaces of Liberty, New Lines of Alliance*, trans. M. Ryan, London: Semiotext(e).

Maniglier, P. (forthcoming), "'Problem-Sharing,'" *Theory, Culture, & Society*.

Osborne, P. (2015), "Problematizing Disciplinarity, Transdisciplinary Problematics," *Theory, Culture, & Society*, 32 (5–6): 3–35.

Osborne, P., Sandford, S., and Alliez, É., eds (2015), "Transdisciplinary Problematics," *Theory, Culture, & Society*, 32 (5–6).

1

Philosophy and History of Philosophy

Deleuze as a Trainee Guard of Philosophy's Epistemological Borders

Giuseppe Bianco

Among the philosophers born in France during the 1920s and the 1930s, Gilles Deleuze (1925–1995) is the one who openly defended a conception of philosophy that one could name "exceptionalist." This conception defends the absolute singularity of the philosophical discipline and its irreducibility to psychological, historical, and social determinations. Deleuze's exceptionalism reaches its peak in *What Is Philosophy?* (1991), the book he coauthored with his friend Félix Guattari (1930–1992). Here, attempting to neatly separate philosophy from doxa and science, Deleuze and Guattari opposed the "plane of immanence," "concepts," "problems," "events," and "conceptual personae," the elements belonging to philosophy, to the "plane of reference," "functions," "solutions," "states of things," and to "psycho-social types," belonging to science. Moreover, at the beginning of the book, Deleuze and Guattari affirmed that, usually, philosophers ask about the nature of philosophy at the end of their lives. The question "what is philosophy?" is a question belonging to "old age," that one can pose concretely only when there is nothing more to be asked.

The following analysis of Deleuze's intellectual trajectory during the 1950s starts from an approach that is grounded in two theses, in contradiction to the one proposed in *What Is Philosophy?*. The first is the following: all exceptionalist conceptions of philosophy, by attempting to preserve the singularity of this discipline, constitute an epistemological obstacle. The second is that a question

---

This essay is one of the outcomes of research funded by the Fundação de Amparo à Pesquisa do Estado de São Paulo (BEPE 2017/15538-7) entitled "Gilles Deleuze: Genesis of a Creator of Concepts."

such as "what is philosophy?" is a question belonging to the youth. The ways in which this question is posed by an author depends from the beginning on her intellectual trajectory, and it is tied to the moment in time when intellectual dispositions become rooted in a permanent way.[1]

I will proceed following three movements. In the first part I will describe the state of the philosophical field in France after the Second World War and the space of possible options offered to Deleuze. I will then take into account a controversy between the two philosophers Ferdinand Alquié (1906–1985) and Martial Gueroult (1891–1976), which started in 1950. At its beginning, this controversy concerned the kind of interpretation one had to give to Descartes's philosophy but soon involved as well a discussion of the task of the history of philosophy and the nature of philosophy itself. In the third section I will try to show that during the 1950s, Deleuze had to occupy an unstable position in search of a synthesis between a scientific and artistic model of the historian of philosophy. Drawing on some archival documents, I will try to show how this position will inform Deleuze's approach to philosophical texts up to the 1960s.

The aftermath of the Liberation of France from Nazi-fascism coincided with the beginning of a process of dissolution concerning the block of antifascist forces formed ten years before and consolidated during the Resistance. This process manifested its irreversible features on June 5, 1948, with the establishment of the Marshall plan and the Soviet response through the Zhdanov Doctrine.[2] This macroscopic polarity indirectly influenced the intellectual field: the journal *Temps modernes* occupied a hegemonic place, popularizing a phenomenological and existential philosophy influenced by the German philosophies of history, Marxism, and Hegelianism. The existentialist attempt to propose a philosophical doctrine able to furnish an original and heterodox reading of Marxism provoked a series of quarrels, especially with communist intellectuals, who were not likely to tolerate an ideological line that did not conform with the one of the French Communist Party (PCF).[3]

During the 1940s and the 1950s, the social sciences did not yet possess a power of fascination drawing in a larger audience, as they would do after the publication of Claude Lévi-Strauss's (1908–2005) groundbreaking *The Savage Mind* (1962). After the dissolution of the Durkheimian school, sociology was dominated by Georges Gurvitch's (1894–1965) eclectic "methodological holism," which combined elements of Weberianism, Marxism, and Durkheimianism with functionalism, imported from Chicago by sociologists such as Gurvitch and Jean Stoetzel (1901–1987) thanks to the Ford Foundation. An independent curriculum in sociology would be created only in 1957, but already in 1946

Gurvitch was at the head of the Centre for Sociological Studies in the framework of the National Centre for Scientific Research (CNRS), where he was animating a research group in the sociology of knowledge.

French psychology, founded at the turn of the century by Théodule Ribot (1839–1916), Georges Dumas (1866–1946), and Pierre Janet (1847–1959), was federating the different new orientations of *Gestalt* psychology, existential psychotherapy, psychoanalysis, Freudianism, reflexology, and behaviorism in syncretic works such as the ones of Daniel Lagache (1903–1972). Lagache was the first psychoanalyst to teach at the Sorbonne, where an independent curriculum in psychology had been created. Two years later Lagache published his famous essay *On the Unity of Psychology*. A few years later, in 1951, his colleague Ignace Meyerson (1888–1983), author of a doctoral dissertation on historical psychology (*Les fonctions psychologiques et les œuvres*, 1947), was elected to the chair of "Comparative Psychology" at the *Ecole pratique des Hautes Etudes*.

In 1947, in the same institution, a department (*section*) of "Economic and Social Sciences" was created, federating history, economics, sociology, and comparative psychology; the same year, the historian Fernand Braudel (1902–1985) had been elected professor at the Collège de France to a chair of "Modern Civilisation"; Braudel presented his discipline as the totalizing knowledge of man, able to federate all the other human sciences, following the path sketched forty years before by Henri Berr (1864–1956), the founder of the journal *Revue de synthèse historique*.

The social and human sciences were therefore slowly emancipating themselves from philosophy, which was, until then, the overarching discipline taught in the Faculty of Letters. Before the war, both psychology and sociology and history were present in this faculty, but they did not constitute an independent curriculum and they were monitored by academics occupying chairs of philosophy and history of philosophy; their implicit role was the one of assigning to these disciplines an acceptable epistemological spot inside the encyclopedic organization of knowledge dominated by the supreme arbiter of philosophy, the "crowning discipline."

Since the beginning of the nineteenth century, namely since the "creation" of philosophy as an academic discipline in France by Victor Cousin (1792–1867) and his pupils,[4] history of philosophy had a solid footing in the academic system. During the 1930s, at the Sorbonne, eight chairs had "History of Philosophy" in their title.[5] This literary genre, established at the moment of the emergence of philosophy as a discipline, was promoting an image of philosophy as a field of knowledge that, since the Ancient Greeks, had a relative coherence. The philosophers proposed themselves as the only ones entitled to produce scholarship about the past of their discipline, the other studies allegedly constituting mere "historical" approaches disregarding the truth-value of the texts. This narrative was a shield used to defend the study of the "philosophical past" from possible interferences coming from psychology, sociology, and history. By underlining the contingent factors that contributed to the emergence of philosophy in Greece, by pointing out the discontinuous development of its heritage and its proximity to religion during the Middle Ages, by showing to what extent Modern Thought constituted an epistemological break and did not have much to do with what was conceived as "philosophy," by suggesting a further possible disappearance of philosophy substituted by the regional positive sciences, certain knowledge-producers were menacing philosophy with a dethronement from its exceptional position as both a discipline between the disciplines and the synthesis of the totality of knowledge. In France, starting from the 1820s the menace was mainly constituted by medicine and neurology,[6] which pretended to substitute itself for spiritualism; from the 1880s it had been the turn of scientific psychology, which was ridiculing the a priori analysis of consciousness; at the turn of the century, it had been Durkheimian sociology, which wanted to replace philosophy as the crowning discipline; and, finally, during the 1930s and the 1940s, the type of history promoted by the historians of the journal *Annales*, who had strong ties to the group of sociologists of the *Année sociologique*.

On an institutional level, because of the relative expansion of the university and the generational turnover, the decade following the end of the Second World War implied a series of academic displacements involving agents teaching in chairs of history of philosophy. Martial Gueroult, professor in Strasbourg University, a pupil of the historian of ancient philosophy Léon Robin (1866–1947), and of the neo-Kantian philosopher Léon Brunschvicg (1867–1944), left his chair in Alsace and moved to the Sorbonne, where he was elected to Brunschvicg's chair in "History of Modern Philosophy," left vacant after his death. Gueroult's chair in Strasbourg was assigned to Jean Hyppolite (1907–1968), another of Brunschvicg's pupils. Following the death of the historian of modern philosophy Jean Laporte (1886–1948), Hyppolite was then appointed to the chair that the first was occupying at the Sorbonne. In 1946, Ferdinand Alquié left his job at the prestigious Henri IV *lycée* and then his job as an assistant at the Sorbonne, for a position as lecturer at the University of Montpellier. Six years later he substituted Emile Bréhier (1876–1952) who supervised the dissertations of both Hyppolite and Gueroult. Bréhier, both the disciple of Henri Bergson and of the Kantian historian of philosophy Victor Delbos (1862–1916), was the author of an impressive *History of Philosophy*, but as well of epistemological texts on the history of philosophy as a discipline. In 1951, Gueroult took the spot left vacant at the Collège de France, by Etienne Gilson (1884–1978), who had just left France to settle in Canada. At this point the situation stabilized. At the end of the 1940s, the other chairs in history of philosophy at the Sorbonne, in "History and Philosophy of Science," "Philosophy and History of Modern Philosophy," "History of Medieval Philosophy," "History of Greek Philosophy," and "Philosophical History of Religious Thought," were respectively occupied by Gaston Bachelard (1884–1962), Jean Wahl (1888–1974), Maurice de Gandillac (1906–2006), Pierre-Maxime Schuhl (1892–1984), and Henri Gouhier (1898–1994).

As it had been since its emergence as a genre, but particularly at this moment, history of philosophy was concerned with a series of debates regarding its nature and its relation with philosophy and with the other disciplines. This interrogation aimed at justifying the peculiar approach to history proper to the philosophers as compared to the one of the "historical psychologists," who aimed at explaining the genesis of cultural productions starting from the development of the structures proper to the human psyche, to the historians of the *Annales d'histoire économique et sociale* school, who were promoting a history of people's "mentalities," considered in the *longue durée*, and to the sociologists, interested in explaining the production of knowledge from the standpoint of social interactions. This interrogation was framed by the growing importance of the German philosophies of history, but most of all, by the growing importance of the Marxist analysis of ideology. What was most important, for the philosophers, was defending history of philosophy as a genre reserved only to philosophers and incompatible with other approach coming from the other disciplines. The constant insistence on the peculiar essence of a philosophical approach to the history of philosophy has to be interpreted as what Jean-Louis Fabiani described, using an expression taken from Bachelard as "the guard of the epistemological borders" (Fabiani 1988). We can find this approach in the multiple publications dealing with what we could call today "epistemology of history of philosophy," produced during the decade following 1944 by authors such as Émile Bréhier, Etienne Gilson, Henri Gouhier, Ferdinand Alquié, Martial Gueroult, and by the phenomenologists Maurice Merleau-Ponty (1908–1961) and Paul Ricœur (1913–2005).

Nevertheless, if the aim of defending the borders of philosophy from the other disciplines was shared by all the philosophers, these agents adopted strategies that were very different one from the other. This multiplicity caused a conflicting context in which Deleuze grew up. At the end of the 1940s, like most of his schoolfellows, he took his distance from Sartre, to whom he had been attached and who contributed to his "conversion" to philosophy.[7] We cannot enter into the details concerning this phase in the space of the present essay, but what has to be said is that Deleuze's Sartrianism implied the internalization of an idea of philosopher that could be defined as artistic and messianic. This model was partially shared by his master Ferdinand Alquié, who represented a kind of academic interlocutor for the "existentialists."

In 1948, when Deleuze passed the *agrégation*, the essential exam qualifying him to be a high school professor in this discipline, he was not any more an enthusiastic "Sartrian," nor yet a charismatic "Nietzschean" philosopher who attracted Trotskyists, junkies, psychoanalysts, Palestinian activists in tiny and smoky classrooms at Vincennes. On the contrary, he was one of the many high school professors in philosophy, a reproducer, looking for a central position in the philosophical field by distinguishing himself from his peers, namely by trying to be a *producer* of philosophy. Since the late 1940s, Deleuze wanted to "himself create a philosophy," as he confessed to his good friend François Châtelet (1925–1985) in 1945.[8]

If one thinks about the young philosophers belonging to Deleuze's generation, their intellectual itineraries depended on the space of possible epistemological choices delimited by phenomenology—in its existentialist or epistemological variants—and Marxism—which could take the form of a humanism or that of the scientific doctrine: the young Jacques Derrida (1930–2004), who was trained at the *Ecole normale supérieure* by Suzanne Bachelard (1919–2007) and until the end of the Fifties considered a phenomenologist, Louis Althusser (1918–1990) as a Marxist epistemologist close to Gaston Bachelard, Michel Foucault (1926–1984) as a philosopher of psychology torn between phenomenology and Marxism. Some Marxist philosophers would convert to sociology, joining the CNRS, through the intercession of Gurvitch, or to psychology, thanks to Lagache. Deleuze may appear as a black swan nowadays, but only because scholarship grounds this assumption on the philosopher's declarations of exceptionality in interviews and texts coming from the 1970s and the 1980s. Like his novelist friend Michel Tournier (1924–2016), who initially tried to pursue a career as a philosopher, Deleuze was attached to the "anti-humanist" Sartre of the *Transcendence of the Ego*[9] and *Being and Nothingness* and he refused the humanist turn of his master, leading to his "*compagnonnage de route*" with the Communist Party. Around 1947 both Deleuze and Tournier stopped being faithful Sartrians, they did not join the Party, nor did they embrace the phenomenological fashion, since both looked like avatars of the humanism stigmatized by Sartre. Just like

Tournier, Deleuze did not belong to the *Ecole normale* élite, therefore he was not involved in the network of communist students present there, nor did he have the opportunity to get to know a less anthropological version of phenomenology that was becoming popular in this institution, thanks to Suzanne Bachelard. Unable to read and speak German, Deleuze could not be involved in the Heideggerian fashion that started being spread by figures such as Henri Birault (1918–1990) and Jean Beaufret (1907–1982) after the publication of Heidegger's *Letter on Humanism* (1947). Because of his Sartrian heritage, he showed no interest in the human sciences, like his two Marxist friends Oliver Revault d'Alonnnes (1923–2009) and François Châtelet, who were close to Ignace Meyerson's *Journal de psychologie*.

A possible allocation left for Deleuze was the one of historian of philosophy. He initially followed the path of his two masters Jean Hyppolite and Ferdinand Alquié, who had been his high school professors during the 1940s. Thanks to the first he obtained a grant to prepare for his *licence* in Strasbourg University. His master's dissertation on Hume had been published in Hyppolite's *Epimethée* book series; thanks to the latter he entered into the *Societé d'études nietzschéennes* and in the *Société des amis de Bergson*, where he presented his first public conference, "L'idée de différence chez Bergson."[10] Thanks to Alquié, he published a series of book reviews in two journals published in the South of France, where Alquié was born: the *Cahiers du Sud*, edited by a friend of him, Jean Ballard (1893–1973), and the *Etudes philosophiques*, directed by the president of the *Société d'études philosophiques du Sud-Ouest*, Gaston Berger (1896–1960). In 1957, Alquié supported Deleuze's application to a position of assistant professor at the Sorbonne, where he would be teaching for four years. A very dense correspondence going from 1945 until 1970 witnesses this close relation between Deleuze and his professor.[11] Alquié was a former member of the surrealist movement, and a contributor to the literary journal *Cahiers du Sud*; therefore he belonged to the figure of the philosopher-creator, compatible with the one embodied by Sartre. But at the same time he was as well a respected member of the academe, being the president of the examination committee of the *Ecole Normale* and of the *agrégation*.

A second philosophical model, much more academic, appeared at the Sorbonne, at the moment in which Alquié left Paris for Montpellier during the fall of 1946: Martial Gueroult. Gueroult influenced Deleuze's generation by embodying the model of the rigorous historian of philosophy, especially when, in 1951, he became professor at the Collège de France, on a chair bearing the impressive title "History and technique of philosophical systems." The examination committee preferred Gueroult to Alexandre Koyré (1892–1964), who was certainly considered too much of an "historian" given his close relations with the group of the *Annales*.[12] Because of his effort in studying internally the coherence of philosophical works, Gueroult was *the* example of the professionalized historian of philosophy. This model was incompatible with the one embodied by Sartre, that Gueroult never confronted, but that he silently despised.

At the beginning of the 1950s, the huge symbolic capital collected by Sartre, thanks to his multiple activities as a novelist, a playwright, a journalist, and a politically engaged intellectual, started being perceived as proof of his lack of seriousness as a specialized philosopher. At this moment of reforms and disciplinarization, academia demanded from its members, even from the philosophers, a type of erudition incompatible with the Sartrian idea of the "total intellectual." As a result, his writings started losing their appeal. Althusser, who often expressed his admiration for the work of Gueroult, wrote that, during the 1950s, at the *Ecole normale*, the habit of his peers was to despise Sartre and existentialism (Althusser 1994: 177). It was especially the humanism expressed in texts such as *Existentialism Is a Humanism* and in *What Is Literature?* that could not be tolerated. In a letter sent to Alquié in 1948, Deleuze wrote in fact:

> Sartre's book on *Baudelaire* [published in 1947], absolutely commercial, and the one of Simone de Beauvoir on ethics [*The Ethics of Ambiguity*, published in 1947] (a mere description of attitudes: there's the adventurer, then the lover, and then the dictator ... etc.) disgust me: normally I claim that philosophy cannot, in any case, start from a description of psychological behaviours, but only from the concept of true philosophy, as an abstract and systematic, even arid, discipline.[13]

After this partial refusal of Sartre, Deleuze's intellectual trajectory started being the result of the synthesis of the model provided by Alquié and the one provided by Gueroult, whose famous polemics about the interpretation of Cartesian philosophy, the task of the historian of philosophy, and the one of the philosopher left a mark on the Fifties.[14] Deleuze started occupying an uncertain epistemological terrain, and he elaborated a series of unstable conciliatory positions. This is evident in his epistolary correspondence with Alquié, where he often seems to attribute to the latter a conception of philosophy that, in reality, is that of Gueroult. For instance, at the end of the passage of the letter quoted above, Deleuze admitted that the reason why he conceived philosophy as "abstract and systematic" was because he considered himself his "pupil."

Nonetheless, if from a philosophical standpoint Alquié's and Gueroult's takes were completely different, on the other hand, if they are analyzed from a broader perspective, which takes into account the interaction between philosophy and the other disciplines, they were aiming at the same objective, the one of defending philosophy's epistemological borders. In a review of Gueroult's book *Descartes selon l'ordre des raisons*, Alquié clearly admits this proximity:

> Both of us [both Alquié and Gueroult] reject the methods that would explain [...] [philosophy] from the exterior, referring to material or social causes, and we believe that philosophical thought can only be understood by referring to its aim, the truth that it aims to seize and express. These convergences are not insignificant. However we cannot agree on the meaning of [Descartes's] text. (Alquié 1953: 115)[15]

Let's come to the reasons of their disagreements in order to understand Deleuze's vision of the history of philosophy. Alquié's theory of philosophy and its history is clear if one takes into account his two doctoral dissertations of 1950: *La découverte métaphysique de l'homme chez Descartes* and *La nostalgie de l'Etre*, often qualified as "existentialist" by the first commentators. I will start from them given that Deleuze discusses them in a series of letters sent to Alquié at the very beginning of the 1950s. According to Alquié, who considered Descartes as the absolute model of the philosopher, philosophy was not reducible to the horizontality of historical time because of the philosopher's privileged, vertical relation with a nonobjectivable "Being" from which he would be separated. This nonrelation is constant in each of the philosophical works coming from the past although it takes different forms. Therefore, philosophy could not consist in a "progress, but in an eternal call of Being" (Alquié 1950a: 34). Each philosophy starts by distinguishing itself from science and by rooting its possibility in the activity of a subject; the philosopher's task is the one of showing that our knowledge is only possible insofar as it depends on the relation to a transcendent Being from which all men are irreparably separated. Philosophy is therefore a paradoxical "knowledge of absence," which starts from an affective experience and results in a rational discourse. Alquié certainly speaks of the "mental structures" of a philosophy, but these structures aren't psychological; they are transcendental. The task of the historian of philosophy is the one of taking into account both the dimensions of philosophy, namely the affective and the conceptual. On this basis Alquié was able to refuse all the psychological, historical, sociological—especially Marxist—explanations, but at the same time he refused as well the structural and synchronic interpretations, insofar as he considered them unable to render the existential dimension of philosophizing, exposing philosophy to the risk of historicism.

In a polemic essay from 1953, Alquié wrote that

> by thinking that the history of ideas is made of opposed [philosophical] systems, one could end up considering the systems as facts, and explaining them using causes [...]. In this case a paradoxical reversal could happen, insofar as only History is important, and the philosophical claims are depreciated, insofar as the philosopher's thought, which wants to reach for the truth, is refused in its foundation and essential project; thinking is transformed into a fact, and this fact is tied to its cause. (Alquié 1953: 95)

In 1956 Deleuze published in the *Cahiers du Sud* reviews of Alquié's *Philosophie du surréalisme* and of his *Descartes, l'homme et l'œuvre*, both published the same year. In the first essay Deleuze described Alquié's conception of philosophy as essential for everyone, insofar as it expresses "the very essence of metaphysics" (Deleuze 2015b: 117). This conception was careful in its examination of the development of the author's thinking but reserved only to philosophers the exclusivity of its deep understanding; it treated the philosopher as an individual able to separate himself from his own epoch's determinations and as having an essential relationship with Being. More than twenty years later, in 1968, in *Expressionism in Philosophy: Spinoza*, Deleuze's doctoral dissertation supervised by Alquié, Deleuze would avow the influence that his professor's diachronic method had on his reading of Spinoza. According to Deleuze, in a series of lectures from 1958, *Nature and Truth according to Spinoza* (*Nature et vérité d'après Spinoza*), it was because of Alquié's focus on the chronological development of Spinoza that Deleuze had been able to understand how the concept of "common notions" in Spinoza constituted a "fundamental discovery," marking a "decisive moment" for the author of the *Tractatus* (Deleuze 1992: 292).

But already in a letter he sent to Alquié in 1960, where he was praising the importance of his lectures on *Kant's Ethics* (*La morale de Kant*), from 1957, Deleuze recognized Alquié's ability to keep together the unity and the evolution of a philosophy:

> [In your lectures] I see two things. First the way following which you demonstrate, according to your own conception, the unity of a radical philosophy [...]. But also a second idea [...], according to which Kant isolated certain motivations [*mobiles*] from their affective determinations in order to transform them into a "mental structure."[16]

In both Alquié and Deleuze, the refusal of a purely systematic reading of philosophical texts did not lead to historicism, sociologism, or psychologism but only to an attentiveness to the progressive encounters between an empirical philosopher and a transcendent dimension. In the second review published in 1956, Deleuze (2015b) praised the way in which Alquié was interpreting surrealism by means of a theory according to which both art and philosophy consist in a series of progressive encounters that an author has with signs that are referring to a transcendent dimension. Deleuze would develop in a personal way this intuition both in his *Proust and Signs* (1964) and in the chapter on the "Image of Thought" contained in *Difference and Repetition* (1968). In *Expressionism in Philosophy*, he attributed to Alquié the merit of having underlined the importance of "this theme of the encounter (*occursus*) in Spinoza's theory of affections" (Deleuze 1992: 386); it is because of his attention to contingency and encounters that Alquié had been able to isolate an order of "fortuitous encounters" or an "order of passions" tied to the "order of reasons" (Deleuze 1992: 283, 303). Finally, already in 1951, in a letter sent to Alquié, Deleuze described the relationship that his master was establishing between the empirical and the transcendental, between man and Being, as a "relationship of expression, of symbolisation."[17]

Let's come to the other pole of the polemic, the one occupied by Gueroult.[18] Although he was located on the same side of the intellectual barricade stacked against all the conquering programs proposed by the human, social, and historical sciences, Gueroult expressed a polite but harsh hostility toward Alquié. This was manifest during the defense of Alquié's dissertation, when Gueroult, a member of the examination committee, treated his dissertation as a "novel" and a "fantasy" (Anonymous 1950). In a letter sent to Alquié a few months after the dissertation, Gueroult accused him of practicing a "novelistic philosophy" and he suggested that he choose between "pure philosophy," where one expresses oneself "directly," and the history of philosophy, where one has to "serve the thought of a genius, instead of enrolling him [...] to serve oneself."[19] The polemics became more violent after the publication of Gueroult's *Descartes selon l'ordre des raisons* (1953) and reached its maximal intensity during the public congress on Descartes held in Royaumont in 1957.[20]

Despite its divergence from the position of Alquié, just like his colleague, Gueroult wanted to preserve the peculiarity of the *philosophical* discourse on the history of philosophy and, at the same time, to justify the differences between different past "philosophical" works. What both of them wanted to avoid was the possible absorption of the study of the history of philosophy into sociology, history, or psychology. According to Gueroult, the only way to escape both skepticism and reductionism was not to appeal to a peculiar "experience" of the nonrelation of the philosopher to Being, as in Alquié, an idea that Gueroult considered to be a way to open the door to historical relativism; on the contrary, Gueroult wanted to root each philosophical work in something able to resist purely historical explanations, even those invoking the chronological order of affective encounters. This something is what Gueroult called, following a terminology coming from Leibniz and Christian Wolff (1679–1754) and then popularized by Kant and by the post-Kantians, the "architecture." The architecture is nothing but the system or the "order of reasons," the set of demonstrations, consisting in posed and solved "problems." Gueroult conceived these entities as the objects of the historian of philosophy, the "technologist" of philosophical systems. Each philosophical system, composed of a set of philosophical works, has to be conceived as an architectonically constructed *monument* emerging from history but resisting the erosive action of time thanks to its rational and demonstrative coherence.

The first time Gueroult explicitly formulated this conception was during his inaugural lecture given at the Collège de France in November 1951, which constituted a philosophical manifesto that left a mark on an entire generation of apprentice philosophers.[21] Following the habit and the style of the inaugural lectures, Gueroult compared his approach to the history of philosophy to the one of his predecessors Henri Bergson and Etienne Gilson, who had taught on the same chair at the Collège de France. According to Gueroult the error committed by the latter had been that of isolating a set of invariable essences, allegedly immanent to each system; by doing that, Gilson limited the possibilities of philosophy and denied its historical dimension. Bergson committed the opposite error: by rooting philosophy in an incommunicable intuition, he devalued its conceptual dimension. If Gilson made the mistake of searching beyond the architectonic element, Bergson made the inverse mistake and searched below it. According to Gueroult both philosophers separated philosophical texts from the problems lying at their origin. Philosophical monuments, systems, are exactly the resolutions of problems. Each problem has its solution, insofar as problems are always contingent and not eternal.

This conception of philosophy as a "problematizing" activity[22] had first been proposed by Bergson in a famous letter to Floris Delattre, where he claimed that philosophy creates new problems and does not only give solutions to preexisting ones. In 1947, the International Institute for Philosophy organized a big conference in Sweden whose title was *Nature des problèmes en philosophie*.[23]

A series of historians of philosophy took part in the first session, entitled "Le problème en philosophie contemporaine": Jean Wahl (1888–1974), Léon Robin (1866–1947), Raymond Bayer (1898–1959), Harald Hoffding (1842–1931), and Emile Bréhier (1876–1952). It is Bréhier's paper, entitled "La notion de problème en philosophie," that inspired Gueroult. However, criticizing the Bergsonian conception, Gueroult underlined the independence of the process of posing or solving a problem from intuition.[24]

Deleuze makes this his conception of philosophy. It exempts the historian from problematizing his "engaged" position as historian and from studying the context in which the intellectual trajectory of the author was deployed. Deleuze disregarded completely the phenomenological and hermeneutic problems that occupied philosophers such as Raymond Aron (1905–1983) in the *Introduction à la philosophie de l'histoire* (1938) or Maurice Merleau-Ponty in the introduction to the collective book *Les Philosophes celebres* (1956) to which Deleuze contributed. The Gueroultian conception freed all historians of philosophy from the necessity of considering the social and psychological trajectory of an author who is the object of a study, as was the case for philosophers influenced by Marxism such as Henri Lefebvre in his *Descartes* (1946) or Sartre in his *Baudelaire* (1947).

A series of accounts—especially by François Châtelet and Revault d'Allonnes—prove that Deleuze regularly attended Gueroult's lectures, both at the Sorbonne and at the Collège de France. Here, from 1951 to 1956, Gueroult explicitly dealt with the problem of the link between "philosophy and history of philosophy" and patiently developed commentaries on texts by Leibniz and Malebranche.[25]

In his autobiography, Tournier speaks about the passion he shared with Deleuze: a passion for philosophical systems and their architectures. The terms used by both are very similar to the ones used by Gueroult:

> One idea that we [Tournier and Deleuze] did not question was that an object or a set of objects is real precisely to the extent that it is rationally consistent [...]. Hence it is possible [...] to conceive entities more consistent than "reality" and hence more real. These entities exist, and are called philosophical systems. They can be counted on the fingers of two hands [...]. Are philosophical systems the work of the great philosophers, as they might appear to the naive causalist? Obviously not [...]. Since philosophy was to be our calling, life for us held only two possibilities. Most of us would become guardians of those [...] citadels of granite [...]. As professors of philosophy we would be responsible for initiating young people into the study of these historical monuments, grander and more majestic than anything else mankind has to offer. But by an improbable decree of fate any one of us might become the first [...] witness to the birth of a new

system and by causalist aberration be named its author [...]. We held, moreover, that in good philosophy the solution always precedes the problem. The problem is nothing but the shadow cast by its solution, a fountain of clarity that spurts *motu proprio* into the empyrean of the intelligible. The existence of God, for instance, only became a problem on the day the ontological argument was invented. Like young Saint-Justs of the intellect, we held our swords aloft and divided all the products of man's mind into just two categories: philosophical systems and comic strips. Anything that was not a system—or a study of a system—was a comic strip. (Tournier 1988: 128–31)

According to Deleuze and Tournier, followers of Gueroult, philosophy is neatly separated from science and literature, it is not meant to find solutions to preexisting problems, but it poses the problems, articulated by the solutions. The philosopher is just a means through which the system develops; therefore both the study of the "engaged" situation of the philosopher in the world and the assessment of the historian of philosophy's position in its relation with the past are useless. Gueroult's views, internalized by both Deleuze and Tournier, were incompatible with those of phenomenology, adopted, for instance, by Merleau-Ponty in his *Eloge de la philosophie*, where he opposed Gueroult by underlining the importance of the centrality of the thinker both as a philosopher and as an historian of philosophy.

The internalization of Gueroult's method is already evident in Deleuze's first book, *Empiricism and Subjectivity* (1953). Here a philosophical theory is defined as a "problem" or "developed theory" and philosophical critique as a "critique of problems." Deleuze writes that the "psychological factors and most of all the sociological ones [...] do not concern the question" (Deleuze 2001: 106). In 1955, he publishes, in *Les Cahiers du Sud*, a review of a posthumous book by Emile Bréhier, Gueroult's mentor, *Etudes de philosophie antique*. Praising the work of Brehiér both as an historian and as a philosopher, Deleuze admired the way in which he was able to demarcate philosophy from science and art in studies such as "The Notion of Problem in Philosophy": philosophy poses new problems, and science answers preexisting questions; the element of philosophy is the concept while art uses images. Deleuze mentions Bréhier forty years later in a footnote in *What Is Philosophy?*

Gueroult's method was also internalized thanks to one of Gueroult's most faithful pupils, Victor Goldschmidt. In a methodological essay first published in 1953, "Temps historique et temps logique dans l'interprétation de systèmes philosophiques" ["Historical and Logical Time in the Interpretation of Philosophical Systems"] Goldschmidt opposed a conference paper by Alquié, entitled "Structures logiques et structures mentales en histoire de la philosophie," and nearly paraphrased Gueroult's lectures at the Collège de France. Goldschmidt distinguished between two methods in history of philosophy, one *genetic*, the other *dogmatic*. While the genetic interpretation, "searching for causes, risks explaining the system below or beyond his author's intention," the dogmatic one is fully philosophical because "it considers a doctrine following its author's intentions and privileges the problem of truth" (Goldschmidt 1970: 14). The first interpretation inscribes the doctrine in time; the second "subtracts it from time" (Goldschmidt 1970: 14). If philosophy is "explanation and discourse," then the historian of philosophy has to render the articulation between logical structures and the progression of the demonstrations that are taking place in what Goldschmidt calls "logical time." The historian of philosophy has to place his analysis in this logical time, repeating, after the author, the philosopher's initial operation (those are the same words used by Revault d'Allonnes). Goldschmidt talks about this method much later in an essay from the Eighties, "Remarques sur la méthode structurale en philosophie" ["Remarks on the Structural Method in Philosophy"]. According to Goldschmidt, it is "useless" for a structural analysis of philosophy to "rely unconditionally on chronology: it is possible to show that the method developed [by Bergson] in the 1911 conference "The Philosophical Intuition" can explain the structure of the four most important books by Bergson, even if the first three come before it." In a footnote, Goldschmidt adds that he had given those hermeneutical "guidelines in a paper given at the 'Associations des amis de Bergson' on 21 February 1953" (Goldschmidt 1984: 264).[26]

Not only was Deleuze one of Goldschmidt's students during the Forties, when Goldschmidt was teaching there as an assistant, but he was also a member of the "Association des amis de Bergson." In 1954, he presented the paper "On the Idea of Difference in Bergson," later published in the *Etudes bergsoniennes*. Deleuze will literally follow Goldschmidt's suggestions in his own reading of Bergson as it appears in *Bergsonism*, where he takes into account Bergson's work only following the order of reasons and logical time. Deleuze does not follow the development of Bergson's philosophy in time; he ignores Bergson's confrontation with the science of his own time; rather he only pays attention to the internal coherence of the "system," to his "order of reasons." The beginning of the book is paradigmatic: "Duration, Memory, Elan Vital mark the major stages of Bergson's philosophy. This book sets out to determine, first, the relationship between these three notions and, second, the progress they involve" (Deleuze 1991: 13).

Nonetheless, contrary to Gueroult's and Goldschmidt's approaches to philosophical texts, Deleuze's approach wasn't "neutral," but instrumental, insofar as it consisted in strategically deforming the structure of past texts, by paying attention to one detail or another. On this point, just as with Alquié, Deleuze was certainly a historian of philosophy, but also a creator, conscious that each interpretation of a philosophical text could allow him to intervene in an epistemological space made of legitimated problems and solutions. He could then "enrol an author at his own service," to borrow the expression Gueroult used against Alquié. In a letter he sent to the latter in 1951, Deleuze was already claiming the following:

> Reading a book, we give it a tension, a movement which is not the one of the author's thought: nothing is more false than the idea according to which reading would mean finding the original movement of the author; that would mean not understanding anything and not reading. To read means to decentre and to read well means to decentre well.[27]

So Deleuze seems to hesitate between two irreconcilable positions—on the one hand the scientific analysis of works, on the other hand the "novelistic" approach, on the one hand logical time, on the other the affective one. Deleuze's ambiguity is manifest in this and in a few letters, where he seems to attribute to Alquié some features, for instance, the analysis of the inhumanity of reasons immanent to philosophical works, which are proper to Gueroult.

> What I find prodigious in the *Meditations* is the fact that they are, in a sense, a chronology of logic: there's an order, a real temporality. Yet this temporality is not exactly human [...]. It is literally heroic [...]. The logical notions, the Ego, God, the World have a temporal intuition, are discovered in a certain moment. If you pass from Descartes to the Cartesians you will have to suppress this order [...]. So what is, in Descartes, this order which is not only logical, because it is temporal, but not human?[28]

This passage already manifests the attempt to operate a synthesis between the order of concepts developing according to a logical time and the order of experiences developing according to a chronological time. *Expressionism in Philosophy* is probably the text where we can best find the mark of this double heritage. In this book, using the concept of expression, Deleuze shows the presence of two levels in the *Ethics*: the manifest level of the demonstrations, and the latent level of the scholia, where Spinoza makes room for the events and affects that alone give meaning to the former.

To conclude, what has to be underlined is that, even if Deleuze's, Alquié's, and Gueroult's positions look completely different from a philosophical point of view, on the other hand, if they are analyzed from a strategic perspective, they had the same aim, namely that of defending philosophy's epistemological borders. In an article from 1956, Alquié clearly admits it:

> Both of us [both Alquié and Gueroult] reject the methods that would explain [...] [philosophy] from the exterior, referring to material or social causes, and we believe that philosophical thought can only be understood by referring to its aim, the truth that it aims to seize and express. These convergences are not insignificant. However we cannot agree on the meaning of [Descartes's] text. (Alquié 1953: 115)

Deleuze would follow the path of a synthesis during the 1950s and the 1960s. Curiously enough, one of the reasons for his breakup with Alquié had to do with the essence of philosophy as distinguished from the sciences. During the discussion that followed his 1967 paper on the "Method of Dramatization,"[29] Alquié would confess that according to him, by multiplying the examples taken from the sciences, he did not underline enough the importance of a purely philosophical approach. Deleuze would respond to this remark by saying that it was precisely Alquié who had taught him the importance of demarcating philosophy from the other disciplines.

Notes

1 See Bourdieu 1990.
2 The Zhdanov Doctrine was a Soviet cultural doctrine developed by the Central Committee secretary Andrei Zhdanov (1896–1948) in 1946 and then adopted by the European communist parties tied to the Soviet Union. According to the doctrine, the world was divided in two camps: the communist and democratic headed by the Soviet Union, and the imperialistic, headed by the United States.
3 For this aspect, see Boschetti (1988).
4 See Bianco 2018: 8–30.
5 See Chimisso 2008.
6 See Bianco (forthcoming).
7 The first "Sartrian" texts Deleuze wrote during the 1940s are now gathered in Deleuze 2015a: 253–305.
8 See Châtelet 1979.
9 See the chapter on Deleuze in Bianco 2015.
10 Now published in Deleuze 2004, 32–51.
11 The correspondence is now held in Ferdinand Alquié's Archive in Carcassone's public library. In 1946, Alquié had even written a review of the issue of the journal *Espace* where Deleuze had published one of his first articles, "From Christ to the

Bourgeoisie" (Ferdinand Alquié, "La vie intérieure et l'Esprit." *Gazette de lettres*, July 20, 1946).

12 For this aspect, see Fabiani 1989.
13 Letter of Gilles Deleuze addressed to Ferdinand Alquié, April 3, 1948, Fonds Ferdinand Alquié.
14 For this polemic, see Peden 2001.
15 For Alquié's hermeneutic approach, see also his *Qu'est-ce que comprendre un philosophe?* (1956). On Alquié, see Marion and Deprun, eds, 1987, Philonenko 1985, Grimaldi 1974, Marion 1984, Vokos 1993.
16 Gilles Deleuze, letter sent to Ferdinand Alquié, November 21, 1960, Ferdinand Alquié Archive.
17 Gilles Deleuze, letter sent to Ferdinand Alquié, December 26, 1951, Ferdinand Alquié Archive.
18 On Gueroult, see Dreyfus 1969, Vuillemin 1977, Vuillemin et al. 1977.
19 Letter of Martial Gueroult, February 7, 1951, archive Ferdinand Alquié, public library of Carcassonne.
20 The proceedings had been published under the title of *Cahiers de Royaumont: Descartes* (Paris: Minuit, 1957).
21 Martial Gueroult, *Leçon inaugurale*, Paris, Collège de France, 1951.
22 See Bianco 2018.
23 See *Actes du colloque sur l'idée de problème*, Hermann: Paris, 1949.
24 The definition of philosophy as the posing and resolution of problems is constant in Gueroult. For instance, see Gueroult 1956, 1974, 1969.
25 See Châtelet 1979: 43.
26 That's exactly the opposite of what Alquié claimed one had to do in his *La découverte métaphysique de l'homme chez Descartes*, namely "reading each of Descartes's" works as if one was ignoring the ones that would have followed (1950b: 10). This approach was inherited from Henri Gouhier, who suggested that if one wants to understand "the Descartes of 1619, one has to forget what he knows of the Descartes from 1637" (1972: 37).
27 Gilles Deleuze, letter sent to Ferdinand Alquié December 26, 1951, Ferdinand Alquié archive.
28 Gilles Deleuze, undated letter to Ferdinand Alquié, but certainly from January 1948, Ferdinand Alquié Archive.
29 Now published in Deleuze 2004, 94–116.

Bibliography

Althusser, L. (1994), *The Future Lasts Forever*, trans. Richard Veasey, London: Vintage.
Alquié, F. (1950a), *La nostalgie de l'être*, Paris: Presses universitaires de France.

Alquié, F. (1950b), *La découverte métaphysique de l'homme chez Descartes*, Paris: Presses universitaires de France.
Alquié, F. (1953), "Structures logiques et structures mentales en histoire de la philosophie," *Bulletin de la société française de philosophie*, 3 (June): 84–111.
Alquié, F. (1956), *Qu'est-ce que comprendre un philosophe?*, Paris: CDU.
Anonymous (1950), "Compte-rendu de la soutenance de Ferdinand Alquié," *Revue de métaphysique et de morale*, 62 (3): 431–36.
Bianco, G. (2015), *Après Bergson. Portrait de groupe avec philosophe*, Paris: Presses universitaires de France.
Bianco, G. (2018), "The Misadventures of the 'Problem' in 'Philosophy,'" *Angelaki. Journal of the Theoretical Humanities*, 23: 8–30.
Bianco, G. (forthcoming), "What Was 'Serious Philosophy' for the Young Bergson? Philosophy and the Sciences of the Psyche around 1880," in A. Lefebvre and N. Schott (eds), *Interpreting Bergson*, Cambridge: Cambridge University Press.
Boschetti, A. (1988), *The Intellectual Enterprise: Sartre and Les Temps Modernes*, trans. R.C. McCleary, Evanston: Northwestern University Press.
Bourdieu, P. (1990), *The Logic of Practice*, trans. R. Nice, Palo Alto: Stanford University Press.
Châtelet, F. (1979), *Chroniques des idées perdues*, Paris: Stock.
Chimisso, C. (2008), *Writing the History of the Mind: Philosophy and Science in France*, Aldershot: Ashgate.
Deleuze, G. (1991), *Bergsonism*, trans. H. Tomlinson and B. Habberjam, New York: Zone Books.
Deleuze, G. (1992), *Expressionism in Philosophy: Spinoza*, trans. M. Joughin, New York: Zone Books.
Deleuze, G. (2001), *Empiricism and Subjectivity. An Essay on Hume's Theory of Human Nature*, trans. C.V. Boundas, New York: Columbia University Press.
Deleuze, G. (2004), *Desert Islands and Other Texts, 1953–1974*, trans. M. Taormina, Los Angeles and New York: Semiotext(e).
Deleuze, G. (2015a), *Lettres et autres textes*, Paris: Minuit.
Deleuze, G. (2015b), "Ferdinand Alquié, *Descartes l'homme et l'œuvre*," in G. Deleuze, *Lettres et autres textes*, 117–19, Paris: Minuit.
Dreyfus, G. (1969), "La méthode structurale et le Spinoza de M. Gueroult," *L'Âge de la science*, 3: 240–75.
Fabiani, J.-L. (1988), *Les Philosophes de la République*, Paris: Minuit.
Fabiani, J.-L. (1989), "Sociologie et histoire des idées: L'épistémologie et les sciences humaines," in *Les Enjeux philosophiques des années 50*, 115–30, Paris: Éditions du Centre Georges Pompidou.
Goldschmidt, V. (1970), "Temps historique et temps logique dans l'interprétation de systèmes philosophiques," in V. Goldschmidt, *Questions platoniciennes*, 13–21, Paris: Vrin.
Goldschmidt, V. (1984), "Remarques sur la méthode structurale en histoire de la philosophie," in V. Goldschmidt, *Écrits 2*, 259–66, Paris: Vrin.

Gouhier, H. ([1924] 1972), *La pensée réligieuse de Descartes*, Paris: Vrin.
Grimaldi, N. (1974), "La Répétition: étude sur l'expérience métaphysique dans la philosophie de Ferdinand Alquié," *Revue de métaphysique et de morale*, 78 (2): 129–50.
Gueroult, M. (1956), "Le problème de la légitimité de l'histoire de la philosophie," in *Philosophie de l'histoire de la philosophie*, 45–68, Paris: Vrin.
Gueroult, M. (1969), "The History of Philosophy as a Philosophical Problem," *The Monist*, 53 (4): 563–87.
Gueroult, M. (1974), "La Méthode en histoire de la philosophie," *Philosophiques*, 1 (1): 7–19.
Marion, J.-L. (1984), "Ferdinand Alquié," in D. Husmann (ed.), *Dictionnaire des philosophes*, Paris: Presses universitaires de France.
Marion, J.-L., and Deprun, J., eds (1987), *La passion de la raison: Hommage à Ferdinand Alquié*, Paris: Presses universitaires de France.
Peden, K. (2001), "Descartes, Spinoza, and the Impasse of French Philosophy: Ferdinand Alquié versus Martial Gueroult," *Modern Intellectual History*, 8 (2): 361–90.
Philonenko, A. (1985), "Ferdinand Alquié ou de la lucidité," *Revue de métaphysique et de morale*, 90 (4): 462–82.
Tournier, M. (1988), *The Wind Spirit: An Autobiography*, trans. A. Goldhammer, Boston: Beacon Press.
Vokos, G. (1993), "Ferdinand Alquié, lecteur de Spinoza," in *Spinoza au 20e siècle*, 105–12, Paris: Presses universitaires de France.
Vuillemin, J. (1977), "Gueroult (Martial)," *Association amicale des anciens élèves de l'École Normale Supérieure*: 59–63.
Vuillemin, J., Dreyfus, G., Guillermit, L., and Goldschmidt, V. (1977), "Martial Gueroult," *Archiv für Geschichte der Philosophie*: 289–312.

2

Guattari, Transdisciplinarity, and the Experimental Transformation of Research

Andrew Goffey

Introduction

For Félix Guattari, research and life were inseparable, joined together in processes of political, clinical, and philosophical experimentation that crisscrossed the segmented boundaries of serialized existence. Neither a scholar nor a scientist, Guattari was nonetheless intensely concerned by research activities and engaged in collective practices of inquiry that actively sought to overcome the political, subjective impasses that long-established institutions of research found themselves in. For Guattari, a dream and its analysis could form as important a material for research activity as could a scientific discovery, a technical machine, or a set of political events, any and all of which might form component parts of broader processes of "axiological creation." His friend and colleague at La Borde, Jean Oury, once remarked, "What obsessed him was research, and his life was a constant work in progress" (Kirkup 1992).

Experimentation, theory, and practice

It will perhaps be of little surprise to find, in the work of an intellectual whose life developed beyond the confines of the academic institutions in which so many of his contemporaries found themselves, a practice of research that challenges many of the assumptions that are made about it and its relationship to other registers of activity. While Guattari was a tireless *theorizer* of what he did, and while his theoretical writings exemplify a recognizably transdisciplinary disregard for the limiting effect on discourse production that Foucault, in his

"The Order of Discourse," attributed to disciplines (Foucault 1972: 222–23), his thinking, its role vis-à-vis research, and his understanding of transdisciplinarity are not easily construed along standard theory-practice lines. A fairly standard reading of French intellectual production from the 1960s, as "Theory," traces this production, via the concept of "structure," back to work in the epistemology of science (Bachelard, then Althusser), overlooking the very considerable complexities of developments outside the academy and the politics of which they were the vector. For Guattari, engaged initially in a problem of institutional creativity, there is a concomitant appraisal of science and of theory that runs counter to this now rather clichéd epistemological view of knowledge production.

Clearly, Guattari was no great respecter of intellectual boundaries, any more than he treated different institutional practices as rigidly separate from each other. He shared with Gilles Deleuze a taste for developing ideas that moved *between* disciplinary confines with a lightness and humor that clearly—deliberately—challenged the firmly rooted seriousness, the tendency to ossification, of territorial propriety. This can be gleaned as much from his early writings on the psychiatric institution, working out the implications of shaking up divisions of labor, as it is in his later writings in ecosophy. His growing distance and eventual break from structuralist psychoanalysis, represented, of course, by the figure of Jacques Lacan, is exemplified particularly in his inventive reworking of Hjelmslevian glossematics (against structural linguistics) to facilitate the productive rewiring of the transcendental and the empirical in a semiotics "flush with the real" and as such susceptible of getting a grasp on the texture of the institution (Guattari 1996). Yet what might, in this respect, reasonably be characterized as a *transdisciplinary* experimentation cannot, for all that, be readily transformed simply into a comfortably academic or unproblematically aesthetic exercise. Not in the least because there was always an institutional dimension to the constructivist research processes in which he was engaged. As he put it in a brief text, originally titled "The Ethico-Political Foundations of Interdisciplinarity" (but translated as "Transdisciplinarity Must Become Transversality"), written in 1991, at a time when he was elaborating the theoretical and practical approach to the production of subjectivity that he had taken to calling "ecosophy,"

> As an internal movement of the transformation of the sciences, an opening onto the social, aesthetics and ethics, transdisciplinarity will not be born spontaneously […] Its deepening implies a permanent "research into research," an experimentation with new paths for the constitution of collective assemblages of enunciation. (Guattari 2015a: 135)

It is difficult, undesirable even, to split up theory and practice when it comes to addressing Guattari's thinking. Experimentation, for example, is central to Guattari's work, yet experimentation is not, for him, something that is directed by theory or an activity that seeks to confirm a theoretically established hypothesis. No doubt informed by the work undertaken by the GTPsi, of which he was a member,[1] Guattari's enduring concern for the indissociability of the theory and practice evident in his experimental, "creationist" approach offered a point of view from which to evaluate the degree of openness evident (or not) in other forms of intellectual production. Indeed, he sometimes seems inclined to associate theory divorced from the environment of its production, absent the assemblage processes generative of its enunciation, as at risk of falling prey to the inhibiting functions of the superego. In a 1966 presentation at the La Borde clinic, for example, discussing briefly Althusser's reframing of philosophy as "class struggle in theory," he ironizes "amateurs keep out!" (Guattari 2015b: 206-07). And discussing some years later Gramsci's arguments about organic intellectuals, he similarly refuses the theory/action distinction in favor of the elaboration of (schizoanalytic) processes in which "the very form of the division of labour between militancy, the analysis of the unconscious and intellectual activity should wither away, to the extent that the practice of theory gives up basing itself on systems of universals—even if they are dialectical and materialist—and action establishes itself in the extension of a liberatory economy of desire" (Guattari 2016: 98). Pointing here to some of the concerns that Guattari expressed with regard to theory—or perhaps better, Theory—is not to say that concepts, or something like them, do not matter for him. Gilles Deleuze once remarked, in a letter to Guattari, that he produced "wild" concepts (Deleuze 2015b: 56). Isabelle Stengers, by contrast, characterizes them as "operative constructs," fabrications that were always engaged in a praxis, emphasizing in this way what she sees, in Guattari's experimental thinking as "a positive divergence both from concepts [because they were produced in order to operate on something] and from scientific functions [because their construction can never claim to be legitimated by what they refer to]" (Stengers 2011:140). Guattari, for his part, recurs to the image of the "toolbox" as a way to characterize his theorizing. The functioning of this is captured well by Deleuze who, in his 1972 discussion with Michel Foucault on intellectuals and power, argues for the different relationship between theory and practice this betokens: "practice is a set of relays from one point in theory to another, and theory a relay from one practice to another" (Foucault and Deleuze 2001: 1175). For the remainder of this chapter, I will refer, for reasons of economy, to Guattari's "concepts" but Stengers's useful contrastive characterization should be borne in mind.

Transdisciplinarity must become transversality

How does Guattari understand research and the research on research if transdisciplinarity is to become a "living" practice? Here we might consider a little more carefully his 1991 discussion of inter- and trans-disciplinarity mentioned earlier. Arguing within this text that transdisciplinarity—a term preferable in his eyes to that of "interdisciplinarity"—"must become transversality," Guattari in fact points his reader in precisely the direction that he had been endeavoring to push knowledge production in the field of the human sciences since the early 1960s and his work in the field of institutional psychotherapy. For the concept of transversality—in this respect as much a name for an evolving series of practical and institutional engagements in which Guattari had invested his own very considerable energies as it is a concept—is at the starting point of an intellectual adventure into the exploration of, and experimentation with, an unconscious that challenged the autonomy and sufficiency of any and every project.

Written in the context of Guattari's growing concerns with ecological issues and his endeavors to address these efficaciously across the natural, social, and mental realms, the text itself thematizes not so much the foundations of inter- or trans-disciplinary research—in any case, by the late-1980s part of the landscape of academic research in France (Genosko n.d.)—as the importance of its *transformation*, the importance of enlarging the horizons of ecological research through the proliferation of "social relays" susceptible of changing the nature of the objects that such research engaged with. Questioning the formal status of objectivity in research emerging out of the human sciences more generally and the concomitant evacuation of subjective factors from such research, he evinces a concern to do this by bringing research processes—those focusing on the urban environment, for example—into a relationship of *recurrence* with their objects. The main focus of his discussion is research into the urban environment, a topic of growing concern for inter- or trans-disciplinary work in the 1980s and 1990s, and already—under the heading "collective equipment"—a particular engagement of the Centre for Institutional Study, Researching, and Training (CERFI). But other examples to which he refers, the case of AIDS medication in particular, education, family life, old age, are indicative of what might be cast as the biopolitical dimension of the fields within which the transformation of research he was interested in was to be found. The relationship of recurrence between research practices and social practices and the modifications that it can bring about that Guattari argues for here is not simply an example of what social scientists might think of as reflexivity (which maintains the stable distinction of roles, if only in the researcher's head) but rather sketches out the possibility and desirability of constituting a *machine*, or, as he puts it in this brief discussion, "in the course of authentic research, one is always caught up in a constructivist process" (Guattari 2015a: 131).[2]

In calling for the transversal transformation of transdisciplinarity, Guattari quite clearly presents himself as someone concerned with the problematic sufficiency of professional expertise as the basis for undertaking research. While written after his engagement with CERFI was over (he withdrew in 1981), the question of the sufficiency of professional expertise would have been an obvious point of concern for him, not only because CERFI had benefitted for a number of years from generous state funding for its research projects without its personnel holding professionally accredited positions but also because of the ways in which that professionalization would change the nature of the processes involved in research practices. As someone who did not have a position as an academic, who worked for many years at the La Borde clinic as well as in his own psychoanalytical practice, and militated extensively not just around obvious political causes but also in significant relation to the possibilities of conducting collective research, Guattari was certainly no stranger to the problematic cloistering and compartmentalization of intellectual expertise or to the deadening effect of bureaucracy on research institutions. Indeed, his own endeavors at reformulating analytical ideas about the unconscious consistently point toward a critique of professional expertise that was central to his toolbox understanding of the role of concepts and their function in the process of relaying.

Transversality revisited

Guattari's formulation of the problem with transdisciplinarity merits further commentary. Obviously for Deleuze and for Guattari, advocating a toolbox approach to thinking, there can be no question of specifying in advance how a concept is to be used (not that this has prevented a generation of Deleuze scholars from endeavoring to do precisely that), and an appeal to origins as a way to denounce misappropriations would itself be rather difficult to square with the transformational, experimental spirit of Deleuze and Guattari's thinking. However, as a number of commentators have noted, it is impossible to miss the way in which the growing popularity of the term "transversality"—as a way of thinking about research, as a way to characterize the "structuralist" vulgate of French thinking in the 1960s, and so on—has tended to excise from this concept much of the connective tissue surrounding it, a tissue of relations that would facilitate its efficacious grafting into other contexts. As Valentin Schaeplynck has noted, referring in turn to the work of Olivier Apprill (2015) and Paul Brétecher (2012), "the notion of transversality has been the occasion for many misunderstandings, in particular when all reference to psychoanalysis, to the unconscious and to the conflictual dimension of processes of institutionalization are erased" (Schaeplynck 2018: 49). Following Schaeplynck, Apprill, and Brétecher, we might say that without the experimental, potentially conflictual but always transformational praxis with which it was bound up for Guattari, there is a distinct risk of transversality simply becoming transdisciplinarity.

The concept of transversality emerged as the fruit of an ongoing and intensive engagement of workers in the field of psychiatry in France with psychoanalysis, and more specifically, with the limits of traditional psychoanalytic technique when faced with patients in an institutional setting. In this respect (although it did not, at least in the first instance, play this role), the concept also forms a part of Guattari's incipient critique of Lacanian psychoanalysis and its insufficiencies with regard to the treatment of psychosis. This in turn precipitated its extension and revision, with the assistance of Deleuze (whose own strategic interest in psychosis was made fully evident in *Logic of Sense*), as part of a more nuanced response to the structuralist ideal in Lacanian analysis. It is, of course, easy to read the development of the concept of transversality retrospectively, in the light of Deleuze's more obviously philosophical proclivities, but doing so can blind us to elements of Guattari's thinking that are of signal importance with regard to his later interest in research as such. As writings from toward the end of his life indicate, the "singular experience" of working at the La Borde clinic where these ideas were first developed not only marked Guattari deeply but informed his understanding of the "ethico-political" roots of all analytic work (Guattari 2012).

In a series of texts written in the early to mid-1960s, Guattari can be found wrestling with the ossified and bureaucratic quality of psychiatric institutions, referring (no doubt in part with Tosquelles in mind) to the experiences of prisoners of war and concentration camps as giving some people a different view of the psychiatric hospital. Given that, as he puts it, the "habitual proliferation of institutions in contemporary society only results in the reinforcement of the alienation of the individual," he asks, "is there a possibility that a transfer of responsibility may be brought about and that an *institutional creativity* might take the place of bureaucracy?" (Guattari 2015b: 62 [translation modified]). In this context, a question about the nature of groups within the psychiatric institution emerges for Guattari, evidently influenced, like numerous others working in the sector, by Sartre's *Critique of Dialectical Reason*. Considering the institutional locatedness of "the mad" and the situation of psychiatry and psychiatrists—as those socially delegated to deal with a group lacking the aptitude for "normal" commerce—Guattari, among others, sought to reformulate psychoanalytic thinking in such a way as to overcome the problems raised, in an institutional setting, both by its reliance on a kind of methodological individualism and its emerging reworking by a focus on language.

Referring even at this early stage to the institutional subject as a "collective agent of enunciation," Guattari's aim was to avoid a situation in which the institution might become a structure, a possibility that he felt would, analytically, imply a reification of the institution. Thinking in terms of groups rather than structures allowed Guattari to retain a concern with praxis and its possibilities vis-à-vis an institution, necessitating in turn a commitment to the transitory in order to make good on the idea of breaking down the barrier between reason and madness in society at large. And making a distinction between subjugated groups (groups that are the object of the discourse of others, the rules for whose functioning are received from the outside) and subject groups (groups that are the subject of their own enunciation, self-founding, themselves prescribing the way they operate), or rather, between these two dimensions as they can be at work in any group, further facilitated the possibility of developing an analytic exploration of the social unconscious operative within the institution. The concept of transversality intervenes here as a way to introduce distinctions between groups with regard to their degree of openness toward, and aptitude for bringing to light, the desire that circulated within the institution. Subjugated groups, bound up in the ritual cultivation of their symptoms, the territorial maintenance of roles allotted to them in a division of labor, would not be apt for doing this. Subject groups, by contrast, accepting the finitude of their projects, assuming the non-sense of the desire of which they are the bearers, carry the performative potential for the production of a process of analysis within the institution—of the institution and the transversal quality of its unconscious (Schaeplynck 2018: 46 on performativity).

Clearly the theorization of transversality and its links to a conceptualization of groups on the basis of the subject/subjugated distinction made a critique of professional expertise not only possible but necessary, for given that those normally in charge of the institution were just as likely to be the objects of other discourses, invested in the vertical dimension of hierarchy both inside and outside the institution, there could be no guarantee that they would be in a particularly good position to bring to light the desire operative within the institution. Hence, in a text from 1962–1963, discussing institutional psychotherapy, Guattari argued for the importance of

> [having] done with the doctor as individual, colleague, citizen, who puts himself forward as the one who "speaks for …," who is the "spokesperson" of the subject that the institution could be. And not necessarily in full knowledge of so doing. Is he not himself as much the unconscious prisoner as the agent of this process, with his conjugal life, his culture, his opinions, etc. (Guattari 2015b: 69–70, translation modified)

In his preface to *Psychoanalysis and Transversality*, Deleuze brings out well a crucial aspect of the functioning of the concept of transversality for Guattari: it breaks down the opposition (even the dialectically complicated one) between analysis and desire. As he put it in typically Deleuzian terms, institutional analysis has the practical aim of

> introducing into the institution a militant political function, constituting a sort of "monster" that is neither psychoanalysis nor hospital practice, even less group dynamics, and which aims to be applicable everywhere, in the hospital, the school, in militancy—a machine to produce and to enunciate desire. (Deleuze 2015a: 19)

From institutions to infrastructures

In the context of Guattari's appraisal of transdisciplinarity, what is particularly interesting about the discovery/invention of transversality is that by "detotalizing" the institution, it implied the need to extend the analytic possibilities of the unconscious out into society more generally, a point that Guattari made readily in a discussion of institutional training written at the end of the 1980s:

> Whilst working on a day to day basis with its hundred or so patients, La Borde found itself progressively implicated in a more global calling into question of health, pedagogy, the penal condition, the condition of women, of architecture, of urban planning. (Guattari 2012: 68)

This implication led in turn to a series of group initiatives that were, as he puts it, set up with a view to exploring "unconscious formations that didn't just concern the two protagonists of classical psychoanalysis but could be broadened out to much larger segments of society" (Guattari 2012: 69). Dosse has suggested that the Federation of Groups for Institutional Study and Research (FGERI), set up in 1965—to which Guattari is alluding in this quote—aimed, in this regard, to "convert intellectual work into a programme of non-academic research" (Dosse 2007: 99), a programme in which research that might otherwise be considered the privileged domain of academic institutions could acquire a different set of connections with the social field. In any case, the editorial of the second issue of the journal *Recherches* that formed the mouthpiece of the federation (and later, the Centre for Institutional Study, Researching, and Training [CERFI]) makes it clear that the transversal approach to research that was envisaged would not be divorced from a concern with the institutions, and consequently, with producing precisely that militant function for the production and enunciating of desire pinpointed by Deleuze:

> *Recherches* is the mouthpiece of every group that works in a social field directed towards the analysis of the institutions in which everyone is inserted and agrees to be constantly addressed by groups planted in other sectors. (Dosse 2007: 100)

The reality of this programme—a testament equally to the political upheavals of the years following the events of May 1968—was doubtless somewhat chaotic. CERFI, which was set up on the back of FGERI in 1967 and became a fully fledged research organization, received numerous grants from the French government, and it is probably true to say that the experimental contestation of the division between analysis and desire it facilitated in relation to research didn't always result in decisions that facilitated the kind of research into research that Guattari wanted. The activities of CERFI have proved to be of interest to scholars interested in aspects of the history of French theory, not least perhaps, because of the involvement of Foucault with some of its projects (see, among others, Mozère 2004). In the present context, CERFI is interesting because a number of the projects that it undertook anticipate, in their foci, the substantive issues that Guattari addresses in his discussion of transdisciplinarity and transversality. Publications that resulted from the third of CERFI's substantial research grants, devoted to studying the "genealogy of collective equipment," are of special note in this regard. In addition to the involvement of Foucault and Deleuze, the focus of this project gives its title to a manuscript written by Guattari while he was working on *A Thousand*

Plateaus with Deleuze, "Collective Equipment and Semiotic Subjugation" (Guattari 2016). Engaging specifically in the study of issues that might now be considered the province of urbanism, town planning, or urban geography, the first of the issues of *Recherches* exploring the loosely conceived genealogy included two interviews with Foucault. And while the discussions are not entirely conclusive, they do point toward some of the ways in which the transversal approach to transdisciplinary research Guattari was interested in extended into a reworking of his understanding of the "social" unconscious, which is flatly identified, in the first of two discussions with Foucault, with "collective equipment as such" (Foucault et al. 2001: 1316). The idea of collective equipment is notably absent from *A Thousand Plateaus*, which is, in some respects, regrettable. It is largely the exploration of collective equipment undertaken by CERFI (and other CERFI projects such as that by Anne Querrien) that informs the concern with machinic enslavement in that book and in Guattari's own later references to the planetary networks of Integrated World Capitalism (Guattari 2013: 36–37). And it is precisely in relationship to the multiplicity of struggles that take place around collective equipment that Guattari sees the rhizomatic potentialities for transformation that duly transversalized analytic practice—an "analytico-militant labour at all scales"—is able to put into operation (Guattari 2016: 68).

Conclusion

Transversal transdisciplinary research, like the work in and on the institution out of which it emerges, more broadly entails a calling into question of the prerogatives vis-à-vis analytic processes that derive from unquestioned hierarchies and the fixed roles that correlate to them. Indeed, what the experimental practice of research entails when following the lines of flight that transversal analytic processes can facilitate is not just a calling into question of all models (including that of the analyst) but a "permanent reinvention of democracy" (Guattari 2015a: 133). The work of cognitive elaboration implied in research is, as he puts it, "inseparable from human commitment and the choice of values it implies" (Guattari 2015a: 133). But these are not values that are given (Guattari is beyond the fact-value distinction) but the values that are, or can be, produced in the construction of new assemblages of enunciation. From this point of view, transdisciplinarity is cognate with what Guattari sometimes calls "axiological creationism."

It is probably true to say that the prospects for the kind of transdisciplinary research that Guattari was envisaging at the end of the 1980s have become considerably more complex, given the transformations that have been effectuated by Integrated World Capitalism since then (cf. Genosko 2003: 136–38). The thread of connections linking Guattari's work with CERFI in the 1970s, the work on collective equipment in particular, and the slightly later work with Deleuze in *A Thousand Plateaus* in some respects anticipates what at the start of the 1990s Guattari characterizes as "machinic transdisciplinarity." Envisaged *prospectively*, beyond the focus on urban research out of which it emerges, in the context of technological developments around informatics, it entails that closer consideration be given to the connections that he sees between technology and science (and hence, in a more academic context, the nebulous construct "technoscience"). There is an optimism to Guattari's thinking here that is bound up with his speculations about what such developments might make possible—machinic transdisciplinarity, a transdisciplinarity "internal" to the language of informatics, that would "position research 'astride' science, art and social communication" (Genosko 2003: 135). Perhaps it's too soon to evaluate this sort of claim, even if the instances to which Guattari was pointing (arising from "hypertextuality") may appear to have floundered or, rather, been crushed by the astonishing pace of commercialization of networked computing. Guattari's optimism was, in any case, accompanied by considerable lucidity about the prospects for the emergence of such research. Transversality offers no guarantees: it opens up possibilities for change because it is addressed to the precarious contingencies of what is or what could be coming into being, the ecology of the virtual. If it draws our attention to the prospects for creative transformation it is, nevertheless, inseparable from broader political struggle.

Notes

1   The Institutional Psychotherapy and Sociotherapy Working Group (Groupe de travail de psychothérapie et de sociothérapie institutionnelles), who worked together for six years, from 1960 to 1966. Their work—and their modus operandi—has been studied in some detail by Olivier Apprill (2015).

2   On "recurrence" see for example the appendix to the original French publication of Gilles Deleuze and Félix Guattari's *Anti-Oedipus* translated as "Balance-sheet Program for Desiring Machines" (1977: 117–18).

Bibliography

Apprill, O. (2015), *Une avant-garde psychiatrique. Le moment GTPSI (1960–1966)*, Paris: Epel.

Brétecher, P. (2012), "Transversalité, chaosmose et cuisine," *Chimères*, 2 (77): 91–107.

Deleuze, G. (2015a), "Three Group-Related Problems," Preface to Guattari, 2015b.

Deleuze, G. (2015b), *Lettres et autres textes*, Paris: Minuit.

Deleuze, G., and Guattari, F. (1977), "Balance-Sheet Program for Desiring Machines," *Semiotext(e)*, special issue on "Anti-Oedipus. From Psychoanalysis to Schizopolitics," II (3).

Dosse, F. (2007), *Gilles Deleuze Félix Guattari. Biographie Croisée*, Paris: La Découverte.

Foucault, M. (1972), "The Discourse on Language," in *The Archeology of Knowledge*, London: Tavistock.

Foucault, M., and Deleuze, G. (2001), "Les intellectuels et le pouvoir," in Foucault, M., *Dits et Écrits I. 1954–1975*, Paris: Gallimard.

Foucault, M., Fourquet, F., and Guattari, F. (2001), "Premières discussions, premiers balbutiements: la ville est-elle une force productive ou d'anti-production," in M. Foucault, *Dits et Écrits 1: 1954–1975*, Paris: Gallimard Quarto.

Genosko, G. (2003), "Félix Guattari: Towards a transdisciplinary metamethodology," *Angelaki* 8 (1).

Genosko, G. (n.d.), "A French Project: Transdisciplinary Microinstitutions and Journal Publishing," no publishing details.

Guattari, F. (1996), "The Place of the Signifier in the Institution," in Genosko, G. (ed.), *The Guattari Reader*, 148–57, Oxford: Blackwell.

Guattari, F. (2012), *De Leros à la Borde*, Paris: Lignes.

Guattari, F. (2013), "Pratiques écosophiques et restauration de la cité subjective," in *Qu'est-ce que l'écosophie*, Abbaye d'ardenne: Lignes/Imec.

Guattari, F. (2015a), "Transdisciplinarity Must Become Transversality," "*Theory, Culture & Society,*" 32 (5–6).

Guattari, F. (2015b), *Psychoanalysis and Transversality. Texts and Interviews 1955–1971*, Los Angeles: Semiotext(e).

Guattari, F. (2016), *Lines of Flight. For Another World of Possibilities*, trans. A. Goffey, London: Bloomsbury.

Kirkup, J. (1992), "Obituary: Félix Guattari," *The Independent*, September 1, 1992.

Mozère, L. (2004), "Foucault et le CERFI: instantanés et actualités," *Le Portique*, 13–14, accessible here: http://leportique.revues.org/642 (last accessed August 08, 2018).

Schaeplynck, V. (2018), *L'Institution renversée. Folie, analyse institutionnelle et champ social*, Paris: Eterotopia.

Stengers, I. (2011), "Relaying a War Machine," in É. Alliez and A. Goffey (eds), *The Guattari Effect*, London: Continuum.

3

The Semiotics of De-Modeling

Peirce and Guattari on the Diagram

Guillaume Collett and
Chryssa Sdrolia

Introduction

While Félix Guattari is often characterized as a restless theoretical innovator, spawning a myriad of seemingly otherworldly abstractions, this productivity risks clouding both his methodology and the contextual stakes of his innovations. This chapter argues that one of the key ways of understanding Guattari's work is by highlighting his method of "metamodelization," by means of which preexisting models across the disciplines are theoretically inhabited in order to track down the points at which they close themselves up and come to stand apart—as "theory," "model," or "structure"—from the singular, historical, practical, and institutional (in short, "transversal"[1]) contexts of their production. Guattari develops the notion of metamodelization in a number of texts and especially in *Chaosmosis* (1992), in which he opposes his better-known creation schizoanalysis to psychoanalysis on the basis that psychoanalysis purports to develop a "universal reading, with scientific claims," whereas schizoanalysis (the "metamodel") is "partial," not totalizing, and orientated by "functional" (Guattari 1995: 11) and "axiological" (Guattari 1995: 34, 55, 84) questions, above all "the way [metamodelization] uses terms to develop possible openings onto the virtual and onto creative processuality" (Guattari 1995: 31).

To metamodel is thus in a way to "de-model" so as to return to the transdisciplinary basis of modeling as such—though the sense of de-modeling implies that this transdisciplinary basis is itself immanent to each process of de-modeling and cannot be itself "modeled" as transcending these singular contexts. Indeed, for this reason, Guattari elsewhere will speak of metamodeling rather as a "*discipline* of reading other systems of modeling," insofar as it is to be approached "not as a general model," at risk in the very notion of a "transdisciplinary" framework, but as "an instrument for deciphering modeling systems in various domains" (emphasis added, quoted in Watson 2009: 8), including within the problematic of transdisciplinarity itself.[2] Others have hence described Guattari's work as a politics of models or, as Éric Alliez (2015) puts it, an "*intervention*" which "mobilize[s] the politics at stake" in the work in question (139, emphasis in the original).

It is in this sense that we propose to examine the notion of *diagram* as a framework for thinking that seeks to promise a greater degree of singularity and processual immanence to its emergent conditions than that found in what we are terming "structure."[3] The term "diagram" is taken from its first innovator within the field of semiotics, Charles Sanders Peirce, whose notion of "semiosis" has precisely these advantages over Saussurian signification. While the first section will explore semiosis' irreducibility to structural or semiological signification in Peirce's work, the flexible adaptability of the diagram will be further emphasized in the second section on Guattari and structural or Lacanian psychoanalysis. While this chapter will not be concerned with reconstructing the precise nature of Peirce's influence on Guattari, nor judging the validity of Guattari's appropriation of his notion, what will be shown is how between these two thinkers, a shared understanding of the diagram emerges as process of de-modeling.

Given that much of Peirce's posthumous reception has focused on his extensive typologies of signs, his association with the critique of structural closure might strike an odd note. Peirce does announce the creation of an architectonic made of "simple concepts applicable to every subject" on several occasions (*CP* 1898: 1.10).[4] Yet anyone who reads his work with a mind to discovering an ultimate philosophical structure is bound to be perplexed. Peirce remains mistrustful of the very demonstrative type of reasoning that would guarantee the definitional simplicity of the concepts in the first place, let alone their foundational value. No sooner is triadism established than it is abducted into divergent series by the very subjects it is supposed to apply to, making each new triad a singular construction. There is a metaphysical triad but also a physiological, a logical, a biological, a phaneroscopic, and a psychological one. To be sure, all of them converge in their triadic makeup; yet they are less the pre-given components of a homogeneous structure than the many geneses of a thought that is decentered every time it inscribes itself in a disciplinary milieu. In turn, this decentering can only be accompanied by the "search for *a* method," the efficacy of which cannot be determined beforehand.⁵ The method itself will have to be *experimented* with while the problems are being constructed—while thought *experiences* itself as contingent to the worlds it taps into and whose vital relations make it mutable, plural, and potentially fallible.

Relying on this experience the philosopher will not be able to elevate any architectonic to the level of an all-encompassing structure. To the extent that the method interacts with the world, the architectonic it enables is merely a system of habitual relations. In this sense, it can only be tested according to the "effects" it distributes in relation to a specific problem (*CP* 1902: 5.2, 1903: 5.196). The philosopher is thus called to a pragmatism *of creation* appropriate to the experimenter, to refrain from the allure of turning an explanatory system into a conceptual structure that would overdetermine the ability of the world to rupture and disprove it. The whole of Peircean semiotics as such a pragmatic affair turns on this point. The world must be acknowledged as speaking in its own signs, as engaging a semiotic process that spontaneously proliferates into multiple directions. If our theories are to be worthy of this spontaneity at all, they need to be taken as the effects of an ever-shifting mutual construction. In his pivotal article "The Architecture of Theories" for *The Monist* in 1891, Peirce is going to make the point in no unclear terms: a theory needs to exhibit a radical evolutionism or nothing at all (*CP* 1891: 6.14). What compels this radicalism is the need to resist what, in his time, has become bad practice—namely, the tendency of scientific positivism to silence the plurivocality of the world by neutralizing it into conceptual structures that aspire to be given once and for all.

By bringing Peirce and Guattari together, this chapter will explore how in the fields of semiotics and psychoanalysis, the two thinkers develop a practice of thought inhabiting a movement that is evolutionary and transversal, respectively. Again, we are not attempting to establish a genealogical link between them or a kind of mutual understanding. Barring Guattari's idiosyncratic reading of Peirce and the fact that they are separated in time as they are in contingency, they situate themselves in different milieus in response to different problems. Peirce's problem is restoring to nature the capacity to speak; Guattari's, on the other hand, is freeing unconscious signs from structural psychoanalysis. Yet insofar as both resist structural closure, they are both participating in the mode of pragmatic creation that Peirce would consider appropriate to philosophy as experimentation and Guattari to a free institution. What is interesting is that in both cases, this pragmatic creation revolves around the creation of a sign that resists overcodification in that it is immanent to its singular milieus and thus reinvents itself every time the relations of its milieus shift.

Peirce's semiotic Diagram

"Semiosis," wrote Peirce in 1905, is "an action, or influence, which is, or involves, a cooperation of three subjects, such as a sign, its object, and its interpretant, this tri-*relative* influence *not* being in any way resolvable into actions between pairs" (CP 1905: 5.484, emphasis in the original). The idiosyncratic use of the term "interpretant" and the respective assignation of sign, object, *and* interpretant as "subjects" should give us a clue of the challenge involved in approaching Peircean semiotics from a structuralist point of view. The problem is not simply that Peirce uses none of the familiar distinctions between signifier and signified that modern semiology inherits from Saussure. The nature of the Peircean "subject" itself as well as the type of relation that requires it are enough to make the grafting of structuralist terminology onto his system nearly impossible. Besides the fact that the otherwise contemporary thinkers oddly miss each other, the language of "double articulation" itself would risk compromising the triplicity of the sign.

For Peirce, this triplicity is already contained in the commonest of definitions: a sign "is something that stands *to* somebody *for* something" (CP 1897: 2.228, emphasis added). Yet the reduction of this "standing for" into the isomorphic correspondence between two distinct planes is avoided from the beginning. A sign is not simply "*to* some thought which interprets it" and "*for* some object to which in that thought it is equivalent" (W2 1868: 223, emphasis in the original). It crucially involves a third articulation: it is "*in* some respect or quality, which brings it into connection with its object" (W2 1868: 223, emphasis in the original). It is this latter quality, simultaneously demanded and enabled by the "connection" itself that the model of bi-univocality, to borrow a term popular in the Lacanian school, does not adequately express.

To understand the irresolvability of the semiotic connection into a dyad that is "self-contained" and motivated by nothing other than the internal relations of the system of linguistic signs (Saussure [1916] 1974: 134), it is essential to linger on what exactly a triad entails. Peirce's writings are dominated by this concern. His experimentations appear as early as 1857 in his "Diagram of the It" mapping the connection of the categories that Peirce at this stage still calls "I, Thou, It."[6] Leaving aside their subsequent evolution into Firstness, Secondness, and Thirdness, their elaboration in 1861 already contains the gist of triadic relations:

> If conceptions which are incapable of definition are simple, I, It, and Thou are so. Who could define either of these words, easy as they are to understand? Who does not perceive, in fact, that neither of them can be expressed in terms of the

others? [...] Though they cannot be expressed in terms of each other, yet they have a relation to each other, for THOU is an IT in which there is another I. I looks in, It looks out, Thou looks *through*, out and in again. [...] True the I may be IT—as when we think of ourselves objectively. The IT may become THOU— in apostrophe. The THOU may become IT—in cruelty or rather hardness. The IT may even become I—in Pantheism. [...] Yet in all the cases [...] the I, the IT, and the THOU are [...] in three different worlds. (*W1* 1861: 45–46, original upper case and emphasis)

The terminological complexity of this passage should not obscure what Peirce proposes: the three categories are irreducible to each other yet they may become one another in their mutual relations; this quality makes them resistant to a clear-cut definition and yet each of them can be singularly experienced. We are here given the portrait of a philosophy whose object is categorical yet impossible to categorize. The importance of this impossibility cannot be overstated: the three categories are neither relata nor relations. Peircean semiotics thus finds its starting point in a paradox inducing structural indeterminacy. The experience of this indeterminacy alone, which is practiced before it is even formalized as such, accounts for the difference in method between semiotics and semiology. The work of the semiotician will never be to look for definite and ultimate prior components to arrive at a structuralist science of signification.[7] Instead, it will evolve as a pragmatic experimentation with semiosis as a process that is to be evaluated in terms of its diagrammatic effects.

Peirce explores the relations of the categories in another manuscript from the same period titled "The Modus of the IT" (*W1* 1861: 47–49). The essay is important not only because etymologically the "Modus" puts the Diagram on the track of what is simultaneously movement and motivation at the heart of the triadic connection. It warrants attention also because this movement reasserts the importance of experience by recalling the familiar problem of synthesis. Before the relations of the categories are laid out, Peirce asks: "How shall sense become consciousness?" (*W1* 1861: 47).

This question gives us the philosophical milieu of Peirce's thought and, with it, another point of difference between his semiotics and Saussure's semiology: whereas the latter does not begin with, or does not require, a metaphysical understanding of the sign, semiotics does. The difference in method between the two approaches is therefore tied to a difference in origin. Peirce's relational triadism needs to be evaluated as responding to the Kantian project and, in particular, the problem of synthesizing the faculties in a way that Peirce would rather envisage as "uncritical" (*W1* 1861–1862: 79). The routes that connect his work to post-critical philosophy are too intricate to do justice to here. Suffice it to say that in his explorations, sense and consciousness are not taken as two preexisting and discontinuous realms necessitating the intervention of a term external to them. Instead of the logic of distillation that Peirce finds in the Kantian project (*CP* [undated]: 1.384), he opts for the logic of "conjunction": sense can only become consciousness by being "conjoined with" a third term that Peirce calls "abstraction" or "experience" (*W1* 1861: 47). The particularity of this third term is that it is not added to a dyad; rather it is the connective tissue that internally co-emerges with the two terms it connects.

The internal operation of the Peircean third becomes clearer as the Modus spirals into a series of trifurcations where the middle term produced by each triad is also required both by that triad and for the next. "Abstraction" may be produced and required by the triad "sense, abstraction, consciousness" but it already partakes in another triad that Peirce calls "time, absoluteness, space" and so on until the Modus arrives at the "I, Thou, It" triad (*W1* 1861: 47). Every middle term is thus selected twice: once for the triad it already occupies and once for the next. The effect of this double selection is that by the time any component is called a second time it has already become other than itself. By means of an operation that is as conjunctive as it is generative of the terms it needs, the Diagram remains ambiguous and open, its potential explanatory circularity being disrupted at every junction.

The mode of connection is elsewhere clarified as follows: any three terms "*A, B, C*" are not to be taken as the preexisting and independent members in a set. To the extent that they are related, they are brought into being by the conjunction itself (*W1* 1861: 85).[8] Peirce uses an example from mathematics: any three terms connect "just as in arithmetic 7 results from 3 *and* 4, though not the same as three *with* four" (*W1* 1857: 15, emphasis added). In the triad (3,7,4), the third term "7" is not the result of a simple aggregation of "3" and "4." We do not have a result isomorphic, identical or equal to its components. At the point of the junction there is the creation of novelty, a term conceived both as "some-thing" required by the union and as the "process" that sets the union in motion (*W1* 1861: 85). We therefore have a tension between structure and process, which qualifies the result of the triadic connection as different from its terms. In this tension we also find the locus of the semiotic paradox: a sign is a whole exceeding the sum of its parts; it is a manifold of continuous or neighboring components that are internally and relationally differentiated at the junction as their mutual limit (*W1* 1861: 462).

The tension between process and structure triggers a series of consequences that are critical for a future semiotics. First of all, on the level of relation alone, the Diagram leaves no room for the Saussurean model of dualistic correspondence. From a Peircean perspective, severing linguistic expression from conceptual content would beg the question of their synthesis again.[9] Even the proposed solution of the simultaneous "cutting" of the expression and content suggested by Saussure's paper-sheet metaphor would be taken to contradict their very autonomy (Saussure [1916] 1974: 113). Instead of addressing the ambiguity between relatum and relation, the signifying dyad would be criticized as disengaging the structured sign from the structuring act of signification. Peirce might agree with Saussure that linguistics "works in the *borderland* where the elements of sound and thought combine" (Saussure [1916] 1974: 113). However, the latter's conclusion that this combination produces "*a form, not a substance*" ends up producing another separation between the system of signs and a reality external to it (Saussure [1916] 1974: 113, emphasis in the original). The problem of motivation regarding the relation between the two orders, which Saussure had sought to resolve through the concept of arbitrariness, would return renewed: if the combination of the planes is only ever formal, if signification is independent from any extra-linguistic determination, why should signs be created in the first place?[10]

The inadequacy of a formal dyadic structure to account for the problem of an implied and generative third term does not exhaust the differences between semiology and semiotics. To the extent that the Diagram is tied to the problem of synthesis, it also entails a new theory of the subject. As is the case with the categories "I, Thou, It," object and subject are no longer divided by a structural gap between them but conjoin in experience as their shared abstract limit. This limit is neither inner nor outer. As Peirce explains, it is "mixed" and nonconscious, "not a world of self but of instances of self" (W1 1865: 167, 168–69). Freed from receptivity, experience becomes the place where the subject is continuously and processually determined with and by its object (W2 1868: 191).

From that point onward, the question "who signifies" is turned on its head. We no longer have a vocal subject assigning meaning to a silent world but a world that is an equal participant in semiosis. That a black cloud stands *to* me *for* rain does not necessarily make me the source of semiosis. Insofar as I am mutually determined by the black cloud, I am also its object or, properly speaking, its "correlate" (W1 1866: 520) and hence a mere channel for the real subject that is the sign "rain." Indeed, if we insist on using the term "subject" at all then we need to be aware that it is "an abstraction," as Peirce warns—a mobile locus that may be a human but not necessarily so. Any-thing and any-body can be a subject (W1 1865: 335). In the rain, I may be said to stand *to* the falling water *for* an obstacle that forces it to change its trajectory. In any semiotic junction, the subject is the middle more properly called an "interpretant" (W2 1868: 223).

The speculative indifference of the interpretant for traditional dualisms has a double effect: it protects semiotics from having to suppose a division between concept and thing *and* from having to connect the two through the route of psychologism. With this gesture, semiotics avoids from the beginning what in structural linguistics eventually becomes a problem. Precisely because he leaves this division unquestioned, Saussure relies on the supposition that the "sound-image" attached to a concept in the sign is not "a purely physical thing, but the psychological imprint of the sound" (Saussure [1916] 1974: 66). However, this solution will not only end up presupposing the very physical real that is to be bracketed from the sign but will also compromise the arbitrariness of signification by tracing it back to a subject having an inexplicable relation with that physical real. Despite its promise to decouple signification from anything external and resist the fallacy that the sign is "freely chosen" by the subject (Saussure [1916] 1974: 71), structural linguistics ends up tethering the sign to the anthropological and signification to phenomenology.

The problem of psychologism allows us to clarify that the internal relations subtending Saussurean signification and the internal movement of Peircean interpretation relate to two very different adventures. The interpretant may be said to be internal to the semiotic junction but this junction is radically open to an outside that defies the psychological internalization of the thing into a closed signifying structure. Peirce's own examples leave little room for doubt. Interpretation is said of a pollen grain standing to the ovule it fertilizes for the plant that the grain comes from (W1 1865: 333); of an "inscription which no one can read, a natural face upon a rock which no one has seen or shall see" (W1 1865: 326); or of the "color of a flower upon the flower" (W1 1865: 326). The effects that the Diagram distributes remain metaphysical: by interpreting itself as red, the red flower literally crosses the limit that enables it to become its own sign, to experience itself in its subjectivity in becoming red. In this sense, the sign does not "represent" any thing without also constructing that thing. The foundational premise of a phenomenology of signs is hereby removed. Signs are not *about* things or phenomena but things themselves. As such they are said to participate in a semiotic process conceived as the abstractly *physical* "machinery of realization" through which the world interprets itself into existence (W1 1861: 88).

The abstractly material sign widens the distance of semiotics from structural linguistics. Contrary to signification, semiosis cannot be conceived as lacking in extra-linguistic motivation. Rather, it is extra-linguistic motivation itself, the impulse that restores to the world its voice—a sense of unconscious purposiveness beyond the strictures of the finality of reason or natural causation. The interpretant is nothing other than the "purpose, effect, or actuality" of the triadic or mediating relation itself (W1 1865: 335). We could call this purpose "a-signifying" or "pre-signifying" but these terms, too, would not fit easily into Peirce's system as the sign is never restricted to signification or representation classically understood.[11] If the transcendent signifier never appears in his semiotics, it is because its condition of possibility never arises. In the Diagram, "the reference to an interpretant arises upon the holding together of diverse impressions and therefore it does not join a conception to the substance [...] but unites directly the manifold of substance itself" (W2 1867: 54).[12] Instead of searching for an invariant formal structure of signifiers, the study of signs will have to employ a different mode of thought—one that follows from the interpretive operation of the Diagram itself.

The mode of thought Peirce turns to is hypothesis or "abduction" as the only inferential process that requires and thrives on an *excess* of material connections. Abduction is particular in that it never simply explicates what is already implied in the premises. In this capacity, its interpretant differs from a deductive one (W1 1866: 459). But what is even more interesting is the difference of an abductive interpretant from an inductive one. This is because, at first sight, both inferential modes seem to increase the "information" of a syllogism—namely, the quantity of the new interpretants in a conclusion (W1 1866: 465–66). Indeed, induction does result in superfluity—in a certain non-isomorphism between premise and conclusion—by increasing the extension of the subject of a proposition (W1 1866: 428). Yet while induction stretches to an infinite degree a valid probabilistic conclusion, abduction infers non-necessarily (W1 1865: 271). Increasing the comprehension of the predicate of a proposition instead, the superfluity of abductive interpretants is not even possible to describe in terms of probability. This is because while induction "infers from one set of facts another set of similar facts [...] hypothesis infers from facts of one kind to facts of another" (CP 1866: 2.642). It is therefore the only inferential movement that does not put *excess* into ordered sets but is primarily *creative* of it. Induction may be said to extend our knowledge and deduction to make it distinct. Prior to knowledge, however, abduction arrives at sheer novelty, which may even be consciously observed. As such, it "[gives] us our facts" (W1 1865: 283). By inferring from fact to fact, from sign to sign, it exemplifies that vital element of differentiation in the Diagram in terms of which the interpreted sign becomes different in kind from their premises (*CP* 1866: 2.642).

As the only genuine leap from the given, abduction becomes the only conceivable starting point for semiotics both logically and experientially: "It is hypothesis with which we must start; the baby when he lies turning his finger before his eyes is making a hypothesis as to the connection of what he sees and what he feels" (*W1* 1865: 283). Hypothesis thus simultaneously involves a lot less and a lot more than what is afforded by the phenomenological reduction of a field of variation into general categories. As Peirce puts it, "[the] moment an expression acquires sufficient comprehension to determine its extension, it already has more than enough to do so" (*W1* 1866: 465). Correspondingly, "whenever we make a term to express any thing or any attribute, there is no way we can make so empty that it shall have no superfluous comprehension" (*W1* 1866: 467). Becoming subject, or becoming interpretant, is becoming the experienced limit where the tremendous superfluity of material flows can find an immanent *though not exhaustive* expression in a sign.

As the by-product and the raw material of interpretation, abduction has two important consequences. On the one hand, it allows us to add a final layer to the question of arbitrariness, as it is clear that Peirce orients it away from the operation of bracketing the real. Insofar as the real fabricates itself in signs, arbitrariness is not needed to guard against the reductive presupposition of things-in-themselves waiting to be labeled. Rather, it comes to refer to the very non-necessity of excessive experiential connections that prevent semiosis from closing onto a structure in the first place. The world may have a say in the creation of a sign but it does not demand that any sign be expressed in a given way. The sign "substance" itself that the interpretant unites directly, as Peirce says, is abducted by a "there is" but this "there is" does not necessitate the same sign for all languages and all circumstances and might not even result in the sign at all. The minimum requirement of interpretation is that the limit be crossed but not in structurally determined way. We thus arrive at the second consequence of abduction: the superfluity of the sign at its genesis is the superfluity of the sign throughout. The sign evolves and must be allowed to evolve. This leads us to the ultimate constraint of a semiotics that, as Peirce puts it, needs to exhibit a "thoroughgoing evolutionism or none" (*CP* 1891: 6.14).

The evolutionary character of the semiotic operation initiated by the Diagram of the It finds its refinement in the mature expression of the categories. Insofar as a sign refers to a quality, it expresses the category of the First. In itself, the First is not "definitely" but only potentially a sign; it only appears as "possibility" when involved in a relationship with a "Second," an existent that is actual in the literal sense (*CP* 1903: 1.532). Involving the First, the Second exists as an actualized fact in reactive reaction to an "other." As a second, any sign is active force established, mutually determined by what it is not—its object. At the junction where signs encounter their objects, we find the intensive Third involving the First and the Second in a relational bond that abducts the sign into "a subject" capable of expressing the passage from potentiality to possibility. As a third, the sign is a habit. This habituation does not exhaust the potential of the first. As per the logic of conjunction, the third is also a first—the law itself that habituates the sign is itself susceptible to change. As such, the habit may always be re-abducted from its neighborhood into new habits, new interpretants (*CP* 1903: 1.532). The ground of semiosis is an ever-evolving limit that signifies only to the extent that it transforms itself.

In the evolutionary triad we find the culmination of the structural indeterminacy at the heart of the Diagram, this time returning as a problem of method. The paradoxical constancy of evolution saves the sign from atomism and semiotics from having to refer variation back to a formal structure. However, the problem of how to account for the novelty involved in the genesis and life of signs remains. What is inexpressible in structural linguistics is inexpressible, in general. The moment we try to talk about the First it vanishes. There is always "some residue of dreaminess in the world, and even self-contradictions" (*CP* 1893: 4.79), which are only ever spoken of from the standpoint of Seconds. And yet inexpressibility is not a problem in itself. The problem arises only to the extent that one is interested in establishing a science of signification and a method that would deduce ultimate non-signifying elements. For Peirce, not only is this pursuit naïve but it is also fueled by a positivist image of science that pragmatism decidedly distances itself from. Against the idea of science theoretically overdetermining the real by purifying experience from superfluity, Peirce will side with scientific experimentalism instead. The very mode that enables experimentalism is none other than abductive speculation. The experimenter can only ever experientially situate themselves in a milieu as one sign among others; they must contend with the fact that they are mutually abducted by the manifold of signs they seek to examine, which as interpretants possess the power to act back on and test the efficacy of a question asked of them (*CP* 1903: 4.529). Put differently, the experimenter can only diagrammatize their way into a semiotic territory, trusting "flight[s] of imagination" (*CP* 1903: 5.196) that might destabilize their systems.

Inasmuch as it is mobilized by such flights, the diagram as method emerges in resistance to the reduction of the semiotic activity of the world to formalisms that would present themselves as objectively general structures. Peirce's own examples, evident in his Existential Graphs (1895–1910), illustrate the point. Although he sets out to formalize the movement of signs, the activity of formalizing is inextricable from the form-giving semiotic process, which no deductive or inductive certainty can fit into a closed structure. The diagram exemplifies the abductive un-conscious operation at the junction between experimenter and semiotic milieu. It simultaneously "synthesizes and shows" (*CP* 1885: 1.339, 1.384) and thus opens up a system to potentially unexpected relations between signs. It is for this reason that "the difference between setting down spots in a diagram to represent *recognized* objects, and making new spots for the *creations* of logical thought, is huge" (*CP* 1892: 3.424, emphasis added).

In its creativity, the diagram compresses the power of the icon, the sign Peirce situates closest to the First. In the icon, the First, which is otherwise impossible to capture as pure potential, is expressed more vividly as it is characteristic of this type of sign to be a "quality that it has *qua* thing" (*CP* 1902: 2.276) and, in a sense, to be monadic. There is such a thing as a pure icon but no icon is a pure First—the icon remains a third, the interpretive junction between quality, object, and subject. Compared to an index, however, which has a direct relation to its object, or a symbol, which has a habitual relation to its object, the icon may refer to an object that may not already exist. If this is the case, "the Icon does not act as a sign" (*CP* 1903: 2.247). Yet, as Peirce explains, "this has nothing to do with its character as a sign. Anything whatever, be it quality, existent individual, or law, is an Icon of anything, in so far as it is like that thing and used as a sign of it" (*CP* 1903: 2.247). At this instance, the conjunctive operation of semiosis allows us to exercise care regarding this "likeness." An icon may be pure to the extent that it draws no "distinction between itself and its object" but this lack of distinction does not entail the identity of the icon with a thing outside it (*CP* 1903: 5.74). As a triadic junction, always indifferent to the distinction between inside and outside, the icon involves differentiation no matter what. To use an example from Kohn's semiotic anthropology, the stick insect does not confuse itself with the stick any more than the anteater confuses its snout with the ant hole. The point is that this difference may not be noticed (Kohn 2013: 85). In the case of the pure icon, what is interpreted is the abductive differential genesis of suchness itself, which is folded into indices and symbols. In Peircean semiotics, no type of sign ever loses its connection to the material flows of the semiotic process.

Insofar as it is an icon the diagram certainly "exhibits a similarity" to what it diagrammatizes (*CP* 1885: 1.369), but it does not codify the real into a structure. It affords no assurance that what it creates exists but this is not the right question to ask of the method in any case. The point is to see "what would be the character of such an object in case any such did exist" (*CP* 1903: 4.447), which allows the creation of and experimentation with new signs as *such*. Tied to the Diagram as process, the diagram as method is as iconic as the icon is diagrammatic (*CP* 1899: 1.369); its success is that it is the expression and agent of semiotic evolution but that may make it unfit to address the new signs it may give rise to. In this final sense, the diagram is rendered "fallible" and cannot be said to serve "science" understood in positivist terms. If the pragmatist famously asks for "clarity," this clarity is not to be achieved at the cost of closing the "path of inquiry" (*CP* 1906: 6.612).[13] Diagrammatically "ascertaining the real meaning of any concept, doctrine, proposition, word, or other sign" (*CP* 1905: 5.6) is contingent on the experiments for which this meaning is to be created as relevant. And if the diagrammatic activity results in typologies, at the very least one needs to ask what the semiotician needs the typologies for. In Peirce's case, these will enable a phaneroscopy, a study of signs as appearing, which freed from psychological connotations is properly transformed into an experimental ethics of the sign.

Guattari, psychoanalysis, and the diagram

In his landmark article "The Unconscious" (1915), Freud argues that while the unconscious system (*Ucs.*) is radically barred, the preconscious system (*Pcs.*) is *potentially* but not actually accessible to consciousness (*Cs.*). Whereas the *Pcs.* is entirely accessible to the *Cs.*, while remaining nonconscious, "secondary repression" operates between the *Ucs.* and *Pcs.* such that communication between them is far less direct. The *Pcs.* is composed of all thoughts that could potentially become conscious, while the *Ucs.* is "censored," so that it cannot directly communicate with the *Pcs.* (and thus with the *Cs.*) (see Freud 1987b: 195–96).

For Freud, the "nucleus" of the *Ucs.* consists of "instinctual representatives which seek to discharge their cathexes" (Freud 1987b: 190) or libidinal investments. These representatives are termed "thing-presentations," which are complexes of "associations made up of the greatest variety of visual, acoustic, tactile, kinaesthetic and other presentations" (Freud 1987b: 221). As mental images, thing-presentations cannot inherently contradict each other or influence one another, and there is "no negation, no doubt, no degrees of certainty" (Freud 1987b: 190). As an earlier text puts it, the *Ucs.* "equate[s] reality of thought with external actuality, and wishes with their fulfilment" (Freud 1987a: 42) or, as "The Unconscious" puts it, there is a *"replacement of external by psychical reality"* (Freud, 1987b: 191, emphasis in the original).[14] But as "contents, cathected with greater or lesser strength" (Freud 1987b: 190), all thing-presentations nonetheless participate in a single organizing principle which makes them "co-ordinate" (Freud 1987b: 190) with one another: the "pleasure–unpleasure regulation" (Freud 1987b: 191). This regulation organizes series of thing-presentations inscribed on the erogenous body according to a principle of repetitive habit regulating a field of experience from which pleasure (as the cancelling of difference and otherness or discharging of cathexes) can be extracted.

Very early on, however, the *Ucs.* is almost completely "overlaid" by the *Pcs.* (Freud 1987b: 192). The *Pcs.* is composed of "word-presentations," all of which are capable of becoming conscious. A "word-presentation" is a "complex presentation" made up of its own "visual, acoustic, and kinaesthetic" associations linked to the process of learning a language (Freud 1987b: 221). However, a word "acquires its meaning" by being linked to a thing-presentation (Freud 1987b: 221). Thus, a word-presentation includes the presentation of the word and the presentation of the thing corresponding to it (Freud 1987b: 207). Though as long as an infant is still learning a language, she largely associates a word-presentation with other word-presentations according to her own associations (Freud 1987b: 218) and thus according to the pleasure–unpleasure series.

Now, an apparent contradiction emerges because, on the one hand, Freud claims that the *Ucs.* is censored by the *Pcs.*, yet on the other, the meaning of the word-presentations forming the *Pcs.* is entirely comprised of thing-presentations, which correspond to the *Ucs.* This is resolved by the *Pcs.*'s function of "hypercathecting" the "first and true object-cathexis" (Freud 1987b: 207) of the thing-presentation, which is its initial libidinal association with an unconscious complex of presentations coordinated by an overarching pleasure–unpleasure series. Hypercathecting the thing-presentation means that the original, unconscious, cathexis and its series of associations governed by the pleasure principle is replaced by a new set of associations governed by the word-presentation corresponding to it. In other words, a particular mental image or presentation loses its unconscious libidinal associations, which are replaced by a preconscious and potentially conscious set of associations completely determined by the word associated with that mental image, as well as with the other words with which the original one can form relations. As such, the connections in the unconscious governed by the pleasure principle give way to the "reality principle," which will determine the associations capable of being formed between words in the *Pcs*. The reality principle requires the individual to submit to the use of language and to such cultural norms as the incest taboo. Any presentation or psychical act that is not put into words thereby remains unconscious or repressed by the *Pcs*.'s censorship of the pleasure principle (Freud 1987b: 207).

Thus, the word-presentation is now to be understood as consisting of a word and a thing-presentation that has lost its unconscious associations or "memory-images" and is now cathected only to "remoter memory-traces derived from [the unconscious memory-images]" (Freud 1987b: 207). The word-presentation is cathected to associations but ones that are determined by a new organizing principle. As such, Freud installs what the Lacanian school—most notably Jean Laplanche and Serge Leclaire in their structural linguistic reimagining of Freud's article "The Unconscious: A Psychoanalytic Study" ([1960] 1972)—view as a structural break located between the unconscious system, on the one hand, and the pre-conscious/conscious systems (*P/Cs.*), on the other, and which they consider as isomorphic to the structural linguistic distinction between signifier and signified. More precisely, signifiers (expressive materials) that can be bi-univocally coupled one-to-one with corresponding signifieds (conceptual contents) as an identity, forming the Saussurian sign (a two-sided unity), come to populate the *P/Cs.* (where they are incorporated into word presentations). Whereas signifiers that cannot be (thus being determined negatively as what Lacan calls a nonsensical and material "letter") are retrojected to the *Ucs*. On the one hand, this layer of nonsensical thing-presentations structurally resists its incorporation into the *P/Cs.*; on the other, this resistance establishes a tension internally animating structure as such as its fundamental driving principle (fantasy).[15]

One of the strengths of this structural approach is that it offers a means to tackle the communication between psychic systems. In "The Unconscious," Freud offers two possible hypotheses to explain how they communicate, without definitively settling on either nor really elucidating the mechanism that accounts for their communication. According to the first hypothesis, cathexes simply re-cathect the conscious representation or "word-presentation" once the infant has negotiated the overlaying of the pleasure with the reality principle during the Oedipal stage of development (during which time the pleasure and reality principles most directly confront one another). According to the second, cathexes are maintained in both series (with "thing-" and "word-presentations"), giving rise to what Laplanche and Leclaire call a continued "double inscription" in both series, even after the formation of a structural split between the two orders with the onset of post-pubescent, genital sexuality. Laplanche and Leclaire opt for the latter option in their article, arguing for the continued return or insistence of the repressed letter within conscious discourse, as evidenced by the classic Freudian *lapsus*. Nonetheless, while offering a rigorous and inventive intervention in Freudian metapsychology that would prove influential in Lacanian circles, Laplanche and Leclaire did not themselves agree on the nature of the general relations between language and the unconscious, Laplanche considering language to merely offer a structure amenable to its incorporation into the workings of the unconscious, whereas Leclaire (sticking more closely to Lacanian orthodoxy) considered the unconscious more as the *effect* of the structure of language.

Lacan himself would respond to this debate in "Position of the Unconscious" (1966), arguing that the *object* of psychoanalysis—the *objet petit a* or object (a), understood as the "object-cause" of desire—takes precedence over purely structural considerations when conceiving of the relations between psychic systems, and between language and psyche.[16] In his work more generally, Lacan argues that the object (a) structures structure (as internally displaced or decentered) by making structure pivot around the *gap* between Ucs. and P/Cs., which it objectifies at the level of its disjunctive synthesis of partial (unconscious) and complete or whole (pre/conscious) objects—for instance the other's gaze or voice as irreducible to the gazing or speaking other person (see Lacan 1998: 67–119).[17] This relation to what Lacan terms the "Symbolic Other" (at once culture, Saussure's *langue*, the unconscious, and superego[18]) *in* the subject's concrete relations to other people (relations dialectically constitutive of the lures, projections, and imaginary ordering of the ego) performatively manifests the distinction between *Ucs.* and *P/Cs.* In short, the object (a) splits the subject, retroactively constituting it as subject of the unconscious (cut off from the imaginary ego of the *P/Cs.*), since while the object (a) contingently embodies and in a way centers the dialectic of the imaginary and the symbolic, it is itself irreducible to that dialectic (as a-structural or "real")—hence the above used term "disjunctive synthesis." Thanks to the object (a), structure is thus conceived by Lacan as embedded in a wider social practice that, while itself structurally mediated (via the dialectic of the imaginary and the symbolic), provides structure with purchase on the real of lived experience that internally ruptures and displaces structure in relation to itself.

In the *Anti-Oedipus Papers* (*AOP*),[19] Guattari explicitly engages these debates by re-reading Freud's "The Unconscious" through the work of the post-Saussurian semiologist Louis Hjelmslev, whose work Guattari semiotically radicalizes by means of Peirce.[20] Guattari's work during this period converges with Lacan's on many key notions, including the sharing of a more or less Freudian basis (repression, psychic systems, libido, etc.), desire's embeddedness in networks of signs, and a relative privileging of the unconscious over its epiphenomena (such as the *P/Cs.* ego). But we will see that the use of the semiotic diagram adapted from Peirce is precisely what enables Guattari's de-modeling of Lacanian psychoanalysis to break with the closure of structure onto the signifier, opening instead onto a conception of the unconscious that is fundamentally schizophrenic and social, drawing on Guattari's experience of institutional analysis.

We see this project at work when Guattari (2006) defines Freud's "thing-presentation" as a (Peircean) *icon* and associates Freud's "word-presentation" with "double articulation" (73), a notion adapted from Hjelmslev by the linguist André Martinet (1960). Double articulation has the advantage over the Saussurian bi-univocal mapping of a signifier onto a signified (and vice versa) of allowing conceptual content to inform the individuation of the expressive material of a sign in a manner that is equally balanced with its opposite (the individuation of a linguistic concept using expressive material).[21] Saussure's schema, by contrast, implies that thought (conceptual content, the signified) is subject to the set of substitutions and permutations permissible within a language taken as set of signifiers or expressive materials defined purely as distinctive oppositions "without positive terms." In short, the notion of bi-univocality belies a unidirectional or at least non-equal structuring relation between signifiers and signifieds. This way, when articulated, the *Ucs.* and *P/Cs.*, for Guattari, are to be viewed not as a grid of bi-univocal relations between signifiers and signifieds (giving way to a substratum of rejected letters) but rather as two coordinate layers of "figures," or equally and mutually formed expressions (expressive materials) and contents (signified concepts).[22]

At a first level, we can already see how Guattari intends to do away with the structural gap between *Ucs.* and *P/Cs.*, as filtered through a reductive grid via the Saussurian reading of its relation, inasmuch as expressions and contents (or from a related angle icons and symbols/indexes)[23] are free to mutually inform one another in a way that bypasses any supposed binary relation between the two orders (or any unidirectional structuring of the one order by the other). Indeed, Guattari writes that whereas in Saussure one must abide by the existence of a structural separation between signifiers and signifieds, without which Saussure's overall framework becomes unworkable (and which Lacanian psychoanalysis then maps onto the break between the *Ucs.* and *P/Cs.*), in Peirce (and to an extent in Hjelmslev, cf. double articulation) there is a "*continuous* passage from the signifier to the signified" (2006: 188, emphasis in the original) and vice versa. Indeed, Guattari's ultimate aim here is to push beyond (Hjelmslev's) figures toward (Peircean) *flows* that are as semiotic as they are material and in which the very distinction semiotic/material loses its sense. Moreover, it is around this distinction between structural separation and continuous passage that will turn Guattari's own attempt to rework the Lacanian object (a) as a *diagram*, understood as the object of institutional analysis (later the object of schizoanalysis).

In the *AOP*, Guattari greatly values Lacan's innovation regarding the object (a) in its relation to structure, particularly appreciating this "machinic" dimension of Lacan's work given Guattari's own attempts to reinsert historical materialism, and to more fully insert the social more generally, into Lacanian psychoanalysis.[24] The machinic will be Guattari's term for any process breaking with structure (and with figure), as well as that which produces structure (or figure)—by being enveloped and trapped within it—to the extent that structure, for Guattari, entails repetition without difference or novelty (see Guattari 1984a: 111), such as Saussure's pre-established set of permissible substitutions and permutations of signifiers within a language. For Guattari, structure conceals or represses a machinic power of singular repetition breaking with generality (1984a: 114) and accounting for any creativity or novelty in a structure, as well as its genesis. Structure repeats or echoes in a register of unproductive or disempowered mimicry the empowered repetition, as production of difference, established by the machine.[25] What is important to bear in mind, however, is that for Guattari one cannot really divorce the one from the other, at least not in the domain of language; indeed, one sees from his writings that, for him, the "power sign" (*signe de puissance*) (as "diagrammatization of the sign," 2006: 46) entails precisely this alliance of generality and singularity.[26] The machinic furnishes structure with its events whereas structure enables machinic effects to be expressed linguistically or more specifically to *signify*.[27]

Now, Guattari argues that Lacan's object (a) indicates a repressive usage of the machine—a usage that has been "archaized" or "overcoded" by the signifier (Guattari 2006: 94, 382). For Guattari, Lacan's discovery of the object (a) is the discovery of a *particular instantiation* of the machine, a "writing machine" (Guattari 2006: 220, 382) that has been perverted by the signifier, insofar as it installs a break between the *Ucs.* and *P/Cs.* (as we saw it structures structure) and brings about the structural repression of letters from the order of signs. Yet, perceivable in the object (a)'s own self-subversion of the structure it installs, as seen earlier, is its true machinic nature. Guattari goes so far as to claim that the object (a)—which contrary to Lacan's claims is not the "object-cause" of desire but merely its *representation* (2006: 152) (or "displaced represented," 2006: 107)— has as its own *reverse side* a fully machinic *diagram* (or "repressed representative" of desire, 2006: 107),[28] which the object (a) covers over due to its historically contingent alliance with the signifier.[29] In short, the object (a) *represses* its diagrammatic nature, giving us moderns "the unconscious we deserve!" (Guattari [1979] 2011: 9), i.e., one "structured like a language" (cf. Lacan).

We can understand this diagram in terms of an articulation of "iconic" thing-presentations freed not only from the grid of the signifier (which reduces icons to signifiers aimed bi-univocally toward signifieds) but also from the figures of double articulation that relatively fix individuated expressive materials in relation to individuated conceptual contents (Guattari refers to these doubly articulated or signifierized icons as "impotent" or "disempowered" images, as opposed to diagrammatic "power signs," Guattari 2006: 212). Articulated diagrammatically, icons enter into a free-flowing state albeit one that is assembled in and as this diagram of relations, i.e., constructively, as a kind of machinic structure of relations. Another way of putting it is that the diagrammatic "power sign" is a "total sign" involving icon, symbol, and index (Guattari 2006: 192), within a continuously varying self-referential entity that produces its own referent ("power sign flow," Guattari 2006: 219) as an effect of its internal relations.

This diagrammatic conception of the unconscious in turn connects with Guattari's understanding of "desiring machines" as "asemiotic encodings" (such as the genetic code) (see Guattari 1984b: 74) that desire as a function of their ability (via "transcoding") to open onto one another. Guattari's classic example of transcoding, which he repeats throughout the *AOP*, is that of the wasp and the orchid—who insert themselves into one another's machinic processes in such a way that the combined effect of their interaction isn't genetically programmed or reducible to the code of either species taken separately (insofar as the wasp does not gain anything from the encounter, believing the orchid to be another wasp, while the orchid gains self-reproducibility via pollination). To desire, desiring machines must therefore engage in transcoding, by which they open onto a becoming-other (as a double capture of the other's code). Icons, as markers of experience and perception, are the primary means by which desiring-machines encounter one another, and so desire (their mutual becoming-other conditioned by transcoding) hinges on icons' ability (in and through power signs) to form relations going beyond any preestablished meaning or direction. Indeed, the openness of their relations (the postponement of closure) conditions desire as such (as contingent upon transcoding), and hence Guattari associates the unconscious with a schizophrenic process or flow diagrammatically constructed by a writing that is "transcursive" (rather than unidimensional or semiologically discursive) and "polyvocal" (contra the bi-univocal signifier).[30]

In agreement with the general framework introduced earlier, Guattari writes that thing-presentations are thus not "prior" to or "beside" word-presentations but "counter-produced" by them (Guattari 2006: 73). Guattari notes that "the unconscious is not primitive, it is the result of the re-assemblage of desiring machines after the intrusion of the Preconscious-Conscious" (Guattari 2006: 73).[31] In this way, Guattari views Lacan's unconscious as ultimately proto-diagrammatic[32] (whereas Freud's is more static) insofar as the object (a), once de-modeled away from the signifier, has the capacity to produce a *new relation* between icons and symbols/indexes (or thing- and word-presentations, respectively) that makes the (schizophrenic or polyvocal) unconscious an internal *effect* of this diagrammatism (Guattari 2006: 74).

As Guattari reads it, the diagrammatic nature of the object (a) is repressed in Lacan because it is treated at the level of an individual logic of fantasy ($\$\Diamond a$) enclosed in an Oedipal binary structure prioritizing neurotic castration anxiety (the phallic separation between *Ucs.* and *P/Cs.*) over schizophrenia (non-binary power sign flow across psychic systems) in its modeling of subjectivity[33]—not least because of its ultimate privileging of the Saussurian signifier in its modeling of the unconscious.[34] As we saw, according to this logic the object (a) is inscribed in the subject's conjunctive–disjunctive ($\Diamond$) relation to the object (a) that disjoins the unconscious subject from its preconscious/conscious ego but also constitutes it as such (i.e., as split subject, or $\$$), as the conjunctive effect of the structural tensions between these two orders. As *institutional* object (Guattari 2006: 107, 114), which is to say as only articulable using a shared set of statements whose pragmatic effects are contingent on the social field in which they are enunciated, the diagram steps outside individual fantasy to a collective production of desire that is as libidinal as it is social. This requires that we move away from treating word-presentations as Saussurian signs in an abstracted language, to seeing them as a-subjective trans-individual discursive (or rather trans-cursive) statements pragmatically embedded in an institutional setting.

Guattari's fundamentally revised notion of fantasy pinpoints his de-modeling of Lacanian psychoanalysis, and we see again that it is the diagram that functions as the site of this transformation. The diagram's self-enclosure within structure at the level of the object (a) is supplanted in Guattari's work by collective and institutional practice. Guattari thus reverses the relation between structure and its (machinic) outside such that structures must be explained rather than explaining psychic phenomena, since as we saw, for Guattari a structure is the effect of a specific institutional instantiation of the machine.[35] To sum up, for Guattari a structure generates itself (as a structure) precisely by repressing its machinic or diagrammatic outside, closing itself off from the context on which it initially modeled itself but which itself continues to change after this modeling. And while sympathizing with aspects of Lacan's work, particularly the a-structural potential of the object (a), it is instructive that Guattari had to import a totally foreign semiotic framework, whose most radical features stem directly from Peirce, in order to complete his de-modeling of Lacanian psychoanalysis.

Notes

1 At its most general level, this term specifies the mutually informing relations between institutions and unconscious desire, the latter being expressed through collective thought and practice thereby embedding the unconscious in a social field. Transversality gives thought and practice a variable degree of creative openness to its fundamentally collective and institutional contexts, being functionally conjoined with them at all times.

2 This is the sense in which we should understand Guattari's (2015) claim that "transdisciplinarity must become transversality," the latter being understood as a "localized modelling, incarnated in a social body whose destiny is in question" (132), which he proposes as an alternative to transdisciplinarity's "bureaucratized" vision (136). With regard to structuralism, Alliez (2011a, 2013) has shown how Deleuze and Guattari's *Capitalism and Schizophrenia* project can be considered as inseparable from Guattari's de-structuring (i.e., "machinic") critique of Deleuze's own earlier identification of a transdisciplinary element unifying French 1960s structuralism—namely the "criteria" by which Deleuze identifies structures within any domain (see Deleuze 2004: 170–92)—an element that is ultimately compromised by the re-disciplinarizing (or modeling) effects of structure's functional self-enclosure or essential synchronicity (see Deleuze 2004: 191, Alliez 2013: 224).

3 On this point, see also Watson (2009: 7–13), who helpfully characterizes Guattari's overall project in terms of the three notions of metamodeling, mapping (with ties to the territorial, political spaces of institutions), and the diagram.

4 Quotations from Peirce's *Collected Papers* (henceforth *CP*) are to be referenced in the standard manner of Peirce scholarship. These include the year after which the first numeral indicates the volume number and the number to the right of the point indicates the paragraph. Wherever the year is not included is an indication that the manuscript in question is undated. In the case of the *Chronological Writings* (henceforth *W*), we will be providing the year, volume, and page number.
5 The "Search for a Method" is the revised title Peirce will give in 1893 to a series of articles he had written between 1867 and 1893, some of which can be found in his *Collected Papers*.
6 It should be noted that there is no direct correspondence between "I, Thou, It" and "First, Second, Third."
7 To sustain this distinction, we will use "signification" to refer to the union of signifier and signified in structural linguistics and "semiosis" to refer to Peirce's project.
8 "1 Whence is *B*. 2 *B* pure and simple is *A*. 3 *A* is no longer *B*. Why. 4 *A* to become *B* must be joined to *B* in its *null* form *C*. What *C* is. 5 What is the *process* by which *A* is combined with *C*? It is B^{2nd}" (*W*1 1861: 85, emphasis in the original). B^{2nd} is the intensive middle where a term becomes other for the next triad.
9 For Peirce, no relation is of a higher nature than the triadic relation and no fourth is necessary as his logic is not the numerical logic of compounds. For his discussion of the matter, see *CP* 1909: 6.323.
10 This question resonates with the critique of this aspect of Saussure's system by post-structuralist linguistics, with figures such as Lacan, Barthes, and Derrida challenging arbitrariness through the *objet petit a* that articulates and thus constitutes the two halves of the signifying structure (Lacan [1966] 2006); the continuous spatial relationship between the two that the bar in Saussure's structure implies (Barthes [1964] 1967); the "trace" at the crossover (Derrida [1967] 1997).
11 We are borrowing these terms from Deleuze and Guattari's reading of Lyotard's theory of pure designation in *Anti-Oedipus* (see Deleuze and Guattari 2004: 222).
12 Substance appears in Peirce's 1866 list of the categories alongside Being and the three accidents, the latter being the only ones that survive in the mature triad. Substance is assimilated into later lists as "suchness" appropriate to the category of the First; it is "the *very thing*," which is "neither predicated of a subject nor in a subject" (*W*2 1867: 49, emphasis in the original).
13 This is an allusion to Peirce's 1878 article "How to Make Our Ideas Clear" (*CP* 1878: 5.388–410).
14 Laplanche and Pontalis (1968) consider the notion of "psychical reality" to "introduce a third category, that of structure," since it is irreducible to the opposition "real-imaginary" (17).
15 Leclaire goes so far as to claim that it is ultimately the *generality* of the conscious representation (sign) that retroactively constitutes the singularity of the

unconscious (considered as set of letters) (Leclaire 1998: 85), by providing a normative and binary oppositional frame.

16 "The effect of language is to introduce the [object-]cause into the subject": the object (a)—as "speech" or concrete instantiation of language/structure—is the *cause* of that of which (as "object") it is the "effect" ("language") (Lacan 2006: 708).

17 Thanks to the foundational role played by the Other's voice in the libidinal organization of an unconscious, as imprinted across thing- and word-presentations, the voice can be said to hardwire the object (a) to the subject's speech as that elusive and meaningless texture or phonic materiality, assuring at all times a displaced point of relay between meaningful discourse and unconscious desire.

18 See Chiesa (2007: 34–59) for a helpful overview of Lacan's Symbolic.

19 These are the collected letters and texts sent by Guattari to Deleuze during the late 1960s and early 1970s during the writing of *Anti-Oedipus*. We will primarily focus on these for the remainder of the chapter as they clearly expose this aspect of Guattari's work, which *Anti-Oedipus* itself obscures. We will treat these fragments or "papers" as constituting a single text (namely "Guattari 2006") to help the reader navigate the references.

20 Alliez (2011b: 267) states that Hjelmslev enabled Guattari to rework Lacan, but we argue instead that it is ultimately Peirce who enables Guattari to "schizophrenize" Hjelmslev (and thus Lacan).

21 As Lucien Sebag indicates (1964: 108), the arbitrariness of the sign (the conventional pairing of a signifier with a signified) effectively bars questions of genesis, especially if meaning is taken to turn on individuated signs. By contrast, Martinet's double articulation distinguishes the phonemic (nonsensical expressive and material) from the morphemic (signifying) component of the sign, functionally folding them into one another to generate sense, thus breaking apart the preestablished unity of the Saussurian sign (see Martinet 1980: 13–24). On expression and content, see Hjelmslev ([1943] 1961: 47–60).

22 It is helpful to compare the term "figure" with Lyotard's contemporaneous critique of the signifier in *Discourse, Figure* ([1971] 2011), in which Lyotard attempts to unearth a figural dimension of the unconscious that is at work beneath and even between signifiers, partially accounting for their own structural relations. For his critique of Leclaire, see Lyotard 2011: 351–53. See also Deleuze and Guattari 2004: 261, 264.

23 Elsewhere in *AOP*, Guattari associates double articulation with Peirce's symbol and index (2006: 243).

24 On this, see Guattari (1984c), and Kerslake (2008).

25 On the two types of repetition, which Guattari derives from Deleuze, see Guattari 1984a: 111.

26 See Guattari 2006: 45, 224–25, 228, 244–45, 249.

27 This shows again that the diagram cannot be considered apart from the models (such as structure) within which it participates so as to de-model them.

28 The terminology repressed "representative" also alludes to Freud's thing-presentations as unconscious "representatives" of instincts.
29 On the "repressed representative" and "displaced represented" of desire, see also Deleuze and Guattari 2004: 193–95.
30 See Guattari 2006: 44, 118, 193, 210, 226, 234–35, 295.
31 Guattari refers to this throughout the *AOP* as the "third articulation" (or elsewhere the "conjunctive synthesis"), namely that of the unconscious (the "first articulation," or "connective synthesis" of desiring machines) and the preconscious/consciousness (the "second articulation," or "disjunctive synthesis"). What is at stake is a diagrammatic conjunction beyond the initial disjunction between unconscious and preconscious/consciousness. See Guattari 2006: 27–29, 46–47, 107–09, 244. This provides the theoretical basis for the theory of desiring machines' three "syntheses of the unconscious," as developed in *Anti-Oedipus*' first chapter.
32 Guattari notes that while Lacan subsequently reduces it to a linguistics of the signifier, he nonetheless points toward a "new polyvocality" that Guattari will fully develop (Guattari 2006: 73, 71).
33 Guattari 2006: 152–53. See also Guattari 1995: 12.
34 Guattari notes in the *AOP* that Lacan "flattened everything by choosing to work with really bad linguistics (Saussuro-Jakobsonian, when in 1946 Hjelmslev was already much more interesting, and mentioned only once in the *Écrits*)" (Guattari 2006: 152).
35 While Guattari considers the signifier as the effect of an archaic writing machine prioritizing linear writing over polyvocal speech, which he traces back to the earliest ("despotic") civilizations, with regard to contemporary institutions Guattari connects the signifier more directly to capitalism (through the bourgeoisie's appropriation of this writing machine). For Guattari, we see this in mercantile capitalism's utilization of an abstracted exchange value or deterritorialized code, and in state monopoly capitalism's extensive use of binary breaks to code the social field (which provides a particularly innovative reading of reification) (see Guattari 2006: 191, 193, 222, 225). In this sense, for Guattari, Lacanian structuralism has the merit of correctly diagnosing capitalism's linguistic structuration of the machinic unconscious, but fails to recognize this process by generally considering its model transhistorical and universal.

Bibliography

Alliez, É. (2011a), "Rhizome (with no return)," *Radical Philosophy*, 167 (May/June): 36–42.
Alliez, É. (2011b), "Conclusion: The Guattari-Deleuze Effect," in É. Alliez and A. Goffey (eds), *The Guattari Effect*, 260–74, London: Continuum.

Alliez, É. (2013), "Ontology of the Diagram and Biopolitics of Philosophy. A Research Program on Transdisciplinarity," *Deleuze Studies*, 7 (2): 217–30.

Alliez, É. (2015), "Structuralism's Afters: Tracing Transdisciplinarity through Guattari and Latour," *Theory, Culture & Society*, 32 (5–6): 139–58.

Barthes, R. ([1964] 1967), *Elements of Semiology*, trans. A. Lavers and C. Smith, London: Jonathan Cape.

Chiesa, L. (2007), *Subjectivity and Otherness: A Philosophical Reading of Lacan*, Cambridge, MA: MIT Press.

Deleuze, G. (2004), "How Do We Recognize Structuralism?," in G. Deleuze, *Desert Islands and Other Texts 1953–1974*, trans. M. Taormina, 170–92, London: Semiotext(e).

Deleuze, G., and Guattari, F. ([1972] 2004), *Anti-Oedipus: Capitalism and Schizophrenia, Vol. I*, trans. R. Hurley, M. Seem, and H.R. Lane, London: Continuum.

Derrida, J. ([1967] 1997), *Of Grammatology*, trans. G. Spivak, Baltimore and London: The Johns Hopkins University Press.

Freud, S. ([1915] 1987a), "Repression," trans. J. Strachey, in S. Freud, *The Pelican Freud Library Vol. 11, On Metapsychology: The Theory of Psychoanalysis*, 145–58, London: Pelican Books.

Freud, S. ([1915] 1987b), "The Unconscious," trans. J. Strachey, in S. Freud, *The Pelican Freud Library Vol. 11, On Metapsychology: The Theory of Psychoanalysis*, 167–222, London: Pelican Books.

Guattari, F. ([1979] 2011), *The Machinic Unconscious: Essays in Schizoanalysis*, trans. T. Adkins, Los Angeles: Semiotext(e).

Guattari, F. (1984a), "Machine and Structure," in F. Guattari, *Molecular Revolution: Psychiatry and Politics*, trans. R. Sheed, 111–19, London: Penguin.

Guattari, F. (1984b), "The Role of the Signifier in the Institution," in F. Guattari, *Molecular Revolution: Psychiatry and Politics*, trans. R. Sheed, 73–81, London: Penguin.

Guattari, F. (1984c), "Causality, Subjectivity and History," in F. Guattari, *Molecular Revolution: Psychiatry and Politics*, trans. R. Sheed, 175–207, London: Penguin.

Guattari, F. ([1991] 2015), "Transdisciplinarity Must Become Transversality," trans. A. Goffey, *Theory, Culture & Society*, 32 (5–6): 131–37.

Guattari, F. ([1992] 1995), *Chaosmosis. An Ethico-Aesthetic Paradigm*, trans. P. Bains and J. Pefanis, Bloomington & Indianapolis: Indiana University Press.

Guattari, F. (2006), *The Anti-Oedipus Papers*, trans. K. Gotman, New York: Semiotext(e).

Hjelmslev, L. ([1943] 1961), *Prolegomena to a Theory of Language*, trans. F.J. Whitfield, Madison, WI: University of Wisconsin Press.

Kerslake, C. (2008), "Les machines désirantes de Félix Guattari. De Lacan à l'objet « a » de la subjectivité révolutionnaire," *Multitudes*, 34 (3): 41–53.

Kohn, E. (2013), *How Forests Think. Toward an Anthropology beyond the Human*, Berkeley, Los Angeles, London: University of California Press.

Lacan, J. ([1966] 2006), "Position of the Unconscious," in J. Lacan, *Écrits: The First Complete Edition in English*, trans. B. Fink, 703–21, London: W.W. Norton & Co.

Lacan, J. (1998), *The Seminar Book XI: The Four Fundamental Concepts of Psychoanalysis (1964)*, trans. A. Sheridan, London: W.W. Norton & Co.

Laplanche, J., and Leclaire, S. ([1960] 1972), "The Unconscious: A Psychoanalytic Study," trans. P. Coleman, *Yale French Studies*, 48: 118–75.

Laplanche, J., and Pontalis, J.-B. (1968), "Fantasy and the Origins of Sexuality," *International Journal of Psychoanalysis*, 49 (1): 1–18.

Leclaire, S. ([1968] 1998), *Psychoanalyzing: On the Order of the Unconscious and the Practice of the Letter*, trans. P. Kamuf, Stanford, CA: Stanford University Press.

Lyotard, J.-F. ([1971] 2011), *Discourse, Figure*, trans. A. Hudek and M. Lydon, Minneapolis, London: University of Minnesota Press.

Martinet, A. ([1960] 1980) *Éléments de linguistique générale*, Paris: Armand Colin.

Peirce, C.S. (1982), *Writings of Charles S. Peirce. A Chronological Edition. Vols 1–6 & 8*, Bloomington: Indiana University Press.

Peirce, C.S. (1931, 1958), *Collected Papers of Charles Sanders Peirce, Vols. I–VIII*, Cambridge, MA: Harvard University Press.

Saussure, F. ([1916] 1974), *Course in General Linguistics*, trans. W. Baskin, London: Fontana/Collins.

Sebag, L. (1964), *Marxisme et structuralisme*, Paris: Payot.

Watson, J. (2009), *Guattari's Diagrammatic Thought. Writing between Lacan and Deleuze*, London: Continuum.

4

Bachelard and Deleuze on and with Experimental Science, Experimental Philosophy, and Experimental Music

Iain Campbell

Introduction: Transdisciplinary Experimentation

Recent work on transdisciplinarity in the humanities has sought to challenge and complicate what has been referred to as the "technocratic" mode of transdisciplinary research (Osborne 2015: 11, Maniglier, forthcoming). This technocratic conception takes as its goal the discovery of solutions to clearly defined problems, especially widely recognized social problems like global environmental and health issues, bringing a variety of disciplinary procedures into the service of "extra-intellectual" needs. As Peter Osborne notes, such a conception of transdisciplinarity has more often taken on the character of meta-disciplinarity. Losing the radical sociopolitical impulses found in strains of interdisciplinary research of the 1970s and 1980s, this research model involves not so much the immanent movement across disciplines that would characterize transdisciplinarity, properly speaking, but rather finds a point of disciplinary unity in its requirement to serve the functions of the neoliberal state (Osborne 2015: 13).

Patrice Maniglier (forthcoming) has recently developed a theory of the problem drawing on the work of Gilles Deleuze and Gaston Bachelard, elaborating on this important yet undertheorized concern of transdisciplinary research. In so doing, Maniglier demonstrates how transdisciplinarity can constitute a distinct form of thought, a creative and critical mode of inquiry that does not merely serve as a means to state or institutional ends. In this chapter, I too will draw on these two thinkers, posing my engagement with them around the figure of *experimentation*: as Éric Alliez makes clear, transdisciplinarity is achieved in Deleuze's work through experimentation, an "experimentation with the complexity of the real" (Alliez 2015: 145–46) that involves a necessarily multiple approach to research and practice.[1]

I will take experimentation as a candidate for a method of transdisciplinary research: a method for establishing the reciprocal meeting of divergent disciplinary systems without returning to a single higher meta-disciplinary order or falling into a merely eclectic relativism. Experimentation would be the means of producing transdisciplinary research outside of the bounds of its highly formalized and institutionalized forms. But this formulation must be nuanced. If we do not want experimentation to take on the role of meta-disciplinary arbitrator of disciplinary interactions itself, it must itself be considered in its role as a transdisciplinary concept. How are we to think of experimentation as a concept that operates in different disciplines, that moves across them in varied ways, and that bears the trace of each in its particular manifestations?

Here I will take the examples offered by Deleuze and Bachelard to engage with three iterations of experimentation and the relations between them. The three disciplines I will be considering are philosophy, science, and music. The reasoning behind engaging with the former two disciplines is evident: it is to these fields that Deleuze and Bachelard, respectively but relatedly, devoted the greatest part of their work, through Deleuze's consistent engagement with and reinvention of the history of philosophy and Bachelard's significant reframings of the philosophy of science. Yet while Deleuze in particular draws heavily from artistic ideas of experimentation, why we should look at music is less obvious. I hope to show, however, that an in-depth consideration of the notion of experimentation in the field of music can tell us much about the divergent tendencies, difficulties, and creative possibilities of experimentation in its transdisciplinary applications.

While in Bachelard's case experimentation is associated with the experiments of the scientific laboratory, in Deleuze's it is more often linked with forms of artistic experimentation defined by a rejection of predetermined codes and structures. A distinction hinted at here points toward the initial resource I will be drawing from musical research, namely a distinction outlined and complicated by Lydia Goehr regarding the experiment and the experimental (Goehr 2016). In this work, the experiment concerns closed and controlled environments in which a privileged observer tests predefined hypotheses. The experimental, on the contrary, involves attempts to relinquish such control and to produce open-ended contexts in which the unknown and the unexpected can arise.

Certainly such a distinction is not exclusive to music scholarship, but recent work on music has shown how these tendencies are not so easily separable into "scientific" on the one hand and "artistic" on the other, and has elaborated on what happens when the experiment and the experimental are found to meet and comingle. A key aspect of this has been identifying how practices proclaimed to be experimental can inadvertently revert into something like a logic of the experiment. I believe this is a lens through which we can learn much about Deleuze and Bachelard, beyond the common images of a Deleuze concerned with unfettered experimental freedom and a Bachelard engaged in a scientistic foreclosure of the role of philosophy under the guidance of the laboratory experiment, common images that may play a role in the relative paucity of work on the relation between these two major figures of the last century of French thought.[2]

More pointedly, the distinction between the experiment and the experimental seems to correspond to a distinction we find in Deleuze's work, a distinction that has produced controversy and confusion. We can witness in the scholarship on Deleuze a significant and productive plurality of ways of looking at Deleuze and science, be it in his references to thinkers of science like Raymond Ruyer and Gilbert Simondon[3] or in influential theorists like Manuel DeLanda taking scientific concepts to be key to unlocking Deleuze's thought (DeLanda 2002).[4] Yet we find in Deleuze's *Difference and Repetition* what seems to be a thorough devaluation of scientific knowledge and a firm separation between philosophy and science. This leads as astute a reader of Deleuze as Joe Hughes to claim that Deleuze's engagement with science in *Difference and Repetition* is merely metaphorical and that science "never leaves the realm of fact, but Deleuze is interested in the constitution of facticity itself" (Hughes 2009: 153). James Williams, by contrast, gives more weight to such scientific ideas (albeit without giving them the priority DeLanda does: see Williams 2006) and suggests that in *Difference and Repetition* Deleuze obscures the relation of his thought to science, arguing that he "evade[s] legitimate questions concerning the role that science may have to play in the development of his own concepts" (Williams 2003: 36).

These problems are compounded, and raise with them other problems, as Deleuze's work unfolds across the following decades. As noted, Deleuze's encounter with Guattari leads his thought into an especially radical form of transdisciplinarity. *A Thousand Plateaus* (1980) in particular is considered an exemplary transdisciplinary text: its logic of the rhizome, a principle of connection between differing kinds of semiotic chains without reduction to the logic of any given one, is reflected in the text's wildly creative lines of flight across diverse fields, displaying little evident concern for disciplinary propriety (Deleuze and Guattari 1987: 7, Alliez 2011). With this in mind, it is evident why the strict demarcation of disciplinary boundaries between the self-sufficient and distinctly "modern" triumvirate of philosophy, science, and art that we find in Deleuze and Guattari's final collaborative text, 1991's *What Is Philosophy?* (Deleuze and Guattari 1994), was met by followers including Isabelle Stengers with a sense of "perplexity and disappointment" and the feeling that "Deleuze and Guattari seem[ed] to turn their backs against all those who had promoted them as the thinkers of productive connections" (Stengers 2010: 39–40).

By working through the pairing of the experiment and the experimental and their comingling, this chapter will attempt to shed light on some aspects of this passage across Deleuze's thought and the difficulties that emerge through it. It will ultimately suggest that the foreclosure found in *What Is Philosophy?* serves precisely as an attempt to defend the experimental from its reduction to the experiment, though the success of this attempt will remain up for debate, and up for debate in a manner that the transdisciplinary operations of musical practices since the 1960s may illuminate.

Putting Deleuze alongside Bachelard will likewise help us to unpick how the experiment and the experimental relate in Deleuze's thought. The longest period of Bachelard's career was spent developing an ever more refined philosophy of science, but in a manner distinct from most of what has come under that field of inquiry, especially in Anglo-American philosophy. As a founding figure in what has come to be termed the French epistemological tradition, Bachelard sought not so much to develop a theory of knowledge concerning what makes knowledge scientific, or guarantees its objectivity, as to understand the historical conditions under which things become objects of knowledge (Lecourt 1975: 12, Rheinberger 2010: 2–3). Dominique Lecourt termed this approach "historical epistemology" (Lecourt 1974), a term that has been revived in the philosophy of science and that Lorraine Daston has argued raises "the Kantian question about the preconditions that make thinking this or that idea possible" (Daston 1991: 283). This is likewise the kind of transcendental question that is key to Deleuze's investigations in *Difference and Repetition*.[5]

That Bachelard takes such a historical approach, yet deploys it in a method of inquiry that hews closely to the details of laboratory practice, leads to Bachelard producing a body of work in which we find the split between the experiment and the experimental radically reduced: inherent in his work is a recognition of their co-implication in the scientific community's gradual development of its practices. By reading Deleuze alongside this understanding of the experiment and the experimental, I hope to both clarify pertinent issues in Deleuze's thought and indicate the continued relevance of Bachelard's thought, not only in the belated uptake of his insights in Anglo-American philosophy of science but also in the echoes heard through the last fifty years of French thought.

With regard to music, we have seen in recent years a distinct plurality of approaches concerned with experimentation. Projects within Ghent's Orpheus Institute have been at the forefront of one such approach, drawing widely on French thought and the philosophy of science to develop a sophisticated discourse on the term "experimental" in a musical context (Assis 2016: 7). The relevance of this work to the work I am unfolding here is evident, but for the moment I am setting it aside. My key concern is rather with a more historical and sociological grouping of research on "experimental music" concerned with how this term, which is purported to be characterized by an open-ended inclusivity, has come to produce a set of limits and exclusions, often on political lines.

This, again, is a problem that I believe can be articulated through a distinction between the experiment and the experimental. By exploring contexts in which music has made connections beyond its own disciplinary bounds, including science but extending to the wide range of multidisciplinary and intermedia projects that emerge from the 1960s onward, I will begin to sketch the transdisciplinary function of experimentation within musical practices. In so doing I will not only use the philosophical insights gained through Bachelard and Deleuze to aid this musical research but also point to how these concrete instances of transdisciplinary work beginning from a musical perspective can tell us a great deal about the transdisciplinary movement of experimentation. In this respect I wish to leave open, for the most part, the question of the specificity of musical experimentation, in comparison to experimentation in the other arts. Likewise, the important question of how Deleuze and Deleuze and Guattari differentiate between the arts—such as the subtle distinction between music and painting in terms of embodiment in Deleuze's *Francis Bacon: The Logic of Sensation* (2003: 54)—will be set aside for another time. In the meantime, I hope that the set of mutual encounters between three distinct fields that I begin to sketch in this piece can contribute to research between and within each.

To begin, I will follow Patrice Maniglier (forthcoming) by engaging with Bachelard and Deleuze on the notion of the problem or, more precisely, the problematic. This notion, coined by Bachelard and adopted by Deleuze, helps us see what their work has in common, but in turn reveals some of the areas in which they differ. I will work through a pairing of their shared non-Cartesian approach to thought, and how they use the problematic to formulate this, in order to elaborate on their distinctive understanding of problems.

Non-Cartesianism and the problematic in Bachelard and Deleuze

Significant attention has been paid recently to the conception of the problem in French thought, in a line of research that promises to inform and challenge some of the received theoretical lineages of the last century.[6] While Maniglier has emphasized the significance of Bachelard and Deleuze and the relationship between the two to this discourse, Craig Lundy has downplayed Maniglier's claims for the importance of the French epistemological tradition in Deleuze's conception of the problem. Lundy argues, on the contrary, for the primacy of Bergson as a predecessor to Deleuze on this matter, offering a close reading of Bergson's introductions to *The Creative Mind* and indicating the affinities not only between Deleuze's own book on Bergson but in the framing of the problem in *Difference and Repetition* (Lundy 2018).

From a somewhat different angle Sean Bowden too suggests a kinship between Deleuze and Bergson that comes at the expense of Bachelard. Following the work of Elie During, Bowden argues that, by placing concepts before facts, the French epistemological tradition takes major steps toward producing an anti-positivist conception of problems, but yet this tradition nevertheless ultimately remains grounded in historical givens and the promise of solutions (Bowden 2018: 47, During 2004: 17). But while During argues that it is in fact Bergson who furnishes us with a fully developed anti-positivist conception of the problem, Bowden claims that it is not until Deleuze that this is achieved.

That I have outlined these positions should not be seen as a challenge to Maniglier: on the contrary, and as I will develop, Maniglier indicates that there is more to be said of Bachelard's challenge to positivism than perhaps Bowden and During allow. However, I also hope to emphasize that it is important to recognize the richness and the plural basis of Deleuze's understanding of the problem and that it is a lens through which we can clarify some important questions in French thought. Not least of these concerns Foucault's famous distinction between the philosophy of the concept and the philosophy of experience, which During notes is already complicated by reading Bergson alongside Bachelard (During 2004: 5).[7] Paying attention to the significance but also to the limits of this distinction could reframe our histories of French thought and Deleuze's place within them. Such an approach, as I will later allude to, could be especially fruitful in Deleuzian musical research and sound studies, fields where Deleuze has generally been interpreted in terms of a neo-Nietzschean ontology of forces and a neo-Bergsonian distinction between the actual and virtual. Addressing how these no doubt crucial aspects of Deleuze's thought are refigured in the intellectual climate of his emergence into intellectual maturity would add much to these lines of research.[8]

The problematic, then, arises in Bachelard's work as a specific articulation of what it means to engage with an object of experience. With this comes a complication of how both sides of this relation and the relation itself are to be understood: namely, through an overcoming of the distinction between subject and object of knowledge (Bachelard 1966: 9–10). Maniglier identifies three features of the problematic to bear in mind as we work through how this is achieved.

The first of these is that concerning the problematic the purpose is not to learn the truths of specific objects "out there" in the world but to try to solve specific, singular problems (Maniglier 2012: 21). This does not yet disassociate the problematic from the "technocratic" posing of problems, and as such the second feature is that the problematic does not correspond to "wonder" or to a Heideggerian sense of questioning, but implies a questioning of our questions themselves, a break with commonsensical questions. It is not enough to solve problems, they must also be posed anew in each case (Maniglier 2012: 22). This indicates that engaging with problems is a creative and productive act: the given and the immediate gives way to the constructed (Bachelard 1968: 122–23). In turn, the third feature is that the problematic is what Maniglier (2012) calls "an operation on the substance of our ordinary life," a posing and reposing of the structures through which at all levels we engage with the world (23).

Bachelard formulates such an understanding of the problematic in *Le rationalisme appliqué* ([1949] 1966).[9] It features here as a development of the non-Cartesian epistemology he articulates especially in *The New Scientific Spirit* ([1934] 1984) (or scientific mind, *esprit*), but also more generally across his most fruitful period of work on the philosophy of science from 1934 to 1940. In this period, as Christina Chimisso (2008) notes, Bachelard developed from the more direct laboratory studies of his earlier work toward using "history as the laboratory of the philosopher who studies the mind" (141).

There are multiple aspects to what Bachelard considers the non-Cartesian character of his epistemology, but perhaps key is the notion that under the new scientific spirit of the twentieth century, intuition, or the relation between thinking ego and world, cannot be immediate and direct. Rather than subject and object as such, we must speak of what Bachelard (2012) calls "the dialectic coupling objective knowledge and rational knowledge" (28–29).[10] On this basis intuition is "preceded by extended study" (Bachelard 1984: 141), and clarity is the *product* of the work of the scientific mind, not, as for Descartes, at its foundation (Bachelard 1984: 24, Lecourt 1975: 63). As Hans-Jörg Rheinberger describes this non-Cartesian relation, "[subject] and object do not face one another directly in the experiment, but are engaged in a process of mutual instruction." The scientific mind "exists only as a history of involvement in and entanglement with the phenomena that it investigates" (Rheinberger 2010: 24). In this mutual instruction we will speak less of the well-defined objects of science that are seen in retrospect than of a process of *objectification* (Bachelard 1984: 167).

For this reason, the problematic is also implicated in a critique of a Cartesian method of universal doubt (Bachelard 1984: 163). For Bachelard (2012), a science founded on universal doubt "will irremediably pulverize the given into a mass of heteroclite facts" (27), and such a doubt is no longer appropriate when we think of the problematic as less an isolated object than a relational field of inquiry and of the problem as an object-bearer that cannot be said to be wholly distinct from the subject. The co-constitutive aspect of this relationship connects the givenness of the objects and the question of doubt on a different level than we find in Descartes. We think here of the object not as a *designated* object but as *instructor* (Bachelard 2012: 29). The scientific object becomes an object of *interest* and one for which objectification has not been wholly achieved. When such an object is posed problematically, we discover a method of doubt that is rationally applied rather than universal, but which yet can be seen as an extension of the Cartesian form (the non-Cartesian is not the anti-Cartesian), insofar as even that which at one time attained certainty can yet, and must, be doubted (Bachelard 1984: 163).[11]

Implied between a method of applied doubt and a problematic understanding of the objects of science, and central to the concerns of transdisciplinary research, is that not only can there be no general method but further that we discover pluralism at every level. This is a key aspect of Bachelard's response to the supposed crisis of the sciences in the early twentieth century: for Bachelard the splintering of the sciences was not the result of a deficit in scientific method but an effect of scientific progress at work. This is manifest both internally, for example, in the "coherent pluralism" Bachelard finds in chemistry (Bachelard 1932) and externally in an irreducibility between the sciences (Bachelard 1984: 14).

This indicates another key aspect of Bachelard's non-Cartesianism: a resistance toward reductionism. For Bachelard, modern science shows us that the path to scientific knowledge is not the reduction of the complex to the simple, but rather "seeking diversity beneath identity" (Bachelard 1984: 139), an increase in complexity and detail, a shift from truths that are "adventitious and clear" to truths that are "factitious and complex" (Tiles 2005: 16). Here we circle back to our starting point. As the intuition of scientific objects comes only in retrospect, not as immediately given, it is important that while they are in the process of objectification, that is, while they are still *active* objects of inquiry, that they remain in some sense ambiguous. In Bachelard's picture, modern science resists a Cartesian image of the clear and distinct perception of objects for one of inexactness (Bachelard 1928), an inexactness that produces the dynamism between subject and object, the dynamism of scientific thought and the scientific mind itself, and the dynamism of the process of objectification that scientific practice produces.

Bachelard's reframing of Descartes's famous wax experiment (Descartes, Med. 2, AT 7:30–34) vividly displays the non-Cartesian epistemology of modern science. It is worth quoting at length:

> [Descartes] rules out any possibility of what I shall call progressive experimentation, any means of classifying or measuring the diversity of what is observed, any way of fixing the variables of the phenomenon in order to distinguish one from another. Descartes's desire was to apprehend directly the object's simplicity, unity, and constancy, and at the first sign of failure he was plunged immediately into doubt of everything. He failed to see the coordinating possibilities in directed experimentation and did not recognize how theory combined with experiment might restore the organic, and hence entire and complete, character of the phenomenon. What is more, by refusing to submit docilely to the lessons of experience, he condemned himself to overlook the fact that the variability of objective observation is immediately reflected in a corresponding mobility of subjective experience. If the wax changes, I change; I change with my sensation, which is, in the moment I conceive of it, the entire content of my thought; for to feel is to think in the broad sense that Descartes attaches to the *cogito*. (Bachelard 1984: 166–67)

This passage reflects all of the features of Bachelard's non-Cartesian epistemology and highlights the complexity, the forms of reciprocity and co-constitution, and the project-oriented character of Bachelard's depiction of modern science. By never doubting "the permanence of the *I* that is the subject of the *I think*" (Bachelard 1984: 167), Descartes can develop a sense neither of the co-implication of subject and object—with its corresponding openness to being changed ourselves by the changes we encounter in our objects of inquiry—nor of the progressive objectification of modern science, its form as a project that sets the conditions for the production of the purified materials, in this case wax, suitable for laboratory experimentation (Bachelard 1984: 167–68).

Many of the features of this non-Cartesian epistemology are present in Bachelard's work from the very beginning, since his 1927 doctoral thesis *Essai sur la connaissance approchée*. So why does he feel the need to introduce the problematic? One aspect of this is that the problematic goes some way toward refining these thoughts and distancing them further still from the philosophical divisions they are posed against, such as firm distinctions between not only subject and object, but, for example, abstract and concrete (Bachelard 1966: 104). There are concepts that the problematic seems to replace or complement, such as that of the field (Bachelard 1966: 56), that perhaps maintained too much of the character of the scientific observer as a distant, arbitrating *cogito*. The problematic is a step further away from such an isolated form of the subject position.

This also illuminates Bachelard's long-standing interest in scientific instrumentation. The scientific observer and scientific thought cannot be located within individual or even collective scientists, but are equally contained within scientific technologies, understood as a kind of materialized form of scientific theory. In *Le rationalisme appliqué* this is expressed in the key coupling between applied rationalism and technical materialism (Bachelard 1966: 5). These extra layers of mutual implication that the problematic offers also do much to clarify the relation between scientific progress and the fundamental discontinuity that Bachelard sees as underlying the dynamics of thought.[12] The problematic maintains something traceable through the breaks, something that marks the rightly speaking materialist sense of instruction, practical rather than doctrinal (Maniglier 2017: 31), that occurs in the specification of objects of knowledge, the way in which scientific value "imposes" itself (Lecourt 1975: 12) in the "pedagogy of the scientific mind" (Bachelard 2012: 31).

There are many points of resonance between this sketch and the manner in which Deleuze makes use of the problematic in *Difference and Repetition*, not all of which I intend to detail here. However, it is useful to bear this depiction in mind when Deleuze, in a short footnote in that text, cites Bachelard as opposing the problem to Cartesian doubt and to what Deleuze calls "the recognition model of philosophy" (Deleuze 1994: 320n9). Here Deleuze is beginning to develop his notion of the problematic Idea, at this moment being described as an object of encounter "which can only be sensed" (Deleuze 1994: 139) rather than being subject to recognition. For Deleuze recognition ensures that "the form of identity in objects relies upon a ground in the unity of a thinking subject" (Deleuze 1994: 133). This, for Deleuze, like Bachelard, effaces the dynamism of thought, the effects of the result of an encounter with the unexpected and the new. In contrast to such an encounter, "the form of recognition has never sanctioned anything but the recognizable and the recognized; form will never inspire anything but conformities" (Deleuze 1994: 134).

Such a notion of that "which can only be sensed," of an encounter the effects of which are not determined in advance, is key to what Sean Bowden terms Deleuze's anti-positivism (Bowden 2018). However, it is likewise central to the connection that Maniglier draws between Deleuze and Bachelard, offering a challenge to the argument that Bachelard reverts to a form of positivism. Maniglier quotes Bachelard:

> The scientific mind forbids us to have an opinion on questions we do not understand and cannot formulate clearly. Before all else, we have to be able to pose problems. And in scientific life, whatever people may say, problems do not pose themselves. It is indeed having this *sense of the problem* that marks out the true scientific mind. For a scientific mind, all knowledge is an answer to a question. If there has been no question, there can be no scientific knowledge. Nothing is self-evident. Nothing is given. Everything is constructed. (Bachelard 2002: 25)

This phrase, the "sense of the problem," is one Maniglier focuses on. He construes it as referring to an attitude to problems where they are not readily identifiable objects to be solved, but rather objects of encounter that will force us to break with our presuppositions or what Deleuze terms "common sense" (Maniglier, forthcoming, Deleuze 1994: 149): the kinds of formulations that Deleuze will characterize with the phrase "everybody knows ... " (Deleuze 1994: 130) and Bachelard the philosopher's "it is said that ... " (Lecourt 1975: 35).

Elsewhere Maniglier speaks of "positivity," that which for Bachelard "can impose itself against what seems 'thinkable'" and "that which can impose itself against all presuppositions" (Maniglier 2017: 34). For Maniglier this echoes the Bergsonian sense of the problem, pointing toward a "positive metaphysics" not concerned primarily with truth but with modifying our presuppositions when faced with novelty (Maniglier 2017: 28–29). This positivity, then, is far from the positivism that During and Bowden have credited Bergson and Deleuze, respectively, with overcoming, and we find here what we could term a positivity contra positivism, challenging the claims of During and Bowden, and indicating that Bachelard has much to offer to an anti-positivist conception of problems.

Returning to our central topic, Deleuze likewise seems to follow Bachelard in associating this particular dynamic of thought with something called experimentation. We hear, for example, that "the concepts of the understanding find the ground of their (maximum) experimental use only in the degree to which they are related to problematic Ideas" (Deleuze 1994: 168–69). But we also find Deleuze warning against the dangers of reducing his own formulation of the problematic to a scientific model. The remarkably sophisticated constitution of the problematic Idea in *Difference and Repetition* indicates why this would be, and the secondary literature on the problematic and the problem in Deleuze reflects its status as a complex and multivalent concept. Sean Bowden, for example, identifies two essential moments paired within the problematic Idea, the first making use of differential calculus and the meta-mathematical theory of Albert Lautman, the second a form of intensive individuation drawing from Gilbert Simondon (Bowden 2011: 102). Craig Lundy has argued for the primary importance of Bergson (Lundy 2018), while Audrey Wasser has passed through Heidegger, Plato, Bergson, and Nietzsche in order to sketch the characteristics of how Deleuze views an investment in problems (Wasser 2017). Equally we could emphasize the importance of thinkers including Kant, Leibniz, and Maimon.

Furthermore, Deleuze will also speak of works of art as being problematic, naming Mallarmé's *Livre* and Joyce's *Finnegans Wake* among such works (Deleuze 1994: 69). Contrary to the model of recognition, "the work of art appears as experimentation" (Deleuze 1994: 68). These problematic works are works that are not susceptible to a single point of view or model of interpretation, and Deleuze associates them with Umberto Eco's notion of the "open work" (Deleuze 1994: 69, Eco 1989: 8), which is itself an intervention into theoretical structuralism, urging us to also consider Deleuze's ambivalent relationship with that mode of thought.[13]

It is evident enough that we are far from Bachelard's focus on the practical specificities of the scientific laboratory. But we can make an initial statement that Deleuze's aim here, as we will see, is not to deny the validity of scientific knowledge as such but to restrict the domain of knowledge per se. This is marked by the centrality of *learning* in Deleuze's formulation of the problematic Idea: while knowledge "designates only the generality of concepts or of a rule enabling solution" (Deleuze 1994: 164), learning accounts for the confrontation with the objectivity of a problem, as an encounter. Yet we see here that this form of learning closely matches one that Bachelard identifies with scientific thought, while in Deleuze's case when posed against science it points toward a shift into a more specifically critical register.

In the opening pages of *Difference and Repetition* we find some critical remarks on scientific experimentation, on the basis of how it is purported to understand repetition and generality. Contrary to Deleuze's opening statement that "[repetition] is not generality" (Deleuze 1994: 1), the experiment, as Deleuze presents it, is founded on the equation of the two through the production of a form of repetition that erases the difference that underlies it. This obscures, says Deleuze, the distinct singularity of each individual instance of a repetition. The scientific experiment, then, operates in terms of laws. For a given invariable form governing how we expect an object of inquiry to behave, the experiment produces a set of conditions under which the scientist can anticipate the same outcome in each instance, a repetition without variation (Deleuze 1994: 3). Outside of the closed environment of the experiment, the form of expectation the law offers cannot be so easily applied, but the structure of the experiment attempts to isolate individual factors and bear witness to them behaving as the law predicts.

A key concern of *Difference and Repetition* is an undoing of the form of generality that law and the experiment attempts to prove. The scientific experiment and its articulation around law provide for Deleuze an exemplary case of a notion of knowledge that throughout history—and Deleuze is broad here, presenting a history spanning Plato to Kant and beyond—has effaced the fundamental difference that Deleuze posits as underlying identity. This is why, when it comes to his use of differential calculus, Deleuze states that "the many philosophical riches to be found here must not be sacrificed to modern scientific technique" (Deleuze 1994: 171), a sentiment in strong contrast with Bachelard's elevation of the scientific mind over the non-scientific or pre-scientific. Despite the adoption of concepts from science and the philosophy of science from thinkers including Bachelard, Simondon, and widely from the field of biology, the positive role of science, and the means by which scientific concepts can take on this positive philosophical role, remains somewhat unclear.[14]

This takes us back to the trajectory of Deleuze's thought following his encounter with Guattari, from the radical transdisciplinarity of the *Capitalism and Schizophrenia* project to the apparent reversion to disciplinary foreclosure of *What Is Philosophy?* and its tripartite scheme of philosophy, science, and art. Deleuze, one might have supposed, was freed from his disciplinary home in philosophy and from the imposition of strong disciplinary distinctions like that apparent between philosophy and science in *Difference and Repetition* by his encounter with Guattari, with Guattarian notions like the transversal and the machine serving to motivate Deleuze's thought with a new mobility and mutability.[15] *What Is Philosophy?* suggests otherwise.

How to unpick what has occurred across this passage of Deleuze's thought is not obvious. To begin to address this, I turn again to the term "experimentation." Certainly Deleuze speaks of experimentation in a positive sense, while speaking of the experiment negatively. What are we to take from this? We can suggest that Deleuze is favoring an artistic form of experimentation, but the diverse and knotty lineages of this term in an artistic context provide no easy route toward clarifying the sense of experimentation in use.[16] But following Deleuze's collaboration with Guattari, and perhaps especially through the distinctive break with psychoanalytical forms of interpretation this produced, Deleuze would go on to develop a distinction between *experimentation* and *interpretation*,[17] which offers us a starting point for exploring these questions further.

Again in *Anti-Oedipus* we find the formulation "art as experimentation" (Deleuze and Guattari 1983: 371), but in this context we find a fuller sense of how this experimentation is to be understood. We hear of an art that rejects aims and concepts, recodings and axiomatics, "art as *process* without goal, but that attains completion as such." They speak again of literature, here of Artaud and Burroughs, and painting, Turner. However, for a precise definition drawing from the arts, they turn to the composer John Cage. Citing Cage, "experimental" is to be understood "not as descriptive of an act to be later judged in terms of success and failure, but simply as an act the outcome of which is unknown" (370, Cage 1961: 13). It is a model of art that does not find itself axiomatically grounded: the experiment cannot be taken as a "method," if method is taken in terms of a "premeditated decision" regarding the approach toward an object of study.[18]

Here Deleuze tacitly reiterates the position outlined in the opening pages of *Difference and Repetition*: the experimental is posed in strong opposition to the scientific experiment. But it is the effects of such a distinction that leads to the disappointment felt regarding the splits introduced in *What Is Philosophy?*: if philosophy and art are the realms of the experimental, and science the realm of the experiment, what is the relation between them to be if not only separation? To work through this question, I will first turn to the contextual source of Deleuze and Guattari's definition of the experimental, to music, and consider how the practical and historical manifestations of this term complicate such a precise distinction or opposition. Engaging with recent work on the experimental in musical research, I will refine the conceptual and practical terms of the distinction between the experiment and the experimental, and move on to considering how this can offer us a route into reappraising Deleuze's thought.

The experiment and the experimental

Cage's definition of the experimental has often been taken as a general characterization of that which falls under the term "experimental music," but recent work has elaborated on how this term is much more contested and conflicted than is immediately apparent. One narrative that has been dominant since at least the 1970s but which stretches back to the 1950s is a strong distinction between American experimental music and the European avant-garde. In 1959 Peter Yates first speaks of the "American experimental tradition" in his lengthy and generally pluralistic bibliography of twentieth-century composers, including figures such as Cage, Henry Cowell, and Edgard Varèse (who lived in the United States from 1915 until his death in 1965) (Beal 2008), but it is with Michael Nyman's 1974 text *Experimental Music: Cage and Beyond* that the term's widely recognized taxonomical form began to solidify. Nyman posits a strong distinction between an American experimental tradition, stemming from Cage, and the post-serialist music of the European avant-garde. Contrary to the latter's posited overriding concern with the exclusively musical factors of form and structure, explored through the careful management of the parameters of sound (Nyman 1999: 61), experimental music takes an interest in chance, process, unpredictability, playfulness, an independence from institutional form and tradition, and an opening toward music's outside, all features of Cage's composition that have been elaborated on by others (Nyman 1999: Ch. 1). No doubt there are real distinctions to be made, but Nyman's formulation has also served to obscure both the internal heterogeneity of "experimental music" and important connections between North American and European music in the twentieth century.[19]

One terrain this distinction has been articulated across is that of the scientificity of approaches to music. The formal, parameter-oriented work of musical serialism and related musical approaches was well suited to developing a theoretical discourse comparable to that of the sciences, and such an orientation toward scientific rigor was emphasized by significant European journals like *Die Reihe* (Mauceri 1997: 192). This approach had North American equivalents, such as through the journal *Perspectives of New Music*, favoring the serialist-inspired music of composers like Milton Babbitt and Elliott Carter (both featured in Yates's bibliography but who go unmentioned by Nyman).

The examples of Babbitt and Carter indicate that this is far from a neat geographical split, and it is complicated further still by what seems to be a third position. The French *musique concrète* pioneer Pierre Schaeffer formulated his own understanding of "experimental music" through his laboratory-like investigations into sound in the context of the *Groupe de Recherche de Musique Concrète* (GRMC), later renamed the *Groupe de Recherches Musicales* (GRM) (Schaeffer 1957), binding musical innovation with technological progress in the use of turntables, magnetic tape, and other electrical and electronic devices (Schaeffer 2012). Yet Schaeffer, drawing from phenomenological approaches, criticized the scientific character of serialist approaches to sound and music, terming these "abstract" music in distinction to his "concrete" music (Schaeffer 2012: 222). Attacks on the perceived scientism of his former collaborator (and, incidentally, former student of Bachelard) Abraham Moles's work on music and information theory (Moles 1966) form a persistent subtext of his major work on sound and music, *Traité des objets musicaux* (Schaeffer 1966).

This points toward an aspect of Cage's work that seems at odds with the "experimental" attitude outlined above, namely his own attitudes toward new technologies. In his early text "Future of Music: Credo," Cage emphasizes the use of technological advances in the service of producing "new sound experiences" (Cage 1961: 4), and we see this exhibited in the coming decades through his use of emerging sound reproduction technologies. How are we to understand the relationship between these technologies that are the result of scientific research and an artistic inclination that seems to strongly dissociate itself from the methods of science? In Cage's case the tensions and contradictions this connection produces become profoundly manifest toward the end of the 1960s.[20]

Even before their collaboration on the 1969 piece *HPSCHD*, the work of Lejaren Hiller provided an intriguing counterpoint to Cage's. Hiller too termed his approach to music "experimental music," but in Hiller's case this term referred to the experiments of the scientific laboratory (Hiller and Isaacson 1959). Hiller took his training as a chemist and applied it to the realm of music, drawing up carefully defined experimental contexts and conducting tests within them. Aesthetically, Hiller's early work did not seek the formal and practical advances of either North American experimentalism nor the European avant-garde, assuming instead well-established principles of music theory as a standard against which to measure his tests (Brooks 2012: 41). As William Brooks describes the method of Hiller's works modeled with his ILLIAC computer (some of the earliest research in computer music), "experiments are conducted—notes, sketches, 'integers' are tested—and the results are kept or discarded depending on whether they conform to a preestablished set of desires, expectations, or theories" (Brooks 2012: 42). With such a strong contrast to Cage's work, it is then of some surprise that they would choose to collaborate, though some of this could be credited to a shared "outsider" status (Cage's persistent refusal of convention alongside Hiller's lack of formal musical training) that Yates names as a key feature of the "American experimental tradition." As Brooks suggests, what we see here in this collaboration is perhaps cultural and biographical factors overcoming technical and aesthetic differences (Brooks 2012: 56).

HPSCHD, then, combined Cage's and Hiller's methods into a large-scale multimedia piece, composed over two years. Despite the success of the piece, its production was troubled: Cage found the ILLIAC supercomputer ill-suited to his methods, and, while stating that the production of computer subroutines could be construed as not an individual achievement but an achievement on the part of society, would later state that the aesthetic character of *HPSCHD* was produced not through but despite its computerized elements (Joseph 2016: 179–80).

Following *HPSCHD*, in the final two decades of his life, Cage would gradually withdraw from his concern with technological innovation and enter into a more insular, retrospective mode of composition. Cage also generally departed from the large-scale collaborative multimedia works of the 1960s like that of *HPSCHD* or the *9 Evenings* performance of his *Variations VII* (Silverman 2010: 229). We see in Cage's move not only an apparent unwillingness to engage with the methods of others but a pull away from the kind of collective, institutional work that was increasingly at the forefront of new musical research, from Hiller's University of Illinois Experimental Music Studio, to the San Francisco Tape Music Center (Bernstein 2008), to France's GRM and, later, IRCAM.

How does Cage's apparent reluctance to put his work into communication with that of others conform with the openness to the unexpected and to change suggested in his understanding of experimentation? Some recent musical research on the topic of experimentation may suggest a route into engaging with this question and orient us back toward the theoretical crux of my argument.

Cage scholars including William Brooks and Christopher Shultis have emphasized the importance to Cage of what Brooks terms a "pure observation" in contrast to the designed and delimited test (Brooks 2012: 49) and what Shultis calls a "transparent I" (Shultis 2013: 62) or a self "among things" (Shultis 2013: 75) in contrast to a projected self that molds nature under its own terms (Shultis 2013: 65). These figures put Cage in the camp of the experimental versus that of the experiment. But we cannot be so quick with this distinction. Donna Haraway is among those who have noted that such a pure observer or "transparent I" is a grounding figure in the birth of modern science. Haraway speaks of a "modest witness," an inhabitant of an "unmarked category" that renders itself invisible in its observations, living in a "culture of no culture" that conceals this scientific subject's social constitution, namely as European man (Haraway 2004: 223–24), hiding in turn the constitutive exclusions this entails.[21] As Haraway vividly describes this modest witness:

> The modest witness is the legitimate and authorized ventriloquist for the object world, adding nothing from his mere opinions, from his biasing embodiment. And so he is endowed with a remarkable power to establish the facts. He bears witness: he is objective; he guarantees the clarity and purity of objects. (Haraway 2004: 224)

Benjamin Piekut translates Haraway's modest witness directly into a critique of Cage, speaking of Cage as a purported "sound's modest witness" (Piekut 2012). Piekut argues that Cage's work is premised on "an absolute ontological distinction between an objective natural world and a subjective social world" (Piekut 2012: 3), and, for Piekut, Cage's call for listeners to "let sounds be themselves" (Cage 1961: 10) makes a claim to lay nature bare, "to see things directly as they are" (Piekut 2012: 12). Piekut's argument, following Haraway and Bruno Latour especially, is that Cage can hold such an objective sense of nature only by eliminating "the contingencies of the social, the subjective, the human." In so doing, for Piekut, following Haraway, the self-abnegation and "modesty" of Cage's position serves only to reproduce the modern, European, masculine power dynamics of science's modest subject (Piekut 2012: 15).

I am not inclined to accept the full force of Piekut's argument, and believe that the fundamental pluralism and complexity of Cage's work and thought offer means to respond to this critique. For instance, I do not believe that Cage has a substantive, contentful notion of nature that would accommodate such a rigid distinction between the subject and its object that is nature. However, Piekut nevertheless diagnoses at the very least a significant tendency in Cage's work, and a tendency that can be found elsewhere within what has fallen under the banner of experimental music.

Other recent work has pointed to the ways in which the ostensibly open-ended and inclusive form of "experimental music" has served to limit and exclude. A founding text of this work is George E. Lewis's "Improvised Music after 1950: Afrological and Eurological Perspectives" (Lewis 1996). Lewis here elaborates on how a racial space has been delineated through the theorization of "experimental music," such as through the formulation of Cage's "indeterminacy" in contrast to the "improvisation" of traditionally black practices like jazz (Lewis 1996: 97). For Lewis, a technical vocabulary and set of qualifiers to the word "music"—not only "experimental" but also "new," "art," "concert," "avant-garde," "contemporary," and so on (Lewis 1996: 102)—have served to render blackness the other of this music, in so doing revealing "whiteness as power" (Lewis 1996: 99–100).

With pointed relevance to Deleuze, Marie Thompson has recently argued that the erasure of the social and political and the obfuscation of subjective situatedness that Piekut diagnoses in Cage's work have been reproduced in what has been termed the "ontological turn" in sound studies, with Thompson naming an uninterrogated whiteness as underlying this turn (Thompson 2017). This orients us toward debate concerning what has been named "Deleuzian sound studies": this ontological turn, like the modest witness, makes a claim to an immediate, affective immersion in a notion of sound that is paired, in thinkers including Christoph Cox and Greg Hainge, with the Deleuzian notion of the virtual.[22]

As suggested by my earlier remarks on Bachelard and Deleuze's non-Cartesian thought, I do not follow Cox and Hainge in associating Deleuze's virtual with immediacy. I do, however, believe that the risk of making such a claim, and of naturalizing the virtual in a manner that obscures social and political questions, cannot be reduced to a misreading of Deleuze's work, but is rather immanent to what I believe are some key turning points in Deleuze's thought and more generally to the formulation of the experimental. To begin to articulate this, I turn to a refined conceptual elaboration on the distinction between the experimental and the experiment I have been engaging with here, that offered by Lydia Goehr.

Goehr engages with the thought of Theodor Adorno and Max Horkheimer to draw a connection between the beginning of modern science, through the figure of Francis Bacon, and the beginning of modern art, through Cage (Goehr 2016: 16). In the opening pages of *Dialectic of Enlightenment*, Adorno and Horkheimer speak of the Enlightenment, and Bacon, in terms of domination, a scientific domination of nature that is coupled with a domination of man (Adorno and Horkheimer 1997: 4). Goehr notes that the manner in which Adorno and Horkheimer speak of Bacon here closely resembles remarks of Adorno's on Cage, as in his ambivalent discussion of Cage's "catastrophe music" (Adorno 1998: 257). Having established this connection, Goehr then elaborates on how while in modernity the experiment and the experimental become competitor concepts (Goehr 2016: 19), the commonly conceived divides between the two are not always so easy to determine. For Goehr, via Adorno and Horkheimer, Bacon and Cage share an attitude of "nobility and respect" rather than "violent intervention" toward nature, yet this is not something they easily maintain: they both promote the experimental, open-ended, revisable, and incomplete

(Goehr 2016: 23), but for Adorno both ultimately walk the "more dangerous path" (Goehr 2016: 18) of the control and domination of the experiment.

Goehr's reading of Bacon puts into question some common conceptions of his scientific approach to nature: Bacon ultimately does not seek to "torture" nature as he has been commonly accused of doing, but rather to urge it toward disclosure (Goehr 2016: 29). Bacon becomes a kind of modest witness. For Goehr it thus becomes clear that modern science, society, philosophy, and art share a set of concerns to the extent that any commonsensical association of the experiment with science and the experimental with art would be mistaken (Goehr 2016: 31). On Adorno's account, the result of this is that Bacon and Cage's ultimate meeting in the overlap of the experiment and the experimental is in a position of complete control, an authoritarian space. Goehr is not so harsh. Rather she seeks only to note that, on the one hand, the experimental and the experiment both lose their effective power when they move too far in the direction of their respective exclusive tendencies (Goehr 2016: 38) and, on the other hand, to warn that "[truth] is fragile and has only the smallest chance of survival. An experimental act usually ends up as an experiment" (Goehr 2016: 37).

Goehr's engagement with Bacon and Cage shows that any distinction between the experiment and the experimental should not be drawn too quickly and can indeed be dangerous if either side is embraced at the expense of the other. Experimentation, in either sense, is a precarious practice, one that cannot presume its essential character in advance and must carefully navigate these questions as it proceeds. This is an elaboration of the experiment–experimental relation we must keep in mind as we move on.

Practicing transdisciplinarity

Let us return now to *What Is Philosophy?*, first to offer a defense of that text's apparent regression into disciplinary isolation and then, drawing on Bachelard and the musical research detailed above, to suggest some reasons why this defense may yet not satisfy.

While we have seen that *What Is Philosophy?* seems to replicate the strong distinction between philosophy and science from *Difference and Repetition*, what is striking is that the apparent normative aspect of this in the earlier text, where science is devalued in favor of philosophy, is largely absent in the later work. Science is even named as a creative discipline in its own right (Deleuze and Guattari 1994: 127), and Deleuze and Guattari criticize the "bad caricature" of science that Bergson and phenomenology (and perhaps, implicitly, Deleuze himself) offer in suggesting that it refers only to the "already-made" (Deleuze and Guattari 1994: 155). In *What Is Philosophy?* we do not find such a philosophical critique of science, and indeed the concepts of philosophy, the affects and percepts of art, and the functions of science generally do not encroach upon one another: the disciplines "approach chaos in a completely different, almost opposite way" (Deleuze and Guattari 1994: 118); they are of different natures (Deleuze and Guattari 1994: 127).

Where we do find such a normative aspect is when Deleuze and Guattari discuss logic and more generally speaking analytic philosophy.[23] For Deleuze and Guattari logic is necessarily reductionist, it "wants to turn the concept into a function" (Deleuze and Guattari 1994: 135). This points toward the purpose of the redisciplinarization of *What Is Philosophy?* following the transdisciplinary adventure of *A Thousand Plateaus*. The premise of *What Is Philosophy?* is a "lack of resistance to the present" (Deleuze and Guattari 1994: 108), the difficult, near hopeless sense of the political context in which it was written. In this it echoes the near-contemporary Deleuze text "Postscript on Societies of Control," which elaborates on a new modulatory form of control that reads almost like a self-critique of *A Thousand Plateaus*, the modernist freedoms named in that text having been readily adopted into the control mechanisms of the state (Deleuze 1992).

Philosophy, science, and art, in their proper functions, are what Isabelle Stengers terms "endangered practices" (Stengers 2010: 42). Just as for Deleuze and Guattari philosophy risks being lost by having the concept replaced by the function, science too may be lost when the act of creation that is the production of a scientific function is replaced by science in the service of industrial innovation (Stengers 2010: 49). *Doxa* threatens each of philosophy, science, and art, it threatens their contact with chaos, it threatens to replace the specificity of their functions with a stultifying circulation of dogmatic "information." *What Is Philosophy?*, then, takes as its starting point a group of historically engrained disciplinary conditions, but disciplinary conditions that, from Deleuze and Guattari's perspective, hold within them something that could allow us to resist the present, an act that without these disciplinary conditions would be impossible.

The disciplinary divisions of *What Is Philosophy?* are also not as rigid as much of the text suggests. In its concluding section, "From Chaos to the Brain," Deleuze and Guattari provide many rich images of the relationship between the disciplines. At the junction of the three planes these disciplines produce is what

Deleuze and Guattari term "the brain" (Deleuze and Guattari 1994: 208), and they speak of the forms of "interference" that can take place between these planes (Deleuze and Guattari 1994: 216).[24] With extrinsic interference, the philosopher can attempt to create concepts of a sensation or a function (Deleuze could be said to be doing this with his own use of artistic and scientific terminology), or the scientist functions of sensations, like color. With intrinsic interference, there is a more thorough slippage, a departure from one's own plane to navigate through the others (Deleuze and Guattari 1994: 217). Deleuze and Guattari name Nietzsche's Zarathustra as an example, but we could equally speak of the transdisciplinary lines of flight of *A Thousand Plateaus* in this manner.

But something remains elusive about these descriptions, more evocative than a catalyst to resistance. Part of the persisting dissatisfaction lies in how, despite the relative contingency of these disciplinary conditions as the forms of creation that happen to have survived and that offer us tools to escape the present, there is a sense of something essential about them, each discipline marking an unchanging form. An aspect of this lies, I believe, in how Deleuze and Guattari note that it is in the "full maturity" of concepts, functions, and sensations that they can intersect (Deleuze and Guattari 1994: 161). As Stengers notes, this puts Deleuze and Guattari's understanding of science in the realm of what she terms, following Bruno Latour, "bearded science," the system of science and its recognized functions, rather than of science "in the making" (Stengers 2010: 42–44). As Stengers notes, this puts the science of *What Is Philosophy?* firmly in the camp of what *A Thousand Plateaus* names "royal science," asking, "[why] do nomad sciences appear nowhere in *What is Philosophy?*" (Stengers 2010: 42). This question allows us to take a final turn back to Bachelard.

In *A Thousand Plateaus*, Deleuze and Guattari distinguish between "royal" science and "nomad" science (Deleuze and Guattari 1987: 367). The former consists in "reproducing," the latter in "following" (Deleuze and Guattari 1987: 372). What this means is that royal science, in a description recalling the opening pages of *Difference and Repetition*, works on the basis of law, treating differences of time and place as variables to be placed under this constant form. Like Haraway's modest witness, this reproductive mode of science assumes "the permanence of a fixed point of *view* that is external to what is reproduced."

Nomad science, on the contrary, is "ambulant": it follows flows, searches for "singularities," engages in "a continuous variation of variables" rather than extracting constants. We will recall here the distinction between the experiment and the experimental. Yet in *A Thousand Plateaus* this distinction is not oppositional as such. Certainly the royal sciences tie up the movements of the nomad sciences under its laws and, at worst, its state utilization in the form of "technologies" or "applied science" (Deleuze and Guattari 1987: 372–73), but this formalization is a necessary feature of the existence of nomad sciences. The nomad sciences invent problems for the royal sciences to solve, and these solutions depend upon the formal structures of state science (Deleuze and Guattari 1987: 374).

We find here a more creative and dynamic image of science than is present in *What Is Philosophy?*, and it is striking to note that it again begins with a brief reference to Bachelard. Deleuze and Guattari credit Bachelard's *Essai sur la connaissance approchée* as being "the best study in the steps and procedures constituting the rigor of the anexact, and of their creative role in science" (Deleuze and Guattari 1987: 555n32). The anexact, drawing also from Husserl, concerns essences that are not of the precise, ideal form that we commonly associate with science, but are vague, "vagabond or nomadic," yet nevertheless rigorous: "*anexact yet rigorous*" (Deleuze and Guattari 1987: 367). It is with such essences that the nomad sciences engage.

Bachelard's own conception of the inexact reinforces much of what was earlier discussed under the terms of his non-Cartesianism. It concerns the fact that reality can never be fully known and that this incompleteness is a catalyst to further investigation, the discovery of new structures and new levels of complexity (Tiles 2005: 161–62). Indeed, Bachelard, like Deleuze and Guattari, affirms that this level of activity works in a somewhat different sphere than that of the utility of technological goals, and the two levels work together to determine the "importance" of how this inexactitude is to be interpreted (Tiles 2005: 163): comparable to Deleuze and Guattari's discussion of the "safety" for which nomad science relies on royal science (Deleuze and Guattari 1987: 374).

Yet Bachelard feels no need for a distinction like that between royal and nomad science. The only comparable distinction in his work is that between "regular" and "secular" science, the former being of the laboratory and the latter "find[ing] its disciples among the philosophers," that is, those who seek to reduce science to their philosophical abstractions (Bachelard 1984: 145–46). What differentiates Bachelard from Deleuze and Guattari here? I would like to suggest that one key aspect of this differentiation, and one that is greatly amplified in *What Is Philosophy?*, is *practice*.

The contemporary reader may find Bachelard's work on science somewhat curious, with what seems like a strong form of social constructivism coupled incongruously with a scientistic rationalism. Yet, as Mary Tiles notes, when putting forward a social constructivism of science Bachelard cannot be read as taking a side in the "science wars" of half a century later. He must rather be seen to be responding to a context in which other philosophers of science "were talking about foundations, simplicity, and observation protocol statements" (Tiles 2005: 157). Bachelard's concern was not aligned with the later anthropological and sociological concerns of Bruno Latour, and this is why, albeit, as Patrice Maniglier notes, harshly on Bachelard (Maniglier, forthcoming), Latour firmly distances himself from Bachelard and any notion of an epistemology, naming epistemologies as having "always been war machines defending science against its enemies" (Latour 1988: 6). On the contrary, Bachelard positions himself immanently to science, its institutions, its modes of knowledge, and, most precisely, its practices.

For this reason Bachelard's picture of science works at many levels, from the minutiae of laboratory procedures and the development of theories, to pedagogical practices and the form of scientific libraries, to the contention with the imposition of philosophical abstractions, albeit, notes Dominique Lecourt, with less concern for the question of ideological or political determinations (Lecourt 1975: 14). Such an investment in practice poses a challenge to, and offers the opportunity to reframe, some paths through Deleuze's thought. As Alberto Toscano notes, the "place" where the "universal ungrounding" of *Difference and Repetition* occurs is unclear, and indeed seems to lie in the experience of the philosopher-individual (Toscano 2006: 199), and Antonio Negri asks, referring to the difficult notion of "practice" in Deleuze's "How Do We Recognize Structuralism?," "[where] is the 'structuralist Hero'?" (Negri 2011: 157), the actor who can enact a change from one structure to another? The encounter with the practically and collectively oriented Guattari softens this difficulty, certainly, and in Guattari's individual work we do not feel the threat of either disciplinary or individual closure. Furthermore, such a practical orientation is one of the aspects of *A Thousand Plateaus* that most allows for its experimental, transdisciplinary character, *pragmatics* being one of the terms that is used to describe the creative character of this text (Deleuze and Guattari 1987: 2) and one that requires a close examination if we are to understand the meaning of practice in Deleuze and Guattari's thought. Yet at points in Deleuze's later work, most of all in *What Is Philosophy?*, an opaqueness of the practical may linger on.

I do not wish to push this apparent favoring of Bachelard too far. While Patrice Maniglier readily extends the "positivities" that Bachelard attributes to science out into "other activities, like arts, politics, games, techniques, passions, etc." (Maniglier 2017: 34–35), I am inclined to be more cautious. Bachelard's elevation of the scientific mind over the nonscientific mind is exceedingly strong, speaking, for instance, of "the enormous superiority of the *scientific object* over the object of everyday experience for metaphysical instruction" (Bachelard 2012: 28). Lacan would criticize Bachelard's severe distinction between ordinary and formalized languages (Eyers 2013: 58), and indeed Bachelard argued, even, that mathematics is not a language, but a thought, thought itself (Lecourt 1975: 56–58).

In addition, Alison Ross has recently pointed to some important distinctions between Bachelard and Foucault that are also significant in this case. As Ross notes, Foucault departs from the French epistemological tradition that precedes him in terms of the status of knowledge. For Foucault epistemology is an object of study, while for Canguilhem and Bachelard alike it is a practice (Ross 2018: 144). I seek to value this practical element, but with a careful concern for the issues that led thinkers like Foucault to seek alternatives to it.

A renewed concern with the practical will, I believe, help us to engage with key concerns that the disciplinary boundaries of *What Is Philosophy?* seem to, or indeed explicitly, exclude. For example, where do the social sciences sit in Deleuze and Guattari's schema (Brown 2010)? How can we appreciate the impact of conceptual art beyond Deleuze and Guattari's quick dismissal of it on account of its apparent confusion of sensation with concept (Deleuze and Guattari 1994: 198)?[25] We lose much of the richness of contemporary art, and indeed of music, the transdisciplinary modes of practice that music has discovered by opening its boundaries to its outside, if we cannot find the value in this artistic moment. The practical challenge may have a major effect on the framework of *What Is Philosophy?* and would raise new difficulties of its own, but this is something that will only be navigated with careful, open-ended, and, indeed, transdisciplinary work.

With a focus on practice, Bachelard may help us with our musical problems too. How is the experimental to be reconciled with a concern with technological innovation? For Bachelard such a pairing is key to his understanding of laboratory work. The "phenomeno-technology" (Bachelard 1984: 13, Chimisso 2008: 143, Rheinberger 2010: 23) that couples applied rationalism and technical materialism undoes any division between the adventure of the experimental and the results of the experiment. It is a lens that may help us navigate between the poles of musical primitivism and technologism.

What Bachelard and recent musical research on the question of experimentation show us is that when engagement takes place at an immanent, practical level, received distinctions between the experiment and the experimental no longer hold so readily. Involvement in either side is risky and requires the careful, constant evaluation of its relationship with its counterpart. For this reason, the apparent foreclosure of *What Is Philosophy?* cannot be easily dismissed: it is evidence of one aspect of the fragility and the danger of experimental work. Just as philosophy can only be saved from a reduction to logic by carefully navigating its own form of experimentation, perhaps so too may "experimental music" act as a mode of resistance toward the commodification or scientification of music only if its experimentation is carefully measured. This is inconclusive, and it need be: while experimentation cannot be a general method, its transdisciplinary passage across disciplines, invested in new ways in each, may help us map out and draw divergent relations between philosophy, science, and art, transforming each and itself throughout the process.

Notes

1. Here I will alternate between speaking of transdisciplinary practices and transdisciplinary research, but we could perhaps speak of a transdisciplinary "study" in the mode of Stefano Harney and Fred Moten, encompassing collective practices of an intellectual, artistic, and social character (Harney and Moten 2013). Deleuze's collaborator Félix Guattari would speak more explicitly of the transdisciplinary than Deleuze did, positing it as a means to position research "'astride' science, art and social communication" and speaking of "a transdisciplinarity that would enable the problematic of one model in relation to another to be clarified" (Guattari 2015: 135). As Alliez stresses, it is indeed ultimately only through Guattari that a full articulation of Deleuze's investment in transdisciplinarity will become clear, beginning with the adoption of Guattari's notion of the transversal in Deleuze's 1970 revision of his *Proust and Signs* (Deleuze 2008). Here, however, I will be setting aside the specificity of this relation to focus on the significance to transdisciplinarity of some other threads passing through Deleuze's work.
2. Patrice Maniglier (2012, forthcoming) and James Williams (2005: Ch. 4, 2006) are two of the few scholars in the Anglophone literature to have indicated the significance of this relationship and the importance of Bachelard to Deleuze's thought. Among the many routes that future research could take, Bachelard and Deleuze's respective work on the concepts of rhythm and of imagination, as well as their shared insights with regard to the limits of phenomenology, seem to me especially rich avenues of inquiry.
3. A significant amount of work is now available on Deleuze's relationship with these figures, especially Simondon. Some of the most recent of this can be found in a volume of *Deleuze Studies* edited by Andrew Iliadis (2017).

4 This diversity of positions, readings, and uses of Deleuze on and with science can be found in edited collections such as Jensen and Rödje (2010) and Gaffney (2010).
5 While Christina Chimisso is reluctant to incorporate Bachelard's work into Anglo-American philosophy of science frameworks, including that recent work by thinkers like Ian Hacking and Daston that has been named historical epistemology (Chimisso 2008: 143), and Dominique Lecourt rules out such an association on the (perhaps reductive) grounds of Bachelard's materialism opposing the purported idealism of Anglo-American philosophers like Thomas Kuhn and Paul Feyerabend (Lecourt 1975: 10), the work of Hans-Jörg Rheinberger has connected and contextualized these strands of thought in a compelling way (Rheinberger 2010).
6 See the recent special issue of *Angelaki*, edited by Sean Bowden and Mark G.E. Kelly (2018).
7 Bachelard's own reading of Bergson, pitting his own favoring of discontinuity against the Bergsonian continuity that is shared, but complicated, by Deleuze, is another compelling line of engagement between Bachelard and Deleuze (Bachelard 2016, Williams 2005).
8 On contextualizing Deleuze's thought with regard to the French epistemological tradition and strands of French thought contemporary to it, see Eyers 2013 and Peden 2014.
9 It is worth considering the significance of the fact that this work followed a long detour from Bachelard's work on science into a series of explorations of the imagination. These two aspects of Bachelard's work are often posed as entirely distinct, indeed seemingly by Bachelard himself, but a challenge to this presumption could be productive.
10 This piece is an excerpt from *Le rationalisme appliqué*.
11 Bachelard's depiction of Cartesian doubt may not capture the complexity of Descartes's position, and the precise function of doubt in Descartes's thought and its relation to the constitution of knowledge is still a topic of great debate. See Della Rocca 2005.
12 On this discontinuity in relation to Deleuze's primacy of continuity, see Williams 2005.
13 Patrice Maniglier (forthcoming) and Étienne Balibar (2003) are among those who consider Deleuze to be following in a trajectory set out by structuralism, contrary to a narrative that would posit his "poststructuralism" as marking a radical break with structuralism.
14 Mary Beth Mader has convincingly argued that at least one such concept, that of intensity, is better read as a philosophical concept than a scientific one (Mader 2017). The means by which she makes this argument, posing the intensity of philosophical concepts against the necessity of extensive expression in scientific inquiry, provides an illuminating angle for some of the movements in Deleuze's thought across his works with Guattari that I will be discussing here.

15 Guattari's text "Machine and Structure," in part a response to *Difference and Repetition* and *The Logic of Sense*, paved the way for Deleuze and Guattari's collaboration by arguing that what Deleuze credited to a structuralist understanding of structure could only be understood through the immanently practical and political concept of the machine (Guattari 1984).
16 Its literary use traces back to, at least, Émile Zola's 1880 text "The Experimental Novel" (1893), though it is not until the twentieth century that it gradually accumulates more widespread and conceptually refined meanings.
17 See, for instance, Deleuze and Parnet 2006: 41.
18 This definition is used by Deleuze in two similarly worded passages in *Nietzsche and Philosophy* and *Difference and Repetition* (Deleuze 2006: 108, Deleuze 2004: 165). Despite this rejection of such an understanding of "method," the question of method remains an important one when engaging with Deleuze, and considering how this "method" differs from, for example, Bachelard's understanding of scientific method will be key going ahead.
19 Not least through the figure of Cage himself: see Iddon 2013.
20 Branden Joseph compellingly details the difficulties and contradictions present in Cage's engagements with technology throughout Joseph (2016).
21 We could align this with Joseph's remarks on Cage putting aside "affect, emotion, desire, and any other irrational or ego-motivated aspects of human behavior" (Joseph 2016: 187), which Joseph associates with an evacuation of the political from Cage's work.
22 I make an intervention into this debate, suggesting that Cage and Deleuze could be read differently than is suggested by Piekut and "Deleuzian sound studies," respectively, in Campbell 2017.
23 Deleuze and Guattari's conception of analytic philosophy is sweeping and would benefit from more nuance. Jeffrey Bell's careful reading is useful in this respect (Bell 2016).
24 Deleuze also uses this term in his discussion of cinema (Deleuze 2005: 268).
25 Or perhaps this is only Deleuze's dismissal: we find elsewhere that Guattari is much more sympathetic.

Bibliography

Adorno, T.W., and Horkheimer, M. (1997), *Dialectic of Enlightenment*, trans. J. Cumming, London: Verso.
Adorno, T.W. (1998), *Quasi Una Fantasia: Essays on Modern Music*, trans. R. Livingston, London: Verso.
Alliez, É. (2011), "Rhizome (with no return)," *Radical Philosophy*, 167: 36–42.
Alliez, É. (2015), "Structuralism's Afters: Tracing Transdisciplinarity through Guattari and Latour," *Theory, Culture & Society* 32 (5–6): 139–58.

Assis, P. de (2016), "Introduction," in P. de Assis (ed.), *Experimental Affinities in Music*, Leuven: Leuven University Press.
Bachelard, G. (1928), *Essai sur la connaissance approchée*, Paris: Vrin.
Bachelard, G. (1932), *Le pluralisme coherent de la chimie moderne*, Paris: Vrin.
Bachelard, G. (1966), *Le rationalisme appliqué*, 3rd edn, Paris: Presses universitaires de France.
Bachelard, G. (1968), *The Philosophy of No: A Philosophy of the New Scientific Mind*, trans. G.C. Waterston, New York: The Orion Press.
Bachelard, G. (1984), *The New Scientific Spirit*, trans. A. Goldhammer, Boston: Beacon.
Bachelard, G. (2002), *The Formation of the Scientific Mind: A Contribution to a Psychoanalysis of Objective Knowledge*, trans. M. McAllester Jones, Manchester: Clinamen.
Bachelard, G. (2012), "Corrationalism and the Problematic," trans. M. Tiles, *Radical Philosophy*, 173: 27–32.
Bachelard, G. (2016), *The Dialectic of Duration*, trans. M. McAllester Jones, London: Rowman & Littlefield.
Balibar, É. (2003), "Structuralism: A Destitution of the Subject?" trans. J. Swenson, *Differences: A Journal of Feminist Cultural Studies*, 14 (1): 1–21.
Beal, A.C. (2008), "'Experimentalists and Independents Are Favored': John Edmunds in Conversation with Peter Yates and John Cage, 1959–61," *Notes*, 64 (4): 659–87.
Bell, J.A. (2016), *Deleuze and Guattari's What Is Philosophy?: A Critical Introduction and Guide*, Edinburgh: Edinburgh University Press.
Bernstein, D., ed. (2008), *The San Francisco Tape Music Center*, Berkeley: University of California Press.
Bowden, S. (2011), *The Priority of Events: Deleuze's Logic of Sense*, Edinburgh: Edinburgh University Press.
Bowden, S. (2018), "An Anti-Positivist Conception of Problems," *Angelaki*, 23 (2): 45–63.
Bowden, S., and Kelly, M.G., eds (2018), *Angelaki (Problems in Twentieth-Century French Philosophy)* 23 (2).
Brooks, W. (2012), "In re: 'Experimental Music,'" *Contemporary Music Review*, 31 (1): 37–62.
Brown, S.D. (2010), "Between the Planes: Deleuze and Social Science," in C.B. Jensen and K. Rödje (eds), *Deleuzian Intersections: Science, Technology, Anthropology*, New York: Berghahn Books.
Cage, J. (1961), *Silence: Lectures and Writings*, Middletown, Conn.: Wesleyan University Press.
Campbell, I. (2017), "John Cage, Gilles Deleuze, and the Idea of Sound," *Parallax* 23 (3): 361–78.
Chimisso, C. (2008), *Writing the History of the Mind: Philosophy and Science in France, 1900 to 1960s*, Aldershot: Ashgate.
Daston, L. (1991), "Historical Epistemology," in J. Chandler, A.I. Davidson, and H. Harootunian (eds), *Questions of Evidence: Proof, Practice, and Persuasion across the Disciplines*, Chicago: University of Chicago Press.

Delanda, M. (2002), *Intensive Science and Virtual Philosophy*, London: Continuum.
Deleuze, G. (1992), "Postscript on Societies of Control," *October*, 59: 3–7.
Deleuze, G. (1994), *Difference and Repetition*, trans. P. Patton, New York: Continuum.
Deleuze, G. (2003), *Francis Bacon: The Logic of Sensation*, trans. D.W. Smith, London: Continuum.
Deleuze, G. (2004), "How Do We Recognize Structuralism?" in *Desert Islands and Other Texts 1953–1974*, ed. D. Lapoujade, trans. M. Taormina, Los Angeles: Semiotext(e).
Deleuze, G. (2005), *Cinema II: The Time-Image*, trans. H. Tomlinson and R. Galeta, London: Continuum.
Deleuze, G. (2006), *Nietzsche and Philosophy*, trans. H. Tomlinson, London: Continuum.
Deleuze, G. (2008), *Proust and Signs*, trans. R. Howard, London: Continuum.
Deleuze, G., and Guattari, F. (1983), *Anti-Oedipus: Capitalism and Schizophrenia*, trans. R. Hurley, M. Seem, and H.R. Lane, Minneapolis: University of Minnesota Press.
Deleuze, G., and Guattari, F. (1987), *A Thousand Plateaus: Capitalism and Schizophrenia*, trans. B. Massumi, Minneapolis: University of Minnesota Press.
Deleuze, G., and Guattari, F. (1994), *What Is Philosophy?*, trans. H. Tomlinson and G. Burchell, New York: Columbia University Press.
Deleuze, G., and Parnet, C. (2006), "On the Superiority of Anglo-American Literature," in *Dialogues II*, trans. H. Tomlinson and B. Habberjam, London: Continuum.
Della Rocca, M. (2005), "Descartes, the Cartesian Circle, and Epistemology without God," *Philosophy and Phenomenological Research*, 70 (January): 1–33.
Descartes, R. (1996), *Meditations on First Philosophy, with Selections from the Objections and Replies*, trans. and ed. J. Cottingham, Cambridge: Cambridge University Press.
During, E. (2004), "'A History of Problems': Bergson and the French Epistemological Tradition," *Journal of the British Society for Phenomenology*, 35 (1): 4–23.
Eco, U. (1989), *The Open Work*, trans. A. Cancogni, Cambridge, Mass.: Harvard University Press.
Eyers, T. (2013), *Post-Rationalism: Psychoanalysis, Epistemology, and Marxism in Post-War France*, London: Bloomsbury.
Gaffney, P., ed. (2010), *The Force of the Virtual: Deleuze, Science, and Philosophy*, Minneapolis: University of Minnesota Press.
Goehr, L. (2016), "Explosive Experiments and the Fragility of the Experimental," in P. de Assis (ed.), *Experimental Affinities in Music*, Leuven: Leuven University Press.
Guattari, F. (1984), *Molecular Revolution: Psychiatry and Politics*, trans. R. Sheed, New York: Penguin.
Guattari, F. (2015), "Transdisciplinarity Must Become Transversality," trans. A. Goffey, *Theory, Culture & Society*, 32 (5–6): 131–37.
Haraway, D. (2004), "Modest_Witness@Second_Millennium," in *The Haraway Reader*, New York: Routledge.
Harney, S., and Moten, F. (2013), *The Undercommons: Fugitive Planning & Black Study*, Wivenhoe: Minor Compositions.

Hiller, L.A., and Isaacson, L.M. (1959), *Experimental Music: Composition with an Electronic Computer*, New York: McGraw-Hill Book Company, Inc.

Hughes, J. (2009), *Deleuze's Difference and Repetition: A Reader's Guide*, New York: Continuum.

Iddon, M. (2013), *New Music at Darmstadt: Nono, Stockhausen, Cage, and Boulez*, Cambridge: Cambridge University Press.

Iliadis, A., ed. (2017), "Ontologies of Difference: The Philosophies of Gilbert Simondon and Raymond Ruyer," *Deleuze Studies*, 11 (4).

Jensen, C.B., and Rödje, K., eds (2010), *Deleuzian Intersections: Science, Technology, Anthropology*, New York: Berghahn Books.

Joseph, B.W. (2016), *Experimentations: John Cage in Music, Art, and Architecture*, New York: Bloomsbury.

Latour, B. (1988), *The Pasteurization of France*, trans. A. Sheridan and J. Law, Cambridge, Mass.: Harvard University Press.

Lecourt, D. (1974), *L'Epistémologie historique de Gaston Bachelard*, Paris: Vrin.

Lecourt, D. (1975), *Marxism and Epistemology: Bachelard, Canguilhem and Foucault*, trans. B. Brewster, London: New Left Books.

Lewis, G.E. (1996), "Improvised Music after 1950: Afrological and Eurological Perspectives," *Black Music Research Journal*, 16 (1): 91–122.

Lundy, C. (2018), "Bergson's Method of Problematisation and the Pursuit of Metaphysical Precision," *Angelaki*, 23 (2): 31–44.

Mader, M.B. (2017), "Philosophical and Scientific Intensity in the Thought of Gilles Deleuze," *Deleuze Studies*, 11 (2): 259–77.

Maniglier, P. (2012), "What Is a Problematic?," *Radical Philosophy* 173: 21–23.

Maniglier, P. (2017), "Post-Metaphysical Meditations: Reflections on 'Speculative Realism'" in T. Griffin (ed.), *The New Existentialism*, Dijon: Presses du Réel.

Maniglier, P. (forthcoming), "'Problem-Sharing,'" *Theory, Culture & Society*.

Mauceri, F.X. (1997), "From Experimental Music to Musical Experiment," *Perspectives of New Music*, 35 (1): 187–204.

Moles, A. (1966), *Information Theory and Esthetic Perception*, trans. J.E. Cohen, Urbana: University of Illinois Press.

Negri, A. (2011), "Gilles-felix," in É. Alliez and A. Goffey (eds), *The Guattari Effect*, London: Continuum.

Nyman, M. (1999), *Experimental Music: Cage and Beyond*, 2nd edn, Cambridge: Cambridge University Press.

Osborne, P. (2015), "Problematizing Disciplinarity, Transdisciplinary Problematics," *Theory, Culture & Society*, 32 (5–6): 3–35.

Peden, K. (2014), *Spinoza Contra Phenomenology: French Rationalism from Cavaillès to Deleuze*, Stanford: Stanford University Press.

Piekut, B. (2012), "Sound's Modest Witness: Notes on Cage and Modernism," *Contemporary Music Review*, 31 (1): 3–18.

Rheinberger, H.-J. (2010), *On Historicizing Epistemology: An Essay*, trans. D. Fernbach, Stanford: Stanford University Press.

Ross, A. (2018), "The Errors of History," *Angelaki*, 23 (2): 139–54.
Schaeffer, P. (1957), "Vers une musique expérimentale," *Revue musicale*, 236: 18–23.
Schaeffer, P. (1966), *Traité de objets musicaux: essai interdisciplines*, Paris: Éditions du Seuil.
Schaeffer, P. (2012), *In Search of a Concrete Music*, trans. C. North and J. Dack, Berkeley: University of Los Angeles Press.
Shultis, C. (2013), *Silencing the Sounded Self: John Cage and the American Experimental Tradition*, Lebanon, NH: University Press of New England.
Silverman, K. (2010), *Begin Again: A Biography of John Cage*, New York: Alfred A. Knopf.
Stengers, I. (2010), "Experimenting with *What Is Philosophy?*" in C.B. Jensen and K. Rödje (eds), *Deleuzian Intersections: Science, Technology, Anthropology*, New York: Berghahn Books.
Tiles, M. (2005), "Technology, Science and Inexact Knowledge: Bachelard's Non-Cartesian Epistemology," in G. Gutting (ed.), *Continental Philosophy of Science*, Oxford: Blackwell.
Thompson, M. (2017), "Whiteness and the Ontological Turn in Sound Studies," *Parallax*, 23 (3): 266–82.
Toscano, A. (2006), *The Theatre of Production: Philosophy and Individuation between Kant and Deleuze*, New York: Palgrave Macmillan.
Wasser, A. (2017), "How Do We Recognise Problems?," *Deleuze Studies*, 11 (1): 48–67.
Williams, J. (2003), *Gilles Deleuze's Difference and Repetition: A Critical Introduction and Guide*, Edinburgh: Edinburgh University Press.
Williams, J. (2005), *The Transversal Thought of Gilles Deleuze: Encounters & Influences*, Manchester: Clinamen Press.
Williams, J. (2006), "Science and Dialectics in the Philosophies of Deleuze, Bachelard and DeLanda," *Paragraph*, 29 (2): 98–114.
Zola, É. (1893), *The Experimental Novel and Other Essays*, trans. B.M. Sherman, New York: Cassell Publishing Company.

5

Diagrammatic Transdisciplinarity

Thought outside Discipline

Kamini Vellodi

Notions of inter-, multi-, or trans-disciplinarity ostensibly presuppose the existence of a number of distinct disciplines capable of being put into relation with each other. In a 1998 collection of essays titled *The Anxiety of Interdisciplinarity*, the editors note the views of Hal Foster and Julia Kristeva, both interviewed for the collection, that to be interdisciplinary one needs "to be grounded in one discipline, preferably two, to know the historicity of these discourses before you test them against each other" (Coles and Defert 1998: 111). But is this in fact the case? Can't the moment of crossing disciplines, "testing" as Kristeva puts it, precede, or even exceed, the formation and forms of disciplines?

Conceptualizing discipline

From its very emergence the notion of discipline has been split. Deriving from the Greek *didasko* ("teach") and the Latin (*di*)*disco* ("learn"), *disciplina* already bore in classical Latin the double sense of knowledge (a knowledge-system) and power (the disciplining of an individual)[1]—both an activity and an attribute.

In the Christian Church from the thirteenth century onward, discipline designated the punishment imposed by ecclesiastic authority or self-imposed as penance. In medieval England, discipline also came to refer to the practice of a disciple/scholar, as well as to branches of knowledge, especially medicine, law, and theology, that comprised the core of the new university—and it was from this that the modern notion of discipline as a branch of knowledge or learning, a particular subject-area, stemmed. Insofar as to be trained in a branch of knowledge allowed one to achieve discipline (that is, the quality of self-mastery), the two senses of discipline as knowledge-system and as regulation were conjoined. A certain, regulative approach to thinking was linked to the formation, preservation, and instilling of a body of knowledge. The dynamics of this conjunction is what Michel Foucault famously and critically called attention to, defining discipline as a "system of control in the production of discourse" and part of a scientific quest to advance knowledge, even when it simultaneously limits the freedom of inquiry.[2]

The notion of what constitutes a knowledge-system has of course changed significantly since the early thirteenth century. The early Scholastic university system, as pioneered by Peter Abelard (founder of the University of Paris in 1200, which became the prototype for most other universities of the Middle Ages), replaced the classical division of subjects into the *trivium* (grammar, rhetoric, and dialectic) and *quadrivium* (arithmetic, geometry, astronomy, music), with "reasoned theology" and abstract philosophy.[3] The notion of discipline transformed radically with the emergence of modern disciplines in the late eighteenth century and early nineteenth century that was made possible by the development of new institutions and practices, initially the development of scientific societies such as the Royal Society and later the rise of the research university (Shumway and Messer-Davidow 1991: 203–04). It was only after this point that disciplines were taken to designate historically specific forms. The emergence of academic departments subsequently enabled the professionalization and organization of knowledge production, which added to the original sense of regulation a further sense of institutionalization (Shumway and Messer-Davidow 1991: 207).[4] By the late twentieth century, discipline was understood to signify "a particular class of legitimizing institution that produces a community of competency" (Reese 1995: 544), "a community based on inquiry and centred on competent investigators [...] who associated in order to facilitate intercommunication and to establish some degree of authority over the standards of that inquiry" (Geiger 1986: 29), and for some, "nothing more than an administrative category" (Jencks and Riesman 1968: 523).[5] Today we can characterize discipline as a regulated, institutionalized, authoritative, normative, and knowledge-orientated form of thought shared by a community and bound together by customs and conventions of method, technique, and tropes, and finally a name.

The development of disciplines has been accompanied by the identification of their borders, the desire to protect and defend these borders (which in the twentieth century has been called "boundary-work")[6] as well as the desire to challenge and transgress these borders (as inter-, multi-, or trans-disciplinary work). One might say that a defense of borders accompanies the regulation of disciplines, while experimenting and deregulating impulses leads to a transgression of borders. In any case, as Peter Osborne has put it, "disputes about the nature, borders and rationales of academic disciplines have a history as long as the disciplines themselves" (Osborne 2015: 3).

Throughout history, each discipline has defined its center in relation to its periphery and frontier disciplines. In the Middle Ages every subject shared a border with theology. Today, economics borders mathematics, psychology, and political science while art history shares borders with sociology, history, and aesthetics. Put in other terms, we could say that each discipline is inseparable from power relations to other disciplines. Certain disciplines at certain moments have attained a methodological and conceptual dominance over others, in the way that theology dominated all other subjects in the Middle Ages, or textuality—as a combination of linguistics, semiotics, and rhetoric—became the master discipline for critical reflection on the arts in the 1970s and 1980s (reviving a nineteenth-century feeling, expressed by Mallarmé when he remarked that literature is at the crossroads of all the other disciplines [Mallarmé, quoted in Kristeva 1998: 3]), or indeed how the social sciences have today become the model for the humanities, overdetermining the meaning and value of "research."

The nature of the borders themselves is of course highly variable. Some disciplines are more fixed, with more impermeable borders, while others are more fluid and metamorphic.[7] A "pure" subject such as pure mathematics is arguably less permeable than an applied one such as sociology, a discipline that has been characterized as having an essentially "interstitial" character as a consequence of it not being "good at excluding things from itself" (Abbott 2001: 5).[8] Some have felt that if the discipline is "strong" and established, then traversing its borders requires force, but if the discipline is "weak" or very young, then interdisciplinarity happens naturally, as part of its development. No doubt ancient disciplines carry the weight of their histories, whereas others, more recent, are not as beholden to the historical circumscription of borderlines. It is fair to assume that academics hired in the relatively young field of Visual Culture, for instance, might not necessarily possess the same sense of certainty over their discipline's identity or boundaries as those working within mathematics or theology. Indeed, this porosity has come to be seen as an asset. In any case, borderlines between disciplines have meant different things at different times and with respect to different fields.

Before the twentieth century, disciplines bled into each other without self-conscious reflection on this process. What has changed is not that disciplines have suddenly embraced the idea of transgressing their borders but that they have become more aware of doing so. The transgressive element is pulled out, examined, and named. This has brought about a marked shift in the nature of the debates.

Even if the practice long predated it, the notion of interdisciplinarity only emerged in 1929, in the context of Anglophone debates in the social and physical sciences, initially to refer to a pluralism of disciplinary methods.[9] It was followed by "multidisciplinarity," which referred to a multiplicity of researches with different disciplinary attitudes and affiliations—an additive juxtaposition of disciplines. Transdisciplinarity, the most recent of these terms, first emerged in 1970 and seemed to offer something different in its sense of "across" borders, and not just "between" or a multiplication of them.[10] Initially associated with the application of systems theory to educational policy and child development, transdisciplinarity was vaunted both as a possibility of an integrated and universal knowledge system (an idea with ancient roots),[11] and—ultimately more influentially—as a new "mode 2" type of knowledge production, which in contrast to conventional "mode 1" disciplinary production of knowledge was developed for "real-world" application and involved expertise from academia, government, and industry (the view proposed by Michael Gibbons et al. in their 1994 publication *The New Production of Knowledge*).[12] In addition to these three dominant terms, a host of other sub-categories have proliferated: indisciplines, antidisciplines, postdisciplines, dedisciplinarization, metadisciplinarity—giving rise to an apparently endless reproduction of prefixes.

The presiding view since the 1960s has been that the transformation of intellectual practice, and the most politically and theoretically adventurous and engaged practice, occurs at the borders of disciplines—that it is from the challenge to and disruption of bordered areas of competence that new theoretical avenues emerge.[13] But such "border work" has also been subject to charges of philistinism: in fleeing from a single designated area of competence does one flee from competence altogether?[14] Furthermore, far from undermining the mastery of disciplines, a practice that traverses a discipline can in fact reciprocally strengthen its hold: as a derivative, the prefix reciprocally reinforces the preposition. Lastly, new offshoots can stabilize themselves as new "interdisciplines," in W.J.T. Mitchell's words, "sites of convergence across disciplinary lines" (Mitchell 1995: 541)—which is to say, the offshoot re-stratifies, becomes instituted and normative, and eventually grows into a new discipline. Again, Visual Culture is a good example of this. While originally functioning as both the "outside" and "inside" of art history (Mitchell 1995: 542),[15] it has now become a thoroughly recognized discipline in its own right, arguably betraying the revolutionary potentials it harbored at its moment of emergence and falling into the trap that haunts every discipline: establishment.

The fact that passage, breakthrough, and transgression are invariably recuperated into the stability of a name and a form complete with its set of methods, concepts, curricula, canon of thinkers has led some to deny that inter- or trans-disciplinarity are even possible. In Stanley Fish's view, for example, the professional canons of knowledge reassert disciplinary norms at every stage (Fish 1989: 21). Today, when inter-, multi-, and trans-disciplinary initiatives have been institutionalized as norms, and made instrumentalized features of the accountability of research and its social agendas, the urgent question is how to retain the disruptive and destabilizing force to disciplines as a site of transformation and production. The point is not to simply add new material for thought while retaining the definitive traits of disciplinary practice (methods, techniques, discourse, a canon, scholarly conventions, an academic community, and so on). Rather, it is to fundamentally disrupt and transform the form of discipline. How can border practices qualitatively transform the respective fields they touch upon, rather than simply extend and recombine consolidated grounds? How can we sustain and affirm the interval?

W.J.T. Mitchell argues that the answer lies in the turbulence of "indiscipline" and incoherence at the inner and outer borders of established disciplines— moments of breakthrough when the continuity of discipline is broken and "the practice comes into question" (Mitchell 1995: 541). Such moments, when a discipline "performs a revelation of its own inadequacy," are not necessarily predicated upon seeking out other disciplines (Mitchell 1995: 541). They can also occur by going more deeply into one's own discipline, by an inward burrowing that (and Mitchell's example here is Jacques Lacan) causes "an explosion of its own boundaries that send shock waves into other disciplines" (Mitchell 1995: 541). Carlo Ginzburg echoed this sentiment: he claimed "there is nothing intrinsically innovative or subversive in an interdisciplinary approach to knowledge" (Ginzburg 1995: 534), that interdisciplinary approaches do not necessarily indicate a significant intellectual program and that often in the history of a discipline the innovative practitioners are those who work within a discipline. Ginzburg cites the example of an art historian working with connoisseurship and shows that, while often critiqued for being narrow and purist, connoisseurship is in fact a hybrid, interdisciplinary practice for it requires expertise in whatever area is demanded by the particular subject at hand. For instance, a connoisseur studying a fifteenth-century painting of flowers is called upon to understand botany and not only the history of artistic representations of plants. Thus, good scholarship, Ginzburg claims, can be interdisciplinary from within rather than interdisciplinary from without (Ginzburg 1995).[16]

That the transgression of discipline may happen from within the discipline invites a thinking of the border not simply as that which exists on the exterior frontier of disciplines. That the "outside" of a discipline, what is foreign and unrecognizable to it, can be found deep within the discipline invites a thinking of the border not simply as a relation between disciplinary terms but as an intensive space within the discipline itself. In the art historian's study of a flower painting, "botany" is not another discipline but part of the reality of art history itself—albeit a mysterious reality. The identification and substantiation of inter-, trans- and, multi-disciplinarity perpetuated by the academy since the latter half of the twentieth century exteriorizes border work, but what Mitchell points to is how border work can occur as intensive ruptures within a discipline. Such intensity is not simply an interiority, for it does not already belong to the discipline. Rather, it is a zone of turbulence, a blind spot that resists integration and upon contact has a destabilizing impact. And indeed, if there is a potential in the prefix trans- (in distinction to the "inter-" and "multi-") it is in the sense of the "across" as beyond disciplinary structure as such, where this beyond is not just exterior to but in excess of. Such is the sense of transdisciplinarity that emerges in the work of Deleuze and Guattari.

Discipline and trans-discipline in Deleuze and Guattari's philosophy

Deleuze and Guattari's work, and the conceptions of transdisciplinarity that it stages and invites, reflects the practice of twentieth-century French philosophy between the 1940s and 1980s as a radically expanded and heterogeneous field, "regenerating itself out of its other."[17] Discipline, if understood as the formalization and regulation of thought such that it assumes an identifiable and recognizable image that can be practiced by a professionalized and institutionalized community for the production of knowledge, is a designation that their philosophy insistently challenges. Even Deleuze's early works, focused on the history of philosophy, stage encounters between philosophy and mathematics, the arts and the sciences, and through these stagings reveal the way in which the history of philosophy has been far from a purified lineage or professional specialism, that metaphysical concerns have always been integrated with extra-metaphysical problems, and that philosophy as a practice of thought continually extends beyond disciplinary and institutional parameters and the images of philosophical thought that already exist.[18]

While the early works are certainly broad in their range, it is with Guattari that Deleuze's work reaches new, almost vertiginous levels of transdisciplinarity. Texts such as *Anti-Oedipus, What Is Philosophy?* and perhaps especially *A Thousand Plateaus* enact a breathless passage across disciplines, exposing the intersections of philosophy with many other disciplines—arts, the physical sciences, social sciences, linguistics, anthropology, ethnography, mathematics, history, geography, to name but a few. Presented here is a rhizomatic motility of thought that counters what Deleuze and Guattari call the "arborescent," tree-like, hierarchical, centered system of thinking that is indebted to a ground and projects a traceable lineage with an origin.[19] In contrast to the latter, rhizomatic thinking is "acentered" and nonhierarchical, traversing systems. The rhizome "connects any point to any other point" in an extended middle (milieu) (Deleuze and Guattari 2003a: 21). With its rhizomatic style, *A Thousand Plateaus* answers to a remark that Deleuze had made in his original preface to *Difference and Repetition*: that "the time is coming when it will hardly be possible to write a book of philosophy as it has been done for so long: 'Ah! The old style ... '" (Deleuze 2001: xxi).[20] In place of any lamentation, what we find in *A Thousand Plateaus* is Deleuze and Guattari taking ownership of the new conditions of thought and writing, putting into practice philosophy as "a thought synthesizer to make thought travel" (Deleuze and Guattari 2003a: 343).

In an interview about *Capitalism and Schizophrenia*, Deleuze and Guattari remark on the role May 1968 had to play in their approach to disciplinarity. Before this moment, "the various disciplines have gotten along by relying on a kind of respect for one another's autonomy" (Deleuze and Guattari 2009a: 59). But after 1968, such autonomy is dangerous and unproductive. The new realities that disciplines must confront cannot be addressed by specialists working in their separate corners. Instead, academics must learn something from schizophrenics, switching "from one register to another," assuming the capacity to "range across fields" (Deleuze and Guattari 2009a: 59). Thus, the challenge to disciplinary divisions does not come from eclecticism, "nor does it have to lead to confusion." Questioning the division of fields of study does not mean dissolving the various sciences, "but rather deepening them, making them worthy of their objects" (Deleuze and Guattari 2009a: 60), in part by addressing their utility. It is in this vein that Guattari defined his practice of "ecosophy" as a "multifaceted movement," open to multiple fields, as opposed to "a discipline of refolding on interiority" (Guattari, quoted in Genosko 2009: 17). While this may sound superficially like the socially driven, policy-oriented agenda of transdisciplinarity advocated by Gibbons et al., Deleuze and Guattari do not mean by utility a neoliberal, technocratic, positivistic solving of real-world problems, but a critique with transformational effect that operates at the level of thought and concepts, which, while immanent to the real, does not positivistically reproduce its coordinates. As such, they point to an enlarging of disciplinary scope that calls "for a profound revision of our conceptual system of today" (Deleuze and Guattari 2009a: 60), an ambition that, as some have noted, is not one usually voiced by today's advocates of transdisciplinarity (Osborne 2015: 14).[21] What Deleuze and Guattari offer, along with many of their French counterparts, is a restitution of a practice of transdisciplinarity as critical, productive, and transformational, where the prefix "trans-" is not beholden to existing structures but operative beyond them.[22]

So when Deleuze and Guattari remark, in the blurb to the French edition of *What Is Philosophy?* that "philosophy is not interdisciplinary" but an "entire" discipline that enters into resonance with others, they are gesturing toward something other than the dissolution of borders between philosophy and other disciplines.[23] That is, they argue for a retention of the integrity and distinction of disciplines, to prevent the generalization of knowledge, while at the same time challenging the closure, autonomy, and historical hierarchies of the disciplines. For them, fleeing from the bordered competencies of a discipline is by no means fleeing from competency as such. With their dazzling erudition, their works reveal transdisciplinarity as polymathy rather than philistinism, an intellectually rigorous practice of crossing and creatively traversing borders that has nothing to do with the superficial borrowing of concepts and tropes as referential or applied motifs. In turn, the conception and practice of philosophy are altered, as is the understanding of philosophy's primary material, concepts. Thus, Deleuze tells us that philosophy is a "practice of concepts" that "must be judged in the light of the other practices with which it interferes" (Deleuze 2005: 268) and that "a philosophical concept can never be confused with a scientific function or an artistic construction but finds itself in affinity with these" (Deleuze 2001: xiv). Philosophy has no supremacy over art or science, which are also practices of thought. Philosophy is a practice of concepts, but concepts are themselves "fragmentary totalities" that do not fit together but link on divergent lines and detours, forming a toolbox that has to be used.

What we see emerging here is a distinction between thought and discipline, and, furthermore, the sense that thought is always more than a discipline.

Indeed, the ongoing preoccupation of Deleuze and Guattari's works is not discipline or even borderline disciplinary activities, but thought. Thought has always had a relation to discipline, but it is irreducible to discipline, and not dependent upon its frameworks. In *What Is Philosophy?* Deleuze and Guattari (2003b) claim that each discipline of art, science, and philosophy must be open and in contact with an "outside"—which they describe as the element of the "nonthought within thought," the element of thought that thought cannot think yet must be thought and the apprehension of which forces thought (59). The contact with this unthought outside renews thought and ultimately renders disciplinary distinctions indivisible. Which is to say, the outside of art, the outside of philosophy, and the outside of science (and presumably the outside of other disciplines too) are integrated into a complex of "connections and secondary integrations" (Deleuze and Guattari 2003b: 211) reacting on one another, in a transversal nexus of thought (that Deleuze and Guattari also call a "brain"). This is not unlike the "indisciplined" moments of chaos at the borders of disciplines that Mitchell invoked, a decade after *What Is Philosophy?*, as antidotes to established practices of interdisciplinarity and other border activities proceeding as recognized activities. Deleuze and Guattari bring philosophical precision to, and activate particular solutions for, diagnoses also made by many others discontent with the institutionalization and instrumentalization of border practices.

In *What Is Philosophy?*, Deleuze and Guattari distinguish three levels of the "interference" between disciplines, from the relative to the absolute. There is a first "extrinsic" type when a practitioner in one discipline attempts to venture into another while remaining on their own plane and proceeding with its own methods and criteria, such as when the painter Paul Klee "creates pure sensations of concepts or functions" (Deleuze and Guattari 2003b: 217). Here, the painter uses the materials and methods proper to painting to explore the domain of another discipline, philosophy. A transdisciplinary relation emerges but both disciplines remain intact. A second, "intrinsic," type of interference is produced when the elements of one discipline leave their plane and slip into another plane to create "complex planes that are difficult to qualify" (Deleuze and Guattari 2003b: 217)—such as we find in Nietzsche's *Zarathustra*, with its passages between philosophy, literature, drama, and allegory. Here, transdisciplinarity begins to confuse borders, and a distinctive space emerges irreducible to any one disciplinary plane. The third type are the non-localizable interferences produced when each discipline is "in an essential relationship with the No that concerns it" (Deleuze and Guattari 2003b: 218), where this "No" is the unthought outside that which refuses to be directly thought by a particular disciplinary practice. This is the moment where disciplinary borders dissolve, where "concepts, sensations and functions become undecidable, at the same time as philosophy, art, and science become indiscernible, as if they shared the same shadow that extends itself across their different nature and constantly accompanies them" (Deleuze and Guattari 2003b: 218).

All three levels of interference appear in Deleuze and Guattari's practice of philosophy as thought rather than simply as discipline. As a discipline, philosophy is an institution, a profession, with a history, canon, set of subdisciplines, and so on. But as a practice of thought, philosophy is nebulous, restless, modulating, dissolving, and reforming, constantly in contact with what exceeds it. In this sense, the outside of a discipline and the outside of thought are not the same thing. What is outside a discipline may one day be grasped by that discipline (or indeed, other disciplines), but the outside of thought resists thought. From a disciplinary perspective, math might be outside art history, and engineering might be outside philosophy: these divisions may, however, be addressed and perhaps traversed. But the outside of thought has no name or assignation and occludes direct access. It is not the possession of another thinker, somewhere else, in a different department, but non-placed, ambulant, itinerant. It is not just a border between two terms but an inexhaustible and turbulent zone beyond terms where traits of disciplines mix and meld with as-yet unthought material. Distinct from the history and continuous development of disciplines and their trans- and inter-disciplinary offshoots, there is a becoming of thought, a movement that nevertheless retroactively mobilizes and transforms disciplines. This is the sense of transdisciplinarity in Deleuze and Guattari's work: the passage of thought "ranging across fields" in a zone of ontological excess, in distinction to trans- and inter-disciplinarity as localizable and institutionalized practices. Transdisciplinary thought is posited against transdisciplinary disciplinarity.

Transversality, transdisciplinarity, and diagrammatics

The transdisciplinarity of Deleuze and Guattari's joint work owes much to Guattari's commitment to the practice of transdisciplinarity, a term that he was one of the few figures at the time to use. In his 1991 text "The Ethico-political Foundations of Inter-disciplinarity," retitled as "Transdisciplinarity Must Become Transversality," Guattari elaborated on the conception of transversality that he had developed through his critique of Lacanian psychoanalysis and structural linguistics. Never affiliated with a university, and as such always practicing outside the departmental identification of disciplines, Guattari had begun to apply the notion of transversality to the relationship between forms of disciplinary knowledge as early as 1964 in his work with the Federation of Institutional Study Groups and Research (FGERI)—whose journal explicitly promoted a radically cross-disciplinary program—and at the Centre for Institutional Study, Research and Training (CERFI), set up on the back of the FGERI in 1967.[24]

In place of structural approaches to the unconscious overdetermined by language, and by what he felt to be the ossified and bureaucratic practices of the "professional," Guattari pioneered—most famously at his work at the La Borde clinic from the 1950s onward—a transdisciplinary schizoanalysis that aimed to capture the "mobility of affect" within the group dynamics of the institution. The aim of this practice was to reconnect the individual with the social and political milieu via "semiotic discordances"—the asignifying material that escapes and exceeds signifying structures and that becomes the site for a new production of signs. For Guattari, transversal transdisciplinarity occurs within the "matter" of the institution: "the entangling of workshops, meetings, everyday life in dining rooms" (Guattari, in Goffey 2015b: 235). Nonhierarchical transversal relations displace both the double impasse of the verticality of hierarchical management structures and the horizontality of groups of similar individuals: "transversality tends to be realised when maximum communication is brought about between different levels and above all in different directions" (Guattari, in Genosko 2009: 51). Transversal matter functions as the asignifying and relational "outside" of institutionalized structures of thinking. As Peter Osborne has neatly surmised, transdisciplinarity emerges in Guattari's work as a post-structuralist and anti-dialectical concept, relocated within a generalized ontology of transversal relations (Osborne 2015: 4).[25]

Transversality is further developed through the notion of the diagrammatic, which emerges in Deleuze and Guattari's notes to *Anti-Oedipus* written between 1969 and 1972, and which itself has a transdisciplinary heritage across semiotics, aesthetics, psychoanalysis, ontology, and politics. In the *Notes*, Guattari talks about what he would later call a "meta-modelling" of the unconscious, a nonrepresentational mapping of transversal relations that unleashes a "deterritorialized polyvocality" (Guattari 2006: 71). If transversality describes the passage across structures, the diagram pertains to the construction of something from this passage. While the senses of the two terms are very close, not least since both prefixes indicate "across" ("trans-" suggesting a movement across many things at once and "dia-" suggesting a movement across two things), diagrams may be thought of as concentrations of transversality. For it is not enough that new interactions within the material of a system are staged or that there is mobility within structures—such relations need to be affirmed and something needs to be constructed from them.

Guattari will develop diagrammatics as a tool for schizoanalysis and the new ethico-aesthetic paradigm in later works such as *Cartographies Schizoanalytiques* (1989) and *Chaosmosis* (1992). Meanwhile, Deleuze independently develops the concept of the diagram in a 1975 essay on Foucault, "Ecrivain non: un nouveau cartographe," where, like Guattari, and in response to Foucault's analysis of power, he too characterizes it as a nonrepresentational map of relations of forces.[26] The diagram receives its most rigorous and in-depth elaboration in *A Thousand Plateaus* in 1980. Here, it is presented as a crucial concept in a pragmatic and asignifying semiotics—a theory of signs not concerned with decoding meaning but rather with signs as agents intervening in and transforming reality (in a non-instrumental utility). Such a semiotics puts into practice Deleuze and Guattari's advocation of thought as a practice that "ranges across fields" and overcomes disciplinary autonomy. Indeed, the theme of the "outside of thought" is already here in *A Thousand Plateaus*—the invocation "to place thought in an immediate relation with the outside, with forces of the outside," which "is not at all another image […] but a force that destroys both the image and its copies" (Deleuze and Guattari 2003a: 377).[27]

Against the structuralist privilege assigned to linguistic signs, a pragmatic and asignifying semiotics foregrounds asignification as a force that ruptures signifying structures and subverts the mechanics of communication "which only works under the sway of opinions in order to create 'consensus'" (Deleuze and Guattari 2003b: 6). For Deleuze and Guattari, signs are no longer referential, but productive. They are not communicative, but what "flashes across the intervals when communication takes place between disparates" (Deleuze 2001: 20). The diagram is a type of generative sign that does not refer or reproduce but produces. It maps what is blocked or overcoded in a regime of signs, permitting "original interactions" in matter and playing "a piloting role" in constructing a new reality, which includes a new reality of thought. It has no substance or form of its own and must be "abstracted from any specific use" (Deleuze 2016: 30). It is not an instrumentalized agent of transformation and production; its being derives entirely from its functioning. In this sense, any transdisciplinary effect of the diagrammatic can only be discovered through its action. "The diagram is not a science, it is always a matter of politics" (Deleuze 1975: 1223). Contrary to its quotidian usage, for Deleuze the diagram does not work within the precedents of a science with methods and regulations; rather it is a politics of disruption and transformation that continually reinvents itself in contact with the real.

Deleuze and Guattari's dissociation of the diagram from C.S. Peirce's concept of the diagram as a type of icon is crucial to the elaboration of this constructive character. While Peirce had defined the diagram as a relational icon, Deleuze and Guattari recharacterize the diagram as a type of sign with a "distinct role, irreducible to either the icon or the symbol" (Deleuze and Guattari 2003a: 531n41). Whereas Peirce understood icons as signs that functioned through resemblance, and therefore bound within referential function, for Deleuze and Guattari diagrams break through all referential structure and are purely productive.[28] Diagrams are relational, but relations are no longer submitted to terms, but external to them, operating in the element of the "outside" (Deleuze 1991: x).

Deleuze and Guattari characterize this element of the outside as material: a diagram maps relations of forces in matter as it is constantly modulating and in its excess to forms. Deleuze revisits this idea in *Francis Bacon. The Logic of Sensation* (1981) where the diagram is understood as a "preparatory" work of painting, an informal and material zone of experimentation that produces new form (that Deleuze calls the "Figure"). Bacon's diagrams map relations of the asignifying traits of color and line, material traits that exceed the pictorial forms of figuration and narration, to conjure the new pictorial reality of the figure. A few years later, in *Foucault* (1986) Deleuze expands on the intimations of his earlier essays on Foucault. He develops the notion of the diagram as "a map of destiny or intensity, which proceeds by primary non-localizable relations" (Deleuze 2016: 32) and which is "different from structure in so far as the alliances weave a supple and transversal network [...] [a] perpetual disequilibrium" (Deleuze 2016: 31). This diagram of forces contrasts with the stratified, historical forms of knowledge: the diagram "is neither the subject of history, nor does it survey history. It makes history by unmaking preceding realities and significations, constituting hundreds of points of emergence or creativity, unexpected conjunctions or improbable continuums" (Deleuze 2016: 30–31).

Diagrammatics, thought, and transdisciplinarity

The analysis in *Foucault* underscores the inextricability of signs and thought in Deleuze's work. That thought happens in signs, that forms of thought can also be understood as regimes of signs, and that the diagram is both a type of sign and an agent of thought whose asignifying matter constitutes the outside of thought are themes running through most of Deleuze and Guattari's major works. In relation to Foucault, Deleuze characterizes diagrammatism as "a new way of thinking" (Deleuze 1975: 1223), where thinking is no longer "the innate exercise of a faculty" but something that "must happen to thought" (Deleuze 2006: 253) through the intrusion of the outside—where the outside is not an exterior form but an intensive locus/milieu of forces that is at once farther than any external world and closer than any internal world (Deleuze 2016: 80). The diagram acts as thought's genetic element in the "formless disjunction" carved by this intrusion of the outside (Deleuze 2006: 253).[29] While "the diagram stems from the outside but the outside does not merge with any diagram, and continues instead to 'draw' new ones" (Deleuze 2016: 74). In this way, the outside is always an opening on to a future.

The function of diagrammatics in the construction of thought can be traced back to Deleuze and Guattari's articulations on the problem of a thought with or without an image, the foundations of which are developed by Deleuze in *Difference and Repetition*. They define an "image of thought" as the image thought gives itself of what it means to think (Deleuze and Guattari 2003b: 37). No thought can proceed without bearings but when these bearings are assumed uncritically—for purposes of identification, regulation, and control, or simply out of habit—then they calcify into images that block thought.[30] Disciplines, as regulated, institutionalized, normative forms of thought bound by customs and conventions and shared by a community, can be understood as one class of such imagistic thinking. No doubt disciplines begin to assume solidified images as they become institutionalized, until eventually the disciplinary image inhibits thought as a set of presuppositions or doxa (opinion). For example, in its incipiency Visual Culture might have assumed certain coordinates—such as media theory, social history of art, and Marxist critique—to help its orientation. In its early expressions, it may have not identified itself as anything distinct but as a "frontier" or fringe practice of established disciplines such as Art History or Cultural Studies. But over time, as the borderline became self-aware and reflexive, such coordinates began to solidify to eventually become integral to the image of Visual Culture. A new border is erected, between what is Visual Culture and what is not Visual Culture, and a new set of presuppositions emerges that blocks new thoughts—the type of thoughts that can transform and reinvent the discipline.

The institution of the act of thought in the image that precedes it is what Deleuze calls grounding. That "everyone knows" erects "the form of representation," permitting communication and consensus among a community of thinkers. And surely this is what a discipline, when it is instituted, becomes—a practice of thinking that knows itself before it begins can recognize itself once it has begun and represent itself through the views of a shared community. Indeed, border practices of inter-, multi-, and trans-disciplinarity that have become established practices of the academy are as plagued by dogmatic images as disciplines are. Not only elements of specific disciplinary images of thought, border practices have become part of the image of academia itself.

Deleuze and Guattari are concerned with the conditions under which we can continue to think despite the sedimentation of images that assail thought from all sides. In contrast to the imagistic thought that recognizes itself in the act of thinking and subjects thinking to a grounding in its representational activity, what Deleuze and Guattari call a "thought without image" is a thought born in its genesis and free from all presuppositions, that represents nothing, and does not know in advance what thinking means. It is not a natural and innate exercise reliant on readymade elements and structures, established values, and recognized methods—a characterization that, again, today applies as much to border practices of inter- and trans- disciplinarity as it does to disciplinarity. Rather, it is a thought that is forced through differences and dissimilarities, and irreducible to any image that arises from it (Deleuze 2001: 167). The claim that thought is born as a shock to thought is rigorously explicated in *Difference and Repetition* and insists throughout Deleuze and Guattari's work. In *What Is Philosophy?* they claim that the disciplines of art, science, and philosophy of thought move "by crises or shocks in different ways" (Deleuze and Guattari 2003b: 203). In *Francis Bacon*, this shock will be spoken of in terms of the act of the diagram, as an assemblage of involuntary marks, where chance is the first moment of a rupture with (painting's) thought as custom. Here, the diagram extracts what is most asignifying of a discipline (the "discipline" of painting) and conjures new relations in this asignifying matter to produce a new reality of thought (the new pictorial thought that materializes as the Figure). How does this construction take place?

The eighteenth-century German philosopher Solomon Maimon's theory of differentials, which he articulates as a "solution" to what he believes to be Kant's neglect of the account for the genesis of thought in the name of regulation, offered Deleuze a way of addressing the construction of thought in terms of difference, process, and the exceptional event.[31] Through Maimon's "genetic method," Deleuze develops the notion of thought's genesis from the matter of what it thinks—namely, the differential field of sensation. No longer just a given feature of experience submitted to what cognition determines is possible to experience, sensation is understood as an intensive reality only perceptible in exceptional circumstances. As such, sensation bears a transcendental element to the a priori structures of thought and to encounter sensation in its "pure" state is to be made to think anew (Deleuze 2001: 68, 143). In what Deleuze calls "transcendental empiricism," sensation furnishes "the conditions under which something new is produced," conditions that are "no wider than the real" but that are not given in ordinary experience. In other terms, the differential field of sensation constitutes the outside of thought. Confronted by pure sensation, the sensibility "finds itself before its own limit and raises itself to the level of a transcendent exercise" and new thought, unregulated, rhizomatic and without image, emerges (Deleuze 2001: 140–43). Thought is made to travel through this inaugural disjunction. This conception of a transcendental genesis of thought further distinguishes Deleuze and Guattari's conception of transdisciplinarity from the empirical putting-into-relation of extant disciplines.

Sensation, art, and transdisciplinarity

This characterization of the outside of thought in terms of sensation persists throughout Deleuze and Guattari's writings. In *Capitalism and Schizophrenia*, it is expressed with respect to the mobility of forces and affects within and across structures. In *Francis Bacon*, it is elaborated with respect to Bacon's diagrams, which Deleuze characterizes as diagrams of sensation not form, where sensation has only "an intensive reality" (Deleuze 2003: 45). And even in *What Is Philosophy?*, where we are led to believe that sensation is the preserve of art such that only art thinks through sensations, Deleuze and Guattari speak of how in "the meeting point of things and thought" it is sensation that must recur and that the brain—the point of connection of the "disciplinary" planes—is a field of sensory excitations (Deleuze and Guattari 2003b: 202, 211).

Such intimations implicate art in a singular way. In *Difference and Repetition* art is attended to in its function for thought, as supplying both the model and the impetus for thought beyond representation. In *What Is Philosophy?* Deleuze and Guattari clarify how art is itself a practice of thought and that artists are as much thinkers as philosophers—that while the philosopher thinks through concepts, artists think through "sensible aggregates." Between these two texts, we are alerted to the double function of art: first, art as a being of sensation the encounter with which forces us to think, art as a provocation to thought; second, art as a disciplinary practice that thinks through sensations. As a discipline, art too is subject to an image of its own thinking. Indeed, art has always harbored and continues to harbor presuppositions about itself, particular dogmatic images by which one recognizes an activity as art—a state of affairs compounded by changes in art education and the professionalization of art and growth of the creative industries over the late twentieth and twenty-first centuries.

However, Deleuze and Guattari are not concerned with art as an institutional and historically specific reality but with art as a creative act of genesis beyond "works of art" themselves. The notion of art as a being of sensation, the encounters with which initiate thought, functions as an alternative to the institution of the disciplinary image of art. As they write in *A Thousand Plateaus*, art is never an end in itself, but

> a tool for blazing life lines, in other words, all of those real becomings that are not produced only *in* art, and all of those active escapes that do not consist in fleeing *into* art, taking refuge in art, and all of those positive deterritorializations that never reterritorialize on art, but instead sweep it away with them toward the realms of the asignifying, asubjective, and faceless. (Deleuze and Guattari 2003a: 208, emphasis in the original)

Insofar as the sensible is not just the medium for thought, or a component of thought, but the occasion for thought, and art as a being of sensation is not exclusive to art as a discipline, or the specific subdisciplines of the various arts, but an element of thought across disciplinary boundaries, all thought (at least, all creative, constructive thought) is artistic insofar as it partakes in this activity of seizing of, in Guattari's words, "creative potentiality at the root of sensible finitude—'before' it is applied [as an image] to works, philosophical concepts, scientific functions and mental and social objects" (Guattari 1995: 112). Indeed, when Guattari states that "art does not have a monopoly on creation, but it takes its capacity to invent mutant coordinates to extremes: it engenders unprecedented, unforeseen, and unthinkable qualities of being" (Guattari 1995: 106), he is gesturing to a paradigmatic process that crosses disciplines and gives expression to the freedom of thinking beyond disciplinary images of thought and the production of knowledge.

Conclusion

Practices of inter-, multi-, and trans-disciplinarity have today become as established as their disciplinary counterparts. Whatever radical and anti-establishment aspects they may have harbored in their incipience has been engulfed and made normative by the insatiable apparatus of the university and the gluttonous character of knowledge within its ambit. When even the thresholds, borders, and frontiers of our disciplines have become institutionalized, thinking is surely in peril. This is why it is important to resuscitate the genuinely critical, creative, and anti-establishment notions and practices of transdisciplinarity that animated twentieth-century continental philosophy and theory.

This chapter has explored the singular contribution made by Deleuze and Guattari to the idea of transdisciplinarity. In contrast to practices of transdisciplinarity as recognized programs supported by the academy that aim to produce new branches of knowledge, Deleuze and Guattari seek to free thought, and thought as transdisciplinary practice, from the predetermined imperative to know and indeed from any predetermined imperative whatsoever. In their work transdisciplinarity emerges as a creative and productive operation that does not set out to dissolve disciplinary borders but in fact strengthens the interrelations between the disciplines and their connection to real experience. The rigors of specific disciplines are not challenged: what *is* challenged are their introspection, self-sufficiency, and hierarchy. And what is offered instead is a problem-led conceptual system able to range across regimes of thought in response to real encounters. To cross borders in response to an experience, to a problem posed in the field of the sensible—rather than as part of a planned enterprise—this is the sense of transdisciplinarity that their work invites.

The history of the twentieth century has shown how border practices of inter-, multi-, and trans-disciplinarity have functioned as intermediary and transitional moments that are either reabsorbed into the original root discipline or consolidated as new disciplines of their own. By contrast, Deleuze and Guattari affirm thought as something more than the provisional and subjective moment in the progressive elaboration of our knowledge systems and as something other than disciplinary regulation and control: namely, thought as violent encounter that shatters extant forms of thought such that it can no longer continue as it has done. Their philosophy offers one way of addressing how transdisciplinarity can be a qualitatively transformative practice, free from predetermined aims and with ends that are not recognizable. Rather than an inter- or trans-disciplinary practice that proceeds, as Julia Kristeva and Hal

Foster suggested, through grounding in the disciplines, Deleuze and Guattari remind us that thought has never been a merely disciplinary matter. Their work suggests that a genuinely transdisciplinary thought is one that ejects itself not from "between" existing disciplinary forms but from the outside that exceeds them and their localizable borders. That is, the "crossing" of disciplines is not based on disciplinary foundations and knowledge, but conducts itself prior to and in excess of discipline. It is in this sense that Deleuze and Guattari affirm the sense of "beyond" (and not simply "between") belonging to the prefix "trans-." In place of transdisciplinarity as an extension and continuation of disciplinarity, grounded in principles of resemblance and recognition, they offer us the notion of transdisciplinary thought as a thought without image that forges itself through dissemblance, fracture, and discontinuity and calls forth "forces in thought which are not the forces of recognition, today or tomorrow, but the powers of a completely other model," beyond any established measure (Deleuze 2001: 136).

Having considered the expression of transdisciplinarity of Deleuze and Guattari's work from its earliest expressions in Deleuze's *Difference and Repetition* to *What Is Philosophy?*, the chapter elaborated on the concept of the diagram. In its character as an agent of construction, an involuntary operation that operates within a regime of signs and breaks through signifying blockages, assembling relations of forces in asignifying material, and producing a new reality, the diagram provides a compelling way of approaching and conceptualizing Deleuze and Guattari's transdisciplinarity with respect to a constructivist ontology of relations. While a discipline may think it engages with its outside when embarking on border work, this is usually only as an externality between terms that is always grounded on them. Through diagrammatics, border work is reclassified as a process occurring not between the terms of discipline but fundamentally excessive to them. The border is not between but beyond.

Linking the semiotic conception of the diagram to Deleuze and Guattari's critique of the "image of thought" and philosophy of transcendental empiricism has further illuminating potential. If discipline, at its most calcified, operates as an overcoded regime of signs and a dogmatic image of thought, diagrammatics affirms the relational, asignifying, and sensible material within disciplines as the source for a "new reality" of transdisciplinary thought without image. The chapter closed with some reflections on how for Deleuze and Guattari art, as a being of sensation, plays a crucial role as a model for and impulse to the genesis of thought. Further analysis is needed of how, in place of current grounding of research agendas on the social sciences, Deleuze and Guattari's philosophy offers an artistic paradigm for a transdisciplinary thought beyond disciplinary coordinates.

Perhaps one of the most surprising—and in today's climate, refreshing—notions to emerge from Deleuze and Guattari's work is that of transdisciplinarity as provoked. That it is not simply an activity intentionally staged within the system of disciplines but an event provoked by encounters with things that are too much for thought, by impositions that strain current systems of thought and reveal blind spots and impasses. A painting of peonies makes a connoisseur shift his thought outside its usual terrain and exposes an intensive zone within art history, a zone of turbulence and indiscernibility where the borders between art history and botany fray. The art historian has not become a botanist. Nor has he produced a new hybrid trans- or interdiscipline. His actions do not need to be extracted, examined, and named. That such moments of mobility often go unnoticed and uncommented upon is arguably part of their effectiveness. For in identifying them, and extracting them as nameable, we change their nature from genetic, enabling agent to a substantial and formalized entity. We can only sustain the interval and affirm its transformative power by repeating its gesture and obstinately retaining relationality as external to terms.

What Deleuze and Guattari offer us is not simply an "alternative" to an institutionalized transdisciplinarity. Rather in their work we find a theoretical crystallization and practical expression of what already occurs within every discipline when it thinks creatively—whenever thought is seized by something it does not recognize and liberated from its home territory, whenever, out of an unnameable necessity, thought is made to roam. Every act of experiment or innovation, however modest, augments a border. Deleuze and Guattari's work reminds us that transdisciplinarity is not something we embark upon from within the safety nets of the institution but an effect that emerges from thought's own adventures, from those vital moments of escape, chanced and blind, that remind us that when we think we are free.

Notes

1 "To call a field a 'discipline' is to suggest that it is not dependent on mere doctrine and that its authority does not derive from the writings of an individual or a school but rather from generally accepted methods and truths" (Shumway and Messer-Davidow 1991: 202).

2   As Goldstein has pointed out, Foucault's notion of the disciplines in his 1975 *Discipline and Punish* is a theory not simply about professionalized subject areas and their practitioners but about operations of power upon the bodies of the masses (Goldstein 1984: 175). Goldstein argues that as Foucault develops the concept, it emerges that those who administer the disciplines are "the 'professional men' of the Anglo-American sociological traditions [...] physicians, psychiatrists, pedagogues, penologists ...." Thus, the "well-disciplined" hospital corresponds to the medical "discipline" (Goldstein 1984: 179). He notes Foucault's description of discipline in *The Archaeology of Knowledge* as a body of knowledge, "groups of statements that borrow their organization from scientific models, which tend to coherence and demonstrativity, which are accepted, institutionalized, transmitted and sometimes taught as sciences" (Goldstein 1984: 179). On Foucault and discipline, see also Osborne 2015.
3   On Abelard's "Christian rationalism as the basis for the new university, preparing the way for philosophical rationalism," see Compayre 1893: 18. See also Schachner 1938.
4   See Goldstein 1984 for an intriguing analysis of the genealogy of "professions" and the contribution of Foucault's theory of discipline to the sociology of professions. See Shumway and Messer-Davidow 1991: 204 on the emergence of modern disciplines.
5   For an excellent overview of the problem of the category of discipline and its history, see Becher 1989. Drawing on the work of several commentators, Becher identifies various characteristics of a discipline: a community, a network of communications, a tradition, a particular set of values and beliefs, a domain, a mode of inquiry and a conceptual structure, a body of concepts, methods, and aims, organized social groupings (Becher 1989: 20).
6   "The development of explicit arguments to justify particular divisions of knowledge and of the social strategies to prevail in them" (Shumway and Messer-Davidow 1991: 208).
7   On this point, see Becher 1989: "Impermeable boundaries [...] are in general a concomitant of tightly knot, convergent disciplinary communities and an indicator of the stability and coherent of the intellectual fields they inhabit. Permeable boundaries are associated with loosely knit, divergent academic groups and signal a more fragmented, less stable and comparatively open-ended epistemological structure" (Becher 1989: 37–38).
8   As Abbott elaborates, unlike mathematics, sociology has "no intellectually effective way" of denying the integration of new fields. Consequently, sociology has become "a discipline of many topics, always acquiring them, never losing them. No form of knowledge is alien to it" (Abbott 2001: 35).
9   Interdisciplinary was first referred to in the sixth annual report of Social Science Research Council (SSRC), New York. Thompson Klein (1990) claims that

interdisciplinary designates a range of activities: borrowing across disciplines, collaborative problem-solving, bridge building between disciplines, and producing new fields.

10 Nowotny (2004) intimated this potential of transdisciplinarity as something more than juxtaposition of disciplines: a joint problem-solving. "The Potential of Transdisciplinarity" http://www.helga-nowotny.eu/downloads/helga_nowotny_b59.pdf (accessed August 01, 2018). Transdisciplinarity was introduced in 1970 at a seminar on interdisciplinarity in universities held at the University of Nice and sponsored by the Organisation of Economic Co-operation and Development and the French ministry of education. It "emerged in the latter part of the twentieth century in response to a host of concerns about the pitfalls of specialization and the compartmentalization of knowledge, a globalized economy, shifts in the centre of gravity in knowledge production, the ethics of research, and environmental crisis" (Bernstein 2015: 13). Jean Piaget is credited with coining the term, as a "higher stage succeeding interdisciplinary relationships [...] which would not only cover interactions or reciprocities between specialized research projects, but would place these relationships within a total system without any firm boundaries between disciplines" (Bernstein 2015: 2). Joseph Kockelmans defines transdisciplinarity as "scientific work done by a group of scientists [...] with the intention of systematically pursuing the problem of how the negative side effects of specialization can be overcome so as to make education (and research) more socially relevant" (Kockelmans 1979: 128).

11 This was the view taken by the Romanian theoretical physicist Basarab Nicolescu, founder of the *Centre international de Recherches et Etudes Transdisciplinaires* (CIRET), which was sponsored by UNESCO, who imparted to this synthetic conception a cosmological one. Nicolescu claimed, "Transdisciplinarity concerns that which is at once between the disciplines, across different disciplines, and beyond all disciplines. Its goal is the understanding of the present world, of which one of the imperatives is the unity of knowledge" (Nicolescu 2014: 19).

12 Gibbons 1994. Transdisciplinarity has been recently defined as a term of research that defines and forms its problems independently from any disciplinary background (Mittelstrauss 2011: 331). See also Osborne 2015: 5.

13 Osborne argues that very few of the most important works in the area of "theory, culture and society" over the last fifty years are "disciplinary" in character or representative of the disciplinary training of their authors and that "all the major thinkers in European theory in the second half of the twentieth century exhibit transdisciplinary conceptual dynamics" (Osborne 2015: 4).

14 As Kristeva (1998) puts it, to describe one's work as interdisciplinary can be tantamount to admitting to only having a limited amount of knowledge of various domains and fragmentary competences (6). Dogan and Pahre argue that

specialization is a necessary phase of knowledge production and that innovation in the social sciences happens naturally, through the dual processes of fragmentation and hybridization, without a declared and explicit interdisciplinary approach. As disciplines grow and produce more knowledge, they become denser and fragment into subfields, which further fragment into specializations. Scholars can then study minor points that would be ignored in an underpopulated field, while those interested in major points go elsewhere: "Density in the core opens up room for innovation at the margins of the field, on the frontiers" (Dogan and Pahre 1990: 32).

15 Mitchell (1995) explains: "On the one hand, visual culture looks like an 'outside' to art history, opening out the larger field of vernacular images, media and everyday visual practices in which a 'visual art' tradition is situated, and raising the question of the difference between high and low culture, visual art versus visual culture. On the other hand, visual culture may look like a deep 'inside' to art history's traditional focus on the sensuous and semiotic peculiarity of the visual" (542).

16 For his argument, Ginzburg specifically draws upon the art historian Fritz Koren's analysis of Martin Schongauer's 1473 painting *The Madonna of the Rose Garden*. The art historian James Herbert puts it in slightly different terms: Interdisciplinarity "begs the question of how disciplines reside within one another" (Herbert 1995: 4).

17 This is Etienne Balibar's characterization, cited in Osborne 2011: 16. Osborne (2015) distinguishes this tendency in French theory from the German, post-Hegelian feeling that philosophy after Marx could only be realized outside philosophy itself, such that transdisciplinarity emerges as the product of philosophical reflection on the limits of philosophy (4).

18 By "image," Deleuze (2002) refers to a "whole organization which effectively trains thought to operate according to the norms of an established order or power, and moreover, installs in it an apparatus of power, sets it up as an apparatus of power itself" (23). In his 1991 preface to the English version of *Difference and Repetition*, Deleuze (2001) states that philosophy needs a new image of thought, "or, rather a liberation of thought from those images which imprison it" (xvii).

19 Maurice Nadeau describes *A Thousand Plateaus* as a book "that is likely to revolutionize many disciplines" (in Deleuze and Guattari 2009b: 89).

20 Indeed in the 1994 preface to the English edition of *Difference and Repetition*, Deleuze (2006) makes this connection claiming that it is his chapter on the image of thought "which now seems to me the most necessary and the most concrete, and which serves to introduce subsequent books up to and including the research undertaken with Guattari where we invoked a vegetal model of thought: the rhizome in opposition to the tree, a rhizome-thought instead of an arborescent thought" (xv).

21 Osborne (2015) argues that there is currently an "exclusive focus on knowledge production as 'research process' to the neglect of concepts" and thinking (14).

22 Osborne points out that nearly all the major texts of twentieth-century European theory that were transdisciplinary in character "either predate the established discourse on transdisciplinarity, with its myth of origin in Nice in 1970, or were produced independently of it" (Osborne 2015: 14).

23 Quoted in Collett, Kosugi and Sdrolia 2013: 157. The passage reads in the original as follows: "La philosophie n'est pas interdisciplinaire, elle est elle-même une discipline entière qui entre en résonance avec la science et avec l'art, comme ceux-ci avec elle; trouver le concept d'une function etc. C'est que les trois plans sont les trois manières dont le cerveau recoupe le chaos, et l'affronte. Ce sont les chaoïdes. La pensée ne se constitue que dans ce rapport où elle risque toujours de sombrer."

24 Goffey 2015a: 125–30. Goffey (2015a) describes the work of FGERI as a "programme in which research that might otherwise be considered the privileged domain of academic institutions could acquire a different set of connections with the social field" (128).

25 Osborne notes that Guattari shares this type of transdisciplinarity with Serres, Foucault, Derrida, Althusser, and Latour.

26 The essay was published in *Critique*, 343 (1975): 1207–77. It was later modified and reprinted as "A New Cartographer" in Deleuze's (1986) *Foucault*.

27 See also p. 23 of *A Thousand Plateaus* on the notion of the book as an assemblage with the outside against the book as an image of the world. Departing from Foucault, Deleuze and Guattari (2003a) characterize the diagram as a mapping "not of power but of desire" (585n39).

28 Any resemblance diagrams do produce is produced through "non-resembling means" and is a "sensible or aesthetic rather than formal resemblance" (Deleuze 2003: 117).

29 Foucault develops the notion of the thought from the outside in his essay on Maurice Blanchot. Literature is a "passage to the 'outside'"; language "escapes the mode of being of discourse—in other words the dynasty of representation—and literary speech develops from itself, forming a network in which each point is distinct, distant from even its closest neighbors, and has a position in relation to every other point in a space that simultaneously holds and separates them all. Literature is not language approaching itself until it reaches the point of its fiery manifestation; it is rather language getting as far away from itself as possible. And if, in this setting 'outside of itself,' it unveils its own being, the sudden clarity reveals not a folding back but a gap, not a turning back of signs upon themselves but a dispersion" (Foucault 1990: 12).

30 On relations between professionalism, habit, and discipline, see Weber 1982: 66.

31 Maimon argues that Kant's conception of the heterogeneity of concepts and intuitions cannot account for the application of the former to the latter, and the theory of conditioning cannot account for reality as more than transcendentally

determined possibility. For Maimon (2010) "differential" refers on the one hand to an infinitesimally small unit of sensation and on the other to the rule of the combination of sensations (22).

Bibliography

Abbott, A. (2001), *Chaos of Disciplines*, Chicago: University of Chicago Press.
Becher, T. (1989), *Academic Tribes and Territories: Intellectual Enquiry and the Cultures of Disciplines*, Milton Keynes, England: Society for Research into Higher Education/ Open University Press.
Bernstein, J.H. (2015), "Transdisciplinarity. A Review of Its Origins, Development and Current Issues," *Journal of Research Practice*, 11 (1): 1-20.
Coles, A., and Defert, A., eds (1998), *The Anxiety of Interdisciplinarity*, London: BACKless Books.
Collett, G., Kosugi, M., and Sdrolia, C. (2013), "Editorial Introduction: For a Transdisciplinary Practice of Thought," *Deleuze Studies*, 7 (2): 157–68.
Compayre, G. (1893), *Abelard and the Origin and Early History of Universities*, London: Heinemann.
Deleuze, G. (1975), "Ecrivian non. Un nouveau cartographe," *Critique*, 343: 1207–27.
Deleuze, G. (1991), *Empiricism and Subjectivity. An Essay on Hume's Theory of Human Nature*, trans. C.V. Boundas, New York: Columbia University Press.
Deleuze, G. ([1968] 2001), *Difference and Repetition*, trans. P. Patton, London: Continuum.
Deleuze, G. ([1977] 2002), *Dialogues II*, trans. H. Tomlinson and B. Habberjam, London: Continuum.
Deleuze, G. ([1981] 2003), *Francis Bacon. The Logic of Sensation*, trans. D.W. Smith, London: Continuum.
Deleuze, G. ([1985] 2005), *Cinema 2: The Time-Image*, trans. H. Tomlinson and R. Galeta, London: Continuum.
Deleuze, G. (2006), "Michel Foucault's Main Concepts," in G. Deleuze, *Two Regimes of Madness*, trans. A. Hodges and M. Taormina, New York: Semiotext(e).
Deleuze, G. ([1986] 2016), *Foucault*, trans. S. Hand, London: Continuum.
Deleuze, G., and Guattari, F. ([1980] 2003a), *A Thousand Plateaus. Capitalism and Schizophrenia*, trans. B. Massumi, London: Continuum.
Deleuze, G., and Guattari, F. ([1991] 2003b), *What Is Philosophy?*, trans. H. Tomlinson and G. Burchill, New York: Columbia University Press.
Deleuze, G., and Guattari, F. (2009a), "Capitalism and Schizophrenia," in F. Guattari, *Chaosophy. Texts and Interviews 1972-1977*, trans. D.L. Sweet, J. Becker, and T. Adkins, 53–68, Los Angeles: Semiotext(e).
Deleuze, G., and Guattari, F. (2009b), "In Flux," in F. Guattari, *Chaosophy. Texts and Interviews 1972-1977*, trans. D.L. Sweet, J. Becker, and T. Adkins, 69–89, Los Angeles: Semiotext(e).

Dogan, M., and Pahre, R. (1990), *Creative Marginality: Innovation at the Intersections of Social Sciences*, Boulder: Westview Press.

Fish, S. (1989), "Being Interdisciplinary Is So Very Hard to Do," *Profession*, 89, 15–22, New York: MLA.

Foucault, M. ([1966] 1990), "Maurice Blanchot: The Thought from Outside," in *Foucault. Blanchot*, trans. J. Mehlman and B. Massumi, 7–58, New York: Zone Books.

Geiger, R.L. (1986), *To Advance Knowledge. The Growth of the American Research Universities*, New York: Oxford University Press.

Genosko, G. (2009), *Félix Guattari: A Critical Introduction*, London: Pluto Press.

Gibbons, M., Limoges, C., Nowotny, H. et al. (1994), *The New Production of Knowledge: The Dynamics of Science and Research in Contemporary Societies*, London: SAGE.

Ginzburg, C. (1995), "Inter/disciplinarity," *The Art Bulletin*, 77 (4 December): 534–52.

Goffey, A. (2015a), "Introduction to Guattari on Transdisciplinarity," *Theory, Culture & Society*, 32 (5–6): 125–30.

Goffey, A. (2015b), "Guattari, Transversality and the Experimental Semiotics of Untranslatability," *Paragraph*, 38 (2): 231–44.

Goldstein, J. (1984), "Foucault among the Sociologists: The 'Disciplines' and the History of the Professions," *History and Theory*, 23 (2 May): 170–92.

Guattari, F. ([1992] 1995), *Chaosmosis. An Ethico-Aesthetic Paradigm*, trans. P. Bains and J. Pefanis, Sydney: Power publications.

Guattari, F. ([1970] 2006), "Psychoanalysis and Polyvocality," in F. Guattari, *The Anti-Oedipus Papers, 1969–73*, New York: Semiotext(e).

Guattari, F. (2009), *Chaosophy. Texts and Interviews, 1972–1977*, trans. D.L. Sweet, J. Becker, and T. Adkins, Los Angeles: Semiotext(e).

Herbert, J. (1995), "Interdisciplinarity and the Pictorial Turn," *The Art Bulletin*, 77 (4 December).

Jencks, C., and Riesman, D. (1968), *The Academic Revolution*, New York: Doubleday.

Kockelmans, J. (1979), "Why Interdisciplinarity?," in J. Kockelmans (ed.), *Interdisciplinarity and Higher Education*, University Park: Pennsylvania State University Press.

Kristeva, J. (1998), "Institutional Interdisciplinarity in Theory and in Practice. An Interview," in Alex Coles and Alexia Defert (eds), *The Anxiety of Interdisciplinarity*, London: BACKless Books.

Maimon, S. (2010), *Essay on Transcendental Philosophy*, trans. Nick Midgley, London: Continuum.

Mitchell, W.J.T. (1995), "Interdisciplinary and Visual Culture," *Art Bulletin*, 77 (4): 540–44.

Mittelstrauss, J. (2011), "On Transdisciplinarity," *Trames*, 15 (4): 329–38.

Nicolescu, B. (2014), "Multidisciplinarity, Interdisciplinarity, Indisciplinarity, and Transdisciplinarity: Similarities and Differences," in *RCC Perspectives*, No. 2, *Minding the Gap: Working across Disciplines in Environmental Studies*.

Nowotny, H. (2004), "The Potential of Transdisciplinarity," http://www.helga-nowotny.eu/downloads/helga_nowotny_b59.pdf (last accessed August 01, 2018).

Osborne, P. (2011), "From Structure to Rhizome: Transdisciplinarity in French Thought," *Radical Philosophy*, 165 (January/February): 15–16.

Osborne, P. (2015), "Problematising Disciplinarity, Transdisciplinary Problematics," *Theory, Culture & Society*, 32 (5–6): 3–35.

Reese, T. (1995), "Mapping Interdisciplinarity," *The Art Bulletin*, 77 (4 December).

Schachner, N. (1938), *The Mediaeval Universities*, London: George Allen & Unwin.

Shumway, D., and Messer-Davidow, E. ([1984] 1991), "Disciplinarity: An Introduction," *Poetics Today* 12 (2 Summer): 201–25.

Thompson-Klein, J. (1990), *Interdisciplinary: History, Theory, and Practice*, Michigan: Wayne State University Press.

Weber, S. (1982), "The Limits of Professionalism," *Oxford Literary Review*, 5 (1–2): 59–79.

6

Hermeticism instead of Hermeneutics

The History of Philosophy Conceived of as Mannerist Portraiture

Sjoerd van Tuinen

Gilles Deleuze once described his works in the history of philosophy as acts of initiation. Like Van Gogh or Gauguin, he writes, one needs to keep painting portraits for a long time before you can move on to doing your own landscapes, and, like them, it might take a while before you dare use the stronger colors (Deleuze and Parnet 2004: "H"). While Deleuze thus emphasizes the slow modesty of his apprenticeship in philosophy, having started out with monographs and texts on classical figures such as Plato, Lucretius, the Stoics, Spinoza, Leibniz, Hume, Kant, Nietzsche, Bergson, and Whitehead, it is clear that the comparison between pictorial and noetic portraits is more than a mere metaphor without consequences (Ginoux 2004). Not only does art have an operational role for a transcendental empiricism that experiments with so-called conditions of the new. It is also essential in the search for new means of expression in philosophy, where what is at stake is the historical self-understanding of philosophy itself. As Deleuze (1994) famously argues: "The theory of thought [i.e. philosophy] is like painting: it needs that revolution which took art from representation to abstraction" (276).[1]

The first time in his published works that Deleuze compares his work in the history of philosophy to portraiture is in the preface to *Difference and Repetition*. He makes an analogy with Duchamp's collage in painting: "a philosophically bearded Hegel, a philosophically clean-shaved Marx, in the same way as a moustached Mona Lisa" (Deleuze 1994: xxi). This analogy would also be taken up by Michel Foucault in his review of *Difference and Repetition* and *Logic of Sense*, which he sees as a *theatrum philosophicum*, a kind of masked ball in which "Duns Scotus places his head through the circular window; he is sporting an impressive mustache; it belongs to Nietzsche, disguised as Klossowski"

(Foucault 1998: 368). What these collages suggest is that Deleuze's "faithfulness" to the thinkers he writes about goes much deeper than their belonging to a common school or an immediate adaptation of concepts. Instead of offering a privileged point of view, the conceptual personae stand for an infinity of complicities and mutual imbrications, each functioning as a seed crystal that engenders the next. Far from general attributes that guarantee the constant identity of philosophy over a classical series of distinguished "thinkers," it is as if the beard and the moustache are turned into ambivalent signs around which multiple metamorphoses take place. As a consequence, the history of philosophy is not one of neat filiation and external resemblances but of strange encounters and hidden alliances in which the various "moments" of the past get mixed up. Instead of a historical history, it is a natural history made up of lines of evolution and involution rather than of descent: "There is a philosophy-becoming which has nothing to do with the history of philosophy and which happens through those whom the history of philosophy does not manage to qualify" (Deleuze and Parnet 2002: 2; see also Deleuze 1995: 49).

Almost twenty-five years later, looking back on his own landscapes ("plateaus") and more strongly colored portraits (of Foucault and Leibniz), Deleuze returns to the analogy between his work on other thinkers and the art of the portrait in *What Is Philosophy?*:

> The history of philosophy is comparable to the art of the portrait. It is not a matter of "making lifelike," that is, of repeating what a philosopher said but rather of producing resemblance by separating out both the plane of immanence he instituted [*instauré*] and the new concepts he created. These are mental, noetic, and machinic portraits. Although they are usually created with philosophical tools, they can also be produced aesthetically. (Deleuze and Guattari 1994: 55)

What both quotes make clear is that we cannot content ourselves with reproducing what a philosopher has said, since we have to find our own means and manners of resembling. In fact, they imply a rather humorous definition of the art of portraiture—an art of the portrait based no longer on representation but on expression. For it implies that there are no a priori criteria of resemblance, which is to say that a produced resemblance is not necessarily "true." Instead, there are many "different means" and manners of resembling, including, but certainly not limited to, those of painting, theater, and philosophy (Deleuze 1995: 135–36).

The multiplication of versions gives us a very concrete example of what it means to reverse Platonism. The shift from "that which is alike differs" (Deleuze 1994: 116) to "only differences are alike" (Deleuze 1990: 261) implies a chiasmic reversal of model and image, of creator and spectator, of reading and writing, of seeing and drawing. The reversed positions belong not just to different perspectives but to different worlds and consequentially also to incommensurable understandings of the means and aims of portraiture. In the second case, "only differences are alike," the reason for constructing a portrait is not to reproduce but to exhibit *how* a philosopher moves back and forth between the concepts for which he has become known and the problems to which they answer, as well as to reinvent this movement in relation to new problems. Just as resemblance is produced as the eternal return, not of the same ("Plato," "Bergson") but of the similar ("Platonism," "Bergsonism"), the portrait is an effect rather than a genre; it is the heterogenesis of a strange, phantasmatic presence, following a brewing, incestuous logic that constantly progresses and regresses from the figurative to the abstract and back.

Is Deleuze's difference and repetition in philosophy driven by a mannerist way of relating to the past? Traditionally mannerism is considered as abnormal: it is interpreted as a divergent characteristic within some historical group-norm and evaluated as a symptom of degeneration. From a Deleuzian perspective, however, mannerism is anomalous: it is the cutting edge of deterritorialization of the group itself. Instead of a single group portrait in the history of philosophy, his portraits of classical figures are so many modalizations or singularizations of philosophy itself. The models are never given in fact, but must gain consistency in the contemplation of the "manners" in which they populate their plane of immanence with concepts. Already in Deleuze's earliest portraits, this paradoxical fidelity lies much deeper than a systematic use of concepts and imitative zeal. It replaces the Platonic ideal of the authorial voice as claim of the philosopher to authenticity or truth with the expressive retrieval of the real, that is, demonic or schizo-genetic conditions of thought. Mannerism is not some epigonal pastiche or servile imitation combined with excessive stylization in the shadow of a greater, more classical Model, but the negentropic betrayal of academic pedantry and its clichéd history of great men.

Since likeness or similarity does concern the relationship not just between reception and production but also between reading and seeing or drawing and writing; the mannerist art of portraiture can be understood literally as a transmedial transfer of procedures and operations from the arts to philosophy. This chapter provides an overview of the main mannerist traits of expression and their exemplary media as mobilized by Deleuze. From the classical arts of design: chiaroscuro and the realism of deformation. From literature: the mannerism of sobriety and free indirect speech as the insertion of a foreign language within language. From music: the amplification of minor content and expressions, and infinite and continuous variation. From theater: the mannerist *mascherata* or doubling. From cinema: the congelation of past and present through serialization and slow motion.

A mannerism of sobriety

Chronologically speaking, mannerism always comes late. To be a mannerist is to be the inheritor of a more established and more classical style. At the same time, and paradoxically, mannerism poses the question of the new. For not only does each mannerist need to decide by himself *how* he will inherit from the models provided by nature and past masters, he is also confronted with the question what can still be done, given that these models have already been "perfected." Mannerist art, in other words, is inseparable from a rivalry with authority or indeed with historical time as such. But unlike the disruptive and subversive gestures of modernism, or the self-sufficient ironizing of postmodernism, it seeks to pervert the tradition from within. How else to account for the treacherous, impersonal humor of mannerist Figures? "For it is difficult to be a traitor; it is to create. One has to lose one's identity, one's face, in it. One has to disappear, to become unknown" (Deleuze and Parnet 2002: 33).[2] This strategy of becoming-imperceptible resembles that of a perfect counterfeit, in which both the tradition and the latecomer lose their face in a double appropriation. It explains why mannerism has no school, no stable identity, and no uncontested unity in the history of art. Mannerism is different. Without needing to break entirely with tradition, it produces a distinction from that which does not differentiate itself from it. Less than a tradition of the new, mannerism's lateness constitutes an untimely becoming of art itself.

Gilbert Dubois once described the difference and repetition of mannerism according to the model of biological filiation: "all of mannerism proceeds from a mimetism," a "differential imitation" which, in the life of forms, is the universal and inescapable generative process. The work of art is placed in the shadow of a "masterly" or "paternal" model of which the artist claims, as an "honor," the right of reproduction, all the while pursuing, by means of exaggeration or perversion, his autonomous and individual expressivity. Through excess of imitative zeal, there is liberated an anarchizing and paranoid energy that is the condition for the mannerist to find the full realization of his "personality."[3] Dubois thus defined mannerism as an "enduring mirror stage," a painful episode of detachedness and despair. This narcissistic trap becomes especially clear in the apparently bloodless severity of the portraits of Florentine nobility by Pontormo, Rosso, or Bronzino, where we witness a kind of feebleness or fracture of the subject, due to its schizographic oscillation between, on the one hand, a dependence on the eternity of the Model and, on the other, the ephemeral present. The artistic aim would be unity, but its consequence is the exasperation of subjectivity and derealization up to the point of hallucination. *Ogni dipintor dipinge se*, as the Renaissance cliché has it, yet it is only in mannerism that the subjectivity of the painter as such is problematized: "Mannerist art is the product of a dialectics between desire and the impotence to satisfy, resulting in a quest of presence indefinitely differentiated" (Dubois 1979: 26–27).[4]

Despite its problematization of the artistic subject, the limitation of the filiative model is obvious. Mannerism is no longer interpreted according to aesthetic criteria, as the work itself disappears into the background. At the same time, the pathology of the artist turns out to be nothing more than his inability to occupy the more stable, Oedipal or symbolic position, which itself remains timeless and classical. Contrast this analysis with Theodor W. Adorno's concept of "late style" (*Spätstil*), which applies to historical epochs no less than to the development of individual artists such as Beethoven. The mannerist treatment of past models would not be the expression of subjectivity that now manifests itself heedlessly, as its classical evaluation would have it, but precisely the gesture by which subjectivity leaves the work of art and exposes the historical clichés for the contingent fragments they are:

> The force of subjectivity in late works is the irascible gesture with which it leaves them. It bursts them asunder, not in order to express itself but, expressionlessly, to cast off the illusion of art. Of the works it leaves only fragments behind […] Touched by death, the masterly hand sets free the matter it previously formed. The fissures and rifts within it, bearing witness to the ego's finite impotence before Being, are its last work. […] As splinters, derelict and abandoned, they finally themselves become expression. (Adorno 1998: 125)[5]

Accordingly, the lateness of mannerist court portraits is no longer defined by the absence of subjectivity, whether that of the model or that of the painter. Rather, the exteriority of the subject allows for disharmony, discontinuity, and negativity to persist in the composition of the painting itself. Instead of merely reflecting the intransparency or weary eccentricity of some anticipated interiority, it is through its fragmentation and unfinishedness that the object itself severs the head from its organic connection with the pointy hands and expresses the alienating forces at work in sixteenth-century court life.

Still it is perhaps only with Deleuze that this autonomy of expression in the work can be fully affirmed. Accordingly, the mannerist use of classical examples has them embark on a line of flight (*faire fuire*), very much like how Francis Bacon, through a number of diagrammatic operations that dis- and re-sociate the eye and the hand in a haptic fashion, decapitates the body of Velazquez' Pope *Innocent X* (1650) by making it escape through the mouth and dissipate into the armature of the painting. There is still a resemblance between the first and the second Pope, but imitation and identity are no longer the means by which we pass from one to the other. On the contrary, the resemblance is the effect of the combination of various traits of expression in a complex "figure"[6]: the finite expression of an infinite becoming.

In literature, likewise, to produce a figure is to insert a foreign language within an already given, "naturally" transmitted language. Herman Melville's figure of Bartleby, whose famous formula or literary mannerism is the repetitive enunciation of "I would prefer not to," emerges as a muted, unlocalizable presence that haunts the common idiom and puts shared meaning in suspense. Here too the problem of the filiative appropriation of language is displaced by a much more perverse use:

> The paternal function is dropped in favour of even more obscure and ambiguous forces. The subject loses its texture in favour of an infinitely proliferating patchwork [...] It is as if the traits of expression escaped form [...] It is still a process of identification, but rather than following the adventures of the neurotic, it has now become psychotic. (Deleuze 1998: 68, 71, 77–78)

Now isn't the philosophical equivalent of this schizophrenic identification the kind of "buggery" that Deleuze applied in his many monographs on classical philosopher? Looking back, he famously describes his approach as an "immaculate conception," in which he imagines himself "arriving in the back [*dans le dos*] of an author and giving him a child, which would be his and which nevertheless would be monstrous" (Deleuze 1995: 6). As a commentator, Deleuze proceeds in such a way that it is irreproachable from the perspective of philology, but precisely in order to be able to put the object itself, and not its interpretation, into variation. The concepts continue to bear the signature of their author, but the problems to which they respond constitute a pre-individual rhizome in which all sorts of unexpected displacements and partial overlaps occur. In this way, "the most exact, the most strict repetition" has as its correlate the "maximum of difference":

> That it really be his is very important, because the author had to really say everything that I made him say. But it was also necessary that the child be

monstruous, because it was necessary to go through all sorts of decenterings, slippages, breakages [*cassements*: breakages, but also burglary and entering], secret emissions that gave me a lot of pleasure. (Deleuze 1995: 6)[7]

The crux of a Deleuzian interpretation of mannerism is perhaps that this kind of deformation is the sign not of a frustrated presence of the subject but of an excessive presence of the a-subjective. As if through a perversion of classic *aemulatio*, Deleuze appeals to art history or the history of philosophy less on account of its conclusions than through a rivalry with its sources (Conley 1997). This community of rivalry places a surplus power of expression at the heart of the "original," which now becomes part of the matter that new manners drag along. What Deleuze's monographs produce are therefore effects, portraits produced in the manner of historical figures, but not as reproductions of their original works. A historical figure is repeated "in the manner of," but the repetition always already happens in the commentator's own manner—in the span from the definitive article to the possessive pronoun an immanent and creative appropriation takes place. There is no return to the model, only its distorted multiplication. In philosophical portraiture no less than in painting or literature, the struggle is therefore not one of representation, of the positioning of the subject at a proper distance to its natural object and the paranoid avoidance of plagiarism, but one with much more indeterminate and heterogenetic forces to which the original is opened up. Here too, distance is everything, but it is expressed through the interstices of the object itself, which is now stretched and made relative to new determinations. Abstraction is this hysteria or hysteresis immanent to figuration. It is what we call a manner, which may be unnatural, but only to the extent that nature's own manners are already reduced to the historically grown matter of artistic and noetic clichés.

In Deleuze's portraits, all the figurative constraints and determinations of the history of philosophy are there, yet he seeks to create a new variation, a new manner, in the tense position between that of the acolyte and that of the maverick. What replaces the question of authenticity—How do I relate to … ?—is the question of efficacy: What becomings does my reading enable? As the young Deleuze wrote to his teacher, the Cartesian Ferdinand Alquié, in a private letter from 1951, the point of portraiture is to strip the model of its unity and maximize its expressive potential:

Reading a book, we give it a tension, a movement which is not the one of the author's thought: nothing is more false than the idea according to which reading means finding the original movement of the author; that would mean not understanding anything and not reading. To read means to decenter and to read well it means to decenter well [...] clarity and distinction have to be dosed in inversed proportions: thus one has to be distinct and obscure.[8]

Just as the modulation of color in painting is a modulation of original, that is, differential relations, the operation of a mannerist reading consists of a combinatory. It suppresses the constants of the major mode or the source text in its received history and amplifies the minor modes in constructing the "new" version. This treatment could thus constitute a work or creative "movement" no less original than the source. There is a filiation, but it is not a natural or biological one. Rather, in mannerism it is the very artificiality of the tradition, the one-sided reading of classicism, that, in being subject to deformation by other manners, is brought to the fore. Classicism is the exception in art history, not the norm. It has been argued that in simultaneously citing and distorting Renaissance perspective, mannerist fine arts turn nature itself into "the citation of an idea of nature" (Oliva 1998: 9, 15).[9] However, the point is not that art follows art instead of nature or life but that life itself contains multiple becomings and thought processes, and that it takes art to tease them out. The suspense of an indoors light, spread unequally and manipulated with candles and curtains as in a theater, renders the natural model in its unstable, multiplicitous constitution. Mannerist imitation, in other words, is not the naked repetition of what is clear but confused in the original work, but a clothed or masked repetition that proceeds through the condensation of distinct but obscure signs in the clear image that we already have (Deleuze 1994: 201).[10]

This procedure through secrecy explains the affinity mannerism has with hermeticism more than with hermeneutics. Instead of producing simulacra as bad copies of a more perfect Idea, processes of semiosis simulate and generate new ideas. In *De Umbris Idearum*, Giordano Bruno—the mannerist philosopher par excellence—explains how by tempering the light and establishing an immanent continuity between difference and unity, chaos and order, past and present, "shadows do not erase but serve" cognition (Bruno 1884).[11] They are the element of an *ars memoriae* that revolves around the taxonomy of emblematic signs and images rather than memories of the already known. As a synthesis of identification and alternation, of filiation and rupture, the technique of *chiaroscuro* prioritizes the plurality of manners over matter and makes for a complex contagion rather than a linear filiation. It functions like a crystal prism reorienting and recomposing whatever offers itself by reflecting its light in the most diverse and unexpected directions. As Bruno (1991) puts it: "We do not understand by any simpleness, condition and unity, but by composition, combination, plurality of terms" (5).[12]

At stake in Deleuze's portraiture as well as in mannerism in general, then, is an ideational movement that does not belong to either the object or the subject. "It is no longer a question of Mimesis, but of becoming" (Deleuze 1998: 78). This suggests a new solution to the problem of adaptation of the classical or indeed that of adaptation in general. The ultimate aim of the betrayal of classicism is an immanent filiation, something that approximates what Deleuze and Guattari in *Kafka: Toward a Minor Literature* describe as a becoming-child: the literary amplification of the child mode inside the adult mode. They refer to the Kafkaesque manner of making a naïve use of bureaucratic language as a "mannerism of sobriety," i.e., a mannerism "without memory, where the adult is caught up in a childhood block without ceasing to be an adult, just as the child can be caught up in an adult block without ceasing to be a child" (Deleuze and Guattari 1986: 79). Even in their own modulation of Kafka, childhood is not the memory of a time now lost to the adult. The mode of existence of childhood implies, after all, that it is without empirical memory. Rather, the point is that the chronological distribution of child and adult loses its fixity. Contrary to a neurotic return to childhood, the psychiatric understanding of "mannerisms" as psychosomatic regressions, the point of a mannerism of sobriety is the attempt of the adult to encounter the world in the mode of a child, indeed to lose his dominant modality and to become a "child of the world." It is a manner of becoming that can only be produced in art, because it breaks with natural filiation in a mutual becoming between the adult and the child. For the same reason, Deleuze needs artistic means of expression to break with the natural development of thought from author to commentator and replace it with a transversal citation.

The ghost and the machine

In her lecture on the art of writing portraits from 1935, Gertrude Stein brings about a break with mimetic filiation, which she describes as "the American way." The movement from portrayed to portrayer consists of a pure movement contained in itself, a continuous beginning again rather than one flowing from one generation to the next or the next moving against the previous: "the American way has been not to need that generations are existing," since "generations are not of necessity existing that is to say if the actual movement within a thing is alive enough" (Stein 1988: 166, 201).[13] Stein develops this vitality of movement by contrasting the concepts of "insistence" and "repetition." While repetition is based on empirical memory and the externality of model and copy, insistence blends past and present in actual becomings. To insist is to repeat actively; it doesn't suggest a presence but creates it autonomously. It is not to repeat somebody's actual words and actions, which are received in an exterior, i.e., reactive or passive fashion, but to repeat the manner of their expression, to which whatever is said and done remains internal:

> In doing a portrait of any one, the repetition consists in knowing that that one is a kind of a one, that the things he does have been done by others like him that the things he says have been said by others like him, but, and this is the important thing, there is no repetition in hearing and saying the things he hears and says when he is hearing and saying them. (Stein 1988: 174)[14]

This attempt at a chiasmic reversal of passive listening and active speaking, but also of looking and writing, reminds one of mannerist attempts to replace the model with the movement that brings it about. As Jean Starobinski (1995) says of Michel de Montaigne: "Writing transforms the initial reader's experience into an author's experience. Simultaneously, it turns the original obedient reading into a critical reading" (27). Contrary to a more symmetrical or hermeneutical approach, in which we remain dependent on the authority of a past original, to talk and to listen at once is to replace the representation of the original with its decentered expression. It is the condition for the recurrence to be most intensively alive, for no longer making an external difference, but for making a difference in the repetition oneself—an asymmetrical but productive procedure that Stein names "genius." Rather than by words of description, genius lies in bringing about a shift in emphasis by which someone is made to look all the more like himself or herself.[15] Beauty and truthfulness are by-products, what matters is the self-contained rhythm of the manner in which they are achieved: "I wanted however to do portraits where there was more movement inside the portrait and yet it was to be the whole portrait completely held within that inside" (Stein 1988: 202).[16] Put differently: Portraiture does not begin with the question "*who is someone?*," but asks "*How* do they *do*?" and replies by continuing this doing itself. This also explains why Stein insists she wants to write portraits instead of novels. Like history books, novels involve memory and tell a story, "which soothes everyone" as it offers more of the same. Portraits, by contrast, are "what was intrinsically exciting" because they repeat a pure "intensity" to which one cannot remain indifferent (Stein 1988: 181–83).

Who could not be astonished by the affinity between Stein and Deleuze? Sharing a Bergsonist inspiration (Posman 2015), what matters in portraiture is not external resemblance but internal difference. They both proceed in the form of an ascesis that liberates the implied vitality in the model from representation and crystallizes it with what it is not. Beyond our individual emphases, Stein discovers a communal modality or duration that obtains outside and beyond our own intervention, but that, instead of being a given, must be maintained by the various historically and sometimes even contemporarily independent ways of embodying it. Instead of the historical monograph remaining external and accidental to the life of the concept, Deleuze seeks a unity of matter and manner, that is, of difference and repetition. The internal repetition of the singular—or of what he calls "true Originals" (Deleuze 1998: 82–84), originals that keep originating—generates a profound and more truthful manner of resembling than any resemblance between copy and original is capable of: not a fiction, but an indiscernibility; not a counterfeit, but a semblance raised to the nth power of the false.

However, this insistence on singularity is not limited to the heyday of twentieth-century modernism. It is tributary to the mannerist revolution, in which substance or essence comes to revolve around modes instead of vice versa. It was the great discovery of early modern philosophers such as Spinoza and Leibniz that it is not through our identities or existences but through our manners that we attain eternity. If all individuation is modal, then there is no difference between generations except between the changing composition of materials ("machines") that realize the different modes of becoming one. In Stein's (1988) words: "The composition we live in changes but essentially what happens does not change. We inside us do not change but our emphasis and the moment in which we live changes" (195). What happens inside us is precisely not a model or essence that passes from one generation to the next, but a heterogeneous modality or event that persists as a degree of power enabling us to continue to generate models that remain forever in the making.

Pace Bergson, it is clear that this notion of pure movement is derived from the serial production of cinema. Instead of a number of portraits held together by memory, the whole series blends into a single portrait, like a moving picture continuously moving between frames: "a portrait that was not description and that was made by each time, and I did a great many times, say it, that somebody was something, each time there was a difference just a difference enough so that it could go on and be a present something" (Stein 1988: 194). In Deleuze, pop art provides another artistic means of expression in which the singularity of the first repeats the series that follows instead of vice versa. But for him, too, the main procedure for making common cause with other authors remains cinematographic:

> Commentaries in the history of philosophy should represent a kind of slow motion, a congelation or immoblization of the text: *not only* of the text to which they relate, *but also* of the text in which they are inserted—so much so that they have a double existence and a corresponding ideal: the pure representation of the former text and the present text *in one another.* (Deleuze 1994: xxii, emphasis in the original)

In slow motion, there is a double becoming of the past and the present that is irreducible to the actual. Memory and actuality repeat each other in that crystalline circuit that defines the mode of existence of cinema, its artistic essence: the time-image. Against all aesthetic purity, it relies on the provisionality and hybridity of montage.[17] By combining the scholarly eye for multiple details and striking passages with an imaginative passion to synthesize beyond the given, one can continue to write the same portrait forever, since every portrait is a "moving image of eternity" (Plato, *Timaeus*, 37D), a continuation of movement or *Pathosformel* of thought.

Ultimately, however, the point is not that cinema would be the precondition for Deleuze's portraiture. Every age and every portraitist has its own machines. Deleuze refers to various portrait machines: Tinguely's machinic portraits of classical philosophers such as Wittgenstein and Bergson (Deleuze and Guattari 1994: 55–56), Gerard Fromanger's portraits of Foucault (Deleuze 2004a: 247–51),[18] as well as his own "machinic portrait of Kant, illusions included" (Deleuze and Guattari 1994: 56–57). What makes these portraits machinic is that resemblance is not achieved through mimetical filiation but through an intensive filiation based on serial processes continuing themselves in infinite and continuous variation. Crucially, the term "machinic" does not yet have its modern connotation of something man-made. On the contrary, it implies a certain modesty vis-à-vis the mechanical. For early modern philosophers, it is precisely nature that is produced through the endless machination of corporeal mixtures and not cultural artifacts. Nothing is ever readymade, such that even the smallest degree of likeness is based on production rather than reproduction (Deleuze 1995: 135). There is transubstantiation from one medium to another just as there is adaptation within one medium, but always with the consequence that what is produced is a work no less original than the "source." It is this insistence on the new, not their technologies as piously distinguished from a transcending *presentia realis*, that makes the mannerists absolutely modern and that makes their mode of filiation properly machinic.

As Deleuze makes clear in his book on Foucault, this machinic filiation allows for jumps in manner not just between generations but also within the same generation. "I've tried to do a portrait of his philosophy. The lines or touches are of course mine, but they succeed only if he himself comes to haunt the picture" (Deleuze 1995: 102). In their functioning the lines and touches produce an effect that refers to nothing but its own mode of production. This modal likeness explains the sometimes-spectral quality of mannerist portraits. In the grotesques of Arcimboldo, the endlessly machined bodies find their consistency less in organic nature than through the disparity of a certain style. We see how the face is a crystallization of animals, fruits, and vegetables. Take one element away and the overall nature of the composition changes. As a consequence, it is no longer clear what is ideal and what is real or at least there is no privileged commitment. Between the figures of art and philosophical discourse, likewise, there is no philosopher=x that serves as their common substratum. Instead there is only a "higher analogy" based on the resonance between autonomous terms, such that the life or manner of a work or body is itself renewed and extended in another body. This analogy is a question neither of memory nor of fantasy but of the constant oscillation between matter and manner, between perfectly substantial forms and almost completely dematerialized, transparent ghosts (Deleuze and Guattari 1994: 171).[19]

The drama of concepts

With his machinic understanding of time as a constant splitting and redoubling into past and present, Deleuze turns against the Hegelian dialectic, which had guided the organization of historical research at postwar French universities. Hegel had reduced thought to a "false movement" of contradictions between propositions that are sublated in the more general continuity of spirit. For what remains unmoved and extratemporal is precisely the history and propositional form of a clear but confused "reason" (logic) that necessarily and systematically presupposes itself and reads its own linear development from beginning to end as mirrored in world history (phenomenology). Buried under the weight of history are the distinct but obscure problems, in other words, the real ideational movements that the philosophers of the past were immersed in. These are deemed to be surpassed, refuted, and reduced to the conceptual solutions that alone count as the necessary steps in the self-development of human thought.

Throughout his work, Deleuze brings back to life these thought movements by demonstrating, within every philosophical expression, the excess of the Idea over representational content. The actual thinking of a past philosopher does not happen at the theoretical level of concepts but through the manner in which these concepts integrate obscure forces. As Stein (1988) says: "The difference between thinking clearly and confusion is the same difference that there is between repetition and insistence" (173). Every time we write the portrait of a philosopher, at stake is therefore the full multiplicity of vital intuitions that give rise to his discourse, among which thought bears an immanent potency of selection and integration. The conceived combination in the concept, the finite and clear but confused explication of a non-totalizable idea, is a living hypothesis that emerges from, and feeds back into, implicitly felt virtualities: "*Concepts* are inseparable from *affects*, i.e. from the powerful effects they exert on our life, and *percepts*, i.e. the new ways of seeing or perceiving they provoke in us" (Deleuze 2006: 238). If Deleuze attaches so much weight to the necessity of "separating out both the plane of immanence [a philosopher] instituted and the new concepts he created" (Deleuze and Guattari 1994: 55), then because whatever the coherence between concepts, this coherence is never itself conceptual but material and practical. Concepts are modes of existence, not of spirit. They are provisional solutions to changing problems without ever directly corresponding to them, and their vital tenor increases or decreases according to the manner in which they manage to reinvent them.

The problem is that the history of philosophy contains an entropic tendency that stabilizes the back-and-forth between concepts and their immanent conditions to the point of conflating them and thus exhausting their vital insistence in naked repetition. Hegel is only the ultimate personification of this problem. "Ah! The old Style …," Deleuze complains at the outset of *Difference and Repetition* with a formula borrowed from one of the most prominent mannerists of the twentieth century, Samuel Beckett. Consisting of the historically sedimented contents and dominant modes of expression of philosophy, its eternal questions and the legitimate ways of posing them, the "natural" or "classical" style of doing philosophy constantly reproduces a "dogmatic image of thought" (Deleuze 1994: xxi, Deleuze and Guattari 1994: 53). Although this image of thought comes in many (empiricist, rationalist, criticist, etc.) guises and is often explicitly rejected or overturned, it holds fast implicitly as the eternal figuration or semblance of philosophy. There is only ever "a single Image in general which constitutes the subjective presupposition of philosophy as a whole" (Deleuze 1994: 132). Because it is a recognizable image, that of a subject who has already identified himself as friend of wisdom, it is always the same image that stabilizes and secures the concept and practice of philosophy at the same time that it hinders the renewed becoming of philosophy itself. It reflects a style that tolerates no other style and that is in denial of itself as a style even in those moments that, full of its own goodwill, it explicitly recognizes style as a pragmatic constituent of philosophy. As it constantly blots out the implicit orthodoxy with which it makes thought represent itself and extort conformism, however, it also lacks the capacity to criticize and overturn its own doxic character, "the image as produced by style" (Deleuze 1973: 148). The canonical philosophers and their concepts acquire a self-importance that puts off so-called non-philosophers by preceding and anticipating everything. The old Style is hence nothing less than philosophy's own Oedipus complex, its own agent of power and intimidation (Deleuze and Parnet 2002: 10, 13). Every attempt to discuss a concept without its history is a priori disqualified as obscurantist: Do not dare to philosophize without first reading the classics, Aristotle, Descartes, and Kant!

From his first books onwards, it has been Deleuze's project to subject this one-dimensional philosophy to formal renewal—not in order to replace the authority of the dominant Style of thought with his own but in order to disconnect philosophy's form from its contents and have it pass into the form of expression of the nonphilosophical. Only by deforming the subjective presupposition of philosophy, the general form of the "I think" as exclusive style and most visible protagonist of thought, does the concept become the affirmation of "thought as heterogenesis" (Deleuze and Guattari 1994: 199) and thus of a variety of other— and more potent—manners of thought.

> The thought of the singular is the most sober thought in the world. [...] One is never oneself remarkable or interesting, on the contrary, the thinker is the extension on a series of ordinaries whereas thought explodes in the element of singularity, and the element of singularity is the concept.[20]

What individuates a concept and constitutes the life of a philosophy, in other words, is not the stable identity of its ostentatious author but the variable stability of a style. It is through the more aberrant and least recognizable or even respectable manners, moreover, that the concept acquires a higher power of thinking. Since a manner can never be entirely formalized, it comes to be known only in accordance with singular terms, that is, proper names or *haecceities*. However, the proper name remains only the index of schizophrenic affects and thought processes that exclude the mediation of the "I think" as their common ground. In the work of "Foucault," for example, Deleuze finds that the sentences strain "toward the movement of concepts" according to a variety of discursive styles, each of which remains an irregular construction built from many attending visibilities and capable of quite other becomings following no other logic of development than the crises they go through.[21] It is the task of the history of philosophy conceived as portraiture to seek out atypical expressions and reanimate this mutant variety of manners of thought, as each of them enables philosophy to begin again.

Instead of constantly reproducing the self-sufficient cliché of the (no doubt very "critical") Thinker in the study of other authors, what the history of philosophy therefore needs is a method of distinguishing the singular from the ordinary manners. Instead of a historicization of philosophy, this would be a method for the philosophicization of history itself.[22] Such is Deleuze's well-known "method of dramatization," which deals with the question of the transdisciplinary "utilization of the history of philosophy" (Deleuze 1994: xxi): "Staging means that the written text is going to be illuminated by other values, non-textual values" (Deleuze 2004a: 144, 98). More than a reenactment of thought, it takes the form of a counter-actualization; it is a replaying of a dormant concept on a new stage, even if doing so turns the original concepts against its author (Deleuze and Guattari 1994: 83). There are no eternal problems, rather, the dualism of theory and practice is surpassed in an experimental reading that situates a body of work among forces that are themselves untimely or outside all narrative history (*hors-temps de l'histoire*) and that perpetually give a new sense to it. This experiment begins by showing that the voice of the philosopher who coined a concept is itself occupied by a variety of other voices, each of which is the implied personification of a series of impersonal thought-gestures that exceeds historical coordinates. As Deleuze and Guattari put it, borrowing from Mikhail Bakhtin's polyphonic and contrapuntal conception of language, the author's name is only the pseudonym of the conceptual personae that are its heteronyms (Deleuze and Guattari 1994: 64–65). Thus a philosophy is no longer a given, but must be constructed. Whodunnit? What happened? Such are the questions of style, of an aesthetics of the concept in which philosophy and art mutually interfere. Their answering demands "vital anecdotes" that unify thinking and feeling/acting. It takes a few narrative fragments, not the weight of an encompassing history, to personalize the powers of imagination and enunciation that schematize the affects and orient the concepts of a certain philosophy (a portrait), that is, those powers of selection and integration that can also be mobilized for an entirely new conceptual system of which the historical authors are only so many heteronyms (a landscape). By discerning, recombining, and multiplying manners of thought, dramatization thus functions like a perpetuum mobile that constantly introduces movement in thought. It strips the classical Style of its dogmatism, enabling philosophy to surpass its history and achieve "a reproduction of philosophy itself" (Deleuze 1994: xxi).

Standing with one leg in the canon, dramatization gives an author an *acte de présence*, making him participate in something beyond the canon to the point that he constitutes a "zone of indiscernibility" between philosophy and life. Since each is the incarnation of a mode of thinking (concepts) as well as of a way of being (plane of immanence), conceptual personae function as marker or referent whenever an ideational movement is to be interpreted and evaluated in terms of its uses and abuses for life, including, but not limited to, the life of philosophy. Indeed, manners can be ranked according to the degree in which they resist coinciding with their own image as philosophy and thus enable the richest or "best" becomings (Deleuze and Guattari 1994: 27–28, 59). What unites the philosophers that Deleuze focuses on is their "charm" or "style," in which "the eternal philosophy and the history of philosophy give way to a becoming-philosophical."[23] Among them, Spinoza famously stands out as the philosopher of absolute immanence, that is, as the very personification of non-philosophy, the "Prince" or "Christ" of philosophers:

> This frugal, propertyless life, undermined by illness, this thin, frail body, this brown, oval face with its sparkling black eyes—how does one explain the impression they give of being suffused with Life itself, of having a power identical to Life? In his whole way of living and of thinking, Spinoza projects an image of the positive, affirmative life, which stands in opposition to the semblances that men are content with. (Deleuze 1988: 12)

With reference to the portrait of Masaniello, the Neapolitan fisherman and revolutionary who caught the interest of Spinoza, Deleuze draws a portrait of Spinoza as "practical philosopher" who divested thought of its theoretical transcendence. His calm Latin, written *more geometrico*, seems to be almost devoid of any style, but this only enables him to create all the more movement and move all sorts of nonphilosophical practitioners. Hence Deleuze repeatedly stresses how Spinoza's *Ethics* is itself the alchemy of at least three different styles: the continuous stream of definitions, propositions, proofs, and corrollaries (concepts), the discontinuous chain of scholia (affects), and the pervading intuitions of book V (percepts)—"three languages" entangled "in his outwardly dormant language."[24] Precisely because both concepts and percepts do not belong to modes of representation but are expressive of nonphilosophical affects, the two movements tend to interfere with and reinforce one another, but each in their own way. This constant modulation at the level of expression is the mannerist potential or vital power of imagination that philosophy shares with art or indeed with all creative practices.

The cult of the implicit

Any portrait of a philosopher with his problem raises the following question: What affective becomings and thoughts is a certain philosophy capable of? The aim is a thought in the present and not in the past, recreating and further developing a certain philosophy not just in the style of the author commented upon but equally in the manner of the commentator—without a hierarchy between the original style and its derivative variations. It is not the particular manner that is in excess over a more general style but the problem that remains implicit in, and is transformed by, both. This is to say that a particular philosophy or another is not the object of commentary but the immanent point of view of an expressive becoming.[25] On the one hand, philosophy is a force that, like all forces, can only appear in the mask in which it is expressed: the concept. The expression, on the other hand, should never receive priority over what it expresses. Instead, the real movement of thought always starts from a departure from what a certain author was assumed to be: "Thought is primarily trespass and violence, the enemy, and nothing presupposes philosophy: everything begins with mysosophy."[26] Deleuze's theater of philosophy therefore takes the form of a mannerist *mascherata*, in which all the masks are maximally betrayed. It does not start by the unmasking procedure of critique, but relies on a "dialectic of camouflage" (Mircea Eliade). As "the difference *in* the origin does not appear *at* the origin," the commentator masks himself with the work commented upon and still appeals to the prevailing image of philosophy, but with "new, bizarre and dangerous ends" (Deleuze 1983: 5–6).

At this point where identification dissolves in the distorted and distorting trace of the original, there arises the mannerist challenge of *virtuosità*. Based on performativity, virtuosity and monstrosity meet in the habitus of the craftsman who makes things gestural. Michelangelo famously claimed that a block of marble already encloses the idea of the work of art, but that it takes a hand to accomplish it. As its implicit principle of individuation, the stone is already charged with an internal difference or expressive force (*virtus*): the inner material movement, character, and resistance that defines its historicity as well as its unfinished potentiality. In order for the stone to acquire the mode of existence of a work of art, the artist must experiment with what it can do, deforming and intensifying its gestures by giving them a new relief. *De la matière à la manière*, writes Deleuze.[27] As Michelangelo's practice of the *non finito* shows, however, it is far from necessary for matter to fully embody its new manner. On the contrary, it effects a sort of infinitization at the level of material realization.

If in the renaissance material difference remains implicit and possible manners are limited by the stability of received practice and organic forms, mannerism seeks an explosion of divergent material explications, each of which demands its own plane of composition with exterior forces. The greater the virtuosity in modulating the stone's texture, the greater the variety of new manners or intensities it can pass into.

Contrary to classicism, moreover, mannerism does not exhaust a given material's potential in a certain form but seeks to transform and improve it. It is not enough for something that remains implicit in a past body of work to become the explicated object of the next, since the explication may well neutralize the various other becomings that it was pregnant with. Thus the explication must also reimplicate future versions. For Bruno, the immanence of the post-Copernican universe means that there is no prime mover but an energetical autarchy. Whenever something passes from potency to act, this also implies a movement from act to potency. The plasticity of expression, not just explication through participation but renewal and change, is what enables the different modes of existence to grow and preserve their potential in a world of constantly varying aggregate states of matter. Lacking the substantiality or generality of essence, a manner is thus always involved in a tortuous circle in which each point is both endpoint and beginning (Bruno 1998: 61–62, 1985: 385–87).

Only that which finds its finality completely in itself, by contrast, is incapable of reinventing itself or being reinvented by something else. Hence the warning of the later Bacon to David Sylvester about his early versions of Velazquez's Pope, that they contain too much explicit distortion and too much figurative violence, whereas what he was after was the scream and not the horror: the grimace as pure event, an inexhaustive modality already virtually present in the layered colorations of Velazquez himself, and that would have been more powerfully sustained in a less ostentatious fashion. Hence also the mannerist imperative, formulated by Deleuze (1994) as an "ethics of intensive quantities" (244): never explicate too much, such that matter and manner continue to reinforce one another. Mannerist virtuosity is the cult of the implicit, an art of involution. What matters is not matter, but the manner in which matter comes to matter. Is a particular material general or singular, entropic or negentropic?

The success of a history of philosophy conceived as mannerist portraiture likewise depends on virtuosity. The mannerist commentator does not interpret what a philosopher "meant," but involves the other in an a-parallel becoming. He must become the philosopher's "double,"[28] yielding to the latter's concepts as far as it goes, but also subtract from them all definiteness and redundancy (n-1) in order to give them the expression of a more impersonal and more abstract voice than that of the commentator. A virtuosic reading of an author repeats what an author has said as well as what he could have said. But instead of merely making explicit what remains implicit in the original, crucially, it must adapt to the *virtus impressa* of an author, as if in a transfer of causality: "one does not go back on a theory, one makes others, one has others to make" (Deleuze 2004a: 206).[29] It asks: What is a body of work capable of? What are its innate ideas? But also: What else is it capable of? What is its virtuosity? How can we revirtualize this work?

Deleuze approaches the history of philosophy in the same way he approaches language, as an implicit order of polyvocal murmuring in which no single voice or literary canon sets the tone by itself. Language knows no original author or fixed structure, but only a generalized indirect speech, in which each voice or manner of speaking implicitly repeats the others in a continuous and infinite variation: "It is not that one leaps from one language to the next, as in bilingual- or pluralingualism, it is rather that there is always one language in another and so on to infinity. Not a mixture but a *heterogenesis*" (Deleuze 2006: 367). In the same vein, the history of philosophy is an open system in which the names and concepts of classical authors continue to play a central role, but only insofar as they express pre-individual and impersonal problems at the level of which they continue to resonate with a multiplicity of other voices and solutions. In language as in philosophy, there is no paternity of ideas. Just as there exists no natural and indiscriminate light that guarantees their evidence and stability, but only the flickering of an artificial chiaroscuro, there is no natural language in which we can neutrally represent an author from the past. With each voice being the zeugmatic assemblage or *agencement* of different voices, it is in the shifting, slipping, dislocations, and hidden emissions that philosophy rejuvenates itself.[30] None of the philosophical voices seems really "new," yet they have never sounded like this before.

If the first determination of language is indirect discourse, then the virtuosity of a great style can be determined as an extended ventriloquy or free indirect discourse. Drawing from Bakhtin but largely following the neo-mannerist film director Pier Paolo Pasolini, Deleuze understands free indirect discourse as the point where the subject of an enunciation and the subject of a statement lose their distinction. "She summons up her strength: *she will rather endure torture than lose her virginity*" (Bakhtin, in Deleuze 2005: 75). The main "she" and the subordinate "she" are not the same subjects, but neither are they entirely different, as if one would be reporter and the other reported. Where a preceding voice implies an actual voice at the same time as it is deformed by it, the two enter a "zone of neighborhood" that makes for an altogether new way of speaking. But when neither the other nor the self can be fixed, they also encounter other, even more indeterminate voices with which they must interact. The more the others become the inseparable intercessors of the self, the more anonymous is the collective assemblage of enunciation, the more active and passive speaking becomes indiscernible, and the less enunciation remains bound to an external point of view, the more free is the discourse. Style therefore "belongs to people of whom you normally say, 'They have no style'" (Deleuze and Parnet 2002: 4). It "requires a lot of silence and work to make a whirlpool at some point, then flies out like the matches children follow along the water in a gutter. [...] All writers, all creators, are shadows. How can anyone write a biography of Proust or Kafka?" (Deleuze 1995: 133–34).

The ultimate criterion for the evaluation of a style can only be a radical antihistorical ascetism: do not impede immanence! Movement always happens behind your back. Not only does virtuosity depend on the power of old age to abstain and be preyed upon by one's proper impotence (Agamben 2016), everything depends on the discretion (*discrezione*, as Lomazzo calls it) with which a difference infects the whole of language in "becoming like everybody else (*devenir tout le monde*)."[31] This goes for philosophy no less than for the philosophical portraitist. "There is no act of creation that is not transhistorical and does not come up from behind" (Deleuze and Guattari 2003: 296). In order not to exhaust philosophy but to continue its vital movement, the portraitist aims for a kind of soliloquy in which one philosopher repeats another, not for the sake of repetition but for the sake of insistence. The shift in emphasis appears like a foreign language within a language, but it is precisely this emphasis that makes repetition possible and successful, especially if it does not appear too much as foreign (Stein 1988: 167, 171). On the one hand, this strategy of writing "with" rather than writing "about" implies the greatest degree of precision or perfection, since it forbids putting words into the mouth of the other. As Stein says, the only difference is a shift in emphasis: "There can be no repetition because the essence of [...] expression is insistence, and if you insist you must each time use emphasis and if you use emphasis it is not possible while anybody is alive that they should use exactly the same emphasis, not even when this emphasis is taught" (Stein 1988: 196). On the other hand, the result aimed for is a sort of hallucinatory confusion: "The succeeding and failing is what makes the repetition not the moment to moment emphasizing [of difference] that makes repetition" (Stein 1988: 196). Becoming no longer proceeds through the law of noncontradiction or the excluded third but through elective affinities (or "vice-dictions"), just as thought is not a dialogue between the multitude of positions of enunciation, but transpires in the various manners in which the personae mediate ongoing processes of conceptual creation (or "negotiations").

This mannerism of indirection is not only Deleuze's "method" in reading other philosophers, but if one were to create a portrait of Deleuze, this would also have to be a mannerist one. In his preface to the English translation of *Anti-Oedipus. Capitalism and Schizophrenia*, Foucault emphasizes the manner, ethical as much as aesthetical, in which the book does what it says in producing the anorganic life that it describes. The authors "care so little for power that they have tried to neutralize the effects of their own discourse. Hence the games and snares scattered throughout the book [...] so many invitations to let oneself be put out, to take one's leave of the text and slam the door shut" (Foucault, in Deleuze and Guattari 2003: xiv). Having initially merely described the heterogenesis of thought, Deleuze himself recounts that he finally felt to have found the freedom of style or expressivity to exercise this heterogenesis himself by way of his collaboration with Félix Guattari (Deleuze and Parnet 2002: 23). At the same time, the book's clear message—the declaration of war against the dualisms and organic wholes that attempt to mediate the grinding of the desiring-machines—still suggests a master voice articulating the categorical imperative of molecular non-stratification. It is a "beginning" (Deleuze 1995: 7) but therefore the mannerism of indirection is not yet fully achieved. In *A Thousand Plateaus*, as Isabelle Stengers (2007) has pointed out, "the problem has changed" and with it, the manner.[32] The problem is still that of "life" and its machination, but the message is less polemical and closer to the words on Spinoza's seal ring: *caute*. As the book refuses to be a model for those accelerationists who would risk their life in the name of the body without organs, it is no longer clear "what the authors want to say" except that the book soberly practices exactly what it says and could not have said it differently, its resistance to redundancy demoralizing the goodwill of its interpreters.

How then to characterize Deleuze's freedom of style, if its aim is to become unrecognizable? In *What Is Philosophy?*, Deleuze warns that in the past, in answering the question of what philosophy is in its relation to science and art, "there was too much desire to do philosophy to wonder what it was, except as a stylistic exercise. The point of nonstyle where one could finally say 'What is it I have been doing all my life?' had not been reached" (Deleuze and Guattari 1994: 7). Although another case of heterogenesis, still emphasized by the fact that it mentions as its authors Deleuze and Guattari (each of whom "was already several"), his last book is conceived as a self-portrait as an old man, virtuous hands and pointy, elongated fingernails included. Its emphasis on lateness does not mean that a unifying style is no longer deemed necessary, but that finally it can be fully problematized. After all, for Deleuze the transdisciplinary "non-" is not a negation but the question of subtractive modesty: it is the very event of style. The climax of mannerism lies at the point where style becomes nonstyle, a point that Deleuze and Guattari suggest that you can only reach late in life, when philosophy no longer has anything to do with a stylistic exercise, when illness and fatigue have exhausted the habits of philosophy and one is left contemplating one's own manner of doing philosophy, a manner for which one is no longer in need of recognition (Deleuze and Guattari 1994: 1).[33] The paradox of lateness is that it is inseparable from a becoming-child, indeed from the innocence of becoming. Coinciding completely with its own practice, nonstyle is "the grand style, or the creation of style in the pure state" (Deleuze 2006: 367). Hence the question that sums up and hierarchizes all of Deleuze's art: "Will we ever be mature enough for a Spinozist inspiration?" (Deleuze and Guattari 1994: 48).

Notes

1 And: "The search for new means of philosophical expression was begun by Nietzsche and must be pursued today in relation to the renewal of certain other arts, such as theatre and cinema" (Deleuze 1994: xxi).

2 Relying on Deleuze's *The Logic of Sense* as well as Lacan and Derrida, Achille Bonito Oliva has shown betrayal to be a crucial aspect of mannerism, but still couches it in traditional subjectivist terms: "The strategy pursued by art rests on that which I define as the ideology of the traitor. The ideology of the traitor is already ideology betrayed, robbed of the superstructure of any theory that expresses group interests, to acquire the virgin force of subversive projectuality" (Oliva 1998: 20). Deleuze develops the concept of betrayal in the context of the distinction between the positional distance or irony of a subject who is merely mannered or affected and the intimate humor of the mime who doubles the event in the manner of an inner distancing repetition. Hence "the ethics of the mime," according to which one must will "not exactly what occurs, but something *in* that which occurs [...] Thus, the actor delimits the original, disengages from it an abstract line, and keeps from the event only its contour and its splendour, becoming thereby the actor of one's own events—a *counter-actualization*" (Deleuze 1990: 149–50, 142–47). And: "to be the mime of *what effectively occurs*, to double the actualization with a counter-actualization, the identification with a distance,

like the true actor and dancer, is to give to the truth of the event the only chance of not being confused with its inevitable actualization" (Deleuze 1990: 161). This counter-actualization is what makes Shakespeare's and Carmelo Bene's character of Richard III a mannerist hero par excellence: He "does not simply want power, he wants treason. He does not want the conquest of the state, but the assemblage of the war-machine: how can he be the only traitor, and betray simultaneously?" (Deleuze and Parnet 2002: 40–42).

3   Claude-Gilbert Dubois 1979: 28–35, 12.
4   Dubois 1979: 26–27.
5   Adorno refers to the late style of individual artists, but we see no reason why his concept would not equally apply to moments that art history sometimes designates as "silver" or "mannerist."
6   In *Francis Bacon. The Logic of Sensation*, Deleuze (2004b: 154–60) discusses these shifts in the relation between hand and eye in terms of the *maniera* that Bacon inherits from Michelangelo.
7   Translation modified and adopted from Terence Blake. See https://terenceblake.wordpress.com/2016/07/12/zizek-on-deleuzes-letter-against-identitarianism/(last visited 23.07.2018).
8   Quoted by Giuseppe Bianco in this volume.
9   See also Sydney Freedberg's (1965) notion of the "quoted."
10 This way of grounding oneself in, and learning from, the past in order to recover its differential beginning and event-like quality by confusing foreground and background was no doubt inspired by Heidegger's procedure of *wieder-holen* and its artful etymology "Ein Anfang wird aber nicht wiederholt, indem man sich auf ihn als ein Vormaliges und nunmehr Bekanntes und lediglich Nachzumachendes zurückschraubt, sondern indem der Anfang ursprünglicher wiederangefangen wird und zwar mit all dem Befremdlichen, Dunklen, Ungesicherten, das ein wahrhafter Anfang bei sich führt" (Heidegger 1953: 29–30, 4, 10, 17).
11 See I, the thirty "Intentions," esp. XII, XV, XVII. Based on the Renaissance use of the image in the mirror, which by its place, material, and distortion makes from one light a variety of appearances, Bruno's *Ars Deformationum* functions as "universal instrument" for passing or folding from one explication of matter-potential in a form (or "mode") to the next. ("De Monade," *Op.lat.* I, 2, 329, 471). For Deleuze's affinity with Bruno, see also: Ramey 2012.
12 And: "the universe […] the full signification of which is, as it were, a sort of living mirror in which is the image of the natural and the shadow of the divine" (Bruno 1991: 5). The English editor of this work was one of the founders of Fluxus and coiner of the term "intermedia."
13 And: "memory should always be a by-product it should never be an end in itself it should not be a thing by which you live if you really and truly are one who is to do anything and so I say I very exactly began again" (Stein 1988: 201).

14. Or: "I had the habit of conceiving myself as completely talking and listening, listening was talking and talking was listening and in so doing I conceived what I at that time called the rhythm of anybody's personality" (Stein 1988: 174).
15. Cf. Deleuze (2004a) on genius as differential presence: "You have to work your way back to those problems which an author of genius has posed, all the way back to that which he does not say *in* what he says, in order to extract something that still belongs to him, though you also turn it against him" (139).
16. And: "I was empty of them I made them contained within the thing I wrote that was them. The thing in itself folded itself up inside itself like you might fold a thing up to be another thing which is that thing inside that thing" (Stein 1988: 199–200).
17. Here Deleuze is closest to Aby Warburg's *Atlas* as well as Walter Benjamin's *Denkbilder*, which the latter conceived of as monads or crystals composed of powers of visibility and readability. Cf. Georges Didi-Huberman 2009, 2010, 2011.
18. On the concept of machinic portrait and French New Figuration, see Ann-Cathrin Drews 2017.
19. Cf. Deleuze's remarks on how Sade, Masoch, Robbe-Grillet, and Klossowski make the phantasm the object of their work, instead of its origin, in Deleuze 2004a: 132.
20. See Deleuze's *Course Notes*, available at http://www.webdeleuze.com/php/sommaire.html 29/04/1980. And: "the act of thinking is a manner of being composed of a unique relation between the elements extracted from a thought flow" (20/04/1980).
21. Foucault's style has "a rhythmic quality, or, as in the strange dialogues with himself with which he closes some of his books, a contrapuntal one. His syntax builds up the shimmerings and scintillations of the visible but also twists like a whip, folding up and unfolding, or cracking to the rhythm of its utterances. And then, in his last books, the style tends toward a kind of calm, seeking an ever more austere, an ever purer line" (Deleuze 1995: 100–01, 164, 140).
22. On this point, see https://www.academia.edu/9689960/Guy_Lardreau_-_History_of_Philosophy_as_Diff%C3%A9red_Practice_of_Philosophy_Deleuze_as_Historian_ (last accessed July 23, 2018).
23. See Deleuze and Guattari 1994: 112, Deleuze and Parnet 2002: 14–15, Deleuze 1995: 6.
24. See Deleuze 1995: 165–66, and Deleuze 1998: 138–51.
25. Through the problem of expression, Deleuze discovers in Spinoza philosophy's "limit-point," being "neither entirely inside nor entirely outside" philosophy, but a "fold" that doubles the history of philosophy, or hollows it out, with a becoming-philosophical. It is this folding that also justifies Pierre Macherey's (1998) chiasmic formula that "Deleuze in Spinoza is also Spinoza in Deleuze" (124).
26. See Deleuze 1994: 139, and Deleuze and Guattari 1994: 92.
27. See Deleuze 1993: 35, and Deleuze and Guattari 1994: 166–67.

28 See Deleuze 1994: xxi. Or, quoting from Foucault's passage on repetition in *The Order of Things*: "I wanted to find Foucault's double, in the sense he gave the word: 'a repetition, another layer, the return of the same, a catching on something else, an imperceptible difference, a coming apart and ineluctable tearing open'" (Deleuze 1995: 84).
29 With a reference to Jorge Luis Borges's story "Pierre Menard, Author of the Quixote," Éric Alliez (2004) has described Deleuze's practice as "the systematic virtualization of the history of philosophy as the mode of actualization of *a* new philosophy, of a *virtual* philosophy whose infinitely variable effectuation does not cease to *make folds* (folds by folds), thus setting Deleuze apart from the author-function and from the false enunciation of the commentator—to the benefit of an infinitely more 'baroque' and Borgesian figure: mannerism" (101–02; cf. Deleuze 1994: xxii).
30 For the concept of zeugmatic assemblage, based on the originary disjunction governing the distribution of singular points along two, at least, diverging series, see Constantin Boundas 1994: 99–116, 100–01.
31 "To be a stranger, even to one's doorman or neighbors. It is so difficult to be like everybody else, it is because it is an affair of becoming. Not everybody becomes everybody. Makes a becoming of everybody/everything. This requires much asceticism, much sobriety, much creative involution: an English elegance, an English fabric, blend in with the walls, eliminate the too-perceived, the too much-to-be-perceived" (Deleuze and Guattari 2003: 279; Deleuze and Parnet 2002: 29–30).
32 For an English translation: https://www.academia.edu/33073747/Isabelle_Stengers_-_Thinking_Life_The_Problem_has_Changed.
33 As Brian Massumi writes, the intrinsic problem of the copious literature on Deleuze and his "philosophical lineage" is not that it is of low quality or too repetitive but that it consists of a "change in manners" between Deleuze's thinking and its digestion by those who want to restore Deleuze as bona fide philosopher to the academy. See https://lareviewofbooks.org/article/undigesting-deleuze/.

Bibliography

Adorno, T.W. (1998), *Beethoven. The Philosophy of Music*, trans. E. Jephcott, Cambridge: Polity.
Agamben, G. (2016), *The Use of Bodies*, trans. A. Kotsko, Palo Alto: Stanford University Press.
Alliez, É. (2004), *The Signature of the World: What Is Deleuze and Guattari's Philosophy?*, trans. E. Ross Albert and A. Toscano, London: Continuum.

Boundas, C. (1994), "Deleuze: Serialization and Subject-Formation," in C. Boundas and D. Olkowski (eds), *Gilles Deleuze and the Theater of Philosophy*, New York: Routledge.

Bruno, G. ([1582] 1884), "De Umbris Idearum," in F. Tocco, H. Vitelli, V. Imbriani, and C.M. Tallarigo (eds), *Opera Latine Conscripta*, Naples: Morano.

Bruno, G. (1985), "De l'infinito, universo e mondi," in *Dialoghi italiani*, 3rd edn, ed. G. Aquilecchia, Florence: Sansoni.

Bruno, G. (1991), *On the Composition of Images, Signs and Ideas*, ed. D. Higgins, trans. C. Doria, New York: Willis, Locker & Owens.

Bruno, G. (1998), *Cause, Principle and Unity and Essays on Magic*, trans. and ed. R.J. Blackwell and R. de Lucca, Cambridge: Cambridge University Press.

Conley, T. (1997), "From Multiplicities to Folds: On Style and Form in Deleuze," *The South Atlantic Quarterly*, 96 (3 Summer): 629–46.

Deleuze, G. (1973), *Proust and Signs*, trans. R. Howard, London/NY: Allen Lane.

Deleuze, G. (1983), *Nietzsche and Philosophy*, trans. H. Tomlinson, New York: Columbia University Press.

Deleuze, G. (1988), *Spinoza: Practical Philosophy*, trans. R. Hurley, San Francisco: City Lights Books.

Deleuze, G. (1990), *The Logic of Sense*, trans. M. Lester and C. Stivale, London: The Athlone Press.

Deleuze, G. (1993), *The Fold. Leibniz and the Baroque*, trans. T. Conley, Minneapolis: University of Minnesota Press.

Deleuze, G. (1994), *Difference and Repetition*, trans. P. Patton, New York: Columbia University Press.

Deleuze, G. (1995), *Negotiations. 1972–1990*, trans. M. Joughin, New York: Columbia University Press.

Deleuze, G. (1998), *Essays Critical and Clinical*, trans. D.W. Smith and M.A. Greco, London/New York: Verso.

Deleuze, G. (2004a), *Desert Islands and Other Texts 1953–1974*, ed. D. Lapoujade, trans. M. Taormina, New York: Semiotext(e).

Deleuze, G. (2004b), *Francis Bacon: The Logic of Sensation*, trans. D.W. Smith, London: Continuum.

Deleuze, G. (2005), *Cinema 1: The Movement-Image*, trans. H. Tomlinson and B. Habberjam, London: Continuum.

Deleuze, G. (2006), *Two Regimes of Madness: Texts and Interviews 1975–1995*, trans. A. Hodges and M. Taormina, New York: MIT Press.

Deleuze, G., and Guattari, F. (1986), *Kafka. Toward a Minor Literature*, trans. D. Polan, Minneapolis: University of Minnesota Press.

Deleuze, G., and Guattari, F. (1994), *What Is Philosophy?*, trans. H. Tomlinson and G. Burchell, New York: Columbia University Press.

Deleuze, G., and Guattari, F. (2003), *Anti-Oedipus. Capitalism and Schizophrenia*, trans. R. Hurley, M. Seem, and H.R. Lane, London: Continuum.

Deleuze, G., and Parnet, C. (2002), *Dialogues II*, trans. H. Tomlinson and B. Habberjam, London: Continuum.

Deleuze, G., and Parnet, C. (2004), *L'Abécédaire de Gilles Deleuze*, DVD, Paris: Editions Montparnasse.

Didi-Huberman, G. (2009, 2010, 2011), *L'Oeil de l'histoire*, vols. 1–3, Paris: Minuit.

Drews, A.-C. (2017), "Painting Machines, 'Metallic Suicide' and Raw Objects: Deleuze and Guattari's *Anti-Oedipus* in the context of French Post-War Art," in S. van Tuinen and S. Zepke (eds), *Art History after Deleuze and Guattari*, 195–216, Leuven: Leuven University Press.

Dubois, C.-G. (1979), *Le maniérisme*, Paris: Presses universitaires de France.

Foucault, M. (1998), "Theatrum Philosophicum," in M. Foucault, *Aesthetics, Method, and Epistemology*, New York: The New Press.

Freedberg, S. (1965), "Observations on the Painting of the Maniera," *Art Bulletin*, 47: 187–97.

Ginoux, I. (2004), "De l'histoire de la philosophie considerée comme un des beaux-arts: le portrait conceptuel selon Deleuze," in J. de Bloois, J.M.M. Houppermans, and F.W.A. Korsten (eds), *Discern(e)ments. Deleuzian Aesthetics – Esthetiques deleuziennes*, 23–49, Amsterdam: Rodopi.

Heidegger, M. (1953), *Einführung in die Metaphysik*, Tübingen: Max Niemeyer.

Macherey, P. (1998), *In a Materialist Way. Selected Essays*, trans. T. Stolze, London: Verso.

Oliva, B.A. (1998), *The Ideology of the Traitor. Art, Manner and Mannerism*, trans. M. Eaton and P. Metcalfe, Milan: Electa.

Posman, S. (2015), "Fluid Writing: Stein, James and Bergson," in S. Posman and L. Luise Schultz (eds), *Gertrude Stein in Europe: Reconfigurations across Media, Disciplines and Traditions*, 107–28, London: Bloomsbury.

Ramey, J. (2012), *The Hermetic Deleuze. Philosophy and Spiritual Ordeal*, Durham, NC: Duke University Press.

Starobinski, J. (1995), *Montaigne in Motion*, trans. A. Goldhammer, Chicago: University of Chicago Press.

Stein, G. (1988), *Lectures in America*, London: Virago.

Stengers, I. (2007), "Penser la vie: le problème a changé," *Revue International de Philosophie*, 241 (3): 323–35.

7

Try Again. Fail Again. Fail Better

The Role of Literature in Deleuze's Transcendental Empiricism

Emma Ingala

In one of his classes at the University of Vincennes-Saint Denis (Deleuze 1987), and through what he deemed to be one of Leibniz's most beautiful sentences, Deleuze outlined the fate of philosophical thinking: "I thought I had reached port, but [...] I was, as it were, carried back into the open sea" (Leibniz 1998: 149, translation modified, see also Deleuze and Guattari 1994: 22). Whenever the philosopher believes she has arrived at a certain conclusion, she sees herself suddenly thrown out again into the wild ocean of uncertainty. This is probably one of the reasons that led Deleuze and Guattari to claim that the act of thinking is a "dangerous exercise" (Deleuze and Guattari 1994: 41).[1]

On a quick first reading, Deleuze's echoing of Leibniz's formula could be interpreted as a pessimistic assessment of the inexorable failure inherent to the discipline of philosophy, similar to Kant's criticism of speculative metaphysics, which he described as a "battlefield of [...] endless controversies" (Kant 1998: 99 [A viii]) where "no combatant has ever gained the least bit of ground, nor has any been able to base any lasting possession on his victory" (Kant 1998: 109–110 [B xv]). Kant's critique intended to put an end to this procedure of "mere groping" and to elevate philosophy once and for all to the dignity characteristic of science (Kant 1998: 110 [B xv]).

Deleuze's thinking, however, points in a quite different direction: the recurring failure of philosophical concepts is not something that needs to be or, indeed,

---

An earlier version of this paper was delivered at the 2012 International Conference "Deleuze, Philosophy, Transdisciplinarity," held at Goldsmiths College, University of London. I would like to thank Gavin Rae for his suggestions and careful reading of this text.

can be overcome; on the contrary, it is a kind of success in that it bears witness to a reality that is constantly changing, to an ontology of pure difference and becoming that cannot be mapped without being betrayed.

As I will show in the following pages, the alliance between philosophy and literature in Deleuze's thought responds to the project of bringing to light this ontology of pure difference. In particular, it is precisely the failure of philosophy that calls for literature as a discipline better equipped to approach the realm of pure difference without domesticating or stabilizing it.

It is frequently recognized that literature pervades Deleuze's work,[2] but what exactly is the relationship between philosophy and literature in his system of thought? To start, it might be easier to approach the question negatively by noting that it is not a philosophy of literature or a philosophy applied to literature. The idea of a philosophy applied to literary texts presupposes that philosophy is a more or less closed corpus of theses, a steady doctrine that can be exported and transferred to a different domain—in this case, literature—to clarify certain of its aspects. The problem with this understanding is that it disregards and negates the failure inherent to philosophy: the fact that its modus operandi always entails a moment of suspension, of being adrift in the open sea.

Against this, Deleuze posits a relationship based on an alliance that serves the purpose not of vanquishing philosophy's failure, but—to say it with Beckett (1989: 101)—of failing better. Philosophy and literature combine their gestures to explore an experience beyond common sense, beyond the ordinary and the identitarian patterns of thought—an experience of pure difference no longer submitted to identity. This alliance sometimes translates into an exchange of methods and styles. For example, in *Difference and Repetition*, Deleuze states that a book of philosophy "should be in part a very particular species of detective novel, in part a kind of science fiction" (Deleuze 1994: xx). Additionally, *The Logic of Sense* is described in its preface as a "psychoanalytical novel" (Deleuze 1990: xiv, translation modified). However, even if philosophy, at a certain point, becomes literary, this does not erase the distinction between the two. Indeed, this distinction must be maintained because literature operates, in Deleuze's conception of thought, as an indispensable outside to philosophy. Specifically, from his early texts to the end of his life, Deleuze always held that philosophy "is born or produced from outside by the painter, the musician, the writer" (Deleuze and Parnet 1987: 74, translation modified). The genesis of thought is thus necessarily a heterogenesis (Deleuze 2007b: 54), which is a genesis that is caused by an outside or other; and literature, according to Deleuze, is one of philosophy's privileged others or outsides.

From this perspective, literature and philosophy, in so far as the latter's birth is frequently prompted by the action of the former, become inseparable. This inseparability, this necessity of literature for philosophy, has, in short, at least two rationales: first, literature provokes, awakens, or engenders from outside the movement of philosophy. Second, literature comes to supplement—never complement in the sense of a completion—the failure of philosophy in the task of expressing the ontology of pure difference. As Philippe Mengue explains:

> There is a real whose truth cannot be said unless there is a part of myth or narration; of literature, hence. Wisdom does not exhaust truth, and in a certain way it hides the truth, at least the truth that is the truth of the real, the limit to the thinkable and sayable, and which we might call "outside" with Deleuze. (Mengue 2003: 92)

This chapter will be devoted to exploring the peculiar relationship between literature and philosophy thematized and developed in Deleuze's early works up to 1969 and more specifically within the context of his project of transcendental empiricism—the label Deleuze chooses at that time to describe his own philosophical system (Deleuze 1994: 56, 143). Although a number of commentators have noted that there is a link between Deleuze's recourse to literature and his transcendental empiricism, they have tended to overlook the function that failure plays in this relationship.[3] Furthermore, the majority of the analyses tend to focus on the texts that Deleuze (and Guattari) explicitly devoted to literature, while I aim to show that his appeal to literature has an eminently ontological concern: namely, to explore an ontology of pure difference.

In order to unfold the complexity of Deleuze's relationship with literature, I first present the main sources and features of his transcendental empiricism, before showing the extent to which Plato and Kant are crucial interlocutors in this enterprise. I then examine the motivation behind—rather than provide an exhaustive list of—Deleuze's references to literature in his works up to *The Logic of Sense* and finish by highlighting what I consider to be the three roles that literature plays in his transcendental empiricism.

Transcendental empiricism: An extraordinary experience, a strange reason

At first glance, the label "transcendental empiricism" might appear to be an oxymoron, a perplexing concoction of two heterogeneous elements: one a priori, belonging to "before" experience and the other a posteriori, being experience in itself. Anne Sauvagnargues describes it as an "impossible relation" (2009: 9) and as a "short-circuit between allegedly separated theoretical operations" (2009: 10). Moreover, Natalie Depraz warns that Deleuze's aim is not to criticize rigid dualisms or to promote mixtures in Merleau-Ponty's vein, nor is it to enter into a logic of dialectical *Aufhebung* in a Hegelian sense.[4] Rather, it is necessary to give up the traditional distribution and meanings of "empirical" and "transcendental," and be ready to admit a twisting of these concepts.

There is a specific lineage of philosophers that prefigure Deleuze's standpoint, among which Bergson, Hume, and Nietzsche stand out. Yet the name "transcendental empiricism" intimates that Kant's philosophy is the surface upon which Deleuze registers his own project.[5] Kant, who invented the concept of "transcendental," classified his position as a "transcendental idealism" and as an "empirical realism" (Kant 1998: 440 [A 491/B 520] and 349 [A 375]). Deleuze's appropriation keeps the adjective part of these syntagms but discards the substantives. He does so because he is not so much interested in the realism versus idealism debate, as in what the transcendental sphere— the sphere of the conditions—can mean from an empiricist perspective. As a consequence of this reshuffling, the notion of "transcendental"—and that of "empirical" as well—is deeply transformed. Deleuze is certainly not the first to move in this direction. Before him, Schelling contorted the concepts of transcendental and empirical and combined them in the formulae "empirical apriorism" and "empiricism of the *a priori*."[6] This led him to invent, as Jean Wahl—one of Deleuze's professors at La Sorbonne—notes, the label "transcendental empiricism."[7]

Ever since his first published book, *Empiricism and Subjectivity*, Deleuze aspired to affirm an empiricism not of ordinary experience but of the extraordinary—not of the experiences of recognition and representation through conceptual identities but of the experience of difference and the new.[8] Hume is, chronologically, the first ally in this mission. According to Deleuze, his philosophy is a "sharp critique of representation" (Deleuze 1991b: 30) that is committed to exploring the realm of what representation cannot represent: relations—a first aspect of Deleuze's difference. Differential relations constitute objects and ideas, which do not preexist these relations.[9] Representation, nonetheless, obliterates these genetic relations and makes objects and ideas appear as if they were originary, as if identity were prior to difference. Common sense and everyday experience are shaped by representation, and for this reason the notion of a world of differences and relations sounds to the ordinary ear like science fiction. "As in science fiction, the world [of differences] seems fictional, strange, foreign, experienced by other creatures; but we get the feeling that this world is our own, and we are the creatures" (Deleuze 2004c: 162).[10]

There are, therefore, two kinds of experience: possible or ordinary experience, which is the experience of objects through their subsumption under pre-given identities or concepts; and real or superior experience, which is the experience of what cannot be represented—the experience of an absolute other, of an absolute outside.[11] Real experience is what Deleuze calls a "transcendental experience," wherein "transcendental" is no longer opposed to "empirical," but both, "transcendental" and "empirical," join forces to overcome and move beyond the blinding limits of ordinary experience. What transcendental experience encounters in transcending these limits is not just the sensible but "the very being *of* the sensible: difference, potential difference and difference in intensity as the reason behind qualitative diversity" (Deleuze 1994: 57). Deleuze insists that the distinction between ordinary and superior experience does not entail that the former is regulated by and submitted to laws and the latter is pure chaos; rather, the former is subordinated to identity and oblivious to what engenders identity, and the latter is capable of apprehending the source of any given: difference. Difference, therefore, is not the absence of reason but the domain of a "strange reason" (Deleuze 1994: 57).

Deleuze praises Kant for having discovered the "prodigious domain of the transcendental" (Deleuze 1994: 135), but accuses him of being too scared to renounce the safety net of common sense (Deleuze 1994: 136). This fear led Kant to stay within the field of possible experience—where the possible always prefigures in advance the real through pre-given identities—without daring to venture into real experience, into what cannot be anticipated (Deleuze 1994: 135). Deleuze goes further by charging Kant with also committing an illegitimate move that he calls the "tracing method" (Deleuze 1994: 135): Kant established that the domain of possible experience is a domain of a priori conditions, but he traced these conditions from actual experience and, even worse, from ordinary experience.

Against this, Deleuze articulates his notion of the transcendental around three main points: (1) it is the site of a genesis, construction, or production[12] of something new, and not merely the realization of a previous possibility—this is why it is not a possible experience,[13] but a real experience; (2) it is the result of conditions that are not general or abstract, not broader than what they condition, not preexistent, but plastic principles that change with what they condition,[14] particular to each case and only valid for that case[15]; and (3) it is an experience wherein the faculties are unhinged, pushed beyond their limit, and forced to apprehend what is impossible to apprehend from the point of view of their ordinary functioning or possible experience (Deleuze 1994: 139–41).

Once this new conception of the transcendental is outlined, Deleuze has to find a way to access it. Two correlative paths open in his texts: first, the failure of ordinary experience, the failure of the structures of common sense in their efforts to represent and recognize, bears witness to and, through this, gives access to a "beyond"; second, literature has the capacity to suspend phenomenological firsthand experiences and express another type of experience "inherently rare, not available in an everyday way" (Zourabichvili 2012: 211). As Jacques Rancière puts it, literature can operate as the laboratory of real experience (Rancière 2013: 11–12). For this reason, every time Deleuze is about to approach and grasp the being of pure difference, he appears to abandon the field of philosophy and plunge into literary examples, which are able to "transcend the experiential dimensions of the visible […] and […] track down, invoke, and perhaps produce a phantom at the limit of a lengthened or unfolded experience" (Deleuze 1990: 20). This, I maintain, is a familiar gesture for Deleuze, one that he already identified and underlined in Plato's use of myths.

Plato's snares

Following Nietzsche, Deleuze describes the task of modern philosophy—where "modern" means "contemporary"—as the reversal or overturning of Platonism (Deleuze 1994: 59, Deleuze 1990: 253). This could induce us to believe that Plato is an enemy, the one responsible for submitting the history of philosophy to the dictatorship of representation and identity. However, against this temptation, Deleuze immediately adds: "that this overturning should conserve many Platonic characteristics is not only inevitable but desirable" (Deleuze 1994: 59). Indeed, he holds that Plato was the first to "overturn Platonism, or at least to show the direction such an overturning should take" (Deleuze 1994: 68).

Deleuze's reading of Plato detects at least two snares (Deleuze 1990: 254) that Plato purposefully includes in his philosophy without his successors noticing. The first has to do with the understanding of division, the procedure Plato often employs when he is looking for the definition or essence (*eîdos*) of something. Aristotle criticized Plato for dividing concepts and beings arbitrarily, lacking a method and a sufficient reason to do so—for example, when he divides arts into production and acquisition in the *Sophist* (Plato 1997c: 239 [219b–c], Deleuze 1994: 59). According to Deleuze, Aristotle's mistake is to interpret Plato's division as a means to split a genus into opposing species when in reality it serves as a tool for selecting the good against the bad or the authentic against the inauthentic, as a tool for making the difference (Deleuze 1994: 59–60, Deleuze 1990: 253–54).

The second Platonic snare becomes manifest, according to Deleuze, in the (non-)accomplishment of the task of division. When Plato is about to reach the end of the division, he seems to renounce the realization of its goal and, to the reader's great surprise, suddenly invokes a myth (Deleuze 1994: 60, Deleuze 1990: 254). The *Statesman*, the dialogue that searches for the authentic politician, interrupts the division and calls upon the myth of the shepherd-King or God; the *Phaedrus*, which inquires about true love or good madness, gives up the conceptual work to elaborate on the myth of the circulation of the souls.[16] Deleuze, however, does not fall for Plato's snare; he apprizes that this appearance of flight or renunciation is just that, an appearance, since "in fact, myth interrupts nothing. On the contrary, it is an integral element of division" (Deleuze 1990: 254–55).

Plato's dialogues, especially those classed as "aporetic," do not reach a definitive conclusion, and sometimes the discussion is postponed to the following day—the promised sequel, of course, is left unregistered in the dialogue. Plato's dialogues fail more often than they succeed, if, in fact, they ever do. Nevertheless, this failure does not correspond to a lack of method in Plato's approach, as Aristotle would have it, but to a structural problem and condition inherent to philosophy.

The figure of the philosopher intimated here is nicely pictured by Diotima's description of the demon of Love in Plato's *Symposium*—which also resonates with Deleuze's appraisal of Leibniz's image of the sea: "he keeps coming back to life, but then anything he finds his way to always slips away" (Plato 1997d: 486 [203e]). In his reading of Plato's *Symposium*, Lyotard insisted that this is the fate of philosophy because it is nominally linked to love (*philia*): "Wisdom is not the object of an exchange, not because it is too precious for anyone to find an equivalent to swop, but because it is never sure of itself, is always lost and always needs to be found again, the presence of an absence" (Lyotard 2013: 36). When at the end of the *Symposium*, a heartbroken Alcibiades fails to understand why Socrates does not agree to exchange his wisdom for the beauty and favors that Alcibiades is offering him, he receives the following response from Socrates: "Still, my dear boy, you should think twice, because you could be wrong, and I may be nothing" (Plato 1997d: 500 [219a], translation modified). Socrates knows that there is no such thing as a perfect deal in philosophy and that reaching the harbor is always a contingent and precarious operation—if it is reached at all.

But then again, this failure is made to fail better through the recourse to a myth. It is true that Plato's writings give the impression that their mission is to achieve a final conclusion and seize the *eîdos* of something: what is true love, what does virtue involve, who is the right statesman, and so on. Dialectics appears to be the method that would give an answer to these questions—an exact one—through division. But at the moment when Plato is about to reach the end of this process and establish the difference—that is, select the correct answer—he abandons the method of division and turns to a myth.

Aristotle was unable to see that this failure was indeed the triumph of Plato's procedure. He failed to understand that it was the only way for it to succeed—and that parting ways with and abruptly finishing the dialogue after the intervention of the myth was the only way to put oneself on the level of the object of study. The appeal to myth is not an interruption of the process but rather its fulfilment: the myth gives a sensible appearance to that which lacks one—the Idea or *eîdos*—yet it does not stabilize what it expresses within the constraints of the concept. At the same time, the myth reminds us that philosophical argumentation is incapable of bringing the Idea into presence.

Plato's recourse to myth is, therefore, neither anecdotal nor dispensable, but an integral part of his dialectics. In a similar vein, Deleuze's recourse to literature is not incidental but essential to his transcendental empiricism. It is not by accident, then, that Deleuze concludes his sections on the reversal of Platonism by appealing to literature. Right when his philosophical exposition is about to reach the realm of pure difference, he seems to stop his discourse and summon a literary figure: James Joyce's *Finnegan's Wake*, Mallarmé's *Book*, or Gombrowicz's *Cosmos* enter precisely at the moment when Deleuze's words fail to name the intensive world of difference.

This recourse, like Plato's recourse to myth, is the culmination of Deleuze's project, the failure that allows it to succeed or, rather, fail better. "The being of the sensible reveals itself in the work of art" (Deleuze 1994: 68). The work of art, and in particular literature, "indicates to philosophy a path leading to the abandonment of representation [...] [to] the lived reality of a sub-representative domain" (Deleuze 1994: 69). There is, however, an important difference in this respect between Plato and Deleuze: whereas for Plato the myth is a mediation, a means for the operation of grounding (Deleuze 1994: 66)—grounding the essence of something—for Deleuze literature is not merely a mediation, an illustration of or a metaphor for difference, but the incarnation and actualization of difference in itself.

However, not every kind of literature has the power to be and express difference. Deleuze specifies that he is not concerned with *mimetic* literature, but with *poietic* literature, a literature that is no longer representation but creation and in particular creation of difference (Deleuze 1990: 260–61, Deleuze 1994: 56–57). This literature produces worlds that feel like science fiction; it engenders what he calls a "monstrosity" (Deleuze 1994: 69). To incorporate this monstrosity into his conception of philosophy, Deleuze supplements his reversal of Plato with a reversal of Kant. On the reverse side of Kant's wakefulness, in his unconfessed nightmares, Deleuze finds instances of the monstrosity that Kant's categories try to keep locked up.

The cabinet of monsters: The spirit-seer and the cinnabar driven crazy

Literature and the transcendental enter into an unexpected liaison in Deleuze's reappraisal of Kant. Kant invented the notion of the transcendental to make explicit the realm of conditions. This new concept served to replace the traditional essences/appearances couple with a new pairing: conditions of what appears/what appears (Deleuze 1978). However, so Deleuze insists, while Kant's philosophy explicitly remained within the limits established by the conditions of possible experience and did not venture into unchartered real experience, his nightmares did—as eventually did, even if only fleetingly, his theory of the sublime.

In order to formulate his own transcendental empiricism and specify the object of real experience, Deleuze focuses on at least two nightmares in Kant, two dark moments or reverse sides of his otherwise mostly luminous philosophy: the threat of a delirious thought and that of a lawless nature, illustrated respectively by Kant's confrontation with the spirit-seer and by his rejection of a cinnabar driven crazy.

The first nightmare is experienced by a precritical Kant fighting with all his might to distinguish himself, a serious philosopher, from the delusional and extravagant spirit-seer Emanuel Swedenborg (Kant 1900 [AA II]). Kant is aware of the dangerous proximity of both: "Moreover, I undergo this misfortune, that the testimony which I have stumbled upon … resembles so uncommonly the philosophical creation of my own brain" (Kant 1900: 100 [AA II: 359]). Furthermore, he is concerned with the risks involved in displaying in public these deliriums, which he compares with a cabinet of monsters:

Although a collector of objects of natural history puts up in his press among the prepared objects of animal procreation not only such as are formed naturally but also monsters, he nevertheless has to be careful not to show them too plainly and not to everybody. For among the curious there might easily be some pregnant persons who might receive an injurious impression. (Kant 1900: 111 [AA II: 366], translation modified)

This perilous mission, the establishment of a sanitary distance between the spirit-seer and the philosopher, anticipates the constitution of Kant's critique as a science of limits.[17] This becomes clear when, in his *Critique of Pure Reason*, Kant describes the dogmatic metaphysician with exactly the same adjectives and characterizations that he used for the spirit-seer. The temerity and madness of both the spirit-seer and the dogmatic metaphysician consist in that they abandon the safe territory of possible experience and illegitimately fly beyond it, imagining supra-natural beings and entities that they take for real—an act that is called "delirium."[18] For Kant, there is no such thing as an experience of the noumenon—the thing in itself, not submitted to the conditions of possible experience. An encounter with the noumenon cannot but be a delusion.

The second nightmare Kant is confronted with does not so much arise from the subject's madness or delirium, but is motivated by the threat of an unhinged or unruly world. Deleuze refers to a passage of the *Critique of the Pure Reason*, removed from the second edition, where Kant establishes three necessary conditions of knowledge: *apprehension* of representations in intuition— which brings unity to a given diversity; *reproduction* of representations in the imagination—which assures that preceding representations remain linked, through their reproduction in the imagination, to those that follow in perception; and *recognition* of representations as being instances of a given concept (Kant 1998: 228 [A 98–99]). Deleuze denounces that, with this, Kant inadvertently introduces empirical contents into the transcendental, for these operations belong to the psychological consciousness and to the structures of common sense (Deleuze 1994: 135). The figures of apprehension, reproduction, and recognition are, according to Deleuze, Kant's implicit defense mechanism against the terrorizing menace of an inapprehensible, irreproducible, and unrecognizable world beyond the scope of representation. Indeed, as Jean-Clet Martin has pointed out (1993: 17–19, 32–42), Kant narrates out loud this nightmare:

If cinnabar were now red, now black, now light, now heavy, if a human being were now changed into this animal shape, now into that one, if on the longest day the land were covered now with fruits, now with ice and snow, then my

> empirical imagination would never even get the opportunity to think of heavy cinnabar on the occasion of the representation of the color red; or if a certain word were attributed now to this thing, now to that, or if one and the same thing were sometimes called this, sometimes that, without the governance of a certain rule to which the appearances are already subjected in themselves, then no empirical synthesis of reproduction could take place. (Kant 1998: 229 [A 100–101])

The "monstrous cinnabar" (Martin 1993: 38) together with the monster of madness are what Kant's science of limits is to disqualify,[19] and are precisely what Deleuze, in his reversal of Kantianism, identifies as objects of real experience and instances of pure difference: absolute others or outsides that force us not to stay within limits but to go beyond them. For Kant, engaging with these monsters would throw us into a "broad and stormy ocean" (Kant 1998: 339 [A 235/B 295]), "into a shoreless ocean" (Kant 1998: 439 [A 396], see also Kant 2002: 353 [AA XX: 259]), whereas his critique keeps us safe on land, even if it is a small island.[20]

There is, however, a furtive and brief moment when Kant relaxes these limits and allows the faculties to work unhinged, liberated from common sense, and, in so doing, points to how to reverse Kantianism. This moment is his theory of the experience of the sublime—something too big for our imagination, something without measure, unrecognizable and unrepresentable. Interestingly, the sea is also the example Kant employs to illustrate this experience: "the broad ocean agitated by storms" (Kant 2007: 76 [AA V: 246]), "the dark tempestuous ocean" (Kant 2007: 86 [AA V: 256]). Deleuze reads Kant against himself, the Kant of the sublime against the Kant of the limits, and uses this measureless or oceanic experience to qualify his transcendental empiricism (Deleuze 1994: 146, 320–21). Transcendental empiricism has to do with plunging into the sea, with being cast back into the sea, with a particular type of movement that the sublime lays out and that literature will, once again, come to enact.

More important than the philosopher is the poet

Deleuze's transcendental empiricism is thematized and gradually developed from his very first works up to *The Logic of Sense*. Although he does not abandon this position afterwards, the problematics he engages with in subsequent books change the focus substantially.[21] *Difference and Repetition* is the text where transcendental empiricism makes its official debut, yet the monographs published before 1968 prepare the terrain and lay out the foundations. Over the course of fifteen years, Deleuze concentrates his energies on thinking difference—and thinking differently—on figuring out how to approach and apprehend, without undermining it, the object of an extraordinary experience.

In 1953, Deleuze published his study on Hume—his first book—which was followed by an eight-year period of silence wherein he produced just a few scattered articles. It is only in 1962 that a new manuscript, *Nietzsche and Philosophy*, saw the light of day. Deleuze subsequently accounted for this muteness in the following way:

> It's like a hole in my life, an eight-year hole. That's what I find interesting in people's lives, the holes, the gaps, sometimes dramatic, but sometimes not dramatic at all [...] Maybe it's in these holes that movement takes place. Because the real question is how to make a move, how to get through the wall, so you don't keep on banging your head against it. Maybe by not moving around too much, not talking too much, avoiding false moves, staying in places devoid of memory. (Deleuze 1995: 138)

Deleuze's silence is as eloquent as Plato's abrupt endings to his dialogues and Socrates' wandering around without reaching the essence or *eîdos* he sets out to find. This eight-year hole is the testimony of philosophy's failure: at first, Hume helped Deleuze to ground and shape an empiricism worth that name, an extraordinary empiricism. However, when Deleuze left the programmatic moment to jump into the effectuation of his project, he found himself at a loss, cast back into the open sea, speechless. How to present the object of this superior empiricism? How to say what cannot be said? How to write about "those things which one doesn't know, or knows badly?" (Deleuze 1994: xxi).

When Deleuze is about to tell us what he found during this eight-year hole, instead of going on, he suddenly interpolates a reference to F.S. Fitzgerald: "There's a fine short story by Fitzgerald, in which someone's walking around a town with a ten-year hole" (Deleuze 1995: 138). Philosophy fails to live up to the grandeur of empiricism; literature comes to the rescue. Or, rather, philosophy necessarily fails when trying to discursively and conceptually capture the object of transcendental empiricism, and this failure is indeed a triumph: the only way to approach the object of an extraordinary, superior, or transcendental experience, the only way to preserve the pure difference and novelty of this object, is to systematically fail in apprehending it. Only literature is exceptionally allowed to overfly this realm, precisely because its power of fiction will not be taken for a dogmatic affirmation, will not stabilize the object into a conceptual identity. In this sense, Deleuze's eight-year hole, instead of being just an anecdotic writer's block, turns into the matter of transcendental empiricism itself. Once he realizes this is the case, he combines philosophy's systematic failure, philosophy's circumventions and encirclements around the object of superior experience, with literature's plunging into the domain of difference.

In this context, reversing Platonism means repeating Plato's snares: make Socrates fail to find the essence or Idea of something and introduce a myth to provide a sensible face to that which does not have one. Plato is not inept when, for example, he sets his characters to inquire about the essence of beauty—in the *Greater Hippias*[22]—or about the essence of true knowledge—in the *Theaetetus* (Plato 1997e)[23]—and they fail miserably. On the contrary, Plato is using this failure as a tool to preserve the Ideas as what they are: something qualitatively different from things. The Idea of Beauty, as the *Greater Hippias* reminds us, cannot be reduced to beautiful things.[24] The way Plato has to oppose the sophists—those who claim that they are in possession of essences, and that they can teach them to others for a reasonable price—is not to challenge them with arguments but to refute them performatively by enacting the failure of any attempt to capture the essence, to reduce the essence to a thing.

Therefore, once Deleuze becomes aware that writing about what one does not know is not a defect that needs to be overcome, but the effectuation itself of transcendental empiricism—because "it is precisely there that we imagine having something to say. We write only at the frontiers of our knowledge, at the border which separates our knowledge from our ignorance and transforms the one into the other" (Deleuze 1994: xxi)—he resumes the activity of writing. This writing, from that moment on, will work closely with literature and, at the time of encountering the object of transcendental empiricism, will itself be literature: science fiction, a detective novel, a psychoanalytical novel.

As we have seen, the object of transcendental empiricism is that which shocked Deleuze into philosophical silence and made him call upon literature. From *Proust and Signs* onwards, Deleuze describes this object as something violent that "robs us peace" (Deleuze 2000: 15). Borrowing from Plato once again,[25] he distinguishes between two kinds of things: "those which do not disturb thought and [...] those which *force* us to think. The first are objects of recognition" (Deleuze 1994: 138, see also Deleuze 2000: 100–01), while the second are objects of an encounter, objects that cannot be recognized and impel us to go beyond common sense.

The first example that Deleuze provides of disturbing objects of an encounter—which can only be called "objects" inadequately, for they do not even have the form of an object—is, unsurprisingly at this point, a literary example: the narrator of *In Search of Lost Time* experiencing jealousy (Deleuze 2000: 8–9).

The lover of Proust's story sees his thought set in an obsessive motion through something compelling and forceful: a mysterious sign that the loved person emits, something undecipherable that contains "unknown worlds [...] worlds that have not waited for us in order to take form, that formed themselves with other persons" (Deleuze 2000: 9). This jealousy does not simply imagine what other lovers could have given to Albertine, since that would still be recognizable or representable; rather, it deals with a *terra incognita*,[26] an unavailable and "unknowable world."[27] Deleuze quotes Proust: "The rival was not like me, the rival's weapons were different; I could not join battle on the same terrain, give Albertine the same pleasures, nor even conceive just what they might be" (Deleuze 2000: 10).

As noted, the procedure of summoning literature whenever it is a matter of engaging with the object of transcendental experience is a recurrent procedure throughout Deleuze's works. A parade of writers and poets join Proust in assisting philosophy's failure: Fitzgerald, Artaud, Gombrowicz, Zola, Roussel, Tournier, Lowry, Carroll, among others, populate the pages of *Difference and Repetition* and *The Logic of Sense*. From this perspective, literature appears as an integral part, if not as the culmination, of Deleuze's transcendental empiricism, to the extent that he writes that "more important than the philosopher is the poet" (Deleuze 2000: 95).[28]

Three roles of literature in Deleuze's transcendental empiricism

Having shown to what extent literature is integral to Deleuze's transcendental empiricism, and how the reversals of Plato and Kant pave the way for this alliance, I will finish by summarizing three roles that literature fulfils in this project. First, literature provides the object of a superior or extraordinary experience. This object is difference, and Deleuze describes it as the "noumenon closest to the phenomenon" (Deleuze 1994: 222). Kant had banned from philosophy any attempt to engage with the noumena, that is, things in themselves, not submitted to the a priori representation or conditions of possible experience. The price philosophy would pay if it dared to challenge this prohibition is not small: it would end up in madness, extravagant delirium, on the same level as the spirit-seer's chimeras.

Deleuze, however, does not see a problem. As José Luis Pardo puts it, "it is as if Deleuze said: yes, of course these ravings of an undisciplined reason are phantasms, because *only through fantastic delirium* (and not through geometrical method, dialectical reason or dialectics of history) *thought can achieve* [...] the conditions of real experience" (Pardo 2011: 105–06). It is because these conditions do not exist "on the surface of the Earth, among all the countries our perception standardizes" (Proust quoted in Deleuze 2000: 41) in everyday experience, that philosophy has to search for them somewhere else. Yet the fact that this "somewhere else" is literature prevents philosophy from falling into dogmatism.

The second role that literature plays in Deleuze's transcendental empiricism has to do precisely with Kant's feared madness. Literature not only provides the object but also gives shape to the subject of an extraordinary experience: a fractured I and a dissolved self (Deleuze 1994: 145). The encounter with an unrecognizable object triggers a process of de-subjectivation wherein the principles and presuppositions that ordinarily regulate the subject's perception and understanding do not hold any more. In confronting this object, the subject faces its own stupidity (*bêtise*) (Deleuze 1994: 150–53), its own powerlessness.

Deleuze synthetizes this with Artaud's desperate formula: "I do not manage *to think*" (Artaud 2004a: 261, Deleuze 1994: 147). As noted, for Deleuze, this failure or inability to think is not a hindrance that should be eliminated but a "fortunate difficulty" (Deleuze 1994: 147) or necessary moment, in so far as it prevents the extraordinary, superior, or transcendental object from being reduced to and suffocated by the ordinary categories of representation. If the subject is empty, pure powerlessness, it will not impose on the object forms that do not belong to them. Deleuze examines Artaud's correspondence with the editor Jacques Rivière (Artaud 2004b, Deleuze 1994: 146–48) and shows how Rivière tries to reduce Artaud's condition to an empirical, contingent, and temporary situation that could be overcome, in a Cartesian manner, with the help of a good method. Against this, Artaud maintains that his experience is, to say it with Deleuze, transcendental. Deleuze, in turn, finds in Artaud the phenomenology of a new thought, the thought required to think difference (and differently):

> A thinking that no longer opposes itself as from the outside to the unthinkable or the unthought, but which would lodge the unthinkable, the unthought within itself as thought, and which would be in an essential relationship to it [...]; a thinking that would of itself be in relation to the obscure, and which by rights would be traversed by a sort of fissure, without which thought could no longer operate. The fissure cannot be filled in, because it is the highest object of thought. (Deleuze 2004b: 92)

The fissure of thought is, henceforth, a necessary condition for this new thought to operate. Deleuze borrows the figure of a fissure or "crack" from F.S. Fitzgerald's homonym autobiographical essay, which starts with the famous line: "Of course all life is a process of breaking down" (Fitzgerald 1936, Deleuze 1990: 154–61).[29] Fitzgerald compares his experience of breaking down with the cracking-up of a porcelain plate, and Deleuze finds in this story another depiction of the failure key to his transcendental empiricism. "The Crack-Up" is a blow that suspends the assumptions of common sense and opens the scope of perception to what lies beyond it. Fitzgerald puts words to Deleuze's eight years of silence: "a feeling that I was standing at twilight on a deserted range, with an empty rifle in my hands and the targets down. No problem set—simply a silence with only the sound of my own breathing" (Fitzgerald 1936). The subject is emptied, fractured, dissolved. This is the result of a blow, a violent encounter with an unrecognizable object, but it also becomes, as Deleuze points out, the object of thought: "henceforth, thought is also forced to think its central collapse, its fracture, its own natural 'powerlessness' which is indistinguishable from the greatest power" (Deleuze 1994: 147). Fitzgerald confirms this: "When I had reached this period of silence, I was forced into a measure that no one ever adopts voluntarily: I was impelled to think. God, was it difficult!" (Fitzgerald 1936). The writer confesses that, before this experience, he had done very little thinking, just adhering to what others thought, just re-presenting what was presented to him. Object and subject do not preexist, but are engendered and configured through the extraordinary experience. Literature serves the purpose of opening a window into that process, a process that cannot be scientifically recorded but only fabulated, for we are always already a result of it.

The third role that literature executes in Deleuze's philosophy is that of being the vanguard. Literature not only comes to the rescue when philosophy runs out of words but also presents philosophy with a style and a procedure that, according to Deleuze, philosophy needs to adopt if it wants to become truly modern, that is, if it wants to overcome once and for all representation:

> Every object, every thing, must see its own identity swallowed up in difference, each being no more than a difference between differences. Difference must be shown *differing*. We know that modern art tends to realise these conditions: in this sense it becomes a veritable *theatre* of metamorphoses and permutations. A theatre where nothing is fixed, a labyrinth without a thread (Ariadne has hung herself). The work of art leaves the domain of representation in order to become "experience," transcendental empiricism or science of the sensible. (Deleuze 1994: 56)

Notes

1. There is a very similar statement by Michel Foucault: "thought, at the level of its existence, in its very dawning, is in itself an action—a perilous act" (Foucault 2002: 357).
2. See, among others, Bogue (2012), who underlines Deleuze's "deep and lasting interest" (286) in literature; Buchanan and Marks (2000), who affirm that "it would be impossible to overestimate the importance of literature to Gilles Deleuze" (1); and Mengue (2003), who goes even further by maintaining that, for Deleuze, literature is "indispensable" to philosophy, that it "haunts" Deleuze's thought and that it has an "almost obsessive presence" (29).
3. See especially Pombo Nabais (2013), who provides an exhaustive panorama of Deleuze's engagement with literature that follows a sequence of three related projects: transcendental empiricism, philosophy of nature, and philosophy of the spirit. Even though my analysis coincides with hers at certain points, my contention—and the path that I follow in order to trace the relationship between philosophy and literature—is that philosophical failure is key to understanding Deleuze's appeal to literature within the project of transcendental empiricism. As I will show, this is one of the reasons why Plato is a crucial interlocutor. Other authors have mentioned the link between transcendental empiricism and literature, but have not developed it, for example Zourabichvili (see particularly the entry "Transcendental Empiricism" in his *Deleuze: A Philosophy of the Event. The Vocabulary of Deleuze* [2012: 211]), or have just focused on a specific author or text, for example Murphy (2000). Smith (1996) has explored Deleuze's theory of sensation in relation to art in general.
4. According to Depraz (2011), "the rigour of Deleuze's thought depends on the upholding of the formal purity of the Kantian transcendental together with the elevation of the empirical to the dignity of a philosophy worth that name" (133).
5. Deleuze's notion of "transcendental" is also indebted to Jean-Paul Sartre and, in particular, his essay *The Transcendence of the Ego: A Sketch for a Phenomenological Description*. Sartre (2004) conceives the transcendental field as impersonal or pre-personal, "*without an I*" (3), in opposition to Kant's understanding of the transcendental as lodged in the subject. Sartre's influence on Deleuze's transcendental empiricism is apparent in *The Logic of Sense*, for example in the following passage: "A transcendental field which would correspond to the conditions posed by Sartre in his decisive article of 1937: an impersonal transcendental field, not having the form of a synthetic personal consciousness or a subjective identity—with the subject, on the contrary, being always constituted" (Deleuze 1990: 98–99). Deleuze, however, goes beyond Sartre and refuses to preserve the form of consciousness for the transcendental field, even if it is an

    impersonal consciousness, because this would entail conceptualizing this field in
    the image of that which it is supposed to ground (Deleuze 1990: 105).
6   In particular, Schelling defined positive philosophy as an "empirical apriorism" or
    an "empiricism of the *a priori*" (1856–61: 130).
7   "The philosopher who perhaps has been the deepest into the essence of empiricism
    is the idealist Schelling, by showing us the fact of the world as something
    irreducible that imposes upon us, and by inventing a sort of transcendental
    empiricism that might be legitimate, and even more legitimate than the
    transcendental idealism" (Wahl 1965: 164).
8   In his article on Hume for François Châtelet's *Histoire de la philosophie*, Deleuze
    defends the need to rescue empiricism from the history of philosophy, which has
    reduced it to a sterile dispute about innatism. Against this, returning to Hume
    restores empiricism as a genuinely creative doctrine, on the same level, for Deleuze,
    as science fiction (Deleuze 2004c: 162).
9   This is Deleuze's synthesis of Hume's philosophy: "Whether as relations of ideas
    or as relations of objects, relations are always external to their terms" (Deleuze
    1991b: 66).
10 This idea is repeated in *Difference and Repetition*: "A book of philosophy should be
    in part a very particular species of detective novel, in part a kind of science fiction"
    (Deleuze 1994: xx).
11 For this account of experience, see, for example, Deleuze (Deleuze 1994: 139–46).
12 Again, this move was anticipated by Schelling: "Schelling [...] introduced, through
    Naturphilosophie, the themes of construction and production into the narrow
    territory of transcendental philosophy" (Toscano 2004: 108).
13 "The idea of the possible appears when, instead of grasping each existent in its
    novelty, the whole of existence is related to a preformed element, from which
    everything is supposed to emerge by simple 'realisation'" (Deleuze 1991a: 20).
14 "A superior empiricism [...] an essentially *plastic* principle that is no wider than
    what it conditions, that changes itself with the conditioned and determines itself in
    each case along with what it determines" (Deleuze 2002: 50).
15 "One must not elevate oneself to the conditions as conditions of all possible
    experience, but as conditions of real experience: Schelling had already proposed
    this aim and defined his philosophy as a superior empiricism; this formulation
    also applies to Bergsonism. These conditions [...] are not broader than what is
    conditioned" (Deleuze 2004a: 35, translation modified).
16 If the *Sophist*, according to Deleuze, does not present a myth, it is because this
    dialogue is not looking for the authentic or the good—which would be the
    philosopher, but for the inauthentic or the bad—the sophist, the impostor (Deleuze
    1994: 61, Deleuze 1990: 257).
17 For a detailed account of Kant's fear of madness and its relationship with his critical
    enterprise, see David-Ménard 1990.

18 *Schwärmen, Schwärmerei*, are translated by Paul Guyer and Allen W. Wood as "enthusiasm." See Kant (1998: 119 [B xxxiv], 226 [B 128], 659 [A 770/B 798]).
19 This disqualification does not get fully accomplished until the third critique, the *Critique of Judgement*. It is in the "First Introduction," which Kant left unpublished and replaced with a shorter text, where the fear of a lawless world and the strong response to it are more apparent. To the threat of a limitless diversity and heterogeneity of natural forms, Kant opposes a "subjectively necessary, transcendental *presupposition*": that this diversity and heterogeneity do "not belong in nature, but that, instead, nature is fitted for experience as an empirical system through the affinity of particular laws under more general ones" (Kant 2007: 324 [AA XX: 209]). For an analysis of the problematic of the multiple in Kant and his response in the *Critique of Judgement*, see Martin (1993: 29–31) and Sánchez Madrid (2011: 11–84).
20 "This land, however, is an island, and enclosed in unalterable boundaries by nature itself. It is the land of truth (a charming name), surrounded by a broad and stormy ocean, the true seat of illusion" (Kant 1998: 339 [A 235–36/B 294–95]).
21 The notion of "transcendental empiricism" resurfaces in Deleuze's last written work, "Immanence: A Life," bearing witness to the fact that this approach has not been given up (Deleuze 2007a: 384).
22 This dialogue famously ends with Socrates's ironic confession of his failure: "Hippias, my friend, you're a lucky man, because you know which activities a man should practice, and you've practiced them too—successfully, as you say. But I'm apparently held back by my crazy luck. I wander around and I'm always getting stuck. If I make a display of how stuck I am to you wise men, I get mud-spattered by your speeches when I display it. You all say what you just said, that I am spending my time on things that are silly and small and worthless" (Plato 1997a: 921 [304b–c]).
23 Deleuze (1994: 149) points out that the failure in this dialogue is precisely motivated by Plato's encounter with difference (*diaphora*).
24 In interrogating Hippias the sophist, Socrates wants to know "not what is a fine thing, but what is the fine" (Plato 1997a: 905 [287e]).
25 In particular, from a fragment that belongs to the *Republic* (Plato 1997b: 1140 [523b–524d]). Note that Plato describes the objects that force us to think, that "summon thought," through a vocabulary of violence: "strike," "provoke," "compel," "awaken," "summon," etc.
26 Deleuze quotes Proust: "It was a terrible terra incognita in which I had just landed, a new phase of unsuspected sufferings that was beginning" (Deleuze 2000: 10, 139).
27 "Jealousy is no longer simply the explication of *possible worlds* enveloped in the beloved (where others, like myself, can be seen and chosen), but the discovery of the *unknowable world* that represents the beloved's own viewpoint" (Deleuze 2000: 139).

28 The centrality of literature and art in general is further emphasized through the role it plays for two philosophers Deleuze is especially influenced by: Nietzsche and Bergson. Art realizes Nietzsche's program (Deleuze 2002: 102–03, 185), while it helps Bergson thematize the true reality and nature of duration against the distorted version of it that science provides. Frédéric Worms reads Bergson's relationship to art in a manner that applies to Deleuze's relationship to literature: "[Bergson] takes *the fact of art as an evidence of the possibility of metaphysics*, as if the practice of the artist had solved in advance (and without knowing it) the problems that the philosopher's theory encounters" (Worms 2013: 155).
29 Émile Zola examines the idea of a hereditary *fêlure* in *La bête humaine*, and this is another source of Deleuze's notion of fissure (Deleuze 1990: 321–34).

Bibliography

Artaud, A. (2004a), "Au docteur Allendy. Paris, 30 novembre 1927," in *Œuvres*, 260–62, Paris: Gallimard-Quarto.

Artaud, A. (2004b), "Correspondance avec Jacques Rivière," in *Œuvres*, 69–83, Paris: Gallimard-Quarto.

Beckett, S. (1989), *Worstward Ho*, in *Nohow On*, 99–128, London: John Calder.

Bogue, R. (2012), "Deleuze and Literature," in D.W. Smith and H. Somers-Hall (eds), *The Cambridge Companion to Deleuze*, 286–306, Cambridge: Cambridge University Press.

Buchanan, I., and Marks, J., eds (2000), *Deleuze and Literature*, Edinburgh: Edinburgh University Press.

David-Ménard, M. (1990), *La folie dans la raison pure: Kant lecteur de Swedenborg*, Paris: Vrin.

Deleuze, G. (1978), *Les cours de Gilles Deleuze*, 14 March. Available online: https://www.webdeleuze.com/textes/58 (accessed May 15, 2018).

Deleuze, G. (1987), *Les cours de Gilles Deleuze*, 12 May. Available online: https://www.webdeleuze.com/textes/148 (accessed May 15, 2018).

Deleuze, G. (1990), *The Logic of Sense*, trans. M. Lester and C. Stivale, London: The Athlone Press.

Deleuze, G. (1991a), *Bergsonism*, trans. H. Tomlison and B. Habberjam, New York: Zone Books.

Deleuze, G. (1991b), *Empiricism and Subjectivity: An Essay on Hume's Theory of Human Nature*, trans. C.V. Boundas, New York: Columbia University Press.

Deleuze, G. (1994), *Difference and Repetition*, trans. P. Patton, New York: Columbia University Press.

Deleuze, G. (1995), *Negotiations*, trans. M. Joughin, New York: Columbia University Press.

Deleuze, G. (2000), *Proust and Signs*, trans. R. Howard, Minneapolis: University of Minnesota Press.

Deleuze, G. (2002), *Nietzsche and Philosophy*, trans. H. Tomlinson, London: Continuum.

Deleuze, G. (2004a), "Bergson's Conception of Difference," in *Desert Islands and Other Texts 1953–1974*, trans. M. Taormina, 32–41, Los Angeles: Semiotext(e).

Deleuze, G. (2004b), "Humans: A Dubious Existence," in *Desert Islands and Other Texts 1953–1974*, trans. M. Taormina, 90–93, Los Angeles: Semiotext(e).

Deleuze, G. (2004c), "Hume," in *Desert Islands and Other Texts 1953–1974*, trans. M. Taormina, 162–69, Los Angeles: Semiotext(e).

Deleuze, G. (2007a), "Immanence: A Life," in *Two Regimes of Madness: Texts and Interviews 1975–1995*, trans. A. Hodges and M. Taormina, 384–89, Los Angeles: Semiotext(e).

Deleuze, G. (2007b), "Letter Preface to Jean-Clet Martin," in *Two Regimes of Madness: Texts and Interviews 1975–1995*, trans. A. Hodges and M. Taormina, 365–67, Los Angeles: Semiotext(e).

Deleuze, G., and Guattari, F. (1994), *What Is Philosophy?*, trans. H. Tomlinson and G. Burchell, New York: Columbia University Press.

Deleuze, G., and Parnet, C. (1987), *Dialogues*, trans. H. Tomlison and B. Habberjam, New York: Columbia University Press.

Depraz, N. (2011), "L'empirisme transcendantal: de Deleuze à Husserl," *Revue germanique internationale*, 13: 125–48.

Fitzgerald, F.S. (1936), "The Crack-Up," *Esquire*, February, March, April. Available online: https://www.esquire.com/lifestyle/a4310/the-crack-up/ (accessed May 15, 2018).

Foucault, M. (2002), *The Order of Things: An Archaeology of the Human Sciences*, London: Routledge.

Kant, I. (1900), *Dreams of a Spirit-Seer Illustrated by Dreams of Metaphysics*, trans. E.F. Goerwitz, London: Swan Sonnenschein & Co.

Kant, I. (1998), *Critique of Pure Reason*, trans. P. Guyer and A.W. Wood, Cambridge: Cambridge University Press.

Kant, I. (2002), "What Real Progress Has Metaphysics Made in Germany since the Time of Leibniz and Wolff?," in *Theoretical Philosophy after 1781*, trans. G. Hatfield, M. Friedman, H. Allison, and P. Heath, 337–424, Cambridge: Cambridge University Press.

Kant, I. (2007), *Critique of Judgement*, trans. J.C. Meredith, Oxford: Oxford University Press.

Leibniz, G.W. (1998), *New System of the Nature of Substances and Their Communication, and of the Union Which Exists between the Soul and the Body*, in *Philosophical Texts*, trans. R.S. Woolhouse and R. Francks, 143–52, Oxford: Oxford University Press.

Lyotard, J.-F. (2013), *Why Philosophize?*, trans. A. Brown, Cambridge: Polity.

Martin, J.-C. (1993), *Variations: La philosophie de Gilles Deleuze*, Paris: Payot.

Mengue, P. (2003), "Deleuze et la question de la vérité en littérature," *E-rea. Revue électronique d'études sur le monde anglophone*, 1 (2): 1–94.

Murphy, T.S. (2000), "Only Intensities Subsist: Samuel Beckett's *Nohow On*," in I. Buchanan and J. Marks (eds), *Deleuze and Literature*, 229–50, Edinburgh: Edinburgh University Press.

Pardo, J.L. (2011), *El cuerpo sin órganos. Presentación de Gilles Deleuze*, Valencia: Pre-Textos.

Plato (1997a), *Greater Hippias*, trans. P. Woodruff, in *Complete Works*, ed. J.M. Cooper and D.S. Hutchinson, 898–921, Indianapolis: Hackett Publishing Company.

Plato (1997b), *Republic*, trans. G.M.A. Grube, rev. C.D.C. Reeve, in *Complete Works*, ed. J.M. Cooper and D.S. Hutchinson, 971–1223, Indianapolis: Hackett Publishing Company.

Plato (1997c), *Sophist*, trans. N.P. White, in *Complete Works*, ed. J.M. Cooper and D.S. Hutchinson, 235–93, Indianapolis: Hackett Publishing Company.

Plato (1997d), *Symposium*, trans. A. Nehamas and P. Woodruff, in *Complete Works*, ed. J.M. Cooper and D.S. Hutchinson, 457–505, Indianapolis: Hackett Publishing Company.

Plato (1997e), *Theaetetus*, trans. M.J. Levett, rev. M. Burnyeat, in *Complete Works*, ed. J.M. Cooper and D.S. Hutchinson, 157–234, Indianapolis: Hackett Publishing Company.

Pombo Nabais, C. (2013), *Gilles Deleuze: Philosophie et littérature*, Paris: L'Harmattan.

Rancière, J. (2013), "Préface," in C. Pombo Nabais, *Gilles Deleuze: Philosophie et littérature*, 11–17, Paris: L'Harmattan.

Sánchez Madrid, N. (2011), "Contingencia y trascendentalidad. La *Primera Introducción de la Crítica del Juicio* y la catábasis reflexiva de la Lógica trascendental," in I. Kant, *Primera Introducción de la Crítica del Juicio*, trans. N. Sánchez Madrid, 11–84, Madrid: Escolar y Mayo.

Sartre, J.-P. (2004), *The Transcendence of the Ego: A Sketch for a Phenomenological Description*, trans. A. Brown, London: Routledge.

Sauvagnargues, A. (2009), *Deleuze: L'empirisme transcendantal*, Paris: Presses universitaires de France.

Schelling, F.W.J. von (1856–61), *Sämtliche Werke*, vol. 6, Stuttgart und Augsburg: Karl Friedrich August Schelling.

Smith, D.W. (1996), "Deleuze's Theory of Sensation: Overcoming the Kantian Duality," in P. Patton (ed.), *Deleuze: A Critical Reader*, 29–56, London: Blackwell.

Toscano, A. (2004), "Philosophy and the Experience of Construction," in J. Norman and A. Welchman (eds), *The New Schelling*, 106–27, London: Continuum.

Wahl, J. (1965), *L'expérience métaphysique*, Paris: Flammarion.

Worms, F. (2013), "L'art et le temps chez Bergson. Un problème philosophique au cœur d'un moment historique," *Mil neuf cent. Revue d'histoire intellectuelle*, 21 (1): 153–66.

Zourabichvili, F. (2012), *Deleuze: A Philosophy of the Event. The Vocabulary of Deleuze*, trans. K. Aarons, Edinburgh: Edinburgh University Press.

8

Deleuze, Practical Philosophy

The Trans/disciplinary Basis of the Deleuzian Conception of Immanence

Guillaume Collett

Immanence: A life

Deleuze's usage of the term "immanence" conflates the immanence of causation (taken from Spinoza) and that of thought with respect to its object (deriving from Kant). For Deleuze, to be immanent is to be expressed by thought—which means not to condition unilaterally (as in transcendental-phenomenological idealism, according to Deleuze), yet also not to merely represent the preconstituted (Deleuze's critique of representation and of the prioritization of identity over difference in philosophy). To remain immanent, immanence must walk a tightrope between the two transcendent poles of thought: thought as re-presentational tracing of preconstituted analytic unities and thought as predetermined synthetic lens for apperceiving the given (both of which Kant conflates by modeling the transcendental on the empirical).[1]

A fully immanent model of immanent causality saves philosophical conceptualization from the traps of both representationalism and idealism, since it provides the necessary framework to think thought's immanence to what is thought—which is to say thought's difference from itself insofar as, when approached immanently, thought is an irreducible cause of itself (and thus a self-divider). In its circular movement of self-division, thought becomes the insubstantial "substance" of immanent causality, acting as a corrective to the traces of identity that Deleuze still identifies in Spinoza's conception of substance.[2] But, contrary to Fichte's absolute Ego, for instance, which effectuates a seemingly similar theoretical move, Deleuze seeks to relocate the absolute to an impersonal stratum of (equally transcendental and lived) experience. This move is not theoretically inconsistent precisely because thought's ontologically univocal self-division, or circularly oscillating duality, enables it to occupy both a transcendental and empirical position, and in its asymmetrical yet circular movement to twist the senses of both terms.

Ultimately, Deleuze seeks to relocate the absolute to life's auto-positional consciousness, to the extent that he subscribes to a conception of vitalism according to which life is "a force that is but does not act," a "pure internal Awareness" or "contemplation without knowledge," in short pre-personal and pre-subjective *habit* (Deleuze and Guattari 1994: 213).[3] Crucially, this entails a receptive passivity without the need for a subject and thus in need of a means of conceptual, semiotic, or asemiotic formation[4]—in short, an active, if still impersonal, formalism or *constructivism*.[5] Life does not spontaneously self-organize in Deleuze; its passivity (or non-teleological open potential) is antithetical to a "bottom up" genesis of life from matter. Hence the centrality to Deleuze's conception of life—and ontology more generally—of a formal process of selection, a double selection or "double articulation," as a progressive sifting of material and conceptual (or more generally formal) elements expressing immanent life as the index of their agreement.

Life, conceived in this way, thus becomes for Deleuze the site of the absolute, consisting as it does of an internal rift that does not counteract but rather assures its immanence; accordingly, the constructivism involved does not merely paste over or liquidate the difference in level (between receptivity and spontaneity, or force and form) but rather affirms it and thus immanentizes it. As he and Guattari put it in *What Is Philosophy?* (*WP*), conceptual thought "adsorbs" (rather than absorbs) the earth (Deleuze and Guattari 1994: 88).[6] The inactive forces of life stick to thought but they don't "fuse" with it[7]—even if thought qua immanence is ontologically "reversible" with them, as two irreducible facets of nonetheless a single entity (Deleuze and Guattari 1994: 38). Immanence—which Deleuze considers as a self-immanent topological "plane" or surface with n dimensions—can be considered somewhat like a Möbius strip, whose obverse and reverse surfaces, or its outside and inside (force and form), are ultimately coextensive with one another if functionally separated at all times.

The reversibility of Deleuze's model is clear from the immanently causal dynamic involved (according to which a fixed starting and end point cannot be determined). Ronald Bogue (2017) has helped clarify the reasons for the non-fusional aspect by showing how Deleuze's critique of the "neo-finalism" of someone like Raymond Ruyer—on whom Deleuze in large part bases his understanding of auto-positional consciousness—uncovers the need to strip out any vestiges of teleology or finality from life's passive consciousness.[8] Distinguishing the active formation of thought—be it ostensibly human (such as in philosophy) or more directly nonhuman (such as in animal biosemiotics)[9]—from the passive forces immanently affecting it enables a break with a preconstituted representationalist naturalism that would guide thought extrinsically.[10]

Rather, the immanent conception of a "Nature-thought" (Deleuze and Guattari 1994: 88–89, 38) or "Being-thought" (Deleuze and Guattari 1994: 88),[11] a dimension of thought flush with yet also disjoined from a dimension of force, enables nature to be conceived as carried away with, to be reconstructed anew by, thought (latched onto its immanent undercarriage or reverse surface). By remaining separate (even when reversible), force and form remain open to their non-exhaustion in one other, to each one's infinite reserve of diversity in its respective domain, and to the inability of either half to ever fully account for the totality of the other. This is the condition for immanent life to be able to generate novelty, as what appears as singular between these two sets or multiplicities. This underscores the dual influence of Kant and Spinoza on Deleuze's conception of immanence: thought (and form more generally) always equals and matches experience with a mutually informing structure (but, contra Kant, the one does not unilaterally trace the other), and the causality of this two-way dynamic must be absolutely equal, or respect the radical irreducibility of both levels, to guarantee its immanence (and, contra Spinoza, through a model of expressionism that prioritizes difference over identity).

When conceived immanently, thought thus constructs a plane of Nature-thought, which is, in principle, irreducible to either of its component halves. This is what makes it a "plane of immanence" (Deleuze and Guattari 1994: Ch. 2)—prioritizing one half over the other, or vice versa, reintroduces transcendence. What guarantees the plane's immanence is thus its univocity: the establishment of *a plane* (in the singular) that manages to wrest itself from the priority of either one of its two irreducible facets over the other (equivocity). Moreover, it is because the plane's two facets or powers never evaporate in their immanence that immanence can be pinpointed beyond the indeterminacy (no beginning and no end) of a model of immanent causality (contra the commonplace misreading of Spinozist substance and Deleuzian immanence that "if it is everywhere, then it is nowhere in particular"[12]). Rather than that of "where" to locate immanence, the question then becomes: What mechanism (or "machine"[13]) is currently in place accounting for an immanent instantiation (or "event") of the articulation of the plane's two halves; or, conversely, what mechanisms are preventing the two halves from being equally articulated? Or rather, how are these mechanisms or machines being either allowed to function or conversely being tampered with?

The two powers or facets of the plane of immanence—"Thought" and "Nature" (Deleuze and Guattari 1994: 38)—are hence hypostatized as the "*matter* of being" and the "*image* of thought" (Deleuze and Guattari 1994: 38, emphasis added, translation modified) (recto and verso), only when thought referentially (or in logic, denotatively), as in the scientific conception of nature as external to thought's construction of it—the scientific "function" (Deleuze and Guattari 1994: Ch. 5) acting machinically to deprive the plane of its immanence. In other words, the two facets of the plane can only be extrinsically opposed (as a substantial equivocity rather than a real equivocity internal to, and bypassed by, univocity) at the risk of transcending and losing touch with the immanent element of their articulation, and indeed thought and nature (or thought and being) when opposed mutate into *matter* and *image*. When thought immanently, nature loses its materiality, merging non-fusionally with its construction by thought (by the machinic concept) as an *incorporeal* (and not ideal) event; conversely, at the same time, thought loses its image and relation of reference (or of logical denotation), itself becoming-one (or rather, non-fusionally, becoming-univocal) with nature's parallel becoming-incorporeal (namely the event that immanent, conceptual, non-imagistic, thought expresses).[14] Put otherwise, the concept is grounded *in the event it expresses*, an event that as incorporeal (and moreover as incorporeal *becoming*) bypasses the distinction between thought (or concept) and nature (that which is singularly expressed as an event of thought beyond thought).[15]

The unity of the plane of immanence—comprised of two absolutely equal "halves" ("Thought" and "Nature," "being" and "thinking" when dualized-hypostatized) (Deleuze and Guattari 1994: 38)—should therefore be understood as the expressed end result of an immanent (i.e., equipoise) and ongoing practice of conceptualizing force; thus the plane is constantly being produced (it is evental and in a constant state of becoming). When force is conceptualized "immanently" (which is to say without prioritizing form or force), an "event" of immanence is expressed by the concept, "immanent" to that singular bundle of forces (which is not to say, of course, empirically induced from it). The philosophical concept must be "constructed" (Deleuze and Guattari 1994: 36) rather than being prefabricated, since it is capable of being immanent (i.e., of expressing events) only to the extent that it is both sufficiently adaptable to forces' singularity *and* adequately able to calibrate its angle of formation so as to still be creative: capable of expressing something *in* force, beyond force, more fundamental than force itself, namely non-teleological and immanent (i.e., conceptually expressed) life-in-process.

In this way, life short-circuits the gap between reality and fiction, practice and speculation, and *is* this short circuit.[16] The immanent measure of this short circuiting is the plane's capacity to retain consistency (or reversibility), which is to say to intra-communicate as a single plane and not to branch off as two separate worlds. The plane is nothing more than the insubstantial or evental effect of the "immanent" (equal or non-prioritizing) articulation of "its" two halves. Yet despite being merely an epiphenomenal secretion, or insubstantial relational void between powers, the plane still grounds—and is thus deeper or more fundamental than—both Thought and Nature when considered separately or outside their co-articulation (if it wasn't, they would transcend it as non-equal halves or powers). This appears to be primarily accounted for by Deleuze's attribution to this plane (in the singular) of an evental (and, importantly, "*non-organic*"[17]) *life* that the concept expresses beyond force (or beyond inactive vitalism),[18] as the expressed substrate or consistency of concept-force relations.[19] Immanence, in short, is the resulting index or symptom of an equally speculative and practical (that is to say immanent) act of thought, which means one close enough to force to be open to the real or outside, yet one with enough novelty or creativity to affirm thought's irreducible power (indeed its absolutely equal power to all of force).

A philosophical event is ultimately an image or visibility *for itself*, an impersonal perception (or "percept"), which traces on the obverse surface of the plane a conceptually mediated movement inseparable (yet not indistinguishable) from a parallel movement on the reverse surface (Deleuze and Guattari 1994: 38), as affect or sensation materially drives the event's impersonal perception yet is in turn immanently guided in its unfolding by the perceptual (and thus affective) avenues opened up by the concept. This happens "at infinite speed" (Deleuze and Guattari 1994: 21, 42), i.e., through the topological continuity (non-fusional reversibility) of affect and percept. Spatio-temporal distance is only reintroduced (as a perceptual distortion) by transcendent centers of subjective synthesis,[20] which serve to "decelerate" events as denotative and dualized images (perceptions *of* affections). In sum, as life spontaneously and non-teleologically surveys itself, conceptual construction intervenes in this process to determinately guide it (producing a "philosophical" event).

For Deleuze, philosophy, as the study of the plane of Nature-thought, thus both studies ontology or life, according to Deleuze's oft-quoted "Philosophy merges with ontology" (Deleuze 2004b: 205), and also *is* an instantiation of this very process. This is why Deleuze immediately continues this quote with the under-discussed "but ontology merges with the univocity of Being" (Deleuze 2004b: 205), which outstrips specifically *philosophical* activity. Philosophy both studies life's auto-positional consciousness, the double articulation of force and form, and *is* a local example of life's constructive self-expression, as the brain conceptually reacts onto its passive sensations or habits (via immanent survey) to express philosophical events.[21] Deleuze and Guattari consider the features of the plane of immanence to ultimately be accounted for by the topological functioning, or auto-positional self-survey, of the brain when close to a chaotic state (Deleuze and Guattari 1994: 209). This makes the brain the "faculty" of the "creation" of concepts (Deleuze and Guattari 1994: 211), but really concepts auto-produce both *themselves and the brain* by intervening machinically[22] in the brain's topological folds to express a "philosophical" instantiation of the brain—rather than an artistic or scientific one, these being the "three aspects under which the brain becomes subject, Thought-brain" (Deleuze and Guattari 1994: 210) (rather than subjected *to* power relations[23]). Philosophy's constructivism (its concepts) is thus immanent to the brain's self-expression, in the sense that the brain does not precede its disciplinary activation even if it is the translational medium that *all* (un-subjected/un-subjectified) disciplines must use to construct life (and indeed the brain) via their irreducible methods, each discipline forging a distinct relation between brain and chaos and thus establishing an autonomous disciplinary plane on which to express life (Deleuze and Guattari 1994: 206, 208).

This allows us to better understand how the plane of immanence can be both philosophy's specific disciplinary object and a "nonphilosophical" or "prephilosophical" presupposition (Deleuze and Guattari 1994: 41) internal to philosophy, as that through which philosophy thinks about ontology (or through which it thinks about that through which philosophy thinks, namely auto-positional consciousness). While this plane is not itself transdisciplinary, manifesting only the philosophical concept's relation to chaos (or its expression of the brain's chaoid state), it still points beyond philosophy to the brain's auto-positional consciousness and moreover to the concept's machinic processes—which I will show in the final section directly immerse philosophy in a kind of transdisciplinary practice. To sum up this section, Deleuze's philosophically unique conception of immanence consists of three essential components: absolute equality of powers (thinking/being or thought/Nature); reversibility of powers (without fusion); constructivism (the contingent construction of expression).

Expressionism in philosophy

Both facets of Nature-thought (passivity and activity, force and form) articulated together thus capture what Deleuze means by an "expressive" schema of being, which is to say one that does not emanate from a higher, transcendent source in which being (or however one terms the absolute) would be more strongly concentrated—where it has a greater "quantity of reality" (Descartes's Christian creationism) or exists as the retroactive *telos* of the process leading up to it, as in Plotinus's "One above being" that compromises his otherwise immanent interweaving of the intelligible and the sensible.[24] Expressionism means that a cause is grounded in its effect, which, since it as *effect* cannot by definition self-ground (otherwise it wouldn't be an "effect"), requires that the ground be opened up in and as that very movement, which is a movement of "self-causation" of a "self" that is internally split and *is* that split itself. Self-causation thus becomes the self-differentiation of what is nonetheless still univocally single (namely the split between cause/effect).

Deleuze conceives of expressionism in terms of a non-dialectical articulation of three terms: that which *expresses* itself, its varied *expressions* (or constructs), and that which is *expressed*. The logic is that what is expressed does not resemble its expression (contra Platonic mimesis) but does not exist outside it (recuperating Plato via an overturning). Expression introduces a difference or creative torsion between what expresses itself and what is expressed (the unsublatable irreducibility of thinking and being). We see this model clearly at work in Deleuze's conception of philosophical immanence. Inactive life or passive force (that which expresses itself) is filtered through the philosophical concept (a contingent expression or construct), expressing something *other* than inactive life, yet that does not resemble the concept itself even if it doesn't exist outside it, namely (conceptually) *activated* life: "Nature-thought," as an incorporeal event or plane of immanence (that which is expressed). Force acts, form reacts, immanence is expressed; or life expresses (i.e., activates) itself only through an open and non-teleological plurality of formal mediations (its expressions or constructs). Thus, immanence does not emanate from being or thought, but is precisely expressed by the concept's reaction onto (i.e., active selection of) force.

In his generally underappreciated 1968 text *Expressionism in Philosophy: Spinoza* (*EPS*), Deleuze reconstitutes an immanent model of expression, primarily drawing on Spinoza's *Ethics* (1677), and he does this ultimately by foregrounding the role of conceptual activity in this process, as a constructive practice of the concept. This has been too often neglected in the secondary literature, which tends to extrapolate expression from Deleuze's univocal reading of the attribute–substance relation (which is only the first of three "periods" of expression studied by Deleuze in the text)[25] or from Deleuze's reconstruction of the history of the concept of expression in the well-known chapter eleven ("Immanence and the Historical Components of Expression"),[26] while sidelining what is most fundamentally at stake in the book: a *practical philosophy* (to allude to Deleuze's much shorter, generally less misunderstood second monograph on Spinoza from 1970). In other words, the *constructivism* integral to EPS (the practice of the concept) is too often subordinated to a supposedly preestablished "ontological" model of expression at work in the text (purportedly self-organizing substance, substance as *causa sui*), whereas, for Deleuze, expressionism and constructivism presuppose one another (the expresser/expressed torsion passes through a contingent expression).[27]

Indeed, the blurb Deleuze wrote for the French edition makes it clear that what singles out this text—alongside its obvious originality in co-articulating Spinoza and the at least manifestly (if not latently) foreign concept of expression (Spinoza himself does not systematically engage the term in the *Ethics*)—is precisely its aim to determine the relations *between* Spinoza's "ontology (the theory of substance)," "epistemology (the theory of the idea)" (including the "genesis of sense"), and "political anthropology (the theory of modes, of passions and actions)."[28] These constitute the three sections of *Expressionism in Philosophy*, each corresponding to a "period" of expression, expression as such being strictly determined in the (indeed inter-expressive) relation between the three.[29]

One of the reasons for the text's underappreciation is likely due to the fact that Deleuze does not explicitly explain how the three periods are co-articulated or how they inter-express one another, and this more generally also accounts for the little attention that has been paid to the text's clear anticipation of *WP*'s explicitly meta-philosophical concerns. One way of putting it is that the book's ultimate focus or conceptual movement goes beyond it, to a problem that is presented as a kind of aporia, necessitating that we step outside the text to appreciate what it's getting at. This is clear from the book's final page, which abruptly and finally announces that "what is expressed" (in short the very object of the book, as a theory of expression) is "sense," a concept far from central to the *Ethics* and by and large ignored in the preceding nineteen chapters of *EPS*, not to mention lacking any detailed analysis when it is finally invoked. While this is more than made up for by *Logic of Sense* (*LS*) from the following year, this nonetheless presents the commentator with an unanswered question, namely how to determine the relation between both these texts and more generally how to establish why it is that expressionism in Spinoza could be said to express "sense."

Moreover, beyond this specific connection to the problematic of sense—which is not ultimately a fundamental concern insofar as I will suggest that for Deleuze it is folded into the larger problematic of immanence—the text opens up, yet does not fully address, the meta-philosophical question of what immanence means for Spinoza. In the book's conclusion, Deleuze all too briefly refers to expressionism in Spinoza as giving rise to a "specifically philosophical concept of immanence" (Deleuze 2005a: 322). This is moreover confirmed by an interview conducted by Martin Joughin (the translator of the English edition) shortly before Deleuze's death, quoted in the translator's preface, in which Deleuze notes that in this book he was attempting to "se[e] in substance a *plane of immanence* in which finite modes operate" (Deleuze 2005a: 11), that is, of making substance turn on the finite modes and on the concept. Even if only unveiled abruptly and even tangentially at the very end of the text, the plane of immanence (or "sense") as *WP*'s "prephilosophical" presupposition seems to tie together the three periods of expression, Spinoza's ontology, epistemology, and political anthropology, and moreover enables Deleuze to salvage what in Spinoza is salvageable after Kant. By writing that these three periods of expression express "sense" (or a "plane of immanence"), Deleuze thus explicitly acknowledges that Spinoza's metaphysics is only completed or held together at the level of implicit meta-philosophical considerations.

In *WP*, Deleuze cuts to the chase and explains that Spinoza was almost unique in the history of philosophy in being able to account, through his metaphysics, for that which is presupposed by all philosophical activity as such (Deleuze and Guattari 1994: 48)—which as I mentioned earlier is the contingent construction of life's auto-positional consciousness, far exceeding specifically philosophical constructivism. There are two components here: firstly, the prephilosophical "plane of immanence" on which philosophical activity relies and secondly the constructive mechanism, or practice of the concept, through which such a plane can be constructed. I will approach these two in this order, showing firstly how *EPS* extracts a meta-philosophical plane of immanence from Spinoza, and how this is further developed in *LS*, and then in more detail I will show how Deleuze develops a practice of the concept, through his reading of Spinoza, which accounts for the expression of this plane.

Deleuze and Guattari write, in the same passage from *WP* mentioned above, that in Spinoza:

> Immanence does not refer back to the Spinozist substance and modes, on the contrary, the Spinozist concepts of substance and modes refer back to the plane of immanence as their presupposition. This plane presents two sides to us, extension and thought, or rather its two powers, power of being and power of thinking. (Deleuze and Guattari 1994: 48)

Here, Deleuze is concerned less with substance, attributes, and modes, considered as positive metaphysical entities, than with the interdependent co-articulation of the "concepts" of substance, attribute, and mode, in the *Ethics*, and with the manner in which their articulation (in not prioritizing any one concept over the other or in articulating them immanently, at least when augmented by Deleuzian expressionism) brings out the plane of immanence inherent to any philosophical work, if buried beneath it.[30] Deleuze's key argument is that Spinoza manages to do this, above all, not because his concept of substance entails an immanent causality (this would be to attribute immanence *to* substance, as a transcendent entity from which immanence emanates) but rather because of the comprehensiveness with which his metaphysical framework lays bare, albeit implicitly, the plane of immanence built into the core of every philosophical work: a non-fusional equality of powers (of thinking and being) yielding an a-subjective, self-positing Nature-thought expressed by a practical construct.

As noted, this argument is prepared for by *EPS*, the second section of which centers on Spinoza's axiom of the equality of powers. The manner in which Deleuze both emphasizes and specifically reads this axiom is one of the text's most original features. These powers, epistemologically accessible via the attributes of thought and extension but far exceeding them, are in Spinoza the "power of thinking and knowing," and the "power of existing and acting" or "being and acting" (Deleuze 2005a: 118, 335)—referred to in the quote above as the plane's powers of "being and thinking."[31] In Deleuze's reading, this gives rise to a strong (yet ultimately only provisional) dualism (or equivocal tension) internal to Spinoza's (univocal) conception of substance (God or Nature). As he writes in the key closing passage from *EPS*, "what is expressed everywhere intervenes as a third term that transforms dualities [...] What is expressed is sense: deeper than the relation of ['real'] causality, deeper than the relation of ['ideal'] representation" (Deleuze 2005a: 335). In short, what is expressed is "the absolute in [both] of its powers, those of thinking or knowing, and being or acting" (Deleuze 2005a: 335). Sense (or immanence) is implicated or enveloped in ideas and in ideas' representations of bodies, but sense or immanence is only explicated and developed in and for itself when considered outside of conditions of reference (where sense is not conditioned by denotation).

The larger context needed to better understand these quotations is one of the book's central claims, developed in chapter seven ("The Two Powers and the Idea of God"), namely that in Spinoza the power of thinking and knowing is absolutely equal to, adequate to (indeed, as we see here, expressive of), the power of existing and acting (hence part two of *EPS*, which develops this notion of serial equality, is titled "Parallelism and Immanence").[32] This derives from the (in principle) power of any idea, in Spinoza, to formally redouble (in the power of thinking and knowing) any object (in the power of existing and acting, including any acting/existent idea), thus giving the attribute of thought (via its access to the absolute's power of thinking and knowing) the same formal extension, in principle, as the infinity of attributes partaking of the absolute's power of existing and acting (Deleuze 2005a: 120). This absolute equality of series combined with their radical difference in kind or parallelism (understood as a "noncausal correspondence" of series[33]), pinpoints the Spinozist absolute, in Deleuze's reading, as the disjunctive univocity of powers (thinking/being) or as a kind of onto-logical parallelism.

It is clear that, ultimately, Deleuze's aim in *EPS* is not to faithfully reconstruct the essence of Spinoza's work since, as we saw in the previous section, the authorial intentionality involved in concept construction only accounts for one facet of life's auto-positional consciousness. For Deleuze, the plane of immanence always exceeds the philosophical work since it is its end-product, the point of mutation where any initial authorial intention is far outstripped by a life of the concept implicated in it and explicated by conceptual elaboration. One of Deleuze's main aims in his reading of Spinoza is to pinpoint this moment of conversion as it occurs in Spinoza's work, Spinoza being for Deleuze the philosopher best able to construct the conceptual plane highlighting this process. This is attested to, above all, by Deleuze's affirmation of a deeper, expressed and incorporeal univocity ("sense") tying together these two irreducible powers, which conceptually owes little to Spinozist substance (other than its immanent causality) and rather marks the aporetic transition point from metaphysics to its prephilosophical presupposition. In general, I would argue that in *EPS*, Spinoza's metaphysical entities (substance, attributes, modes) are not so much discarded by Deleuze as fundamentally reoriented in relation to the novel discovery of a prephilosophical foundation at work in the *Ethics* (and in philosophy at large). This makes *EPS* harder to read in a sense than *WP* and *LS*, since it disengages its notion of immanence or sense from Spinoza's work by oscillating between Spinoza's metaphysics and Deleuze's own immanent problematic, whereas the latter texts are more securely fastened to a meta-philosophical overflight surveying the history of philosophy immanently.[34]

Indeed, this "third term" alluded to earlier, as stated, spans *EPS* and its sequel *LS*, where "sense" (now fully deployed as a metaphysical but post-critical "sense-event") is formulated in terms that shed much light on *EPS*'s cryptic conclusion and concealed project to develop a plane of immanence. *LS* formulates sense as irreducible to either conceptual signification or the designation of bodies in a spatio-temporal state of affairs ("real causality and ideal representation," as *EPS* puts it), in short words and things, bodies and language. Sense cuts across, or rather is presupposed by, this distinction (which, in terms of *WP*, is ultimately a "logical" or "scientific" distinction, rather than a philosophical one) and even *is* nothing else than the cut between concept/body. We see this clearly in the following quotation from *LS*'s "Fourth Series of Dualities":

> Although sense does not exist outside of the proposition which expresses it, it is nevertheless the attribute of states of affairs and not of the proposition. The event subsists in language, but it happens to things. Things and propositions are less in a situation of radical duality and more on the two sides of a frontier represented by sense. The frontier does not mingle or reunite them (for there is no more monism here than dualism); it is rather something along the line of an articulation of their difference: body/language. (Deleuze 2004b: 30)

Even if the terminology of "propositions" and "sense" is ultimately extraneous to Deleuze's overall understanding of the plane of immanence—*LS* being precisely an investigation of the plane of immanence when the *construct* in question is language (hence the term "expression" is used throughout the work in relation to, but far exceeding the remit of, the linguistic proposition)—articulated in this quotation is nothing else than the notion of a plane of immanence, as Deleuze will later formulate it in *WP* and already in *EPS*.[35] The plane of immanence, or sense, cuts across the exclusive disjunctive alternative "either monism *or* dualism" and presents instead a disjunctive synthesis or univocal cut ("an articulation of their difference"), whereby the difference or cut is ontologically prior to its relata and grounds them as such—even if, following the causal model of expressionism, their articulation "expresses" this cut, which thus does not precede them (even if, paradoxically, it is presupposed by them). This way, the absolute (the cut) and its powers (being and thinking) are laid out on the same ontological plane, wherein the one does not emanate from the other but rather they collectively express a plane of immanence.

In terms of Deleuze's reading of Spinoza, this enables the antiquated pre-Kantian notion of substance to be displaced from considerations of the absolute, such that the latter is no more "substantial" than the difference or cut between "its" two powers, whose parallelism expresses this cut as an index of the powers' equal articulation, as constructed through a practice of the concept that I will now explore further.

The three kinds of knowledge

For Deleuze, in Spinoza the genetic development of the three kinds of knowledge (imagination, reason, and intuition),[36] or the construction and articulation of concepts on the basis of affects, functions as the construct undergirding expressionism as such, amounting to the practical expression of a plane of immanence embedded in ethical praxis and—as I will discuss in the next section—in the philosopher's sociopolitical milieu.

In *EPS*, and throughout Deleuze's texts on Spinoza, the three kinds of knowledge return as central to his reading of the philosopher, pointing beyond a merely epistemological and practical means of engaging with substance, to a constructivism accounting for the expression of the absolute as such. Indeed, in *Spinoza: Practical Philosophy* (1970/81), Deleuze attributes much of Spinoza's evolution—from an ontology developed using the geometric method in the *Treatise on the Emendation of the Intellect* (1677) toward a practical ontological ethics—to the theoretical-practical discovery of the "common notions" (cf. Spinoza's second kind of knowledge).[37] Above all, it is the hinge between concept and affect provided by the common notions that gives them this central role in the *Ethics*, for Deleuze, practically and contingently accounting for the parallelism substance purportedly maintains itself, in Spinoza, between attributes and between powers. In short, in a reading that severs immanent causality from its reliance on substance as analytic principle of unity, projecting immanent causality instead onto a constructive auto-positional consciousness inhabiting the work, the common notions are needed to provide the constructive basis for this operation—functioning as a machine that zips together the two powers of the absolute (as manifested at the level of concepts and affects) so as to constitute it as such.

For Spinoza, the first kind of knowledge relates to ideas of affections, telling us as much about our own bodies as they do about those bodies affecting us (see *Ethics*, Book III, D1–2). As Deleuze puts it, this knowledge is imaginary or inadequate since while it "involves" the external cause of the affection, this cause is neither "explained" nor expressed by this knowledge (Deleuze 2005a: 147). Imaginary knowledge consists in this way of referential signs pointing outside themselves to a supposedly external cause (Deleuze 2005a: 147). In a later text from 1993, "Spinoza and the Three 'Ethics,'" Deleuze calls this knowledge "scalar" (Deleuze 1998: 139) since it involves the comparative knowledge of bodies ("this is further away than that," "here is warmer than there," etc.), situated in relation to a fixed or subjective point of view and through discrete and quantifiable measurement on a single scale.[38]

Nonetheless, in the same text, Deleuze disengages a second kind of imaginary sign from the scalar signs or ideas of affections, which he terms "vectorial" (Deleuze 1998: 139) and which are ideas of *affects*. Affects are derived from the affections but cannot be reduced to them. They still point to relations between bodies, but this time relations measurable not on an extrinsic scale of spatio-temporal extensity but rather on an intrinsic scale of intensity or *power*. Affects point essentially to relations of joy and sadness—joy in Spinoza being the affective index of bodily composition or ethical agreement (its converse being the affect of sadness).[39] Correspondingly, joy indicates an increase in power (sadness a decrease) or a "becoming-active" (Deleuze 2005a: 288) relative to the degree to which one incarnates the power of existing and acting—understood as a continuous scale, with decompositional materials (such as poison) at one pole and God (as *causa sui*) at the other. Affections are passive insofar as they affect a larger and more powerful individual into which they are actively absorbed as one of its immanent causes. Thus blood is composed of the passive affections of lymph and chyle (which itself subsumes lymph), while blood is a passive affection with respect to muscle tissue, and so on; whereas the human body conceived as an individual incorporates these smaller and less powerful collections. Affects are thus "vectorial" in that they have a magnitude or a degree of power, and a direction since their magnitude expresses bodily relations of composition and decomposition actualizing this magnitude.

Unlike the corporeal affections, imprinted directly on our body, the affects could be said to be incorporeal, gliding over the surface of bodies like events.[40] This is not to say that they are events befalling bodies as if they were distinct from them, nor that as events they are any less in touch with a body's essence than is an affection. Rather, the reverse is the case, since the being of bodies (their power of existing and acting) is ultimately change (variable relations of composition and decomposition contingent on their ongoing encounters), whereas affections only take positional snapshots of this change. Indeed, in one of his most daring (re)formulations of Spinozist metaphysics, Deleuze considers that the being of bodies (their power of existing and acting) hinges on their encounters with other bodies, and thus on their relations, rather than solely on their essences. Deleuze accepts that a mode's essence is fixed, pointing in his rather Scotist reading to an "intensive quantity" (Deleuze 2005a: 196) whose critical thresholds determine that mode's capacity for being affected by other modes.[41] The greater the mode's intensive quantity, the greater its power of existing and acting (i.e., the more individuals it can be affected by as passive relative to it). Yet, this does not lead to an ontological prioritization of essence over relation, in Deleuze's account.[42]

Looking at the attribute of extension, a mode's essence or intensive quantity provides a vital capacity for being affected, which *expresses* relations of mechanical causality between it and the bodies affecting it (Deleuze 2005a: 227–28). Yet the crucial point is that while a mode's essence vitally expresses modes affecting it mechanically (via this vital capacity for being affected relative to its modal essence), contingent encounters between existing bodies (relations of mechanical causality) "actualize" the variations of this essence (Deleuze 2005a: 211), as well as the passage from one modal essence to another. Encounters that exceed a mode's capacity for being affected by another mode (e.g., lymph + chyle relative to blood) actualize the essence of a third mode that subsumes them (here blood). Hence Deleuze (Deleuze 2005a: 195) considers a mode's essence to be distinguished from the essence of another mode, and from the attribute itself (conceived of as an undifferentiated intensive continuum), through these external, contingent encounters. Modal essence thus expresses modal existence—through a preconditioning vital capacity for being affected—but modal existence *actualizes* and individuates modal essence (a kind of processual Sartrian Spinozism).

This is indeed the purpose of much of Deleuze's overall reading of Spinoza in *EPS*, namely to make "substance turn on finite modes" (Deleuze 2005a: 11) and indeed on modal existence. From the point of view of affects, and the three kinds of knowledge, what this means, most fundamentally, is that a body's essence expresses, but does not unilaterally determine, its being—namely its power of existing and acting, and more deeply its "absolute" power. A body's relation to the continuous scale of the power of existing and acting (what I will term the "scale of power") is instead determined by at least three factors: firstly, a mode's essence, secondly, the contingent interactions that actualize a mode's essence or determine it to fall under the essence of another mode (which cannot be entirely reduced to its modal essence), and thirdly (in the third kind of knowledge), its relation to the "absolute" equality of powers (of being and thinking).

The second kind of knowledge—reason—involves the construction of adequate ideas (via the common notions), which are adequate precisely because they map out relations between bodies on the basis of their objective, which is to say intrinsic, ontological agreement (composition and decomposition), and not through an imagined, merely epistemological reconstruction of this agreement established by measuring their extrinsic relations.[43] Indeed, Deleuze's signal contribution to the literature on the common notions is arguably his claim that they are constructed not on the basis of affections but of a particular type of affection—or rather affect—the passive joys (Deleuze 2005a: 282).[44] According to Deleuze, the construction of a common notion is induced from the experience of particular relations of bodily composition and occurs once enough passive joys have been accumulated, through a slow, empirical apprenticeship (Deleuze 2005a: 149, 212, 265, 283). He notes that they are constructed on a progressive scale of particularization, moving from the most general common notion— which models what is common to all bodies (the infinite mode of movement and rest)—to the most particular ones, which model what is common to two or more bodies (Deleuze 2005a: 275–76).[45]

Nonetheless, the common notions, when articulated in the second kind of knowledge, appear to be as constrained as the scalar signs and equally subject to a transcendent, subjective viewpoint, even if this is now on the basis of relations of intrinsic, objective agreement. While common notions establish a rational break with the bodily habits initially inducing their formation,[46] and thus invoke the power of thinking and knowing, this bodily origin nonetheless means, for Deleuze, that an individual's accumulated network of common notions retains coded within it a trace of the notions' formative milieu and thus of the subjective viewpoint of the scalar signs (Deleuze 1988: 54–55, Deleuze 1998: 144).[47] As he puts it, common notions initially actually *reduce* our ability to become-active because they fixate on the "traces" of joyful passions (attempting to "preserve" joys and "ward off" sadness) (Deleuze 2005a: 246).[48] As such the common notions' strength is also their weakness, namely their rigorous basis in empiricism and their modeling of the world as it is (but not as it could be). What is missing in the second kind of knowledge is thus a certain margin of creativity or the untapped speculative-practical and experimental power of the common notions when fully dis-anchored from bodily habit, which brings us to the third kind of knowledge.

In the third kind of knowledge—intuition—we move from the adequate idea of bodily composition to adequate knowledge of "the essence of things" (*Ethics*, Book II P40S2 and Book V P25). Deleuze's entire reading of expressionism in Spinoza ultimately hinges on this shift and on the two distinct manners in which Deleuze formulates the Spinozist concept of adequacy through the concept of expression.[49] While for Deleuze an adequate idea is an expressive idea (Deleuze 2005a: 133–34),[50] he makes it clear that expressionism at the level of the idea is not expressionism *tout court*, but invokes only one power of the absolute: the power of thinking and knowing or the capacity of God's mind to formally redouble any object as an idea, expressing an idea-object pair or individual (Deleuze 2005a: 120, 132). Likewise, we saw that when it is applied to modal essence in the attribute of extension (the question "what can a body do?"), the concept of expression engages only the power of existing and acting. To cut to the chase, Deleuze develops no less than three concepts of expression, one corresponding to each power of the absolute (existing and acting, and thinking and knowing, or being and thinking in short) and a third (expressionism as such) corresponding to the absolute itself (the absolute equality of the two powers). This third conception (expressionism as such) builds on the first two but reformulates adequacy, reorienting both powers (and their modes of expression) in relation to it.

This shift from one conception of adequacy to another itself turns on Deleuze's reading of parallelism in Spinoza. While it is well known that Spinoza posited a non-relation between attributes (*Ethics*, Book I P2–3) that gives rise to a parallelism—or noncausal correspondence—between attributes in Book II P7 ("the order and connection of ideas is the same as the order and connection of things"), what is generally ignored is that two distinct conceptions of parallelism seem to emerge from this proposition. While claiming that attributes exist in a noncausal correspondence seems to necessitate that their "parallelism" be merely epistemological, in Book II P7S, Spinoza turns this on its head by claiming that a mode of extension and its idea are "one and the same thing, but expressed in two ways." This gives rise to what some commentators, including Deleuze, consider to be two distinct conceptions of parallelism in Spinoza, one epistemological (P7) the other ontological (P7S)[51]—the second of which appears to emerge in the transition to the third kind of knowledge, which we saw moves from an "adequate *idea* of certain attributes" to "an adequate *knowledge* of the essence of things" (Book V P25, emphasis added). Yet the key point, at least for Deleuze, is that ontological parallelism must pass *through* epistemological parallelism (Deleuze 2005a: 113), meaning that the non-relation of attributes (and dualism of powers—see Book II P7C) is not negated but bypassed.

While the psycho-physical parallelism of the second kind of knowledge is a species of epistemological parallelism, knowledge of the third kind uses such knowledge to drive the production of the very substance undergirding epistemological parallelism itself, namely the scale of power and, more completely, absolute, univocal sense. While we saw that knowledge of the second kind is not barred from such a production of ontological parallelism through its conceptual practice (preserving joy and warding off sadness), I noted that its engagement with the scale of power is nonetheless hindered by the conceptual and habitual form of its network of common notions. Thus, as Deleuze conceives it, the third kind of knowledge implies a process of de-subjection and dis-individuation through which the common notions disarticulate themselves from habit and memory (in short, from "ideal representation") and thereby reopen anew onto an objective affective field.[52] Yet this reopening does not simply imply a return to the pre-conceptual affects and signs of the first kind of knowledge, but rather entails what I would argue in Deleuze's reading is an ontological parallelism, or absolute equality, of concepts and *post-conceptual affects* freed from habit,[53] wherein the very distinction concept/affect is displaced (if not negated) in favor of the vectorial *sens* (meaning and direction in French) they collectively express, cutting through and animating them internally.[54]

Returning to the earlier quotation from the last page of *EPS*, what is then "deeper" than the expressionism of the power of thinking and knowing (the power to particularize or to create idea-object pairs), and deeper than the expressionism of the power of existing and acting (the vital expression of mechanical causality or more generally of modal existence by modal essence), is "sense" considered as the absolute in both of its powers (essentially, "what is expressed"). If as stated in my first section, Deleuze subscribes to a conception of inactive vitalism, then we can see here how the third kind of knowledge uses the power of thinking and knowing to *express* the power of existing and acting (the inactive, non-teleological capacity for being affected), activating life in the plane thought constructs in its immanence to being.[55] Hence, *Natura naturans*, the *expressing* power of existing and acting (what is retroactively individuated as modal *essence* or the vital capacity for being affected more generally), is *expressed* by contingent encounters as modal existence (*Natura naturata*). We can say that the third kind of knowledge causes a plane of immanence to insinuate itself into the curve of this torsion, bringing the contingency of conceptual practice to bear on the necessity, or ontological expressivity, of the power of existing and acting, thus reexpressing its being in the expressive immanence of the expressed to the expresser: in short, vectorializing modal essence through conceptual practice.

Ultimately, as seen, the point of Deleuze's theory of expression—as extracted from, modified, and projected back onto Spinoza's work—is to determine within the movement of expression the practical construction of a plane of immanence and to use this movement of expression to account for the immanent functioning of this plane.

The milieu of immanence

While it is well known that Deleuze and Guattari posit the plane of immanence as philosophy's "prephilosophical" presupposition, what is generally much less discussed is their complementary conceptualization of what we could term the "pre"-prephilosophical element philosophy presupposes. In terms of the model of the three kinds of knowledge discussed above, if we have seen that philosophy's relation to the plane of immanence is located in the relation of the second to the third kind of knowledge, this "pre"-prephilosophical element is located in the relation of the first to the second kind.[56] Deleuze alludes to this in "Spinoza and the Three 'Ethics,'" writing that even after the formation of the common notions, the sad passions of knowledge of the first kind continue to "subsist" beneath knowledge of the second, "doubling" the common notions with a dark or nonconceptual backdrop from which absolute rationalism's infinite "light" or infinite speeds cannot fully wrest themselves—which Deleuze compares in this text to the Leibnizian *fuscum subnigrum* (Deleuze 1998: 144–45). While, for Deleuze, the second kind of knowledge is indeed founded on the joyful affects of the first, it is instructive that in two of his last texts (*WP* and "Spinoza and the Three 'Ethics'"), it is rather the concept's relation to the sad passions that is equally emphasized. This amounts to philosophy's "pre-"prephilosophical element, namely the sociopolitical milieu of the philosopher—what *WP* terms the "*milieu of immanence*" (Deleuze and Guattari 1994: 87)—and what we can call the biopolitical construction of life.

While the first section of this chapter presented philosophical practice in Deleuze in terms of a construction of inactive life, this in turn needs to be supplemented with a consideration of the manner in which this constructive relation is always (bio)politically mediated and thus of how philosophical practice has a directly political function to the extent that it is capable of reexpressing, or breaking free from, its political construction or capture.[57] This supplementary dimension concentrates the shift undergone by Deleuze's conception of philosophy after his encounter with Guattari, though my main argument here is that Deleuze does not so much modify his understanding of philosophical practice after Guattari, as politicize a preexistent feature of it, namely his lifelong commitment to philosophy's "exceptionalism"[58] or disciplinary irreducibility. Moreover, this politicization of what is ultimately philosophy's *expressivity* (its capacity to conceptually express, and politically reexpress, incorporeal life), appears as a late vindication of the theory of expression of the 1960s after an initial critique undergone by it.

In what we could term Deleuze and Guattari's "first" political philosophy (their *Capitalism and Schizophrenia* project of 1972–1980), one finds a consistent critique of expression on the basis that it is ultimately idealistic,[59] its primary effects being localized within its own domain (the conceptual expression of incorporeal events).[60] What is criticized is precisely expression's *conceptual* mediation, or the philosophical practice at stake, according to which immanent life would be expressed at the edge of conceptual articulation alone. Instead, Deleuze and Guattari develop a dual framework according to which expression constitutes only one (namely, conceptual) means of formalizing experience—at least when considering the domains of language and the political—the other (drawing on Hjelmslev) they term a "form of content," which is radically nonconceptual (at least when articulated together with conceptual expression).[61]

If in *A Thousand Plateaus* (1980) the two levels are involved in an ongoing relation of mutual presupposition or "double articulation"—as an application of expressionism's absolute equality (its model of immanence) to the relation *between* expression and content—this does not in any way soften the edges of their absolute equalization of the conceptual and the nonconceptual. Thus, if expression in the early Deleuze itself turns on the equality of the conceptual and the nonconceptual, or concepts and affects/percepts, this is nonetheless developed *strictly from the viewpoint of the conceptual* (it is an ultimately *philosophical* model of expression). In his collaborative work with Guattari, in an attempt to push beyond the limitations of his earlier merely "philosophical" (if nonetheless immanent and nonhuman) model, Deleuze will therefore seek to arrive at a level of analysis where not only will the nonconceptual be given an autonomous, irreducible mode of formalization (later termed a "logic of sensation"),[62] but more deeply, they will aim to identify a transdisciplinary element accounting for both the conceptual and the nonconceptual, and which cannot be derived from either, which they refer to as a "diagram" (or "abstract machine").[63]

In the context of sociopolitical milieus, Deleuze and Guattari are particularly influenced in their conceptualization of the diagram by Foucault's work. In *Discipline and Punish* (1975), Foucault refers to Jeremy Bentham's unrealized plans for a "panopticon," which would survey prison inmates without their knowing, as "the diagram of a mechanism of power reduced to its ideal form" (Foucault 1979: 207), and prior to the distinction between the discursive and the non-discursive (if necessarily expressed through them). Deleuze and Guattari will extend further Foucault's claim that such a diagram must be "detached from any specific use" (Foucault 1979: 207), pointing to a latent organizational model (or abstract machine) spanning the sociopolitical milieu in which Bentham was writing, by considering the diagram to be "coextensive with the entire social field" (Deleuze and Guattari 2004b: 593n16),[64] which is to say immanent to its ongoing negotiation both from the side of power relations and from the side of resistance to them.[65] Indeed, for them (beyond Foucault), "the diagram and abstract machine have lines of flight that are primary, which are not phenomena of resistance or counterattack in an assemblage, but cutting edges of creation and deterritorialization" (Deleuze and Guattari 2004b: 585n39). Conceiving of resistance—and, beyond resistance, creation—as essential to the diagram's functioning has the benefit of dynamically implicating active processes of subjectivation (primarily at the level of collective thought and action, in *A Thousand Plateaus*) within the diagram's relations of power, so that the former are no longer largely passively subjected to the latter, as one tends to find in Foucault.[66]

When Deleuze and Guattari write that the philosophical plane of immanence implies its own "diagrammatic features" (Deleuze and Guattari 1994: 39–40, 75), we should bear in mind the twofold nature of the Deleuzo-Guattarian diagram: both passive subjection and active subjectivation—the latter of which they frame in terms of 'creation's *"resistance to the present"* (Deleuze and Guattari 1994: 108, emphasis in the original), which is to say expression's reexpression of biopolitical construction. Moreover, I would argue that *WP* takes the diagram one step further, establishing a final stage in Deleuze and Guattari's political philosophy largely absent from their earlier work,[67] in that not only does active subjectivation inhere in diagrammatic processes but the effect of creation is ultimately to break *with* the diagram and its milieu (if by means of them). *A Thousand Plateaus* primarily frames its politics in terms of active processes of subjectivation turning the diagram against relations of power, and so its model of resistance appears grounded in a transdisciplinary understanding of the diagram bypassing the distinction between the conceptual and nonconceptual formation of thought and action. This work reflects the post-1968 radical politics and social movements of the 1970s, which experimented with new social, psychic, and identitarian forms, engaging the very same diagrams (or "rhizomes") through which capital dynamically traversed society and psyche during the postwar years,[68] but does so with the aim of rerouting these diagrams against capitalism itself. By contrast, in ultimately emphasizing a break with the diagrammatic as such, or rather its embeddedness in a transdisciplinary practice, *WP* seems to adopt a more pessimistic stance toward collective political action, arguably cemented by France's post-1984 conjuncture after the capitulation of the communist faction of the Mitterrand government[69] and more generally in light of the creeping totalization of globalized capitalism during this period (what Guattari called the "Winter Years").

Hence, Deleuze and Guattari will characterize the establishment of a philosophical plane of immanence in terms of a process of "absolute deterritorialization" from its milieu of immanence (Deleuze and Guattari 1994: 87). At one level, through its diagrammatic features, a plane of immanence connects to a milieu's "geographical, historical, and psychosocial" movements of relative de- and re-territorialization (Deleuze and Guattari 1994: 88), in short a milieu's spatio-temporal extensity and its concrete social actors and socioeconomic processes. Whereas philosophical concepts are strictly speaking not diagrammatic but "intensive" features of the plane (Deleuze and Guattari 1994: 39–40, 75), having no extension only intensive quantity or quanta of immanence relative to their degree of absolute deterritorialization from transcendence and milieu.[70] Through a diagrammatic process ending in creation, the "infinite speeds" of absolute survey leave behind the relative speeds of the milieu. Nonetheless, these absolute speeds of creation are never fully separable from the plane's milieu of immanence (Deleuze and Guattari 1994: 88), meaning that one can never hope to establish a fully immanent plane of immanence, only the "best" plane, namely the one that "inspires the fewest illusions, bad feelings [sad passions], and erroneous perceptions" (Deleuze and Guattari 1994: 60).

Deleuze and Guattari thus consider that "thinking takes place in the relationship of territory and the earth" (Deleuze and Guattari 1994: 85), or of relations of relative de- and re-territorialization, on the one hand (milieu), and absolute deterritorialization on the other (creation). While Deleuze had long determined thought's outside (being) in terms of chaos (understood as the chance encounter of forces prior to their synthesis[71] or unsynthesized "purely disjunctive diversity"[72]), the notion of "earth" specifies further that thought's relation to being is always mediated by politics (as geopolitics).[73] The "earth" (*terre*) names the trace of chaos within territory, a territory's point of greatest intensity,[74] whose aberrant line thought must constructively map so as to be creative, which is to say expressive of a counter-earth (a Nature-thought or rather Earth-thought) resisting the *terre*'s *territoriali*zation in a milieu.[75] Relative de-/re-territorialization becomes the general name in Deleuze and Guattari's work for the transdisciplinary and diagrammatic hinge between thought and being. Talk of the concept "circling" chaos at "infinite speed" seems to invoke a spontaneous relation between philosophy and chaos (or the earth), but it is important to stress that this relation is always mediated by the sociopolitical milieu's relative de-/re-territorialization of chaos, or from a biopolitical angle its "control" of impersonal affects/percepts[76] and/or its subjectification of them as the affections/perceptions of hegemonic "opinion." In principle, for Deleuze, the brain is coextensive with the whole of nature through its spontaneous contraction of sensations or habits, which it immanently surveys opening thought onto being[77]; but this requires a creative act of subjectivation to first free the brain (as "brain-subject," Deleuze and Guattari 1994: 211) from both control and the transcendent centers of subjective synthesis that habitually subject the brain to the relations of power in a milieu.[78]

The relation between the plane of immanence's diagrammatic features and its concepts, and between the plane and its milieu, is ultimately accounted for by Deleuze and Guattari's theory of "conceptual personae," which is the third and final component of philosophical activity discussed in *WP*—after the concept and the plane (see Ch. 3).[79] Conceptual personae refer to the philosopher's impersonal, multiple, and unsynthesized (or schizoid) habits (as expressed in her affects and percepts); they refer to the brain's habitual inscription of presubjective, inactive forces, as the basis for philosophy's bio-expressionism (the expression of Nature-thought) (Deleuze and Guattari 1994: 64). If philosophy expresses life by conceptually activating it, the concept's relation to life is mediated by these schizoid habits.[80] Moreover, they write that these habits are irreducible to "psychosocial types," but not entirely divorced from them either (Deleuze and Guattari 1994: 88).[81] Rather, thanks to the diagram, the conceptual personae appear to straddle the milieu, on the one hand, in which they are actualized as historically and geographically determined psychosocial types, and where they are subjected to diagrams of power; and, on the other, the Nature-thought they express as a reexpression (or rehabituation) of the biopolitical construction of their experience.[82] If the latter moment points to an active process of subjectivation pitted against relations of power in a milieu, this is nonetheless expressed as an impersonal and incorporeal event understood as a becoming breaking with history (and geography) entirely (Deleuze and Guattari 1994: 70, 96, 110).[83]

While we have seen that philosophical expressionism in *WP* retains many of its earlier features, with regard to Deleuze's theory of philosophical practice from the 1960s, its key innovation is arguably to account for the plane's constructive element—that which mediates between the two sides of Nature-thought—in terms of the concept's articulation with a sociopolitical diagram. Thus, politics is to be seen as internal to philosophy itself, as its pre-prephilosophical genetic element. Philosophical practice consists in the expression of life, but to do so it must first deconstruct its own diagram (so as to reexpress life's biopolitical construction). In short, for Deleuze, philosophy amounts to the *counter-actualization* of sociopolitical diagrams. Politics, and practice more generally, appears therefore as philosophy's internal transdisciplinary element, but philosophy constitutes its autonomous practice by re-disciplinarizing this element or breaking free from it (if using it so as to achieve this very result). If the conceptual personae are thus philosophy's means of interfacing with the world, ensuring that philosophy has directly practical effects on habit, (conceptually expressed) immanence is what assures the regulation of this interface, providing a selective test for habit and an axiological orientation for thought.

Notes

1 See Deleuze 2006d: 385, 2004b: 122.
2 Almost the entry point for Deleuze's analysis of Spinoza is the substance-mode relation, which he considers to be ultimately equivocal insofar as their causality seems to asymmetrically privilege substance ontologically (2004a: 50). Donagan (1988: 63–64) has developed well the critique of Spinozist substance on the basis that it constrains and compromises a far more radical theory (that of immanent causality). Likewise, by critiquing its implicit self-identity and analytic unity, Deleuze seeks to differentially immanentize substance by making it "turn around the modes" (Deleuze 2004a: 377).
3 Regarding habit, see Deleuze 2004a: 90–100.
4 Guattari speaks of "non-semiotic encodings," such as the "genetic code," as "forms of code" (Guattari 1984: 74). Deleuze and Guattari discuss this in *A Thousand Plateaus* (1980) in terms of "forms of expression" (in relation to the organic strata, see Deleuze and Guattari 2004b: 65–66). See Eyers (2013: 162–70) for an interesting comparison of Deleuze's and Canguilhem's respective vitalist formalisms.
5 In relation to philosophy, see Deleuze and Guattari (1994): "Philosophy is a constructivism," involving "the creation of concepts and the laying out of a plane" (35–36).
6 See also Deleuze 2004b: 237.
7 "This is not a fusion but a reversibility, an immediate, perpetual, instantaneous exchange [...] there is only a fold from one to the other" (Deleuze and Guattari 1994: 38).
8 In Ruyer's (1952) terms this auto-positional consciousness is a "true form" (113) or, as Deleuze and Guattari (1994) put it, a "*form in itself*," which "surveys *itself* independently of any supplementary dimension" (210, emphasis in the original).

9   See Deleuze and Guattari 2004b: Ch. 11.
10 Here I agree with Montebello (2008) who clears Deleuze of the charges of falling into a naïve pre-Kantian "realism of being," "positive naturalism," "materialism," or "energeticism" (223, translations mine).
11 They also write it "Thought-Being" (Deleuze and Guattari 1994: 65), which seems preferable since it makes the equality of the two halves clearer.
12 Meillassoux 2007: 66.
13 In *WP*, the term used is "diagram."
14 On the philosophical concept's expression of a non-referential and incorporeal "event," see Deleuze and Guattari 1994: 21.
15 See also Montebello (2008): "*Physis*" in Deleuze is "insubstantial, impermanent, informal and impersonal" and "can only be thought" even if it is entirely real and not merely ideal (23, translations mine).
16 "Ethical *joy* [bodily agreement] is the correlate of speculative affirmation" (Deleuze 1988: 29). On the dynamic relation between the "speculative" and "practical proposition," see Deleuze 2006a: 186.
17 See Deleuze 2006c: 178.
18 See Deleuze 2005a: 227–28, 2004b: 215, and Deleuze and Guattari 2004a: 47.
19 See Deleuze 2006d: 385–86. What he terms "a life" is precisely this reverse side of the plane of immanence consubstantial with its events.
20 Deleuze and Guattari (1994) call these science's "partial observers" (129) because they lack the plenitude of immanent survey where perception is infinitely and equally distributed throughout the perceptual field. On Deleuze and Guattari's (1994) critique of Husserlian phenomenology, see pp. 142–45.
21 Deleuze and Guattari (1994: 211) highlight sensation or habit and immanent survey as the two functional and nonidentical halves of the brain.
22 I.e., through co-articulation with the "diagram" (see below).
23 Deleuze and Guattari (1994) speak of these three disciplines as the "disciplines of creation" insofar as they directly engage chaos (and thus the "Thought-brain"), constructively expressing life through their irreducible methods, contrary to the hegemonic "opinions" formed in sociopolitical milieus that have the reverse effect (covering over chaos and normalizing the Thought-brain) (204, 206–07, 209). Science, however, seems to straddle these two groupings as it relies on centers of subjective synthesis.
24 These are discussed in Deleuze 2005a: Chs. 10–11, esp. pp. 169–75, and in Deleuze and Guattari 1994: 44–46.
25 See, for instance, Nail 2008.
26 See, for instance, Beistegui 2010.
27 On the inseparability of expressionism and constructivism in Spinoza and Deleuze, see Alliez 2004a: 12–14. On constructivism in the *Ethics*, see Deleuze 2004c.

28 Translations mine.
29 The original blurb is reproduced here: http://www.leseditionsdeminuit.fr/livre-Spinoza_et_le_probl%C3%A8me_de_l%E2%80%99expression-2011-1-1-0-1.html (last accessed May 12, 2018).
30 See also Deleuze 2005a: 11.
31 Equating being with action and existence follows quite directly from *Ethics*, Book I, D1, D3.
32 Deleuze extracts this axiom from Letter 40, to Jelles, March 1667, III.142 [233] (quoted in Deleuze 2005a: 87): "The power of Thought to think about or to comprehend things, is not greater than the power of Nature to exist and to act [...] [A]ccording to [this axiom] the existence of God follows very clearly and validly from the idea of him." See also *Ethics*, Book II P7C, "God's [actual] power of thinking is equal to his actual power of acting." These two powers are dealt with in Books IV and V of the *Ethics*, on the "powers of the affects" and the "power of the intellect," respectively. Accordingly, Deleuze will often emphasize Spinoza's absolute rationalism, the idea's potential adequacy to the whole of being (for instance with regard to the "infinite speeds" of philosophical concepts in *WP*). Melamed (2015) has recently developed a similar thesis of absolute equality regarding the *Ethics*, but contra Deleuze concludes that this makes Spinoza a kind of dualist. Deleuze instead rediscovers univocity at the heart of equivocity (one finds the same strategy at work in his closely connected reading of Bergson). Montebello (2008: Ch. 7) has developed an interesting account of this cross-reading of Spinoza and Bergson as it pertains to the problem of immanence in Deleuze.
33 See Deleuze 2005a: 327, 335.
34 If *WP* develops a reading of the history of philosophy "from the viewpoint of the instituting of a plane of immanence" (44), *LS* develops something like a history of thought's topology conceived from the viewpoint of sense, distinguishing between the immanent "surface" (Stoicism, but also Carroll and structuralism), the ideal "heights" (Platonism, analytic philosophy), and the corporeal "depths" of thought (pre-Socratic philosophy, Heidegger and Nietzsche, Antonin Artaud) (see particularly Chs. 18–19). Again, in this text, metaphysics is not discarded as such, but rather reoriented in relation to sense as its prephilosophical presupposition and in relation to psychoanalysis and structuralism, which provide it with its practical or constructive and genetic milieu, all of which Deleuze also relates to explicitly ethical concerns (drawing primarily on the Stoics, Nietzsche, and Freudian psychoanalysis) (see particularly Chs. 20–21).
35 *LS* develops deep analyses of all three components of the plane of immanence mentioned in the first section above: serial equality and disjunction (here, of bodies/language), sense's univocal reversibility or topological folding (disjunctive synthesis), and detailed analysis of the kind of constructive machinery needed to express sense. It also develops thorough analyses of the event, considered

as incorporeal and inorganic life and as auto-positional consciousness, and in its phantasmatic theory of the "infinitive verb" develops a prototype of the philosophical concept. Nonetheless, Deleuze and Guattari will later consider the text to be compromised by its use of a structuralist and psychoanalytic constructive framework (both of which they comprehensively critique in *Anti-Oedipus* [1972]). WP will later explicitly reject the linguistic basis of the plane of immanence and its association with sense (Deleuze and Guattari 1994: 22), and will depend instead on the (anti-structuralist) model of the sociopolitical "diagram" (see below).

36 See *Ethics*, Book II P40S2.
37 See also Deleuze 2005a: 292.
38 Deleuze and Guattari (1994) imply that such knowledge can to an extent be conflated with the disciplinary domains of science and logic, which also operate through reference, quantification, fixed subjective or perceptual viewpoints, and via an exteriority of relations (subjects and objects), and more generally with the hegemonic "opinions" formed in sociopolitical milieus.
39 In Spinoza, joy is the affect by means of which the mind perceives the body's passage from a lesser to a greater perfection (a greater closeness to God as *causa sui*)—see *Ethics*, Book III P11S. Spinoza discusses the relations between the affects (joy and sorrow), the power of action, and the imagination, throughout Books III–IV in particular.
40 Deleuze develops this point most explicitly, both with regard to Spinoza and more generally, in Deleuze and Guattari 2004b: 283–92.
41 Deleuze (2005a: Chs. 12–13) develops this reading at length.
42 The reverse reading is nonetheless quite common in the literature (see, for instance, Hammond 2010: 228–29).
43 Spinoza introduces the common notions in the *Ethics*, Book II P40S1. Deleuze's reading of the common notions is found primarily in Deleuze 2005a: Chs. 17–19, and Deleuze 1988: Ch. 5. On this reading, see Hardt 1993: Ch. 3.
44 For a critique of Deleuze on this point, see Macherey 1997: 152–55.
45 See *Ethics* Book II P39–40, especially P40S1.
46 On the first kind of knowledge and habit, see Deleuze 1988: 49.
47 In terms of Deleuze and Guattari's terminology, we can call such an acquired network a *plan*—in the sense of both a spatial mapping and a transcendental plane or image of thought.
48 Hence, if common notions themselves are adequate, the syntactical networks they form to constitute a plan (on the basis of habit and memory) are subjective and belong to "ideal representation" (2005a: 335).
49 Indeed, in WP, Deleuze considers the plane of immanence to emerge precisely in Book V where the third kind of knowledge is elaborated (Deleuze and Guattari 1994: 48).

50 Adequacy first appears in Definition 4 of Book II of the *Ethics*, where Spinoza defines an adequate idea as "true" in excess of the epistemological contact with its object (i.e., true in God's mind and not only in the idea as a filled denotation). Adequacy thus goes beyond representation and indication to the "internal conformity of the idea with something it expresses" (Deleuze 2005a: 133–34).
51 See Melamed 2015 and Deleuze 2005a: 113, 127.
52 This point is particularly emphasized in Deleuze (1988: 23–24, 29), where he argues for the connection between the third kind of knowledge and the unconscious or at least the non-egoic or non-individualized. In *EPS*, Deleuze emphasizes more the dis-individuating effects of constructing an idea of God, with which one's own individuality merges (Deleuze 2005a: 304).
53 In the third kind of knowledge, or in ontological parallelism, Deleuze claims that the "commonality" of common notions changes to mean univocity: concepts become expressive of univocity (2005a: 300).
54 Macherey (1997) puts it as follows: "The logic of expression that Deleuze finds in Spinoza is a logic of univocity, where things are thought in their being, since the act of thinking something is the same act that produces it, by which it comes to be" (146). We find this logic of univocity above all in *LS*, where Deleuze thematizes the Stoic dictum that when one says "chariot," a chariot passes through one's lips.
55 Hence Deleuze (1988) writes that in knowledge of the third kind, "there is no longer any difference between the concept and life" (130), life here being understood precisely as a post-conceptual affect. For the sake of clarity, it should be pointed out that incorporeal sense-events (or as Deleuze (1998: 149) puts it, "percepts") and post-conceptual affects (or "a life") are not one and the same entity but the two sides of the absolute's surface (Thought/Nature, recto and verso). On the percept's immanent "survey" and Spinoza's third kind of knowledge, see Deleuze 1998: 149. On the concept's internal "straining" in Spinoza toward the affects and percepts constituting the limit of conceptual thought as well as the essence of conceptual syntax, see Deleuze 1995a: 164–65.
56 More specifically, it is located in the relation between scalar signs and concepts, affects, and percepts.
57 This point has been generally underemphasized in the literature, along with *WP*'s directly political theses. Moreover, this reading of *WP* in a way reverses or adds a twist to Alliez's (2004b) claim that Deleuze's philosophy moves from a model of bio-philosophical expressionism (before Guattari) to a critique and counter-strategy of biopolitical constructivism—and indeed, for Alliez (2013), to an analysis of the biopolitical construction *of* bio-philosophical expression—insofar as I argue that, in *WP*, the former is then recuperated beyond and against the latter.
58 I am borrowing this term from Bianco's chapter in this volume.

59 See Deleuze and Guattari 2004a: 6, 25–26, and 2004b: 6–7.

60 The target and impetus of this critique become clearer if we consider the reliance of Deleuze's 1960s theory of expression on sense, language, and in *LS* (and implicitly in *Difference and Repetition*) a structuralist and psychoanalytic framework. On this point, see Alliez (2011, 2013). Correspondingly, *WP* will return to the earlier model of philosophical expressionism but subtract from it any reference to language and sense (Deleuze and Guattari 1994: 22).

61 This interplay of two forms, one conceptual the other nonconceptual, is particularly found in *A Thousand Plateaus*, Chs. 4–5 (on language and politics), where conceptual activity is examined in terms of discursive statements or "order words" doubly articulated with the non-discursive formations they presuppose and which are presupposed by them. On the conceptual, expressive, basis of order words in *A Thousand Plateaus*, see the reference to Stoic expressibles (*lekta*) and incorporeal events (Deleuze and Guattari 2004b: 95–100), shared with the philosophical concept in *WP* (Deleuze and Guattari 1994: 21). In short, what this means is that *A Thousand Plateaus* cannot account for the concept independently of the nonconceptual (and diagrammatic), hence the level of analysis of *WP* (the philosophical concept developed independently from any autonomous nonconceptual logic, determined in *WP* in relation to art) is methodologically prohibited in the earlier text. Similarly, in *The Fold: Leibniz and the Baroque* (1988), Deleuze will speak of "a regime of expression and a regime of impression" (2005c: 114), one conceptual the other nonconceptual, both "folded" into a single process that does not prioritize one over the other.

62 See Deleuze 2005b, and Deleuze and Guattari 1994: Ch. 7.

63 See Chs. 4–5 of *A Thousand Plateaus* for discussion of the diagram and abstract machine in relation to the social field.

64 See also Deleuze 2006b: 32, see also 30, 74.

65 See Alliez 2013: 219–20.

66 Deleuze and Guattari's (2004b) reformulation of Foucault is summarized in a footnote (585n39), where they signal their distance from him (within a larger affirmation of great proximity) in terms of a prioritization of *desire* over power, which they understand through the Guattarian notion of "transversality" (understood as the mutually constitutive and actively dynamic relation between deterritorializing desire and territorial institutions). The book develops this in terms of its concept of "assemblage" (*agencement*), conceived as the production of a collective agential subjectivity.

67 Although less central *politically*, this absolute deterritorialization is nonetheless anticipated by the 'refrain's processual development through its three stages, in *A Thousand Plateaus*, Ch. 11: chaos, milieu (and territory), cosmos (or plane).

68 See this volume's Introduction.

69 See, for instance, Deleuze and Guattari's 1984 text, "May '68 Didn't Happen" (Deleuze and Guattari 2006: 233–36). Compare also *Anti-Oedipus*' "accelerationist" thesis concerning globalization's radical potential (Deleuze and Guattari 2004a: 260) with *WP*'s far less ambiguous critique of globalization (Deleuze and Guattari 1994: 56, 58).

70 Transcendent concepts such as emanation, Subject, or Substance would have small or negligible quanta of immanence because they are still overdetermined by their sociopolitical milieu (for instance by theological and anthropological notions belonging to the philosopher's society more than to philosophy itself). Deleuze and Guattari (1994) speak of "sympathetic" versus "antipathetic" conceptual personae and of "repulsive" (as opposed to "intense") concepts (65, 76).

71 See Deleuze 2006a: 24–25.

72 See Deleuze 2005c: 86.

73 Territory's relation to the earth is first developed in *Anti-Oedipus*, Ch. 3, and then further elaborated particularly in the chapter on the "refrain" from *A Thousand Plateaus*, as well as throughout *WP*.

74 See Deleuze and Guattari 2004b: 359.

75 Deleuze and Guattari (1994) refer to this as a "new earth" for a "new people" (99, 101, 108).

76 See Deleuze 1995b.

77 See Deleuze 2005c: 127, and Alliez 2004a: 58.

78 On the relation between the brain, subjectivation, and power, see Deleuze and Negri 1995: 175–76.

79 As Deleuze and Guattari (1994) put it, "*The role of conceptual personae is to show thought's territories, its absolute deterritorializations and reterritorializations*" (69, emphasis in the original).

80 As Deleuze and Guattari (1994) put it, philosophy only "invents modes of existence or possibilities of life" on a plane of immanence that "develops the power of conceptual personae" (72–73).

81 Deleuze seems to have therefore slightly advanced upon his earlier stance regarding philosophical exceptionalism, if not breaking with it entirely.

82 Deleuze and Guattari (1994) write that conceptual personae form a "system" of "perpetual relays" between their psychosocial determinations and the absolute deterritorializations they can elicit (70). In short, "conceptual personae and psychosocial types refer to each other and combine without ever merging" (Deleuze and Guattari 1994: 70).

83 Conceptual personae clearly have the structure of an event: they are corporeally caused by actions and passions, worldly habits, but irreducible to them (via what we could call the concept's "double-" or "quasi-causality"). On history and becoming in the later Deleuze, see Sauvagnargues 2016.

Bibliography

Alliez, É. (2004a), *The Signature of the World: What Is Deleuze and Guattari's Philosophy?*, trans. E. Ross Albert and A. Toscano, London: Continuum.

Alliez, É. (2004b), "The BwO Condition or, The Politics of Sensation," in J. de Bloois et al. (eds), *Discernements: Deleuzian aesthetics/esthetiques deleuziennes*, 93–112, Amsterdam: Editions Rodopi.

Alliez, É. (2011), "Rhizome (with no return)," *Radical Philosophy*, 167 (May/June): 36–42.

Alliez, É. (2013), "Ontology of the Diagram and Biopolitics of Philosophy. A Research Program on Transdisciplinarity," *Deleuze Studies*, 7 (2): 217–30.

Beistegui, M. (2010), *Immanence. Deleuze and Philosophy*, Edinburgh: Edinburgh University Press.

Bogue, R. (2017), "The Force That Is but Does Not Act: Ruyer, Leibniz and Deleuze," *Deleuze Studies*, 11 (4): 518–37.

Deleuze, G. ([1962] 2006a), *Nietzsche and Philosophy*, trans. H. Tomlinson, London: Continuum.

Deleuze, G. ([1968] 2004a), *Difference and Repetition*, trans. P. Patton, London: Continuum.

Deleuze, G. ([1968] 2005a), *Expressionism in Philosophy: Spinoza*, trans. M. Joughin, New York: Zone Books.

Deleuze, G. ([1969] 2004b), *The Logic of Sense*, trans. M. Lester and C. Stivale, London: Continuum.

Deleuze, G. ([1969] 2004c), "Gueroult's General Method for Spinoza," in G. Deleuze, *Desert Islands and Other Texts, 1953–1974*, trans. M. Taormina, 146–55, London: Semiotext(e).

Deleuze, G. ([1970] 1988) *Spinoza: Practical Philosophy*, trans. R. Hurley, London: City Lights Publishers.

Deleuze, G. ([1980] 2006c), "Eight Years Later: 1980 Interview," in G. Deleuze (ed.), *Two Regimes of Madness: Texts and Interviews, 1975–1995*, trans. A. Hodges and M. Taormina, 175–80, New York: Semiotext(e).

Deleuze, G. ([1981] 2005b), *Francis Bacon: The Logic of Sensation*, trans. D.W. Smith, London: Continuum.

Deleuze, G. ([1986] 2006b), *Foucault*, trans. S. Hand, London: Continuum.

Deleuze, G. ([1988] 2005c), *The Fold: Leibniz and the Baroque*, trans. T. Conley, London: Continuum.

Deleuze, G. ([1989] 1995a), "Letter to Reda Bensmaïa," in G. Deleuze, *Negotiations, 1972–1990*, trans. M. Joughin, 164–66, London: Columbia University Press.

Deleuze, G. ([1990] 1995b), "Postscript on Control Societies," in G. Deleuze, *Negotiations, 1972–1990*, trans. M. Joughin, 177–82, London: Columbia University Press.

Deleuze, G. ([1993] 1998), "Spinoza and the Three 'Ethics,'" in G. Deleuze, *Essays Critical and Clinical*, trans. D.W. Smith, 138–51, London: Verso.

Deleuze, G. ([1995] 2006d), "Immanence: A Life," in G. Deleuze, *Two Regimes of Madness: Texts and Interviews, 1975–1995*, trans. A. Hodges and M. Taormina, 384–90, New York: Semiotext(e).

Deleuze, G., and Guattari, F. ([1972] 2004a), *Anti-Oedipus: Capitalism and Schizophrenia, Vol. I*, trans. R. Hurley, M. Seem, and H.R. Lane, London: Continuum.

Deleuze, G., and Guattari, F. ([1980] 2004b), *A Thousand Plateaus: Capitalism and Schizophrenia, Vol. II*, trans. B. Massumi, London: Continuum.

Deleuze, G., and Guattari, F. ([1984] 2006), "May '68 Didn't Happen," in G. Deleuze, *Two Regimes of Madness: Texts and Interviews, 1975–1995*, trans. A. Hodges and M. Taormina, New York: Semiotext(e).

Deleuze, G., and Guattari, F. ([1991] 1994), *What Is Philosophy?*, trans. G. Birchill and H. Tomlinson, London: Verso.

Deleuze, G., and Negri, A. ([1990] 1995), "Control and Becoming," in G. Deleuze, *Negotiations, 1972–1990*, trans. M. Joughin, 169–76, London: Columbia University Press.

Donagan, A. (1988) *Spinoza*, Harvester Wheatsheaf: London.

Eyers, T. (2013), *Post-Rationalism: Psychoanalysis, Epistemology, and Marxism in Post-War France*, London: Bloomsbury Academic.

Foucault, M. ([1975] 1979), *Discipline and Punish*, trans. A. Sheridan, London: Vintage Books.

Guattari, F. (1984), "The Role of the Signifier in the Institution," in F. Guattari, *Molecular Revolution: Psychiatry and Politics*, trans. R. Sheed, 73–81, London: Penguin.

Hammond, M. (2010), "Capacity or Plasticity: So Just What Is a Body?," in S. van Tuinen and M. McDonnell (eds), *Deleuze and the Fold: A Critical Reader*, New York: Palgrave Macmillan.

Hardt, M. (1993), *Gilles Deleuze. An Apprenticeship in Philosophy*, Minneapolis: University of Minnesota Press.

Macherey, P. (1997), "The Encounter with Spinoza," in P. Patton (ed.), *Deleuze: A Critical Reader*, Oxford: Blackwell Publishers.

Meillassoux, Q. (2007) "Subtraction and Contraction: Deleuze, Immanence, and *Matter and Memory*," *Collapse* (3): 63–107.

Melamed, Y.Y. (2015), *Spinoza's Metaphysics: Substance and Thought*, Oxford: Oxford University Press.

Montebello, P. (2008), *Deleuze. La Passion de la Pensée*, Paris: Vrin.

Nail, T. (2008) "Expressionism, Immanence and Constructivism: 'Spinozism' and Gilles Deleuze," *Deleuze Studies*, 2 (2): 201–19.

Ruyer, R. (1952), *Néo-finalisme*, Paris: Presses universitaires de France.

Sauvagnargues, A. (2016), "Becoming and History: Deleuze's Reading of Foucault," in N. Morar, T. Nail, and D.W. Smith (eds), *Between Deleuze and Foucault*, 174–99, Edinburgh: Edinburgh University Press.

Spinoza, B. ([1677] 1996), *Ethics*, trans. E. Curley, London: Penguin Books.

9

Architectonics without Foundations

Edward Willatt

It seems that the term "architectonics" has fallen out of use in philosophy and would certainly seem to have little chance of revival in the work of Gilles Deleuze and Félix Guattari. If we understand architectonics as the attempt to provide the foundation and hierarchical organization of the disciplines of knowledge it seems to be alien to their concerns. In *A Thousand Plateaus* Deleuze and Guattari elaborate a rhizomatic method in order to remove all roots or foundations from thought. In their final collaboration, *What Is Philosophy?*, different disciplines are related by their engagements with chaos. These terms alone are surely enough to drive a wedge between their work and the architectonics that was ambitiously practiced until around the mid-nineteenth century. Despite this we find in their work an approach that shares certain fundamental concerns with the methodology of architectonics. In this chapter we will first consider Immanuel Kant's notion of architectonics and this will allow us to grasp what is at stake in this very idea. It will also enable us to situate similar concerns in Deleuze and Guattari's writings. We will show how the principles of a rhizomatic method provided in *A Thousand Plateaus* are applied to the relations of the disciplines in their *What Is Philosophy?* This should help us develop our sense of the continuity and fundamental concerns of Deleuze and Guattari's collaborations. This will also place us at the heart of debates over the nature of transdisciplinarity as the relations between disciplines within an architectonic will be seen in a new light.

I would like to dedicate this chapter to my wife, Laura, and children, Patrick and Richard.

Architectonics

The architectonic that we find in Kant's work provides the basis for a unified reading of his *Critique of Pure Reason* but its unifying ambitions also look beyond this text. The architectonic unity of this book must refound the work of cognition that up to now has not been founded upon an account of how the cognition of experience is possible in the first place. It is on the basis of this new foundation that we can then organize all the work of cognition, all of its disciplines and bodies of knowledge. The term "architectonic" is also extended by Kant's *Critique of Practical Reason* and *Critique of Judgement* that concern the foundations of moral judgment, aesthetic judgment, and teleological judgment. We see this unfolding in the second edition Preface to the *Critique of Pure Reason* when Kant refers to a "metaphysics of nature" that is to complement a "metaphysics of morals" (Kant 1996: 39–40, Bliii).[1] Both presuppose the work to be completed in the *Critique of Pure Reason* that provides the a priori elements of the cognition of nature and makes room for morality by distinguishing theoretical cognition from the cognition of the postulates of practical reason that make morality possible. This forms part of a distinction between the different interests of reason that are the concern of Kant's three *Critiques*. If theoretical cognition is the main concern of the *Critique of Pure Reason* it is the foundation of practical or moral reasoning that is the starting point in the *Critique of Practical Reason*. The *Critique of Judgement* proceeds to consider how judgments are made, which are aesthetic and teleological in order to complete this systematic account of reason's interests in different realms of philosophical inquiry. This shows how architectonics concerns the systematic unity of both the disciplines of knowledge and the interests of reason that distinguish different areas of philosophy.

We encounter Kant's use of the term "architectonic" in his introduction to the *Critique of Pure Reason* where it is first of all concerned with how this particular text is organized as an account of the cognition of possible experience. He writes that "a science that merely judges pure reason, its sources, and its bounds may be regarded as the *propaedeutic* to the system of pure reason" (Kant 1996: 64, A11/B25). This is the first sense of the term "architectonic" in the *Critique of Pure Reason*. It is the account of experience that, as propaedeutic, prepares the way for considering how all of knowledge is gathered by different disciplines. The second use of the term refers to "the system of pure reason." This systematic organization of all disciplines of knowledge must carry forward the account of the cognition of possible experience provided in the *Critique of Pure Reason* as propaedeutic. Kant envisages a system of all the principles of a priori cognition that found and characterize the different disciplines of knowledge. These principles allow "genuine" sciences to rigorously analyze matter, to deal with it in ways that are a priori rather than based upon experience and liable to change. Architectonics therefore has the task of providing what Kant calls "an *organon* of pure reason [which] would be the sum of those principles by which all pure a priori cognitions can be acquired and actually brought about" (Kant 1996: 64, A11/B24–25).

An instructive example of the role of this organon is the distinction it makes between empirical psychology and the sciences that study motion. In the *Metaphysical Foundations of Natural Science* Kant derives two of Newton's laws of motion by applying a priori concepts from the *Critique of Pure Reason* (Hatfield 1992: 218). Here the propaedeutic is being realized in an organon of principles for the sciences. Newton's laws of motion are to be secured by showing that they are not derived from experience but from concepts that make experience possible in the first place. Motion is considered as quantity and quality, as quantum and force, on the basis of the preparatory account given in the *Critique of Pure Reason*. This foundation provides an a priori framework within which the sciences are defined by their a priori ways of rigorously analyzing matter.[2] Their activity is to be founded upon the table of categories presented in the *Critique of Pure Reason* that has quantity and quality as its first two divisions. In this way the study of movement by science is prepared for by an account of how experience is possible that is not liable to revision through experience but is given once and for all in a table of categories. Thus, a science is given an a priori framework, distinguishing this science from a discipline that has no such foundation.

This consideration of the place of natural science in Kant's architectonic allows us to place empirical psychology. It has no a priori principles because in studying the temporal succession of psychological or inner experience we have merely a compilation of perceptions or what Kant calls, in his *Anthropology from a Pragmatic Point of View*, "a diary of an *observer of oneself*" (Kant 2006: 20). This temporal flow of inner experience does not provide something to which we can apply the a priori concepts established in the *Critique of Pure Reason* as propaedeutic. It does not provide a science with matter that can be analyzed in a priori ways. This brief sketch shows how for Kant architectonics provides a propaedeutic and an organon, establishing an organization and hierarchy of disciplines by setting out principles that must govern their relations with matter.

Rhizomatics

Can we identify similar concerns in Deleuze and Guattari's work? It might seem that there is little reason to even consider this question given their view that "philosophy does not consist in knowing" (Deleuze and Guattari 1994: 82). A textbook definition of knowledge might suggest that it is essentially a representation of reality mediated by concepts such as those found in Kant's *Critique of Pure Reason* at the heart of his architectonic. It seems intuitive to speak of "knowing that x" or "knowing about y" so that knowledge is essentially concerned with representing reality. We find a consistent critique of representation in Deleuze and Guattari's work and in Deleuze's solo writings (for example, Deleuze and Guattari 1988: 23, 86; Deleuze 2004: Ch. 3). They seek to articulate and put into practice direct connections between different materials of thought without mediating this process through forms of representation. As we shall see, rather than founding thought upon certain concepts that justify a knowledge-claim they seek to produce new and unfamiliar concepts through unregulated connections. In approaching their work we are well advised to emphasize their attempts to think *with* the world as opposed to thinking *about* the world (Holland 2013: 37).

However, I will argue that we neglect key aspects of Deleuze and Guattari's philosophy if we allow their critique of certain concepts to limit the potential of those concepts within their thought. Their critique of representation does not mean that they neglect the problem of accounting for what is important or *makes a difference* in thought, something that animates Kant's architectonic method. While Kant seeks to capture what is significant in the propositions of knowledge that *re*-present sensations, Deleuze and Guattari set themselves the challenge of realizing what is "Interesting, Remarkable or Important" (Deleuze and Guattari 1994: 82). If knowledge is solely concerned with representation through a priori concepts, then Deleuze and Guattari have no interest in this concept. However, insofar as it concerns the creation of new concepts that realize ever wider connections it expresses a problem they share.[3] I've argued elsewhere that Deleuze's solo work draws upon a Kantian methodological framework that can be identified with the architectonic of the *Critique of Pure Reason* (Willatt 2010: 6, 122f). In what follows I will seek to find a framework in Deleuze and Guattari's collaborations that echoes the Kantian architectonic insofar as it shares the ambition of drawing together and setting out the principles of a method that fully realizes what is important in our encounters with the world. This will lead us to engage with the central concern of transdisciplinarity to rethink the relations between disciplines. The framework envisioned by architectonics will be shown to engage directly with problems concerning our ability to work across disciplines and overcome their boundaries.

In the first chapter or "plateau" of Deleuze and Guattari's *A Thousand Plateaus* they seek to articulate the direct connections, unmediated by representation, to which we've just referred. The notion of the "rhizome" is presented as a way in which to "do away with foundations, nullify endings and beginnings" (Deleuze and Guattari 1988: 25). They argue that if we understand thought using the model of a tree and its arborescent root system we always consider how things grow from a central root. This beginning is something that "endlessly develops the law of the One that becomes two, then of the two that become four" (Deleuze and Guattari 1988: 5). They identify an alternative to this arborescent-system in a radicle-system, with its fascicular root: "This time, the principal root has aborted, or its tip has been destroyed; an immediate, indefinite multiplicity of secondary roots grafts onto it and undergoes a flourishing development" (Deleuze and Guattari 1988: 5). This ensures that growth is free to develop in new ways through grafting. With fascicular roots we have growth in a bundle or bunch, thanks to the abortion or destruction of the central root.[4] However, for Deleuze and Guattari this means that we merely shift the unity of this system to another level, to a higher dimension where it still subsists. They write: "This time, natural reality is what aborts the principal root, but the root's unity subsists, as past or yet to come, as possible" (Deleuze and Guattari 1988: 5). As a higher and supplementary unity the principal root subsists as something always lacking, as a lack that is always at work in thought. It is at work in perpetuating a cyclical unity where the grafting together of things is understood as the sign of a unity that is currently lacking but is located in a higher dimension "as past or yet to come" (Deleuze and Guattari 1988: 5). At this point in *A Thousand Plateaus* we must ask how Deleuze and Guattari intend to realize this lack of foundation, beginning or end. If the real we seek is not a deeper or higher dimension that we can never reach, how is it to be understood?

In order to combat arborescent and radicle systems Deleuze and Guattari provide what we shall seek to understand as their own organon of principles. In *A Thousand Plateaus* these principles constitute a rhizomatic method that seeks to eradicate all roots and that ranges across different disciplines. It must show how the rhizome functions and, on this basis, provide basic principles that apply to different disciplinary practices in their dealings with matter. We must proceed according to these principles, without deep roots or higher dimensions providing unity to our activity, and solely with the resources of a flat plane and the relations between materials that proliferate upon it. Deleuze and Guattari call this a "plane of consistency" because upon it the consistency grasped by different disciplines is to be staged and developed. The organon of principles of the correct functioning of the rhizome must put us directly in touch with this plane and prevent us from looking above or below it.[5] Thought must be staged in the immanence of the real and this is the working or functioning of the rhizome.

If we consider the botanical model that Deleuze and Guattari employ here we can see that the move made is from roots to stems. Rhizomes are stems that grow horizontally underground and tend to be rich in food (Robbins et al. 1964: 114). This allows them to live throughout the winter and to send up new shoots the following spring. Abundant food is stored in tubers, an example being the potato that principally stores starch (Robbins et al. 1964: 116). In horticulture and agriculture this removes the need to balance what is underground and overground, something that is vital in the case of arborescent systems. This is the problem of balancing the manufacture of carbohydrates by the overground shoot system and the supply of water and mineral nutrients by the underground root system (Robbins et al. 1964: 123).[6] Instead of this balance between height and depth, our attention is turned toward the horizontal and flat plane provided by the functioning of the rhizome.[7] The vigor and aggression of rhizomatous plants is the result of their dense colonies, which exclude other species, and their abundant food resources, something that allows them to compete more effectively than seedlings (Ashby 1961: 132). We will now examine the principles that make up Deleuze and Guattari's organon in *A Thousand Plateaus* in order to see how this botanical model contributes to their account.

The principles of connection and heterogeneity

These two principles entail that "any point of a rhizome can be connected to any other and must be" (Deleuze and Guattari 1988: 7). This follows from Deleuze and Guattari's concern to be rid of foundations, beginnings, and endings. It might seem that the immanence of the real constitutes an absolute beginning or a break with what went before because it breaks with all transcendence. However, for Deleuze and Guattari it in fact ensures that there is only the re-commencement of a process that is always already underway. With connection through heterogeneity or difference we never pursue thought in a void. Such a starting point would be the deep rooted or higher dimension, the abstract space for a beginning or ending, that would unify our thought in advance. Instead we are in touch with the real on a plane of consistency because this plane is the very proliferation of the real through connection and heterogeneity.[8] Deleuze and Guattari write: "A rhizome has no beginning or end; it is always in the middle, between things, interbeing, *intermezzo*" (Deleuze and Guattari 1988: 25). Connection and heterogeneity are thus able to bring about strange alliances because they are in-between things rather than being rooted in the identity of things. This has significant consequences: "This conjunction carries enough force to shake and uproot the verb 'to be'" (Deleuze and Guattari 1988: 25). However, as well as being destructive in this way the principles of connection and heterogeneity are constructive, something that leads us to the third principle of the rhizomatic method.

The principle of multiplicity

This is what the rhizome constructs by connecting through difference or heterogeneity rather than on the basis of the roots that are uprooted and exceeded by this very process. A multiplicity is never rooted in depth or supplemented by a higher dimension but operates in and through the plane Deleuze and Guattari present as flat and without beginning or end.[9] It embodies and develops this plane of consistency and its principles, making things consistent without relying upon either deep roots or higher dimensions of unity. Deleuze and Guattari write: "The rhizome itself assumes very diverse forms, from ramified surface extension in all directions to concretion into bulbs and tubers" (Deleuze and Guattari 1988: 7). This understanding of the growth of thought can be developed by turning to botany and ecology where the ability of the rhizome to stabilize sand dunes and tidal mud has been studied. This is part of a key process for understanding how such infertile environments become fertile. Marram-grass is rhizomatous and stabilizes the sand dune or tidal mud that has been deposited by the sea, which then retreats (Ashby 1961: 130–31). The marram-grass has made the sand dune stable and this leads to increasing fertility as it is succeeded by other plants. Taller and heaver growing hardwood trees like the oak will eventually dominate after a succession of other species because of their superior ability to reach the sun's light and to draw water and mineral nutrients from the soil. This model might seem to privilege the tree and its arborescent root system as the ultimate stage of this process of succession.[10] However, when trees fall or are destroyed by fire succession resumes. This also happens when the sea reclaims land and deposits new sand dunes and mud flats. The ground is cleared by these events, showing that this process of succession is by no means exhausted by the arrival of a forest of hardwood trees and that it does not privilege this outcome. This model of succession places the rhizome at the heart of reality and undermines the tree as a stopping point in rhizomatic connections: "There exist tree or root structures in rhizomes; conversely, a tree branch or root division may begin to burgeon into a rhizome" (Deleuze and Guattari 1988: 15). When Deleuze and Guattari introduce a principle of multiplicity this must stabilize and make fertile a reality that has no unity in height or depth. It must draw together diverse and disunified materials, embodying the principles of connection and heterogeneity, and in this way account for all that arises in our encounters with reality.

The principle of asignifying rupture

This fourth principle again follows from the lack of any beginning or ending in the functioning of the rhizome upon a flat plane of consistency. Any rupture must not be seen as signifying a deeper or higher dimension, some beginning or ending that would constitute the real as something lacking in thought.[11] There must be a rupture that does not signify anything: no beginning, ending, deep root or higher dimension. This is because Deleuze and Guattari are concerned to leave open the meaning or signification that might result from a rupture by making it an opening onto the heterogeneous connections that take place on the plane of consistency. Is this rupture genuinely asignifying if it seems to *refer* to the plane upon which it occurs? It can be seen as genuinely asignifying only if this plane does not provide it with a signification because it offers only heterogeneous connections that do not establish meaning in advance. Rather than a source of signification, the plane upon which ruptures occur embodies the openness of a process of heterogeneous connection. For Deleuze and Guattari we must always renew connections upon the plane of consistency rather than assuming that any rupture is final. Rather than signifying an end point, ruptures embody "an active and temporary selection" (Deleuze and Guattari 1988: 10). We see Deleuze and Guattari establishing in principle that even when ruptures occur, things that are genuinely forceful and transformative, this is never the end point of an open-ended process of connection.

The principles of cartography and decalcomania

The final two principles in Deleuze and Guattari's organon ensure that the rhizome is a map and not a tracing. It is the mapping of "an experimentation in contact with the real" (Deleuze and Guattari 1988: 12). The real is again found neither in depth nor in height but is immanent to a flat plane of consistency. The rhizome experiments in constructing consistent multiplicities through connection and heterogeneity. Deleuze and Guattari are concerned to avoid the tracing of foundations, beginnings, or endings: "What the tracing reproduces of the map or rhizome are only the impasses, blockages, incipient taproots, or points of structuration" (Deleuze and Guattari 1988: 13). This would violate the fourth principle by making ruptures into events that signify a unity that is always lacking because it is found in depth or height. It would neglect the immanent and asignifying role of ruptures or events in the functioning of the rhizome. Instead they want to resituate tracings on the map (Deleuze and Guattari 1988: 14), to open them to the rupturing connections made through heterogeneity that occur in the ongoing formation of the rhizome.[12] The principle of decalcomania develops this because it refers to a process of transferring engravings and prints to pottery and other materials.[13] Rather than working from or toward a preconceived object this artistic process multiplies the incarnations of an engraving or print. It makes connections between different materials and incarnates something differently every time. It does not involve a beginning, ending, or "preconceived object" because, like cartography, it does not trace from a higher or deeper reality but makes connections between materials upon a flat plane in order to realize something differently.

We have sought to understand Deleuze's and Guattari's rhizomatic method as containing an organon of principles. Like Kant's architectonic the aim is to capture what is important in our encounters with reality by setting out a method for realizing this open-ended process in the creation of new concepts. How does this approach relate the different disciplines as we saw Kant doing within his architectonic? Brian Massumi argues that for Deleuze and Guattari "philosophy frees potential from the captivity of disciplinary self-policing" (Massumi 2010: 4). Their rhizomatic method makes demands upon other disciplines in the ways that they deal with matter. Deleuze and Guattari complain:

> We're tired of trees. We should stop believing in trees, roots, and radicles. They've made us suffer too much. All of arborescent culture is founded on them, from biology to linguistics. Nothing is beautiful or loving or political aside from underground stems and aerial roots, adventitious growths and rhizomes. (Deleuze and Guattari 1988: 15)[14]

They refer to the way in which grass grows between and among other things (Deleuze and Guattari 1988: 19), embodying the first two principles of the organon. Rather than being centered or unified this weed is able to make connections between the most different things because it operates "in between." How do different disciplines proceed on the basis of this lack of foundation that is for Deleuze and Guattari the source of an organon of principles and of a very full picture of the matter with which disciplines work? It presents disciplines at work in the midst of a very concrete world, one where nothing is lacking in multiplicities, no hidden depth or higher dimension, but which is made consistent by the rhizome and its principles of operation. We have both a concern to provide principles for a method of thought and a concern to avoid providing foundations that would limit the relations between disciplines. This is a transdisciplinary conception that makes use of an architectonic method by proceeding according to principles that work across disciplines and have the potential to overcome their boundaries. To explore this we will turn to Deleuze and Guattari's *What Is Philosophy?* where this issue is explicitly addressed.

Founding disciplines upon chaos

In *What Is Philosophy?* we find that the nature and relations of disciplinary practices are center stage. Deleuze and Guattari write: "What defines thought in its three great forms—art, science, and philosophy—is always confronting chaos, laying out a plane, throwing a plane over chaos" (Deleuze and Guattari 1994: 197). These disciplines are organized according to their relation to chaos and their unique ways of extracting from it the materials for presenting those aspects of reality that concern them. This helps us to define the word "chaos" as Deleuze and Guattari use it. Rather than simply undermining knowledge, it must offer material for thought to construct the planes that characterize different disciplines. They develop this constructive role of chaos when they write:

> Chaos is defined not so much by its disorder as by the infinite speed with which every form taking shape in it vanishes. It is a void that is not a nothingness but a *virtual*, containing all possible particles and drawing out all possible forms, which spring up only to disappear immediately, without consistency of reference, without consequences. Chaos is an infinite speed of birth and disappearance. (Deleuze and Guattari 1994: 118)

In this way chaos provides materials for the work of different disciplinary practices. Disciplines extract things that appear suddenly and then disappear. They are distinguished by what they extract from chaos in order to construct planes. The "plane of immanence" is the plane constructed by philosophy and

Deleuze and Guattari refer to it as a sieve. It sieves chaos in order to select infinite movements of thought (Deleuze and Guattari 1994: 118). They define these infinite movements as "events." These move too fast to be anything that could be established or fixed as an object of knowledge. The task is to relate these infinite movements or events on a plane so that they attain the consistency of concepts.[15]

In the case of philosophy a plane is always a particular philosophy, such as Cartesian philosophy or Kantian philosophy. Such planes of immanence relate their own concepts and also those that form part of other planes so that we have what Deleuze and Guattari call a "geophilosophy." Connections and neighborhoods form the horizon of concepts (Deleuze and Guattari 1994: 91–92). Connections take place both on the same plane and between the different planes that represent a particular philosophy but are not limited to it. This makes a particular philosophy a plane of concepts. It makes philosophy in general into the relations between these planes on the model of the relations of geological strata that is embodied by the geologic timescale.[16] We find that for Deleuze and Guattari the thing that distinguishes philosophy most of all is that its concepts are events. This makes the concept singular, the singular extraction of an event from chaos. It then becomes specific to a particular plane but can be reactivated, thanks to the relations between different planes of immanence. Thus we reactivate a Cartesian concept on a Kantian plane but here its relations to specifically Kantian concepts play a part in producing a new philosophy or way of making the world consistent.[17] Concepts can be reactivated at any time and on any plane rather than being isolated by a chronological and linear succession of time.[18] This geophilosophy develops the rhizomatic method we found in *A Thousand Plateaus* by showing how a lack of foundation, a rootlessness and encounter with chaos, is the preparation for attempts to realize all that is *interesting, remarkable, or important*.[19] Philosophy is now decentered because it is always confronting chaos and its concepts relate between different planes. Concepts and the planes of immanence they form are situated in a temporality that is transversal rather than chronological.[20] This shows us how philosophy is defined and put in its place through its relation to chaos. We will now consider how it is differentiated from other disciplines.

For Deleuze and Guattari, planes are constructed by different disciplines using the materials of thought which they extract from chaos. As we've seen, philosophy constructs planes of immanence. Science presents us with a "plane of reference" and art with a "plane of composition." We will limit ourselves to considering the differences between philosophy and science.[21] Our concern is with the ways in which these disciplines are related. We've seen that for philosophy we must retain the infinite speed of chaos and so have events that are singular concepts that are made consistent by their relation to other concepts on a particular plane. For science there is a need to slow down chaos in order to extract the finite and stable points of a plane of reference.[22] Thus while philosophy seeks to retain the infinite, but to provide concepts that have a consistency specific to the event that chaos throws up, science seeks to give a reference to the virtual which makes it part of a stable and measurable plane. Deleuze and Guattari understand this scientific plane of reference as made up of limits that slow chaos down in order to secure points of reference.[23] Science's functions are always a "slow-motion" (Deleuze and Guattari 1994: 118). This is not presented as a negative or limiting move but as the operation specific to science and its creative practice. It allows the universe to be understood in terms of certain borders or limits.

Deleuze and Guattari give the examples of the speed of light, absolute zero, and the Big Bang (Deleuze and Guattari 1994: 119). The slowing down performed by science is not the negation of processes or a move toward their end point. Instead it is "a condition coextensive with their whole development" (Deleuze and Guattari 1994: 118). The boundaries or limits that make reference possible are therefore the immanent limits of scientific processes extracted from chaos through this slowing down. In this way the creativity of science is made possible and thought is enriched by the slowing down of chaos. However, if philosophy is distinguished because it is capable of retaining the infinite movements of chaos, of extracting events, this leaves us wondering if it is made superior to science. Is philosophy closer to chaos and so more profound in its insights than science? In other words, do Deleuze and Guattari introduce a depth specific to one discipline and thus found a hierarchy upon chaos?

Gregg Lambert argues that we find an organizing tendency in *What Is Philosophy?*, something that resonates with Kant's architectonics. He writes:

> Here we can perceive a bit of an organizer in Deleuze, a trait which can be linked to Kant despite his own protests to the contrary, and here we recall that Kant had earlier defined the role of philosophy in comparison to other activities within a veritable division of labor, by relegating to the different faculties their own proper duty and precinct. (Lambert 2002: 154)

By seeking to relate disciplines through chaos, to find here their unity and their differences, Deleuze and Guattari risk privileging philosophy as the discipline closest to chaos.[24] Indeed, Lambert compares what Deleuze and Guattari do in *What Is Philosophy?* to Kant's 1798 work *The Conflict of the Faculties*. Here Kant defended the authority of philosophy against the faculties of law, theology, and medicine, arguing that these disciplines must be subject to scrutiny by philosophy.[25] The division of work between the disciplines in *What Is Philosophy?* seems to reflect the same concern because while all three extract different things from chaos, philosophy alone is able to create concepts by drawing upon the infinite speed of chaos.[26] It alone can realize the singular events that are so singular that they have vanished a moment later. Does this commit Deleuze and Guattari to a hierarchical organization of the disciplines that confront chaos?

John Protevi and Mark Bonta take a positive view of the tendency common to Kant and Deleuze in their book *Deleuze and Geophilosophy* where they argue that Deleuze is "the Kant of our time" (Bonta and Protevi 2004: vii). They point to Kant's role in providing the philosophical "grounding" of classical modern science, something we saw in his attempts to establish Newtonian laws of motion in his organon of principles. Newtonian principles must be grounded in the a priori concepts found in the table of categories of the *Critique of Pure Reason*. Bonta and Protevi argue that, like Kant, Deleuze seeks to provide a philosophy for the science of his times. His philosophical concepts make sense of "our world of fragmented space (the so-called anticipatory effects of systems that sense their approach to a threshold), and the non-linear effects of far-from-equilibrium thermodynamics" (Bonta and Protevi 2004: vii–viii). The limits or boundaries that Deleuze and Guattari find on science's plane of reference are not then to be understood as limiting or as a sign of science's estrangement from chaos. For Bonta and Protevi, Deleuze provides us with the philosophy related to the science that presents material systems that increase in complexity and exhibit systematic behavior without having to rely upon "external organizing agents" (Bonta and Protevi 2004: 3).

It is thus between philosophy and science, in their relation, that this immanent understanding of complexity in material systems is developed. Philosophy captures the *evental* nature of this process and science its limits or boundaries, the points of reference at which change occurs from one state of matter to another with a resultant increase in complexity. It follows that these disciplines develop through their relations, making thought a "heterogenesis" rather than a hierarchical activity rooted in the superiority of any particular discipline (Bonta and Protevi 2004: 199). No field of thought has the privilege of access to a deeper or higher dimension but through their relations there emerges a process that is animated and made possible by both events and limits. In this way Deleuze and Guattari can be said to construct a transdisciplinary conception that overcomes disciplinary boundaries and hierarchies between disciplines.

This understanding of the relations between the disciplines needs to be interrogated further if we are to assess Deleuze and Guattari's attempt to avoid a hierarchical conception. How do they ensure that in seeking to relate areas of thought they are not establishing a higher or meta-level of conceptualization? Éric Alliez argues that in reading *What Is Philosophy?*, "we must start again from the question of the establishment of a non-hierarchical and non-hierarchizing difference (between science and philosophy)" (Alliez 2005: 41). Different disciplines are related by their activities in extracting diverse materials from chaos and using them to construct planes.[27] We must consider whether this account of the common relation of all disciplines to chaos does not imply the unique role of philosophy in providing such a conceptual account of disciplinary activities. In order to avoid this Deleuze and Guattari write: "Philosophy, art, and science are not mental objects of an objectified brain but the three aspects under which the brain becomes subject, Thought-brain. They are the three planes, the rafts on which the brain plunges into and confronts the chaos" (Deleuze and Guattari 1994: 210). This notion of the Thought-brain is intended to account for thought by drawing upon all three disciplines. They are necessary conditions for the emergence of an impersonal Thought-brain that is capable of dealing with chaos and is the junction of philosophy's concepts, science's functions, and art's percepts and affects.[28] It is constituted by the meeting of these disciplines and as such is not merely philosophy's concept but must also involve scientific and artistic processes. How does the Thought-brain constitute the meeting place of three disciplines without being limited to one discipline?

Is the Thought-brain a philosophical concept that expresses the superior role of philosophy's conceptualization of the activity of other disciplines? Éric Alliez suggests a way in which Deleuze and Guattari avoid such a conclusion: "This so-called crisis of foundations is answered by the reaffirmation of the privilege of the living, of a world alive from top to bottom, where the pressure of the virtual ceaselessly expresses the 'lived experience' of things" (Alliez 2005: 78). In answer to the crisis in foundations that results from the role of chaos in thought, Deleuze and Guattari could be seen to introduce a higher level of conceptualization to replace the loss of foundational depth. This would privilege philosophy by drawing upon its unique role in creating concepts and would diverge from the rejection of height and depth that we found in *A Thousand Plateaus*. However, Alliez argues that Deleuze and Guattari present a world alive with philosophy's singular concepts, the functions of science, and the percepts and affects of art. These directly touch the Thought-brain, thanks to the construction of planes by these disciplines, and this ensures that it draws upon chaos rather than being a confused and passive spectator. They also seek to account for its emergence as a concretion of the materials extracted from chaos, just as bulbs and tubers emerge directly through the functioning of the rhizome. The Thought-brain emerges through the meeting of concepts, percepts, affects, and functions because it thinks chaos through philosophically, artistically, and scientifically.[29] It is not then a philosophical concept but a transdisciplinary construction: "this *I* is not only the 'I conceive' of the brain as philosophy, it is also the 'I feel' of the brain as art. Sensation is no less brain than concept" (Deleuze and Guattari 1994: 211). Rather than rising above other disciplines as a philosophical concept, the Thought-brain is to emerge from the concretion of materials provided by every discipline. All of life is to be accounted for and organized by activities that extract from chaos that which emerges by chance and disappears instantaneously but which can be related on a plane that is consistent "*here and now.*" This process ensures that the Thought-brain is a mobile point, continually drawing upon thought as this is extended by the three disciplines in ways that differ but also relate. We see this when science and philosophy concern themselves with Newtonian science in Kant's time and with complexity theory in Deleuze's era. The world is therefore alive in many ways—alive with concepts, functions, percepts, and affects—and through the work of the three disciplines these materials directly touch the Thought-brain.

Is this a convincing account of a nonhierarchical conception of the disciplines? We saw that Alliez finds all the disciplines united in the concrete processes of extracting materials from chaos. However, this very conception can seem to set philosophy apart in its architectonic ambitions. Deleuze and Guattari's attempt to make every discipline equal in their relation to chaos may be compromised by the philosophical task they undertake. However, we've seen how they place the emphasis upon the open-ended creative practices of each discipline and upon particular cases of extracting materials from chaos. They draw our attention to the ways in which these processes distinguish science from philosophy rather than seeking to isolate its essence or define its nature and scope. Instead of asking "what is science?" they aim to find within its practices processes that are defined only by the way they extract materials from chaos. If the Thought-brain is the meeting place of the disciplines these disciplines must also go their own way and relate through their differences. This is what makes possible cases where "two entities [...] pass into each other in a becoming that sweeps them both up in an intensity which co-determines them" (Deleuze and Guattari 1994: 66). The equality between the disciplines comes from their being related through the differences between their autonomous activities. We find in this a more creative relation than would be the case if their relations were traced from a higher or meta-level conceptualization.

Conclusion

We have sought to show that *A Thousand Plateaus* and *What Is Philosophy?* share some of the key concerns of an architectonic method. This seemed doubtful when we compared their work to Kantian architectonics with its representational theory of knowledge. Deleuze and Guattari's rhizomatic principles laid waste to representation and its root-concepts. We also found that Deleuze and Guattari resist a hierarchical conception of philosophy's role in thinking about other disciplines and their relation to chaos. Yet it is in the methodological framework provided by architectonics that we do find a positive relation with Deleuze and Guattari's work. Architectonic method brings to the fore Deleuze and Guattari's concern that the *interesting, remarkable, or important* is not simply made chaotic or lost in the proliferation of the rhizome. They seek to realize what is singular and to capture what is different about disciplines in their creative relations with chaos. They reject representation as a means of doing this and seek to overcome hierarchy among the disciplines. However, they set out principles and distinguish disciplines in their creative practices just as Kant seeks to preserve knowledge and its distinctive fields. Deleuze and Guattari want to achieve an openness of thought that they do not find in representation or hierarchy and yet in seeking to realize this openness they draw upon the methodological concerns we identified in Kant. In order to secure an ambitious method for realizing the full potential of thought, Deleuze and Guattari make significant claims that must not be played down. They do not seek to be modest when they reject roots and hierarchies but to realize the full potential of thought. We found that, in their transdisciplinary concept of disciplines relating in open and unlimited ways, they make use of an architectonic framework for ensuring that disciplines do not become distant from the rhizome or from chaos. We also saw that a nonhierarchical account of the disciplines can be found in Deleuze and Guattari's work. This echoes the concern of transdisciplinarity to avoid privileging a particular discipline or subsuming some disciplines into others in order to genuinely think across disciplines. While we must not simply conflate Deleuze and Guattari's work with the architectonics of thinkers like Kant, we do find that some of the central concerns and ambitions of architectonics are realized in new ways in their writings. Kant's methodological ambitions are developed by Deleuze and Guattari using models and principles that may well be non-Kantian in nature.

In considering the contribution this reading of Deleuze and Guattari's work might make to wider debates concerning trandisciplinarity, we can offer a number of rather speculative suggestions. The work we've done here might lead us to formulate a response to issues arising in the current age of information and the increasing specialization of the disciplines. Deleuze and Guattari's rootless architectonics and nonhierarchical organization of the disciplines does not give up on an attempt to relate different areas of thought using transdisciplinary concepts. Do we have to specialize to be able to work at the forefront of our field or can we simultaneously work at the boundary or in-between disciplines? Is the only scope for common understanding between disciplines to be found in popular or journalistic summaries and surveys that do not participate in the extension of knowledge itself? Deleuze and Guattari's work might contribute to the methodology of interdisciplinary or transdisciplinary projects, making us aware that disciplines must be both highly specific in their relation to concrete subject matters and yet not rigidly specialized in their horizons. Thus, they write in *What Is Philosophy?* of how philosophical writers or artists "install themselves" within the difference between art and philosophy (Deleuze and Guattari 1994: 67). This is not to generalize about, or abstract from, the relation between these two disciplines but to take a very concrete position that overcomes rigid specialization or hierarchy. These are merely suggestions that we cannot develop here but what they suggest is that disciplines should not simply accept the isolation threatened by specialization. Nor should they accept the dominance of information over the ambitions of knowledge-formation. Rather than surrendering to a flood of information, Deleuze and Guattari seek to realize the *interesting, remarkable, or important* in the disciplinary "planes" we saw them elaborate. Thought thus retains the force of the singular and so creates new and transformative philosophical concepts, scientific functions, and artistic percepts and affects. A wider, transdisciplinary account of thought like the one we find in Deleuze and Guattari's work has the potential to relate subject-matters beyond the scope of any specialism and to show that the fragmentation evident in the proliferation of information is in fact the source of relations that intensify the *singular* and *remarkable* rather than undermining it. In this way, architectonics deserves our attention as we face the pressing issues of transdisciplinarity thrown up by the current developments in knowledge and its disciplines.

Notes

1. When citing this text I will first give the page number in Werner S. Pluhar's translation (Hackett 1996) and then the standard *Academie* edition pagination of this text.
2. "The concept of matter had therefore to be carried through all four of the indicated functions of the concepts of the understanding (in four chapters), where in each a new determination of this concept was added" (Kant 2004: 12). In the *Critique of Pure Reason* there are four divisions of the table of categories or pure concepts of the understanding. These are named quantity, quality, relation, and modality. The four chapters referred to must show how these four divisions provide a framework for dealing with matter scientifically. This argument relies upon the preparatory work done in the *Critique of Pure Reason* that translates the categories into temporal processes, via the schematism, in the Analytic of Principles. This makes them into ways of dealing with matter that are a priori and in time.
3. In his solo work Deleuze came to identify Kant as a "creator of concepts." Despite finding Kant's philosophy to have "a completely stifling atmosphere," he believes that beneath this "northern fog" a creation of concepts takes us beyond representation and its confines: "When I said to you that a great philosopher is nevertheless someone who invents concepts, in Kant's case, in this fog, there functions a sort of thinking machine, a sort of creation of concepts that is absolutely frightening" (Deleuze 1978).
4. This is developed in botany where a fibrous root system is one that is relatively shallow while a tap root system penetrates considerably deeper into the soil (Robbins et al. 1964: 125). The fibrous root system of cereal crops is made up of a mass of roots and all are of similar size, including the main roots: "All the roots are slender and fiber-like; no one root is more prominent than the others" (Robbins et al. 1964: 125). By contrast, the tap root system of vegetables like the carrot, beet, radish, turnip, and parsnip has one main root that grows directly downwards. As we shall see, Deleuze and Guattari consider these distinctions between root systems as being less important than the distinction between roots and stems.
5. Deleuze and Guattari articulate the flatness of the plane of consistency by talking about the relations of the materials that compose it: "There are only relations of movement and rest, speed and slowness between unformed elements, or at least between elements relatively unformed, molecules and particles of all kinds" (Deleuze and Guattari 1988: 266). This is explored at pages 124–25 of Bonta and Protevi (2004).
6. This accounts for the need to prune a tree that has been moved. The inevitable damage to its root system caused by moving it disturbs the balance between the productive capabilities of its stem system and its root system (Robbins et al. 1964:

124). Of most importance is the relation between the total leaf surface and total root surface (Robbins et al. 1964: 123). Only by removing some of the leaves and stems, which manufacture carbohydrates, can the physiological balance be restored.

7   "Horizontal growth of the rhizome below ground will achieve lateral spread" (Ashby 1961: 131).
8   "The plane of consistency is the abolition of all metaphor; all that consists is Real" (Deleuze and Guattari 1988: 69). In other words, rather than relying upon metaphor as a means of signifying the real, we are directly in touch with it upon a plane of consistency.
9   "All multiplicities are flat, in the sense that they fill or occupy all of their dimensions: we will therefore speak of a plane of consistency of multiplicities, even though the dimensions of this 'plane' increase with the number of connections that are made on it" (Deleuze and Guattari 1988: 9). The way in which the plane of consistency is both multidimensional and flat is developed using the model of felt in contrast to fabric (Deleuze and Guattari 1988: 475–76). Eugene Holland notes that in the case of fabric, two strands would not intersect but remain separate, thanks to the rigid organization of this cloth. However, felt involves the intersection of any two strands, introducing multiple connections that cannot be anticipated in advance (Holland 2013: 38). Felt is smooth without being homogenous because the "microscales of the fibers" become entangled (Deleuze and Guattari 1988: 475).
10 This was the conclusion of Frederic E. Clements in his *Plant Succession* (1916). He located the end point of plant succession as a "climax community," which is a community of plants where an equilibrium or steady state has been reached. It is composed of those species that are best adapted to the environment they find themselves in.
11 It follows that "there is a rupture in the rhizome whenever segmentary lines explode into a line of flight, but the line of flight is part of the rhizome" (Deleuze and Guattari 1988: 9). In other words, thought is not an abstraction from the concrete world of the rhizome. To think is to remain part of the rhizome, to participate in its heterogeneous connections. Therefore, the real is not lacking but the rhizome and the thought it embodies are fully real.
12 In other words: "Plug the tracing back into the map, connect the roots or trees back up with a rhizome" (Deleuze and Guattari 1988: 14).
13 Decalcomania took on a life of its own in the work of artists such as the surrealist Oscar Domínguez. Domínguez embraced decalcomania as a form of "pictorial automatism" allowing him to work "without preconceived object" (Alexandrian 1970: 108). He was able to create fantastic landscapes using this technique, an example being his *Decalcomania* of 1937 (Alexandrian 1970: 109).
14 They add: "It is odd how the tree has dominated Western reality and all of Western thought, from botany to biology and anatomy, but also gnosiology, theology,

ontology, all of philosophy ... : the root-foundation, *Grund, racine, fondement*" (Deleuze and Guattari 1988: 18). They present this as a phenomenon of the West that follows from its dominant relation to the forest, something that does not hold in the eastern world. This of course raises a huge issue concerning the relation between geography and philosophy.

15 "Now philosophy wants to know how to retain infinite speeds while gaining consistency, *by giving the virtual a consistency specific to it*" (Deleuze and Guattari 1994: 118).

16 Deleuze and Guattari argue that "thinking takes places in the relationship of territory and earth" (Deleuze and Guattari 1994: 85). While the geologic timescale is concerned with the events that take place in the formation of the earth, with the timing and relations of these events, territory locates us in the "here and now."

17 An example is the Cartesian ego or Cogito. Its incarnation can be traced from the Cartesian plane ("I think therefore I am") to the Kantian plane (the passive self located in time and the active self or transcendental unity of apperception elaborated in the *Critique of Pure Reason*) and then to the Deleuzian plane (the fractured self of *Difference and Repetition* (Deleuze 2004: 216–17) and the formula "I is an other" that is taken from the French poet Arthur Rimbaud). "I is an other" is explored in Deleuze's "On Four Poetic Formulas That Might Summarize the Kantian Philosophy" in his *Essays Critical and Clinical* (Deleuze 1998: 29–31) and referred to in *What Is Philosophy?* (Deleuze and Guattari 1994: 211) in order to explicate the "Thought-brain," which we shall shortly explore.

18 For Deleuze and Guattari difference or heterogeneity is the principle of the relations between the planes: "Each created event on a plane calls on other heterogeneous elements, which are still to be created on other planes: thought as heterogenesis" (Deleuze and Guattari 1994: 199).

19 Cliff Stagoll brings geophilosophy down to earth, to the level of everyday, concrete experience. He writes that for Deleuze and Guattari "one's world is organized anew around some relevant concept or set of concepts, such that a new plane of immanence is constructed, providing the temporary consistency of thinking upon which meaning depends" (Stagoll 2005: 205).

20 In other words, planes are "transvered" by their relations rather than the chronological succession of planes dictating the relations that can hold between different planes. To be "transversal" is to cross or intersect with something else, it allows for relations between different elements of a system, for unpredictable relations between things. This takes forward the principles of rhizomatics that we explored and we are led to recall the already quoted precept that "any point of the rhizome can be connected to any other and must be" (Deleuze and Guattari 1988: 7). A transversal time embodies this principle by relating events in the formation of reality without being restricted by their chronological order of succession.

21 For Deleuze and Guattari (1994), art is immanent to a single plane (195–96). They distinguish between the aesthetic and the technical (Deleuze and Guattari 1994: 195–96), and this serves to make art a singular and autonomous discipline, one that makes possible aspects of thought and experience rather than relying upon something external as the measure or model of its technical competence.

22 "Science approaches chaos in a completely different, almost opposite way: it relinquishes the infinite, infinite speed, in order to gain *a reference able to actualize the virtual*" (Deleuze and Guattari 1994: 118). Éric Alliez writes that "whilst philosophy must engage the infinite speed of chaos in order to select and extract the infinite movements of the thought that cuts through it—thereby giving consistency to the virtual through concepts (so that the event, a virtual become consistent, can then breathe its specific life into the concept)—science relinquishes the infinite in order to produce a reference capable of actualizing the virtual by *functions*" (Alliez 2005: 36).

23 "Science is haunted not by its own unity but by the plane of reference constituted by all the limits or borders through which it confronts chaos" (Deleuze and Guattari 1994: 119).

24 The relation of philosophy and art is different because artistic planes of composition make direct use of, or extract (Deleuze and Guattari 1994: 176), the materials of chaos rather than operating a scientific "slowing down" of chaos. This direct use of the chaotic real to create enduring "percepts" means that "art preserves and it is the only thing in the world that is preserved" (Deleuze and Guattari 1994: 163). How does this differ from philosophy's creation of concepts? It seems that art is closer to chaos because its work is much more direct and concrete than conceptual philosophy. However, Deleuze and Guattari ensure that the division between concrete practice and abstract thought is undermined by their conception of disciplines confronting chaos. Philosophy is not at a distance from chaos because it creates concepts. Instead, as we've seen, concepts are the singular extraction of an event from chaos. The creation of concepts is just as much a concrete and engaged practice as artistic creation. In other words, philosophy does not distance itself from chaos in order to form general concepts but engages with it directly in order to create singular concepts. Thus, if we want to see how close art and philosophy are to chaos for Deleuze and Guattari we must understand them both as concrete practices engaging directly with chaos in order to produce different creations ("percepts and affects" and "concepts," respectively).

25 Kant's concern with this issue is clear when he is discussing the right of philosophy to examine the foundations of other faculties: "But the businessmen of the three other faculties [law, theology and medicine] will always be such miracle-workers, unless the philosophy faculty is allowed to counteract them publicly—not in order to overthrow their teachings but only to deny the magic power that the public

superstitiously attributes to these teachings and the rites connected with them—as if, by passively surrendering themselves to such skillful guides, the people would be excused from any activity of their own and led, in ease and comfort, to achieve the ends they desire" (Kant 2002: 51).

26 "The concept belongs to philosophy and only to philosophy" (Deleuze and Guattari 1994: 34).

27 In *A Thousand Plateaus* Deleuze and Guattari argue that "royal" or "major" science and "nomadic" or "minor" science take radically different approaches to matter (Deleuze and Guattari 1988: 362). The minor is associated with the concrete and molecular, with events that are not recognized as important by major sciences. The major is associated with the state and the work of settled rather than nomadic populations (Deleuze and Guattari 1988: 368). However, Éric Alliez points out that Deleuze and Guattari do not set up a hierarchy between major and minor science but make the two inseparable: "Major science has a perpetual need for the inspiration of the minor; but the minor would be nothing if it did not confront and conform to the highest scientific requirements" (Deleuze and Guattari 1988: 486, Alliez 2005: 48n28).

28 Deleuze and Guattari (1994) warn us not to confuse percepts and affects with perceptions and feelings, which gives these materials real autonomy (24, 164).

29 Is this the classical subject of knowledge? It is clear that it is not constituted as the activity of representing the world but is instead directly touched by the materials of thought. It emerges through the activities of different disciplines rather than rising above them. It is something that emerges from, and is immanent to, the world as opposed to the classical subject of knowledge. As we've seen, the activity of thinking *with* the world replaces the activity of representing it. In footnote 17 we charted the incarnations of the Cartesian Cogito and saw that, in his solo work, Deleuze fractures this classical subject in order to reconceptualize it.

Bibliography

Alexandrian, S. (1970), *Surrealist Art*, London: Thames and Hudson.
Alliez, É. (2005), *The Signature of the World: What Is Deleuze and Guattari's Philosophy?*, trans. E. Ross Albert and A. Toscano, London and New York: Continuum.
Ashby, M. (1961), *Introduction to Plant Ecology*, London: Macmillan.
Bonta, M., and Protevi, J. (2004), *Deleuze and Geophilosophy: A Guide and Glossary*, Edinburgh: Edinburgh University Press.
Clements, F.E. (1916), *Plant Succession: An Analysis of the Development of Vegetation*, Washington D.C.: Carnegie Institute of Washington.
Deleuze, G. (1978), Seminar Transcript of 14 March 1978, trans. M. McMahon, http://www.webdeleuze.com/php/sommaire.html (last accessed December 3, 2013).

Deleuze, G. (1998), *Essays Critical and Clinical*, trans. D.W. Smith and M.A. Greco, London and New York: Verso.

Deleuze, G. (2004), *Difference and Repetition*, trans. P. Patton. London and New York: Continuum.

Deleuze, G., and Guattari, F. (1988), *A Thousand Plateaus: Capitalism and Schizophrenia*, trans. B. Massumi, London: The Athlone Press.

Deleuze, G., and Guattari, F. (1994), *What Is Philosophy?*, trans. G. Burchill and H. Tomlinson, London and New York: Verso.

Hatfield, G. (1992), "Empirical, Rational, and Transcendental Psychology: Psychology as Science and as Philosophy," in P. Guyer (ed.), *The Cambridge Companion to Kant*, 200–27, Cambridge: Cambridge University Press.

Holland, E.W. (2013), *Deleuze and Guattari's A Thousand Plateaus*, London and New York: Bloomsbury.

Lambert, G. (2002), *The Non-Philosophy of Gilles Deleuze*, London and New York: Continuum.

Kant, I. (2002), *The Conflict of the Faculties*, trans. M.J. Gregor, Lincoln: University of Nebraska Press.

Kant, I. (1996), *Critique of Pure Reason*, trans. W.S. Pluhar, Indianapolis: Hackett.

Kant, I. (2004), *Metaphysical Foundations of Natural Science*, trans. M. Friedman, Cambridge: Cambridge University Press.

Kant, I. (2006), *Anthropology from a Pragmatic Point of View*, trans. R.B. Louden, Cambridge: Cambridge University Press.

Massumi, B. (2010), "What Concepts Do," *Deleuze Studies*, 4 (1): 1–15.

Robbins, W.W., Weier, T.T., and Stocking, C.R. (1964), *Botany: An Introduction to Plant Science*, New York: John Wiley and Sons.

Stagoll, C. (2005), "Plane," *The Deleuze Dictionary*, Edinburgh: Edinburgh University Press.

Willatt, E. (2010), *Kant, Deleuze and Architectonics*, London and New York: Continuum.

10

Independence, Alliance, and Echo

Deleuze on the Relationship between Philosophy, Science, and Art

Gavin Rae

While Gilles Deleuze maintains that philosophical thinking is intimately connected to and even dependent on the nonphilosophical, he never clearly or consistently outlines what this relationship entails. This an important issue not only because Deleuze returns to it again and again—especially in his later writings—but also because it has been relatively ignored in the secondary literature.

When it has been discussed, two positions dominate. Mary Beth Mader (2017) examines the philosophy—science relation through the lens of the notion of "intensity" to claim that Deleuze's philosophical use of the term is not simply lifted from contemporary science but is developed from his differential ontology, with the consequence that philosophy and science are different in kind. This seems to support the conclusion that philosophy and science cannot interact with one another because, even when they use the "same" sign, each gives it a fundamentally different sense, which prevents meaningful interactions and exchanges. The problem with this conclusion is that, while Mader highlights the difference between philosophical and scientific conceptions of "intensity," it is questionable whether this actually tells us anything about the types of relations possible between these two modes of thinking. At most, it seems to reveal that philosophy and science do not share the same notion of "intensity," but this

---

This chapter forms part of the activities for the Conex Marie Skłodowska-Curie Research Project "Sovereignty and Law: Between Ethics and Politics" co-funded by the Universidad Carlos III de Madrid, the European Union's Seventh Framework Program for Research, Technological Development and Demonstration under Grant Agreement 600371, The Spanish Ministry of the Economy and Competitivity (COFUND2013-40258), The Spanish Ministry for Education, Culture, and Sport (CEI-15-17), and Banco Santander. More information about the research project can be found at https://sovereigntyandlaw.wordpress.com/.

does not engage with whether there are other mediating concepts or similarities between the modes of thought that might permit the disciplines to act together.

Indeed, other commentators have engaged with the issue from a different perspective and lens to come to an alternative conclusion. Éric Alliez (2013), for example, examines the relationship between a type of aesthetics and philosophy to determine the ways in which the former can help the latter overcome the model of representation and develop a response to the question of transdisciplinarity. Similarly, Isabelle Stengers (2005) affirms a complementary relation between science and philosophy with the former engaging with the actual state of affairs and the latter focusing on the virtual event that creates the actual. However, while interesting, the fundamental problem with their positions is that, in their rush to develop a transdisciplinary program from Deleuze's thinking, Alliez and Stengers simply take it for granted that, within Deleuze's differential ontology, there is a mediating factor that allows the very different forms of thinking to communicate and create from one another. However, as Mader's analysis indicates, this cannot just be assumed; it has to be outlined.

Therefore, rather than follow Alliez and Stengers in simply assuming that Deleuze's differential ontology permits transdisciplinarity—which I understand to refer to a form of relation that allows disciplines to cross their distinctive boundaries to act in concert with others in a way that creates synergies—or, as in the case of Mader, dismissing this possibility having examined only one mediating concept, this chapter takes a more expansive and holistic approach to examine the *types* of transdisciplinary relations explicitly affirmed within or made possible by Deleuze's differential ontology. To do so, I first briefly outline Deleuze's ontological categories, paying particular attention to his notions of being, multiplicity, and difference before showing that his epistemology—or analysis of the different forms of thinking—is rooted in his differential ontology. From here, I outline the various concepts that are either explicitly used by Deleuze or permitted by his ontology to describe three different ways (grouped under the terms "independence," "alliance," and "echo") in which the various forms of thinking can relate to one another. Whereas the notion of "independence" maintains the absolute difference between the disciplines, I argue that with the concepts of "alliance" and "echo" Deleuze affirms two specific forms of transdisciplinarity: *inter*-disciplinarity, tied to alliances, where two distinct disciplines remain "external" to one another but simply aggregate their insights to produce results, and *intra*-disciplinarity, manifested through echoes, where an "internal" bond is created from two otherwise distinct forms of thought so that the insights and structures of each "enter" to influence and shape the structure, processes, and conclusions of the other. This allows me to (1) show that Deleuze's epistemology is rooted in his ontology, (2) describe the various structural conditions of the forms of thinking constitutive of Deleuze's epistemology, (3) determine the ways in which he thinks that the different disciplines are capable of relating with one another, and (4) identify that there appears to be a tension within Deleuze's thinking concerning the relationship between his ontological affirmation of difference and epistemic claims regarding the possibility of inter-/intra-disciplinary work. Rather than resolve this issue, I leave it open to conclude that any attempt to affirm a Deleuzian trans-disciplinary research agenda must contend with the questions of if and how it is possible to reconcile Deleuze's insistence that the disciplines are defined by distinct transcendental conditions that secure their difference in kind with the claim that they are entwined in ways that allow them to inter-/intra-act.

Deleuze on being, multiplicity, and difference

Deleuze's ontology famously starts with the claim that there has only ever been one ontological proposition: being is univocal (Deleuze 1994: 35). Univocity returns us to medieval Scholasticism and, more specifically, the difference between "being as univocal" and "being as equivocal." Equivocity means that being is affirmed in different ways "in" each thing (substances, modes, attributes, and so on) and that these have no common measure (Deleuze 2004a: 162–63). In other words, God, man, and animal are imbued with different senses of being. Univocity, in contrast, means that being has only one sense that is said in the same sense across everything. The univocity of being refers, therefore, to the idea that the being of each thing maintains the same sense of being found in other entities. As Deleuze explains, "the univocity of being signifies that being is voice that it is said, and that it is said in one and the same 'sense' of everything about which it is said. That of which it is said is not at all the same, but being is the same for everything about which it is said" (Deleuze 1990: 179).

While it may be thought that this posits a fixed, singular sense of being that runs throughout, and so unites, all that is expressed through it, Deleuze's particular innovation is to show that, if univocity is thought in terms of difference, univocity does not reduce being to a singular or same point of reference. While being is univocal and so always speaks with the same voice, the voice through which being speaks is difference manifested differently "through" multiple beings. As Deleuze (1994) puts it, "Being, this common designated, in so far as it expresses itself, is said in turn *in a single and same sense* in all the numerically distinct designators and expressors" (35). Being is univocal because these multiple entities are expressions of the singular voice of being. But they are not the "same" because being "is" difference, meaning that the voice spoken throughout the multiple expressions of being is always different.

Contrary to Alain Badiou's (2000: 10, 16, 25) understanding, however, Deleuze's insistence that being is univocal does not mean that being is a closed, singular, undifferentiated, transcendent totality from where all else emanates. Being's different/ciating becoming is thoroughly affirmative and "comes first and foremost from the explosive internal force, which life carries within itself" (Deleuze 2004c: 40). In other words, contrary to accounts that posit a unified, transcendent ground, Deleuze claims that being is an immanent becoming and so does not precede its expressions. There is not a division between being and its manifestations; being, as an immanent univocal, rhizomic-becoming, is nothing other than a process of "self"-different/ciation, which is immanently expressed as different multiplicities. While being is singular, this singularity is not the singularity of identity but "is" pure difference that continually different/ciates with this different/ciation occurring immanently (= from being itself) rather than from an external source. As a consequence, being (as substance) is singular, and so is univocal, but this univocal singularity is difference (= multiple), which is immanently expressed differently (= multiply) and continues to different/ciate.

With this, Deleuze describes a process whereby being becomes in a number of different ways simultaneously without this becoming being contained or constrained within an overarching unity. Deleuze introduces the concept "multiplicity" to describe this, claiming that, rather than emanating from or culminating in a unitary source or being contained within an overarching unity, being as multiplicity becomes through a process of continuous, spontaneous, *open-ended* different/ciation. This requires a brief preliminary note on the distinction between different*i*ation and differen*c*iation. As Deleuze (1994) explains, "We call the determination of the virtual content of an Idea differen*t*iation; we call the actualization of that virtuality into species and distinguished parts differen*c*iation" (207). In other words, differentiation relates to the different but undifferenciated (meaning non-spatiotemporally designated) virtual Ideas, which are transformed into spatiotemporal designation and thus made actual by a process of differenciation. For this reason, difference "resides" in both the virtual and actual aspects of multiplicities with the consequence that Deleuze (1991: 42)[1] claims being is nothing but a different/ciating process and, for this reason, is synonymous with the process of becoming different/ciated. Indeed, we find that "being is difference itself" (Deleuze 1994: 64).

As a consequence, multiplicities are not (1) fixed or closed beings but are constantly becoming or (2) formed by coherent, strict, unitary boundaries that distinguish them from others. While they may appear to be coherent and unified, multiplicities are composed of various lines that constantly branch out in unexpected ways (Deleuze 1995d: 161). If we perceive a boundary, it is not because there is a strict boundary that encloses multiple parts but because the multiple elements that compose the multiplicity have coalesced in such a fashion that the multiplicity appears to form a coherent, closed whole. Rather than identity creating multiplicities, "multiplicity indicates a group of lines or dimensions that cannot be reduced to one another" (Deleuze 2007a: 310). Because multiplicities are "the real element in which things happen" (Deleuze 1995c: 146), Deleuze claims that unity (= identity) does not precede or create multiplicities; "unifications are in fact processes which are produced and appear in multiplicities" (Deleuze 2007b: 315). As the configuration of the multiplicity alters due to being's different/ciation, so too does the subject, totality, and identity that result from that particular multiplicity. Multiplicities are not then closed totalities but are open, flexible amalgamations of different and distinct component parts, which are themselves fluid constellations of parts that constantly become. For this reason, being's different/ciation "cannot be brought back to Some Thing as a unity superior to all things, nor to a Subject as an act that brings about a synthesis of things" (Deleuze 2007c: 389). Being different/ciates itself immanently through an auto-poietic, affirmative act (Deleuze 2004a: 173–74) with the result that its rhizomic-becomings are chaotic, disordered, random, multiple, immanent, and open-ended (Deleuze 2004a: 7–8, 13–14).

Rather than think difference from negation or opposition, Deleuze's attempt to think being's becoming as an immanent different/cial process brings him to claim that difference must be thoroughly affirmative. Only this ensures that being becomes because of its own activity as opposed to an action imposed on it from without. To outline this "concept of difference without negation" (Deleuze 1994: xx) he turns to the question of difference itself; not difference in relation to identity or difference between two multiplicities but "pure difference, the pure concept of difference, not difference mediated within the concept in general, in the genus [or] the species" (Deleuze 1994: 60). Engaging with the concept "difference" leads Deleuze to recognize two fundamental types of difference: differences in kind and differences in degree. Difference in kind refers to the fundamental spatiotemporal difference between two multiplicities.

The second form of difference, termed difference in intensity or degree, entails a form of internal difference, "which constitutes the being 'of' the sensible" (Deleuze 1994: 236). Linking difference in intensity to difference itself means that there are two senses of this form of difference: (1) a primordial, transcendental sense of difference in intensity relating to difference itself, which (2) finds expression, through the differenciation process, in empirical reality in terms of different actual multiplicities. Importantly, given that external difference fails to think difference itself or explain the generation of multiplicities, Deleuze privileges internal difference as the truest form of difference because it entails an affirmative form of difference and, due to its self-different/ciation, explains the process through which actual multiplicities are generated (Deleuze 1994: 28). For this reason, Deleuze not only links internal difference to being or life itself (Deleuze 2004c: 40) but also maintains that it is upon this affirmative, spontaneous act of internal self-different/citation that negation depends. With this, he accounts for why identity arises, undermines its historical privileging by showing that it emanates from difference, and affirms difference in non-oppositional, spontaneous, and self-generating terms.

There is, of course, much more to Deleuze's ontology than univocity, difference, and multiplicity,[2] but what is important for our purposes is that Deleuze maintains that each multiplicity is an expression of being's continuous becoming that is radically different in kind. We will shortly see that this ontological claim lies "behind" his epistemic claim that each form of thinking is a manifestation of being (= difference) and that, as a consequence, philosophical, scientific, and artistic forms of thinking not only have unique purposes but are radically different from one another. To show this, I now turn to focus on Deleuze's epistemology and, in particular, the transcendental conditions that he maintains define philosophical, scientific, and artistic forms of thinking.

The transcendental conditions of philosophical thinking

Traditionally, philosophy has occupied a privileged position in relation to other disciplines. Plato, for example, famously maintains that only philosophy is capable of securing access to the Ideas; Hegel insists that only the philosophical consciousness is capable of truly understanding the truth of spirit,[3] and Heidegger holds that philosophy is superior to art and science because only it is capable of answering its purpose and content within its own parameters. However, with the rise of other disciplines, such as biology, computer science, linguistics, psychoanalysis, logical analysis, and marketing, Deleuze (and Guattari) recognize(s) that philosophy has found itself under attack (2004b: 10). This is because philosophy has focused on universals instead of recognizing that its purpose is to create concepts with the consequence that it has become unclear "what [i]s at stake" (2004b: 10). As such, other disciplines have been able to co-opt philosophy's rightful concern with concept-creation for their own ends: "the most shameful moment came when computer science, marketing, design, and advertising, all the disciplines of communication, seized hold of the word *concept* itself and said: This is our concern, we are the creative ones, we are the *ideas men!* We are the friends of the concept, we put it in our computers" (Deleuze 1994: 10).

Rather than abandon philosophy as a result, Deleuze responds by affirming a unique, non-privileged place for philosophy among alternative disciplines. Outlining philosophy's new place requires a primordial engagement with the exact content of philosophy, one that reaffirms its connection to concept-creation. This leads Deleuze (and Guattari) to question and ultimately reject long-standing understandings that link it to contemplation, reflection, or communication because, in the first instance, those activities are not the special preserve of philosophy meaning that philosophy cannot lay special claim to them. Furthermore, contemplation, reflection, and communication are not foundational but depend on and occur through concepts. This leads to the tentative suggestion that philosophy is the "art" of "forming, inventing, and fabricating concepts" (Deleuze 1994: 2), which is refined shortly thereafter to a more rigorous definition that states that philosophy is the discipline that involves "*creating* concepts" (Deleuze 1994: 5). In turn, this leads to a subtle, but fundamental, alteration in the status and purpose of the philosopher away from his traditional Greek-inspired role as the friend of wisdom, toward his new role as the friend of concepts (Deleuze 1994: 5). This is necessary because the problem with the Greek version of the philosopher is that it (1) assumes a truth to be discerned by philosophy, (2) states that it is only the philosopher who has a unique, privileged relationship to wisdom or the truth, and (3) maintains a specific conception of friendship involving a relationship between an observer (the philosopher) and the truth observed. As such, the philosopher is to represent the singular, eternal, and ready-formed truth (Deleuze 1994: 3–5).

Deleuze opposes this because his differential ontology rejects the transcendence inherent in the notion that there is an already-formed world that the philosopher is in represent. Deleuze's differential ontology claims that multiplicities, in this case philosophical concepts, do not lie there ready-made but are created through an immanent process of different/citation. This will be explained as we proceed, but one consequence of it is that philosophical concepts have to be created with this act of creation being the job of the philosopher. There is, therefore, a constitutive bond between the concepts that define a particular philosophy and the philosopher who created those concepts. Philosophy is always linked to the embodiment of the philosopher who produced that particular philosophy and, as such, is not an abstract system of thought; it is an endeavor produced from concrete reality that always refers to concrete reality by virtue of the concepts and conceptual schema it creates to explain, create, and deal with the problems thrown up by concrete reality. As Miguel de Beistegui (2005) puts it, "thought is irreducibly *of* the sensible, generated by and directed towards it" (85), with the consequence that each philosopher's thought is shaped by and responds to problems he encounters in his life.

Rather than follow Plato in holding that concepts are defined by a unitary, ahistoric truth, Deleuze and Guattari insist that concepts entail a fragmented, open, and changing arrangement of components (Deleuze and Guattari 2004b: 16, 19). The consistency of the concept depends on the content of its components, which are themselves multiplicities, the relationship between the various components, which are mobile, and the problem it is orientated toward (Deleuze and Guattari 2004b: 19–20). Furthermore, because Deleuze claims that thought is always of the sensible, meaning that it emanates from and is always orientated toward the being of the sensible, philosophy's concept-creation is always a consequence of, reaction to, and manifestation of being's immanent "self"-different/ciation.

Thinking of concepts in terms of multiplicities is necessary for Deleuze because it avoids, what he considers to be, the great failing of Platonic thought; that is, the way Platonic thought groups the various conceptions, or representations, of a concept under a fixed, unitary meaning. In contrast, Deleuze maintains that each conceptualization is not unified by a universal true essence but entails a unique configuration of component parts that creates an entirely different concept. Two conceptions of a concept do not entail two representations of the same universal concept but actually entail two different concepts. Different philosophers may, therefore, use the same concept, but, because each thinker conceptualizes it in a specific way and addresses it to specific sociohistorical problems, each use or conception is unique. For this reason, each concept must be engaged with through the responses given to the questions that support it and the configuration of its parts. If the answers given are unsatisfactory or no longer deal with the problem they attend to sufficiently well, new answers must be given. This changes the constellation of the component parts of the concept and results in a new concept.

For example, the concept "the other" may be found in different philosophical systems but conceptualized in fundamentally different ways. This does not mean that the various conceptualizations are united by a true, transcendent, universal meaning of the concept; "the other" gains its meaning through the allocation and combination of different components including responses given to questions of space, time, and notions of the self (Deleuze and Guattari 2004b: 16). More specifically, what the concept "the other" actually entails depends on the answers given to a range of related questions including, but not necessarily limited to: Is the self or other primary in the relation or do they come to be others for each other simultaneously? Does the other gain meaning through this relationship or does it have an a priori meaning? And, at what point does the other become other?

Rather than simply being a collection of random concepts, however, each thinker's thought forms a unified and coherent system of thought because each concept is embedded within a preconceptual background, called the "plane of immanence" (Deleuze and Guattari 2004b: 35). Understanding what exactly the plane of immanence entails is, however, somewhat difficult for the simple reason that its nonconceptuality poses problems for any philosophical discussion of it. For this reason, it has been suggested that the plane of immanence is better thought of as a "quasi" (Beistegui 2005: 84) concept that, far from emanating from thought, is a condition of thought itself.

Indeed, the relationship between philosophy's conceptuality and its dependence on the nonconceptuality of the plane of immanence highlights another Deleuzian issue: philosophy is dependent on and intimately connected to the nonphilosophical (Deleuze and Guattari 2004b: 218). As a consequence, a full treatment of the relationship between philosophical and nonphilosophical thinking in Deleuze has to occur across two lines: (1) a discussion of the nonconceptuality "underpinning" philosophical conceptual thinking, and (2) an analysis of the relationship between philosophical and nonphilosophical forms of thinking. While the nonconceptual plane of immanence can never be captured through the conceptuality of philosophical thinking, the plane of immanence is the nonphilosophical condition of philosophical thinking that philosophical thinking can *point toward*. This allows Deleuze (and Guattari) to outline some of its features.

First, the plane of immanence is not anything other than a becoming. The plane does not precede concepts nor does it lie there fully formed waiting for concepts to populate it. The plane has no content other than the composition and constellation of its concepts (Deleuze and Guattari 2004b: 36), although this does not mean that the plane is synonymous with them. The plane forms the horizon that holds the various concepts of a philosopher's thinking together (Deleuze and Guattari 2004b: 36). Importantly, the becoming of the plane of immanence depends on the shape and formation of the concepts that populate it (Deleuze and Guattari 2004b: 36). For this reason, philosophical creation is a constructivism that occurs on two levels: the creation of concepts and the simultaneous setting up of a plane of immanence (Deleuze and Guattari 2004b: 34–35).

A further crucial feature of the plane of immanence is its nonconceptuality (Deleuze and Guattari 2004b: 34). This aspect of his thinking is heavily indebted to Jean-Paul Sartre's distinction between pre-reflective and reflective consciousness and so a brief divergence into his thought may illuminate Deleuze's position. While Sartre maintains that consciousness is unified, its unity is differentiated into two complementary aspects: pre-reflective self-awareness and reflective self-understanding. While this may appear to form a dualism, in actuality, reflective, thetic consciousness is grounded in pre-reflective, non-thetic consciousness. Rather than entailing a fundamentally different level of consciousness, reflectivity entails a specific *modification* of the pre-reflective consciousness (Sartre 2003: 9). For Sartre, reflective, conceptual thought emanates from, is dependent on, and entails a modification of a pre-reflective, nonconceptual horizon.

Although Deleuze is highly appreciative of Sartre's understanding, he does make some important modifications to it. First, he decenters the reflective/pre-reflective division from consciousness ensuring that the pre-reflective field is pre-personal. And second, he insists that pre-reflectivity does not form a transcendent field of consciousness but entails an immanent becoming "of" being. Deleuze holds that being is a pre-personal, non-transcendent, nonconceptual horizon that becomes rhizomically, insofar as it is immanently manifested in an array of different entities. Conceptual thought is dependent on and entails a modification of this pre-personal, non-transcendent, nonconceptual horizon.

At least, three consequences arise from this: First, there is always an aspect of being that escapes conceptual thought. This excess can never be understood philosophically because, as the preconceptual horizon of thought, it cannot, by definition, be conceptualized in the way necessary to allow philosophical thought to understand it. Philosophy's inability to think the nonconceptuality of being means that its traditional purpose of finding and revealing the truth can only ever be frustrated: philosophy simply does not have the means available to it to think the nonconceptuality upon which its conceptuality depends. As a consequence, it is never able to reveal the truth it has traditionally sought. Rather than seek to abandon philosophy as a result, Deleuze salvages philosophy by reconceptualizing its purpose away from its traditional search for the truth toward a discipline that offers innovative conceptual solutions to problems.

Second, while it might be thought that distinguishing between conceptuality and nonconceptuality sets up a dualism between conceptuality and pre-, or non-, conceptuality, where conceptuality is opposed to and dependent on preconceptuality, this is not so. While different, the conceptual and preconceptual are not simply opposed to one another, nor is one transcendent to the other. Conceptuality entails a *modification* of preconceptuality and for this reason does not establish a duality with, nor does it exist in strict opposition to, the preconceptual. The preconceptual plane of immanence is the "nonthought" within conceptual thought (Deleuze and Guattari 2004b: 59). The important role that the plane of immanence plays in philosophical thinking ensures that, third, there is a deep, intimate, if not always appreciated, relationship between philosophical and nonphilosophical thought.

Defining philosophy as the creation of concepts and insisting that its conceptuality is dependent on a preconceptual horizon leads Deleuze and Guattari to claim that philosophy is intimately connected to and, ultimately, dependent on the *pre-philosophical* (Deleuze and Guattari 2004b: 40). This does not mean that the pre-philosophical, preconceptual horizon exists ready-made prior to the moment that philosophy creates its concepts. The conceptual and preconceptual develop immanently, wherein the conceptual is brought together by and entails a modification of the preconceptual, while the preconceptual only becomes that by virtue of the concepts that populate it. Not only is conceptual thought dependent on the nonconceptual, but the nonphilosophical is "perhaps closer to the heart of philosophy than philosophy itself" (Deleuze and Guattari 2004b: 41). For this reason, philosophy cannot be content with simply being understood "philosophically or conceptually"; it is "addressed essentially to non-philosophers as well" (Deleuze and Guattari 2004b: 41).

Philosophers want their works to find a large non-philosophical audience and non-philosophers listen to philosophers because what philosophy orientates itself toward (being) appears to be what non-philosophy orientates toward, albeit in a non-, or pre-, conceptual manner (Deleuze 1995e: 164). Their common intentionality breaks down, however, because philosophers and non-philosophers approach being through fundamentally different means: the philosopher engages with being through concepts, while—as we will see shortly—non-philosophers engage with it through affectivity in the case of artists or quantifiable functions in the case of scientists. For this reason, (1) philosophy both attracts interest from non-philosophers and simultaneously appears alien to them, and (2) each discipline finds it so difficult to engage with the other disciplines: while they are orientated toward (a manifestation of) being, being is always manifested differently for each mode of cognition, thereby ensuring that each discipline not only discusses a different "thing" but does so through different means.

Besides concepts and the plane of immanence, there is a third aspect to Deleuze and Guattari's conception of philosophy: conceptual personae. These are characters invented to present and bring to life the concepts and worldview created. There are two types of conceptual personae. The first relates to the concrete, individual philosopher that created the concept and plane of immanence upon which the concept exists. While the philosopher's name may not be mentioned in the text, he exists implicitly in the background. His implicit presence accompanies the text and allows the reader and, indeed, the concepts created, to have a consistency. Thus, we get Aristotle's "substance," Descartes's "*cogito*," Leibniz's "monad," Kant's "condition," Schelling's "power," and Bergson's "duration" (Deleuze and Guattari 2004b: 7). The second type describes the creation of characters to speak or discuss the concept and entails a literary technique whereby the concept is presented by a character who is taken to be other than the author. Classic examples of this type of conceptual persona include: Plato's Socrates, Descartes's madman, Kierkegaard's "Knight of Faith," and Nietzsche's Zarathustra (Deleuze and Guattari 2004b: 64).

It is important to note, however, that conceptual personae are not singular. There are many features and aspects to them, which change, both in terms of content and constellation, as a philosopher's thinking changes. For this reason, each persona has "several features that may give rise to other personae, on the same or a different plane: conceptual personae proliferate" (Deleuze and Guattari 2004b: 76). Indeed, conceptual personae may also be intimately linked to antipathetic conceptual personae. Deleuze (and Guattari) are thinking here of the ape or clown that follows Nietzsche's Zarathustra or the sophist that is always connected to Socrates (Deleuze and Guattari 2004b: 76). Furthermore, while two philosophers can appear to use the same conceptual personae, a conceptual persona is unique to each philosopher. Descartes's idiot is not the same as Dostoyevsky's idiot. Each conceptual persona is unique, differing from others in terms of its "internal" structure and the problems toward which it is orientated (Deleuze and Guattari 2004b: 62).

The transcendental conditions of scientific and aesthetic thinking

Philosophy is not, however, the only discipline that creates; science and art also create, albeit in different ways. While philosophy creates concepts, art creates percepts and affects, and science creates functions that explain the world quantifiably. As such, although philosophy is exclusively defined by the right to create concepts and, from this, obtains a function, philosophy does not obtain any privileged status as a consequence, "since there are other ways of thinking and creating, other modes of ideation that, like scientific thought, do not have to pass through concepts" (Deleuze and Guattari 2004b: 8). In line with Deleuze's differential ontology, Deleuze and Guattari hold that philosophy, science, and art cannot be placed in a hierarchy of importance, creativity, or legitimacy. Each attempts to understand being and create different ways of seeing the world and each is as legitimate and necessary as the others.

Starting with science, Deleuze and Guattari claim that, while philosophy creates concepts to offer a conceptual solution to the problems formulated from being's rhizomic different/ciation, science creates functions, which are complex multiplicities composed of elements called functives that explain the nature of being in quantifiable terms. Importantly, functions do not simply exist on their own but derive "all their power from reference, whether this be reference to states of affairs, things, or other propositions" (Deleuze and Guattari 2004b: 138). Given that functions gain their meaning through points of reference, the background horizon to scientific functions is not the same as the background horizon that informs philosophical concepts. While philosophy sets up a plane of immanence, science sets up a plane of reference constituted by fixed, constant points that give it a consistency lacking from the plane of immanence. As such, the plane of reference is not limitless but is structured around constants. These are not created from the plane of reference but are the conditions that define the plane of reference and, by extension, the creation of scientific functions.

To further explain the difference between philosophy and science, Deleuze and Guattari introduce the notion of "chaos," which is defined not by

> disorder [but] by the infinite speed with which every form taking shape in it vanishes. It is a void that is not a nothingness but a virtual, containing all possible particles and drawing out all possible forms, which spring up only to disappear immediately, without consistency or reference, without consequence. (Deleuze and Guattari 2004b: 118)

This is a complex passage that requires unpacking, especially with regard to the notion of the "virtual." To do so, it will be remembered that, for Deleuze, thought is an immanent expression of being, which, as mentioned, is a continuous, rhizomic, different/cial becoming. In *What Is Philosophy?*, Deleuze and Guattari describe being's rhizomic-becoming in terms of chaos (Deleuze and Guattari 2004b: 202) with the consequence that the different modes of thinking always refer to and orientate themselves from this chaos. More specifically, they claim that art, science, and philosophy "cast planes over the chaos" (Deleuze and Guattari 2004b: 202) so as to make sense of "it." In other words, the different modes of thinking respond in different ways to being's different/ciation by exploring it through different horizontal lenses: in philosophy's case, a plane of immanence; in science's case, a plane of reference; and in art's case, a plane of composition. These planes provide the parameters through which each of the modes of thinking creates its particular mode of expression.

Second, and complementing this, Deleuze and Guattari link chaos to the virtual. While a difficult concept, virtuality is central to Deleuze's differential ontology, insofar as being's different/ciation entails a movement from what Deleuze calls virtuality to actuality where the virtual refers to the intensive "possible" traits that give rise to actual extensive multiplicities. For Deleuze, every actuality is composed of a variety of limited traits, habits, and features. These do not, however, exhaust the "being" of the multiplicity because there is always a virtual aspect to each that entails a changing reservoir of "potential"/"possible"[4] traits that are made actual in a particular manner. Each virtual–actual movement is unique and creative and gives rise to a different actuality. As such, philosophy, science, and art are different expressions of being's chaotic virtual becoming.

One of the ways in which these modes of thought differ is in terms of how they relate to being's virtual chaos. Philosophy, for example, wants to retain the virtual's infinite speeds all the while giving the virtual a "consistency specific to it" (Deleuze and Guattari 2004b: 118). It does this by selecting specific "infinite movements of thought" (Deleuze and Guattari 2004b: 118) and creating concepts that give consistency to this infinite movement. By creating open-ended concepts, philosophy is able to give the virtual a degree of consistency, thereby allowing it to think being's virtuality.

In contrast, science approaches chaos "in a completely different, almost opposite way: it relinquishes the infinite, infinite speed, in order to gain a reference able to actualize the virtual" (Deleuze and Guattari 2004b: 118). To do so, it imposes specific points of reference on the infinite speed of the virtual's becoming, thereby slowing it down, and thinks the actual from these points of reference (Deleuze and Guattari 2004b: 205). This is the role that "the speed of light, absolute zero, the quantum of action, the Big Bang: the absolute zero of temperature [at] minus 273.15 degrees Centigrade, the speed of light, 299,796 kilometres per second, where lengths contract to zero and clocks stop," play in scientific thinking (Deleuze and Guattari 2004b: 119). They are the points of reference from which scientific thinking orientates its analyses of actuality. It is only by placing the virtual chaos of being within this "freeze-frame" (Deleuze and Guattari 2004b: 119) that it can be observed, measured, and quantified (Deleuze and Guattari 2004b: 121). This reveals an important distinction between philosophy and science. While both modes of thinking are different manifestations of being's rhizomic-becoming, they approach being's becoming in different ways: philosophical thinking focuses on the virtual aspect of being's becoming, whereas science focuses on the actual aspect (Deleuze and Guattari 2004b: 133).

However, given that science results from and entails a process of observation, it requires an observer who sets up and observes the results in relation to the constants of the plane of reference. They are the ones who set up the experiments, ensure they conform to strict methodological procedures, collate results, and delineate the conclusions from those results. As such, scientific observers are different to philosophy's conceptual personae in that, while the latter are part of the act of philosophical creation, scientific observers do not create the results of their experiments. They create functions and monitor and calibrate the results of the experiments set up to test these functions in accordance with the constants that define the underlying plane of reference.

To summarize, therefore, whereas philosophy creates concepts, sets up a plane of immanence, and invents conceptual personae to provide conceptual solutions to the problems that emanate from constantly changing chaos that is being's continuous self-differentiation, science establishes constants that define a plane of reference that lead to the creation of functions that are tested by experiments, which are observed by observers who collate the data from these experiments to chart the variations of being within the parameters established by its plane of reference. Furthermore, while philosophy's relationship to virtuality means that it must break with its history to think being's pure virtual becoming, science's focus on actuality means that it takes its cue from its history and develops experiments and functions based on the data collected from previous experiments. This is not to say that science always works on the same plane of reference, just that science alters its plane of reference less frequently than philosophy alters its plane of immanence. Scientific becoming is less heterogeneous and radical than the becoming inherent to philosophical creation (Deleuze and Guattari 2004b: 124).

Importantly, however, science and philosophy are not the only forms of thinking. Art is defined not by functions or concepts but by the creation of percepts and affects. While art's relationship to creativity has long been noted, Deleuze and Guattari insist that it entails a specific form of creativity based on the senses (Deleuze and Guattari 2004b: 164). Sensation is not, however, unitary or singular but entails, among others, vibration, withdrawal, embrace, joy, and wonderment (Deleuze and Guattari 2004b: 168). Sensations do not simply arise out of the blue; much like philosophy and science, the percept needs to be created and is created from a background horizon. Whereas philosophical concepts are tied to a plane of immanence, and scientific functions gain meaning through a plane of reference, artistic creation entails the laying out of a plane of composition. This plane of composition forms the background assumptions, style, and content that accompanies the creation of specific percepts and affects. While philosophical creation creates concepts unhindered by constraints and limits, and science entails the creating of functions that map variations in being within the constraints of its plane of reference, art aims to create sensation that opens up possibility. As such, Deleuze and Guattari claim that art thus enjoys a "semblance of transcendence" expressed not in a "thing to be represented" but in the "paradigmatic character of projection" and in the "'symbolic' character of perspective" (Deleuze and Guattari 2004b: 193). Artistic creation aims to inspire thought to transcend actuality.

For this reason, artistic creation has a different relationship to virtuality and actuality than philosophical or scientific thinking. Whereas philosophical thinking is linked to virtuality and science to actuality, Deleuze and Guattari write that artistic creation does not "actualize the virtual event" but "incorporates or embodies it: it gives it a body, a life, a universe" (Deleuze and Guattari 2004b: 177). Artistic creation embodies the virtual to create an actuality imbued with sensation that aims to express possibilities that will allow thought to transcend actuality. As such, artistic creation is not orientated around the virtual (philosophy) or actual (science) but the possible (Deleuze and Guattari 2004b: 177–78) with the consequence that, whereas philosophy aims to continuously and freely create concepts that explore the chaos of being, and science creates functions to chart the variations of being within fixed points of reference, the "peculiarity" of art is to "pass through the finite in order to rediscover, to restore the infinite" (Deleuze and Guattari 2004b: 197). Artistic creation aims to sensually express the infinity of virtual being in finite form.

Importantly, each act of aesthetic creation is "grounded" in a specific plane of composition that differs from artist to artist depending on the sensation to be created and the techniques to be employed (Deleuze and Guattari 2004b: 192). While this is similar to philosophy in that philosophical creation is also highly individualistic, it distinguishes art from the sciences, which are based on a homogeneous method that ensures the replication of experimental results (Deleuze and Guattari 2004b: 167). This allows art to explore new avenues and possibilities and means that its creative endeavors are more heterogeneous than those of the sciences.

Furthermore, Deleuze and Guattari maintain that art does not relate to conceptual personae or observers but to figures, which entail sculptures, landscapes, faces, and visions (Deleuze and Guattari 2004b: 177). While it may be thought that aesthetic figures and philosophical conceptual personae are similar, the configuration of figures in philosophy and art are different as are the roles they play in each discipline (Deleuze and Guattari 2004b: 177). Philosophy's conceptual personae are linked to concepts and occur on a plane of immanence whereas aesthetic figures are linked to sensations that occur on a plane of composition. Additionally, philosophy's conceptual personae are always subordinate to the concepts created; while, in art, there exists a symbiotic relationship between figures and sensations in that it is through the presentation of the figure that the sensation arises (Deleuze and Guattari 2004b: 65, 177).

For Deleuze (and Guattari), therefore, (1) philosophy creates concepts with this creation expressing a plane of immanence, which is limitless, invents conceptual personae, and entails a process of pure differential self-generation; (2) science occurs through functions, which refer to specific planes of reference that delineate the parameters of experiments observed by an observer who charts variations as these exist within and refer to the constants of its plane of reference; and (3) art creates and occurs through sensations that are tied to a plane of composition and figures. The important point to highlight is that, for Deleuze and Guattari, thinking is thought through "concepts, or functions, or sensations" and not one of these thoughts is "better" than another or "more fully, completely, or synthetically 'thought'" (Deleuze and Guattari 2004b: 198). Philosophy, science, and art are equal forms of thought that are, nonetheless, different in kind to each other.

While this secures a unique place for the various forms of thinking, their radical difference in kind appears to lead to another question, one that occupies a central place in Deleuze's later writings: What is the relationship between the disciplines? After all, if philosophy, science, and art are different in kind, there should be no commonality between them. While it might be thought that they are united by their common focus on "being," it must be remembered that what being is for each mode of thought is always unique and particular. For this reason, it seems that each discipline exists in its own realm, applies its own methods, and comes to conclusions that appear to be not only independent from but also incapable of being used by or combined with the insights of the other disciplines. As noted, this explains the bafflement that tends to greet philosophers and nonphilosophers when they read each other's work: what "being" means for each and, indeed, the way they approach and engage with "it" are antithetical to one another.

Thinking the relationship(s) between the disciplines

While Deleuze's insistence that philosophy, science, and art are different in kind is supported by his (1) insistence that being is nothing but pure differential onto-genesis that resists and lacks common unity that would allow the various disciplines to influence or speak to one other, and (2) comments on the difficulty with which philosophers and nonphilosophers have engaging with one another, he does, at times, come to a different conclusion. For example, he notes that, while philosophy and art are distinct forms of thought, concepts are not opposed to percepts and affects; concepts have perceptual and affectual significance (Deleuze 1995c: 137, Deleuze 1995e: 64), thereby ensuring that philosophy and art "often pass into each other in a becoming that sweeps them both up in an intensity which co-ordinates them" (2004b: 66). Similarly, philosophy has a "fundamental need" for the science that is "contemporary with it" because science "constantly intersects with the possibility of concepts," and because concepts always include "allusions to science that are neither examples nor applications, nor even reflections" (2004b: 162).

Furthermore, while Deleuze and Guattari leave it to scientists to determine whether science has need of philosophy, they clearly think that there is a reciprocal relationship between the two (2004b: 162) and show this by distinguishing between two types of scientific statement, one that is exact in nature, quantitative, and mathematical, which can only be alluded to by philosophers and artists through metaphor, and another that is "essentially inexact yet completely rigorous, that scientists can't do without, which belongs equally to scientists, philosophers, and artists" (Deleuze 1995a: 29). In turn, this latter sense points to an intimate relationship between science and art, insofar as scientific functions can have affectual significance. Scientists have, after all, been known to speak of the beauty of an equation or the emotional impact an equation has when truly understood. Deleuze and Guattari clearly believe, therefore, that the disciplines interact with and shape each other. This raises a number of questions, the most important of which include: Can philosophy, science, and art be placed on the same background, horizontal plane to allow them to interact with one another? If they are, does this not collapse them into one another in a way that risks obliterating the need for conceptual distinctions between philosophy, science, and art? Can the modes of thinking, which Deleuze claims are so different, actually talk to one another? And assuming a positive answer to the last question, how do the various disciplines, which entail different kinds of thought, interact with and influence each other?

Deleuze's response to these questions is never fully worked out, but we can tease out some tentative lines of retort from the statements he does make. While his differential ontology appears to affirm the *independence* of different modes of thinking, I will suggest that Deleuze also claims that the relationship between the various forms of thought can also be defined by *alliances* and *echoes*. Support for the former is found in the "Preface" to the English edition of *Difference and Repetition* where Deleuze points toward the possibility that the different disciplines can work together by forming "alliances" (Deleuze 1994: xvi). While a philosophical concept can never be conflated with a scientific function or aesthetic percept, Deleuze nevertheless claims that it finds itself in "affinity" (Deleuze 1994: xvi) with these modes of thinking in particular domains. This ties into the claim, made at the end of *What Is Philosophy?*, that it is possible to have relationships between the disciplines built on external interferences where each discipline "remains on its own plane and utilizes its own elements" (Deleuze and Guattari 2004b: 217). While merely mentioned, it appears that, with this, Deleuze is pointing toward the possibility that the various disciplines not only must interact with one another, but, linked to this, can work together to uncover perspectives on being. The preservation of their difference means that this cannot entail the idea that the disciplines synthesize with one another, but Deleuze recognizes that art, science, and philosophy seem to be "caught up in mobile relations in which each is obliged to respond to the other, but by its own means" (Deleuze 1994: xvi).

While he does not develop this further, my suggestion is that, with the notion of alliance, Deleuze is claiming that the various disciplines can enter into a form of transdisciplinarity where they work independently from one another, utilize their particular forms of thought, and having created in accordance with the transcendental conditions of their respective modes of thinking, look to the creations of the other disciplines to determine if and where it is possible to use their *results*. In other words, having arisen and worked independently from one another to create their individual perspectives on being (in its different manifestations), the various disciplines are nevertheless brought together by virtue of sheer proximity and from this coming together are able to form alliances with the other disciplines to either combine results already created or work together to solve a particular problem. This working together does not, however, mean that the various disciplines impact on each other's methods or content. The various disciplines direct their creativity toward the "same" issue and come up with solutions independently from one another to then combine the results after they have been independently created in accordance with the understanding, purpose, and content of their respective disciplines.

The important point regarding this form of transdisciplinary interaction is that the various disciplines remain independent from one another but come together to pool their conclusions or insights to aid further creation. A relationship based on alliances entails a purely external relationship, insofar as the various disciplines work together despite maintaining their fundamental difference in kind. While allowing the disciplines to speak to one another and so appearing to contradict Deleuze's comments regarding the apparent irreducibility of the three disciplines, this form of relationship continues to maintain the fundamental and irreducible independence of the disciplines.

While transdisciplinarity work based around the notion of alliances starts to break through the absolute irreducible difference that Deleuze's ontology appears to maintain exists between the disciplines, Deleuze points toward another form of relationship between the disciplines that is far more entwined and internally constitutive. In the 1985 essay "Mediators," he claims that, while philosophy, science, and art entail different forms of thinking, there are "echoes and resonances between them" (Deleuze 1995b: 123). While the three disciplines are structured around different ways of perceiving and creating, the content of each echoes—with this resonating—throughout the others. Whereas I have suggested that alliances are tied to external interferences, I would argue that Deleuze and Guattari tie the notion of echo to an "intrinsic" type of interference (Deleuze and Guattari 2004b: 217) where concepts and conceptual personae "seem to leave a plane of immanence that would correspond to them, so as to slip in among the functions and partial observers, or among the sensations and aesthetic figures, on another plane; and similarly in other cases" (Deleuze and Guattari 2004b: 217). For example, they note that partial observers introduce into science "sensibilia that are sometimes close to aesthetic figures on a mixed plane" (Deleuze and Guattari 2004b: 217). Furthermore, while it *may* be possible to identify what and, indeed, when there are slips between the disciplines, Deleuze and Guattari also point to interferences that cannot be "localized" (Deleuze and Guattari 2004b: 217–18) but which, nevertheless, can justifiably be considered to bind the disciplines "internally" because, in its own way, each distinct discipline is "in relation with a negative: even science has a relation with a nonscience that *echoes* its effects" (Deleuze and Guattari 2004b: 217–18, emphasis added). For this reason, "*philosophy needs a nonphilosophy that comprehends it; it needs a nonphilosophical comprehension just as art needs nonart and science needs nonscience*" (Deleuze and Guattari 2004b: 218, emphasis added).

To highlight what he has in mind with the notion of "echoes" and "intrinsic interferences," Deleuze points toward some concrete examples, including the way Riemannian space, which sets up little neighboring portions that can be joined in infinite ways, echoes through cinema in the form of different perspectives on the same scene or different takes on the same plot. This does not mean that cinema is Riemannian, or that the cinematic director is Riemann, but that the spatial coordination of Riemann finds expression in and through cinema. This is not to say that cinema mirrors or copies the example of Riemann but that Riemannian space dissipates imperceptibly through the different forms of thought, each time taking on new, sometimes explicit, sometimes implicit, forms and directions (Deleuze 1995b: 124).

Another example given comes from physics and, in particular, its notion of a baker's transformation, which involves the stretching and folding of a square in on itself. Deleuze maintains that the film *Je t'aime, je t'aime* employs the same technique with regard to time so that the hero is taken back to one moment in his life, which is folded into another to create a disjointed, overlapping, and "very striking conception of time [that] echoes the 'baker's transformation'" (Deleuze 1995b: 124). The conclusion drawn is that "there are remarkable similarities between scientific creators of functions and cinematic creators of images [...] The same goes for philosophical concepts, since there are also concepts of these spaces" (Deleuze 1995b: 124–25). We may also point toward Deleuze's own philosophy, which borrows from or is influenced by botanics, Riemannian mathematics, music, and the baroque, to name but a few of the echoes of other disciplines found in his works. Importantly, however, the relationship between the disciplines is not that of a mirror, nor does the same thought flow linearly between the various disciplines; thought echoes through the various disciplines with the echo being different each time.

Concluding remarks

The notion of echo is important because it points toward an intimate relationship between the three disciplines that overcomes their difference in kind. This is not an external relationship based on alliances but an internal one, wherein the content of the various disciplines infiltrates and shapes the content of the others. This is very different to an alliance where both disciplines remain distinct during their individual processes of gestation to subsequently come together to combine results. Indeed, the difference between a relationship based on an alliance and one based on an echo may best be summarized by Karen Barad's distinction between "inter-action," defined as the idea "that there are separate individual agencies that precede their interaction" (Barad 2007: 33), and "intra-action," which "recognises that distinct agencies do not precede, but rather emerge through, their intra-action" (Barad 2007: 33) with the "distinct" agencies of intra-action only being "distinct in a relational, not an absolute sense; that is, *agencies are only distinct in relation to their mutual entanglement; they don't exist as individual elements*" (Barad 2007: 33, emphasis added).

Alliances are *inter*-active insofar as the disciplines remain distinct from one another and subsequently interact by pooling their conclusions, while a relationship based on echoes is *intra*-active insofar as the disciplines emanate from their mutual entanglement. The way each shapes the other is never singular, or linear, but develops and occurs through the becoming of each, thereby ensuring that the disciplines are "separate melodic lines in constant interplay with one another" (Deleuze 1995b: 125). Importantly, however, the echo is not a thought-out occurrence, nor is it located in any specific point of reference; it reverberates through the disciplines at the pre-reflective level, thereby allowing each to spontaneously shape and impact on the conclusions and mode of thinking of the others (Deleuze 1995b: 125).

We see then that while Deleuze's differential ontology appears to necessarily lead to an epistemology that insists on the independence of each form of thinking, his actual comments on the type(s) of relationship conceivable recognize that it is possible to develop an inter-active relationship based on alliances *and* an intra-active relationship based on echoes that resonate throughout the disciplines to play an onto-genetic role in their individual formation. This does, however, reveal a tension in the relationship between Deleuze's ontology and epistemology, insofar as the former appears to necessitate the conclusion that each mode of thinking is independent and different in kind while, in relation to the latter, the notions of inter- and, especially, intra-active relationships hold that the modes of thought are capable of combining to shape the "internal" structures, processes, and conclusions of the others.

In turn, Deleuze's thinking on the relationship between philosophical and nonphilosophical thought tries to reconcile two contradictory positions. The first details a specific content and unique purpose for philosophy that posits a radical distinction between it and other forms of thinking. The second tries to think philosophy's relationship to nonphilosophical thinking through the inter-/intra-disciplinary connections linking them. There is, unfortunately, no clear explanation as to how these two positions can be or are to be coherently reconciled and so it seems that Deleuze leaves us with an antinomy, wherein we either take a critical perspective that questions the tension identified between his differential ontology and insistence that the various modes of thinking are united by a connection that allows them to inter-/intra-act (Rae 2014b) or, more charitably, we affirm Birgit Kaiser's conclusion that, through his appeal to the notions of "alliance" and especially that of "echo," he challenges us to think whether "something can be different without being separate" (Kaiser 2010: 209). For this reason, the fundamental issue that any attempt to affirm a Deleuzian transdisciplinary research agenda must contend with is that of reconciling Deleuze's insistence that the disciplines are defined by distinct transcendental conditions that secure their difference in kind with the claim that they are entwined in ways that allow them to inter-/intra-act.

Notes

1 While it may be tempting to separate Deleuze's commentaries on others from his "independent" philosophical works, I quote Deleuze's commentary on Bergson here because I want to suggest that his commentaries give insights into his own philosophy. Far from excluding Deleuze's commentaries, I take them to be a crucial part of his philosophical thinking.

2 For a more detailed discussion of the ontological categories of Deleuze's differential ontology, see Rae 2014a: Ch. 6.

3 For a discussion of this, see Rae 2011.

4 I have placed quotation marks around "potential" and "possible" because, strictly speaking, the virtual does not entail a potential to be made actual or a possibility to be made real. The virtual is distinguished from (1) possibility, because it has a reality of its own whereas reality is added to possibility to make it real (see Deleuze 2007c: 392), and (2) potential, because Deleuze claims that potential entails a becoming that occurs within fixed parameters (Deleuze 2004b: 30). The virtual, in contrast, is *pace* possibility, real and, *pace* potential, "an" open-ended rhizomic-becoming.

Bibliography

Alliez, É. (2013), "Ontology of the Diagram and Biopolitics of Philosophy: A Research Programme on Transdisciplinarity," *Deleuze Studies*, 7 (2): 217–30.

Badiou, A. (2000), *Deleuze: The Clamour of Being*, trans. L. Burchill, Minneapolis: University of Minnesota Press.

Barad, K. (2007), *Meeting the Universe Halfway: Quantum Physics and the Entanglement of Matter and Meaning*, Durham: Duke University Press.

Beistegui, M. (2005), "The Vertigo of Immanence: Deleuze's Spinozism," *Research in Phenomenology*, 35: 77–100.

Deleuze, G. (1990), *The Logic of Sense*, trans. M. Lester and C. Stivale, New York: Columbia University Press.

Deleuze, G. (1991), *Bergsonism*, trans. H. Tomlinson and B. Habberjam, New York: Zone Books.

Deleuze, G. (1994), *Difference and Repetition*, trans. P. Patton, New York: Columbia University Press.

Deleuze, G. (1995a), "On *A Thousand Plateaus*," in *Negotiations: 1972–1990*, trans. M. Joughin, 25–34, New York: Columbia University Press.

Deleuze, G. (1995b), "Mediators," in *Negotiations: 1972–1990*, trans. M. Joughin, 121–34, New York: Columbia University Press.

Deleuze, G. (1995c), "On Philosophy," in *Negotiations: 1972–1990*, trans. M. Joughin, 135–55, New York: Columbia University Press.

Deleuze, G. (1995d), "On Leibniz," in *Negotiations: 1972–1990*, trans. M. Joughin, 156–63, New York: Columbia University Press.

Deleuze, G. (1995e), "Letter to Reda Bensmaïa, on Spinoza," in *Negotiations: 1972–1990*, trans. M. Joughin, 164–66, New York: Columbia University Press.

Deleuze, G. (2004a), *Expressionism in Philosophy: Spinoza*, trans. M. Joughin, New York: Zone Books.

Deleuze, G. (2004b), "Bergson, 1859–1941," in *Desert Islands and Other Texts*, trans. M. Taormina, 22–31, New York: Semiotext(e).

Deleuze, G. (2004c), "Bergson's Conception of Difference," in *Desert Islands and Other Texts*, trans. M. Taormina, 32–51, New York: Semiotext(e).

Deleuze, G. (2007a), "Preface to the American Edition of *Dialogues*," in *Two Regimes of Madness: Texts and Interviews, 1975–1995*, trans. A. Hodges and M. Taormina, 309–12, New York: Semiotext(e).

Deleuze, G. (2007b), "Preface to the Italian Edition of *A Thousand Plateaus*," in *Two Regimes of Madness: Texts and Interviews, 1975–1995*, trans. A Hodges and M. Taormina, 313–16, New York: Semiotext(e).

Deleuze, G. (2007c), "Immanence: A Life," in *Two Regimes of Madness: Texts and Interviews, 1975–1995*, trans. A. Hodges and M. Taormina, 388–93, New York: Semiotext(e).

Deleuze, G., and Guattari, F. (2004a), *A Thousand Plateaus*, trans. B. Massumi, London: Continuum.

Deleuze, G., and Guattari, F. (2004b), *What Is Philosophy?*, trans. H. Tomlinson and G. Burchell, New York: Columbia University Press.

Kaiser, B.M. (2010), "Two Floors of Thinking: Deleuze's Aesthetics of Folds," in S. van Tuinen and N. McDonnell (eds), *Deleuze and the Fold: A Critical Reader*, 203–24, Basingstoke and New York: Palgrave Macmillan.

Mader, M.B. (2017), "Philosophical and Scientific Intensity in the Thought of Gilles Deleuze," *Deleuze Studies*, 11 (2): 259–77.

Rae, G. (2011), *Realizing Freedom: Hegel, Sartre, and the Alienation of Human Being*, Basingstoke and New York: Palgrave Macmillan.

Rae, G. (2014a), *Ontology in Heidegger and Deleuze: A Comparative Analysis*, Basingstoke and New York: Palgrave Macmillan.

Rae, G. (2014b), "Traces of Identity in Deleuze's Differential Ontology," *International Journal of Philosophical Studies*, 22 (1): 86–105.

Sartre, J.P. (2003), *Being and Nothingness: An Essay on Phenomenological Ontology*, trans. H. Barnes, Abingdon and New York: Routledge.

Stengers, I. (2005), "Deleuze and Guattari's Last Enigmatic Message," *Angelaki: Journal of the Theoretical Humanities*, 10 (2): 151–67.

Index

A Thousand Plateaus 1, 43–5, 75, 93–4, 96, 111, 116, 121, 127 n.19, 128 n.27, 153, 201–2, 205 n.4, 210 n.61, 210 n.63, 210 n.67, 211 n.73, 214, 218–24, 227, 229, 235 n.27
abduction (Peirce) 55–6
actual, actualization 2, 57, 60, 79, 140–1, 143–4, 151, 154–5, 157 n.29, 164, 167, 195–6, 204, 207 n.32, 216, 234 n.22, 238, 240, 242, 246, 250–2, 259 n.4
    counter-actualization 2, 5, 11, 147, 154, 155 n.2, 205
Adorno, T. W. 91–2, 136, 155 n.5
aesthetic, aesthetics 3, 10–11, 36, 88–9, 107, 115, 128 n.28, 133, 136, 143, 147, 153, 215, 234 n.21, 238, 253, 255–7
    "ethico-aesthetic" paradigm (Guattari) 3, 116
affects, affections 23–4, 26, 30, 91, 93, 100 n.21, 115, 120, 145–9, 154 n.2, 184, 186, 201, 204, 227–8, 230, 234 n.24, 235 n.28, 248–9, 252, 254–5
    Spinoza 25, 30, 148, 194–7, 199–200, 207 n.32, 208 n.39, 209 n.55, 209 n.56
    joy and sadness 195–7, 199–200, 206 n.16, 208 n.39
Alliez, É. 2, 13 n.7, 48, 67 n.2, 69 n.20, 73–4, 76, 98 n.1, 157 n.29, 206 n.27, 209 n.57, 210 n.60, 227–8, 234 n.22, 235 n.27, 238
Alquié, F. 6, 13 n.3, 16, 18–26, 28, 30–1, 31 n.11, 32 n.15, 32 n.26, 138
Althusser, L. 20, 22, 36–7, 128 n.25
analytic philosophy 93, 100 n.23, 207 n.34
anthropology 58, 111, 189–90, 216
Anti-Oedipus 45 n.2, 63, 68 n.11, 69 n.19, 70 n.31, 86, 111, 153, 208 n.35, 211 n.69, 211 n.73
    Anti-Oedipus Papers (Guattari) 63–6, 69 n.19, 69 n.23, 70 n.31, 70 n.32, 70 n.34, 70 n.35, 115

arborescence 111, 127 n.20, 218–20, 222
architectonics 11, 26–7, 48–9, 214–17, 222–3, 225, 228–30
architecture 42
Aristotle 146, 165–7
art, arts 8–10, 12, 13 n.5, 16, 20, 25, 28, 45, 74–7, 84–6, 88, 91–4, 96–8, 98 n.1, 107, 110–14, 118–21, 123–4, 127 n.15, 128 n.23, 132–6, 138–9, 142–4, 147–50, 153–4, 154 n.1, 154 n.2, 155 n.5, 155 n.10, 165, 167, 175, 176 n.3, 179 n.28, 187, 210 n.61, 222–4, 227–8, 230, 232 n.13, 234 n.21, 234 n.24, 242–3, 248–50, 252–6
    abstract 88, 134, 138, 154
    art history 107–10, 114, 118, 124, 127 n.15, 127 n.16, 135, 138–9, 155 n.5
    conceptual 97
    contemporary 97
    fine 139
    pop 142
Artaud, A. 86, 173–4, 207 n.34
assemblage (*agencement*) 36–7, 44, 66, 119, 128 n.27, 151–2, 155 n.2, 157 n.30, 202, 210 n.66. See also subject, subjectivity
    collective assemblages of enunciation 36, 41, 152, 210 n.66

Bachelard, G. 8, 19–20, 36, 73–85, 88, 91–2, 94–7, 98 n.2, 99 n.5, 99 n.7, 99 n.9, 99 n.11, 100 n.18
Bacon, F. (painter) 117, 120, 137, 150
Bacon: The Logic of Sensation 77, 117, 119–20, 155 n.6
Badiou, A. 3, 13 n.5, 240
Bakhtin, M. 147, 151
beauty 141, 166, 172, 222, 255
Beckett, S. 145, 161
becoming 2–3, 10, 65, 114, 121, 133, 135, 137–41, 143, 145–6, 148–50, 152,

154, 156 n.25, 157 n.31, 161, 185, 195, 204, 211 n.83, 228, 240–2, 245–6, 250–2, 254, 258, 259 n.4
being, beings 2–3, 10, 23–6, 68 n.12, 116, 121, 123, 128 n.29, 136, 148, 164–5, 167, 169, 184–5, 187–8, 191–3, 195–6, 198–9, 203–4, 206 n.10, 206 n.11, 207 n.31, 207 n.32, 209 n.54, 220, 238–42, 244–52, 254–6. *See also* ontology
Bergson, H. 18, 21, 26–7, 29, 78–9, 83–4, 93, 99 n.7, 132, 134, 141–3, 163, 177 n.15, 179 n.28, 207 n.32, 248, 259 n.1
biology 85, 222, 232 n.14, 242
    botany 110, 124, 220, 231 n.4, 232 n.14
brain 12, 93–4, 113, 120, 168, 187, 204, 206 n.21, 206 n.23, 211 n.78, 227–8, 233 n.17
Bréhier, É. 18–19, 27–8
Bruno, G. 139, 150, 155 n.11, 155 n.12
bureaucracy 39–41, 115, 140. *See also* technocracy

Cage, J. 8, 86–92, 100 n.19, 100 n.20, 100 n.21, 100 n.22
calculus (mathematics) 84–5
Canguilhem, G. 97, 205 n.4
capitalism 3–5, 44–5, 70 n.35, 202–3
    Integrated World Capitalism (Guattari) 44–5
Capitalism and Schizophrenia 5, 11, 67 n.2, 85, 111, 120, 153, 201
causality, causation 6, 23–4, 27–9, 31, 39, 55, 62, 65, 69 n.16, 151, 161, 182–4, 188–9, 191–9, 208 n.39, 211 n.83
    immanent 182, 184, 189, 191–2, 194–5, 205 n.2, 208 n.39
    quasi-cause 211 n.83
CERFI 38–9, 43–5, 115
chaos 11–12, 93, 113, 128 n.23, 139, 164, 187, 203–4, 206 n.23, 210 n.67, 214, 223–9, 234 n.22, 234 n.23, 234 n.24, 241, 249–52
Chaosmosis 47, 116
cinema 100 n.24, 135, 142–3, 154 n.1, 257
classicism 139–40, 150
Collège de France 17, 19, 21, 26–7, 29

common notions (Spinoza) 24, 194, 196–7, 199–200, 208 n.43, 208 n.48, 209 n.53
communication 5, 45, 98 n.1, 106, 115–16, 119, 125 n.5, 243
concept, conceptual 2–4, 7, 10–11, 15, 22–4, 26, 28, 30, 37–9, 48–50, 53–5, 59, 61, 63, 65, 74–5, 78, 82, 84–6, 93–4, 97, 99 n.14, 109, 112–14, 121–2, 125 n.5, 127 n.21, 128 n.23, 128 n.31, 133–4, 137, 142, 144–51, 153, 160, 163–7, 169, 171, 177 n.5, 182–94, 199–205, 205 n.5, 206 n.14, 207 n.32, 208 n.35, 209 n.53, 209 n.55, 209 n.56, 210 n.61, 211 n.70, 211 n.83, 216–17, 222, 224–30, 231 n.2, 231 n.3, 233 n.19, 234 n.22, 234 n.24, 235 n.26, 237–8, 241, 243–57
    non-conceptual, pre-conceptual 199–202, 210 n.61, 245–7
    scientific 75, 85, 99 n.14, 185, 237
conceptual personae 15, 133, 147–8, 204–5, 211 n.70, 211 n.79, 211 n.80, 211 n.82, 211 n.83, 248, 251, 253, 256
consciousness 13, 18, 30, 51, 55, 107, 169, 176 n.5, 184, 242, 246
    auto-positional 183–4, 187, 190, 192, 194, 205 n.8, 208 n.35
    Freud 59–62, 66, 68 n.15, 70 n.31
    pre-reflective 13, 246, 258
constructs, constructivism 3, 7, 11, 26, 36–7, 39, 44, 48–9, 54, 65–6, 79, 83, 95, 112, 115–19, 121, 123, 134, 139, 146–7, 164, 177 n.12, 183–94, 196–7, 199–200, 202–5, 205 n.5, 206 n.23, 206 n.27, 207 n.34, 207 n.35, 209 n.52, 209 n.57, 220, 222–4, 226–8, 233 n.19, 246
creation 2–3, 5, 7–10, 17, 20–1, 26, 30, 35–7, 41, 44–5, 47–9, 52–3, 55–6, 58–9, 64, 67 n.1, 73–6, 79, 92–6, 112–13, 117, 121–2, 124, 133–5, 138–9, 141, 145, 148, 152–4, 157 n.31, 168, 177 n.8, 186–8, 197, 202–4, 205 n.5, 206 n.23, 217, 222, 225–9, 231 n.2, 231 n.3, 233 n.18, 234 n.24, 238, 241, 243–4, 246–53, 255–7
critique 28, 39, 41, 67 n.2, 68 n.10, 69 n.22, 80, 90, 93, 112, 114, 118, 123, 149,

160, 163, 169–70, 182, 200–1, 205 n.2, 206 n.20, 217
Cultural Studies 118

Derrida, J. 20, 68 n.10, 128 n.25, 154 n.2
Descartes, R. 16, 22–5, 27, 30–1, 32 n.20, 32 n.26, 80–2, 99 n.11, 138, 146, 174, 188, 224, 233 n.17, 248
 anti-Cartesian, non-Cartesian 77–82, 91, 95
 Cogito 81–2, 233 n.16, 235 n.29, 248
desire 37, 39, 41–3, 62–3, 65–6, 67 n.1, 69 n.17, 70 n.29, 88, 100 n.21, 128 n.27, 136, 210 n.66
diagram 7–9, 11, 48, 50–9, 63–7, 67 n.3, 69 n.27, 70 n.31, 115–20, 123, 128 n.27, 128 n.28, 137, 201–5, 206 n.13, 206 n.22, 208 n.35, 210 n.61, 210 n.63. *See also* Peirce, C. S.
difference 2, 9–10, 12–13, 21, 29, 52, 54–6, 58, 60, 64, 85, 89, 93–5, 108, 114, 119–20, 129 n.31, 133–7, 139, 141–2, 145, 149–53, 155 n.10, 156 n.15, 157 n.28, 161–8, 170–5, 178 n.23, 182–4, 188, 192–3, 196, 205 n.2, 209 n.55, 217, 219–20, 222, 224–5, 227–8, 230, 233 n.18, 237–59, 259 n.2
 "different/ciation" 2, 240–50
Difference and Repetition 2, 10, 12, 13 n.4, 25, 75–6, 78, 82, 84–6, 92, 94, 96, 100 n.15, 100 n.18, 111, 118–20, 123, 127 n.18, 127 n.20, 132, 134, 145, 161, 170, 173, 177 n.10, 210 n.60, 233 n.17, 255
disciplines, disciplinarity 1–6, 8–9, 11–13, 13 n.5, 15, 17–20, 22–3, 36, 47–8, 73–4, 76–7, 85, 92–4, 96, 98, 105–16, 118–24, 124 n.1, 125 n.2, 125 n.4, 125 n.5, 125 n.7, 125 n.8, 126 n.9, 126 n.10, 126 n.11, 126 n.12, 126 n.13, 127 n.14, 127 n.16, 127 n.19, 128 n.23, 128 n.30, 160–1, 187, 200, 206 n.23, 208 n.38, 214–19, 222–30, 234 n.21, 234 n.24, 235 n.29, 238–9, 242–3, 247–9, 253–9
 boundaries 36, 76, 97, 106–7, 109, 121, 125 n.7, 126 n.10, 178 n.20, 218, 223, 226, 230, 238

hierarchy 11–12, 112, 214, 216, 225–30, 249
indiscipline 108–9, 113
metadisciplinarity 8, 12, 73–4, 108
redisciplinarization 4, 67 n.2, 93, 205
dogmatism 11, 29, 93, 119, 121, 123, 145, 147, 169, 171, 174
double articulation 50, 63–5, 69 n.21, 69 n.23, 183, 187, 201
Durkheim, É. 16, 18

Earth 174, 183, 203, 211 n.73, 211 n.75, 233 n.16, 233 n.19
ecosophy 7, 36, 45, 111
empiricism 7, 10, 25, 36, 120, 123, 132, 140–1, 145, 162–4, 169–72, 174, 176 n.4, 177 n.6, 177 n.7, 177 n.8, 177 n.14, 177 n.15, 178 n.19, 182–3, 185, 197, 216, 242. *See also* transcendental empiricism
epistemology 6, 12–13, 15, 17–20, 22–3, 30–1, 36, 76, 78–9, 81–2, 96–7, 99 n.5, 99 n.8, 125 n.7, 189–91, 194, 197–8, 209 n.50, 238–9, 242, 258. *See also* knowledge
equivocity 184–5, 191, 205 n.2, 207 n.32
ethics 22, 24, 36, 59, 126 n.10, 150, 154 n.2, 194
events, event 2, 5, 13 n.4, 15, 30, 35, 43, 64, 119, 124, 142, 150, 154, 154 n.2, 155 n.10, 184–8, 193, 195, 201, 204, 206 n.14, 206 n.19, 207 n.35, 209 n.55, 210 n.61, 211 n.83, 220, 222, 224–6, 233 n.16, 233 n.18, 233 n.20, 234 n.22, 234 n.24, 235 n.27, 238, 252
experience 9–11, 23, 26, 30, 40, 49, 51–4, 56–7, 60, 62–3, 65, 78–9, 81, 88, 96–7, 120, 122, 141, 161–5, 168–75, 177 n.11, 177 n.15, 178 n.19, 183–4, 197, 201, 204, 215–16, 227, 233 n.19, 234 n.21
experimentation 1, 3, 6–8, 35–8, 40, 43–4, 49–51, 57–9, 73–7, 80–2, 84–92, 94, 96–8, 100 n.16, 107, 117, 124, 132, 147, 149, 197, 202, 221–2, 251, 253
expression (philosophy) 2, 9–11, 24–5, 120–1, 124, 132–8, 140–2, 144–53, 154 n.1, 156 n.25, 165, 167–8, 182–205, 205 n.4, 206 n.14, 206 n.23,

206 n.27, 209 n.50, 209 n.54, 209
n.57, 210 n.61, 227, 239–40, 242,
250, 252–3
Expressionism in Philosophy: Spinoza
24–5, 30, 188–94, 196, 199, 209 n.52
signs 50–1, 53, 56–9, 61, 63–5, 69 n.21

facticity 75, 81
fantasy 25, 61, 66, 134, 144, 156 n.19, 174, 208 n.35
figure, figuration 9, 63–5, 69 n.22, 117, 119, 134–5, 137–8, 144–5, 150, 156 n.18, 157 n.29, 167, 169, 175, 253, 256–7
Fitzgerald, F. Scott 171, 173, 175
force 10, 57, 79, 107, 109, 113, 116–21, 123, 136–8, 145, 147, 149–50, 154 n.2, 164–5, 170, 172, 175, 178 n.25, 183–8, 203–4, 216, 220–1, 230, 240
Foucault, M. 20, 35–7, 43–4, 78, 97, 106, 116–18, 125 n.2, 125 n.4, 128 n.29, 132–3, 143, 146, 153, 156 n.21, 157 n.28, 176 n.1, 201–2, 210 n.66
foundations, founding 4, 7, 11–12, 17, 24, 36, 38, 41, 48, 54, 69 n.17, 76, 80, 85, 90, 96, 106, 114, 118, 123, 126 n.11, 155 n.12, 170, 192, 200, 214–19, 222–7, 233 n.14, 234 n.25, 243, 257. *See also* ground, grounding
Freud, S. 17, 59–63, 66, 70 n.28, 207 n.34

Genesis 6, 19, 37, 52–3, 56–8, 64, 69 n.21, 116, 119–21, 123, 135, 161, 164, 183, 189, 254
   heterogenesis 134, 146, 151, 153, 161, 226, 233 n.18
genius 25, 141, 156 n.15
Genosko, G. 38, 45, 112, 115
geophilosophy 12, 203–4, 224, 226, 233 n.19
Ginzburg, C. 109–10, 127 n.16
globalization 4–5, 126 n.10, 203, 211 n.69
Goehr, L. 74, 91–2
ground, grounding 1, 15, 20, 78, 83–4, 86, 89, 96, 99 n.5, 105, 109, 111, 118–19, 123, 146, 155 n.10, 167, 171, 177 n.5, 185–6, 188, 193, 202, 220, 226, 240, 246, 253. *See also* foundations, founding

Guattari, F. 3, 5, 7–9, 35–45, 47–9, 63–7, 69 n.19, 69 n.20, 69 n.23, 69 n.25, 70 n.31, 70 n.32, 70 n.34, 70 n.35, 85, 96, 98 n.1, 100 n.15, 100 n.25, 111–12, 114–16, 121, 128 n.25, 205 n.4, 210 n.66
Gueroult, M. 6, 16, 18–19, 21–3, 25–31, 32 n.18, 32 n.24

habit 22, 26, 40, 49, 57–8, 60, 118, 128 n.30, 149, 154, 156 n.14, 183, 187, 197, 199, 204–5, 205 n.3, 206 n.21, 208 n.46, 208 n.48, 211 n.83, 250
Haraway, D. 89–90, 94
Hegel, G. W. F. 16, 127 n.17, 132, 144–5, 163, 242
Heidegger, M. 21, 79, 84, 155 n.10, 207 n.34, 242
Hjelmslev, L. 36, 63–4, 69 n.20, 69 n.21, 70 n.34, 201
human sciences 4, 17, 21, 38. *See also* social sciences
Hume, D. 21, 132, 163, 171, 177 n.8, 177 n.9
   Empiricism and Subjectivity 28, 163
Husserl, E. 95, 206 n.20
Hyppolite, J. 18, 21

idealism 5, 99 n.5, 163, 177 n.7, 182, 201
image of thought 25, 118, 123, 127 n.18, 127 n.20, 145, 185, 208 n.47
   thought without image 119, 123
immanence 7, 10–11, 15, 48, 133–4, 145, 148, 150, 152, 178 n.21, 182–94, 199–205, 206 n.19, 207 n.32, 207 n.34, 208 n.35, 208 n.49, 211 n.70, 211 n.80, 219, 223–4, 233 n.19, 245–53, 256
incorporeality 2, 185, 188, 192, 195, 200–1, 204, 206 n.14, 208 n.35, 209 n.55, 210 n.61
information 55, 88, 93, 230
institution 3, 7, 9, 17–18, 21, 35–6, 38–44, 47, 49, 66–7, 67 n.1, 67 n.3, 70 n.35, 73–4, 89, 96, 106, 109–11, 113–15, 118, 121–2, 124, 125 n.2, 128 n.24, 210 n.66
   Federation of Groups for Institutional Study and Research (FGERI) 43, 115, 128 n.24

institutional analysis 7, 38, 42, 45 n.1, 63-4. *See also* schizoanalysis
intensity 25, 57, 68 n.8, 84, 99 n.14, 110, 117-18, 120, 124, 141, 143, 149-50, 164, 167, 195-6, 203, 211 n.70, 228, 230, 237, 242, 250, 254
interdisciplinarity 1, 3, 5, 36, 38, 73, 105, 107, 109, 112-14, 124, 125 n.9, 126 n.10, 126 n.14, 127 n.16, 128 n.23, 230, 238
    intradisciplinarity 238-9, 259
    multidisciplinarity 1, 77, 108, 110
interference (Deleuze and Guattari) 1, 12-13, 18, 94, 113-14, 255-7
interiority 110, 112, 136
interpretation 16, 19, 22-3, 25, 28-30, 50, 54-8, 79, 84, 86, 95, 134, 136-8, 148, 150, 153, 160, 165

Joyce, J. 84, 167

Kafka, F. 140, 152
Kant, I. 10-12, 18, 24, 26, 51-2, 76, 84-5, 119, 128 n.31, 132, 143, 146, 160, 162-4, 168-70, 173-4, 176 n.4, 176 n.5, 177 n.17, 178 n.18, 178 n.19, 178 n.20, 182, 184, 190, 193, 206 n.10, 214-17, 222, 224-6, 228-30, 231 n.2, 231 n.3, 233 n.17, 234 n.25, 248. *See also* transcendental
    Critique of Judgement 178 n.19, 215
    Critique of Pure Reason 169, 215-17, 226, 231 n.2, 233 n.17
    Sublime 168, 170
knowledge 4-6, 11, 17-19, 23, 36, 38, 42, 55, 75-6, 79-85, 96-7, 99 n.11, 105-6, 108-10, 112, 115, 117, 121-3, 125 n.2, 125 n.6, 125 n.8, 126 n.10, 126 n.11, 126 n.14, 127 n.21, 169, 172, 183, 194-200, 208 n.38, 214-17, 223-4, 229-30, 235 n.29. *See also* epistemology

La Borde 35, 37, 39-40, 42, 115
Lacan, J. 8, 36, 40, 48, 50, 61-7, 68 n.10, 69 n.16, 69 n.18, 69 n.20, 70 n.32, 70 n.34, 70 n.35, 97, 109, 114, 154 n.2
Latour, B. 90, 94, 96, 128 n.25
learning 4, 60, 79, 84, 105, 155 n.10
Lecourt, D. 76, 80, 82-3, 96-7, 99 n.5

Leibniz, G. W. 26-7, 84, 132-3, 142, 160, 166, 200, 248
libido 59-60, 63, 66, 69 n.17
life 4, 6, 27, 35, 57, 73, 83, 89, 121, 135-6, 139, 142, 144-6, 148, 153-4, 161, 166, 171, 175, 183-4, 186-8, 190, 192, 199-201, 204-5, 206 n.19, 206 n.23, 208 n.35, 209 n.55, 211 n.80, 228, 232 n.13, 234 n.22, 240, 242, 244, 248, 252. *See also* vitalism
literature 10, 22, 28, 86, 107, 113, 128 n.29, 134, 137-8, 140, 161-2, 165, 167-8, 170-5, 176 n.2, 176 n.3, 179 n.28
Logic of Sense 40, 100 n.15, 132, 154 n.2, 161-2, 170, 173, 176 n.5, 189-90, 192-3, 207 n.34, 207 n.35, 209 n.54, 210 n.60
Lyotard, J.-F. 68 n.11, 69 n.22, 166

machine, machinic 7, 8, 35, 39, 42, 44, 64-5, 67, 67 n.2, 70 n.35, 85, 133, 142-4, 153, 156 n.18, 184-5, 187, 194, 201, 210 n.63, 231 n.3
    desiring machine 65-6, 70 n.31, 153
    "Machine and Structure" (Guattari) 100 n.15
    machinic transdisciplinarity 45
    war machine 96, 155 n.2
    writing machine 64, 70 n.35
Maimon, S. 84, 119, 128 n.31
Mallarmé, S. 84, 107
Maniglier, P. 4, 13 n.4, 73, 77-9, 82-3, 96, 98 n.2, 99 n.13
mannerism 9-10, 134-45, 148-51, 153-4, 154 n.2, 155 n.5, 157 n.29
Martinet, A. 63, 69 n.21
Marx, Marxism 16, 19-21, 23, 27, 118, 127 n.17, 132
matter, materialism 2, 5-6, 9-10, 12, 23, 31, 37, 55-6, 58, 61, 63-5, 69 n.17, 69 n.21, 82, 97, 99 n.5, 109, 113, 115-19, 123, 136, 138-9, 142, 144-5, 149-50, 155 n.11, 171, 183, 185-6, 195, 206 n.10, 216, 218, 221-4, 226-8, 231 n.2, 231 n.5, 234 n.24, 235 n.27, 235 n.28, 235 n.29
May 1968 5, 43, 111, 211 n.69
Merleau-Ponty, M. 19, 27-8, 163
metamodelization 47-8, 67 n.3, 115
    de-modeling 7-8, 47-8, 66-7, 69 n.27

metaphysics 11, 24, 48, 51, 54, 83, 97, 110–11, 160, 169, 179 n.28, 190–3, 195, 207 n.34, 215–16
Middle Ages 18, 106–7
mimesis 135, 140, 143, 154 n.2, 168, 188
Mitchell, W. J. T. 108–10, 113, 127 n.15
modernism 93, 135, 142
multiplicity 145, 151, 184, 218, 220–3, 232 n.9, 238–44, 249–50
music 8, 10, 74–7, 79, 86–92, 97–8, 161, 257

National Centre for Scientific Research (CNRS) 17, 20
nature, naturalism 90–2, 135, 138–9, 143–4, 168, 176 n.3, 178 n.19, 178 n.20, 184–8, 191, 203–4, 206 n.10, 207 n.32, 209 n.55, 215
neoliberalism 8, 73, 112
Nietzsche, F. 20–1, 79, 84, 94, 113, 132, 154 n.1, 163, 165, 171, 179 n.28, 207 n.34, 248
  Zarathustra 94, 113, 248

object, objectivity 23, 38, 51, 58, 76, 80–1, 84, 90, 196–7, 199
  objectification (Bachelard) 80–2
  Objet petit a (Lacan) 62, 64–5, 67, 68 n.10, 69 n.16
Oedipus complex 61, 66, 136, 146
ontology 2–5, 7, 10–13, 28, 79, 90–1, 114–15, 123, 161–2, 183, 186–7, 189–90, 193–4, 196, 198–9, 205 n.2, 209 n.53, 233 n.14, 237–9, 242–3, 249–50, 255–6, 258–9, 259 n.2. *See also* being, beings
opinion 42, 83, 90, 116, 118, 204, 206 n.23, 208 n.38
organon 216, 218–19, 221–3, 226
original 10, 30, 138–9, 141–3, 147, 149, 151, 154
Osborne, P. 4, 13 n.7, 73, 107, 112, 115, 126 n.13, 127 n.21, 128 n.22, 128 n.25
outside of thought 114, 116, 118, 120

painting 10, 77, 86, 109–10, 113, 117, 119, 124, 127 n.16, 132–3, 136–9, 161. *See also* portraiture
  landscape 132–3, 147, 232 n.13, 253

Peirce, C. S. 7–8, 48–59, 63–4, 67, 68 n.4, 68 n.5, 68 n.7, 68 n.9, 68 n.12, 68 n.13, 69 n.20, 69 n.23, 117. *See also* diagram
  icon 58–9, 63, 65–6, 117
percepts 93, 145, 148, 186, 201, 204, 209 n.55, 209 n.56, 227–8, 230, 234 n.24, 235 n.28, 249, 252, 254–5
phenomenology 16, 19–21, 27–8, 54, 165, 174, 182, 206 n.20
physics 257
Plato 10, 84–5, 133–4, 143, 162, 165–8, 171–3, 176 n.3, 178 n.22, 178 n.23, 178 n.24, 178 n.25, 188, 207 n.34, 242, 244, 248
pleasure and reality principles 60–1
politics, political 3, 5, 7, 9, 11, 13 n.5, 22, 35–6, 38–40, 42–3, 45, 48, 67 n.3, 73, 77, 91, 93, 96, 100 n.15, 100 n.21, 107–8, 114–17, 166, 189–90, 194, 200–5, 206 n.23, 208 n.35, 208 n.38, 209 n.57, 210 n.61, 210 n.67, 211 n.70, 222
polyvocity 66, 70 n.32, 70 n.35, 115, 151
polyphony 147
portraiture 9–10, 51, 132–4, 136, 138, 140–5, 147–50, 152–3, 156 n.17. *See also* painting
positivism 49, 57, 59, 78, 83, 112
  anti-positivism 78
potential, potentiality 41, 44, 57–8, 121, 138, 148–50, 155 n.11, 164, 183, 250, 259 n.4
practice 2–4, 6–9, 11, 35–9, 42, 44, 49, 51, 62, 67, 67 n.1, 74–7, 81, 90–3, 95–7, 98 n.1, 105–6, 108–16, 118–22, 127 n.15, 145, 147–50, 153–4, 157 n.29, 178 n.22, 179 n.28, 185–90, 194, 199–202, 204–5, 218, 223, 225, 228–9, 234 n.24
praxis 37, 40–1, 194
pragmatism 7, 49, 51, 57, 59, 66, 96, 116, 146
problems, problematics 2, 4, 6, 8, 13 n.4, 15, 26–30, 32 n.24, 48–9, 51, 53, 57, 73, 75, 77–80, 82, 84, 95, 97, 98 n.1, 111–12, 122, 125 n.9, 126 n.10, 126 n.12, 134, 136–7, 144–5, 147, 149, 151, 153–4, 156 n.15, 170, 178 n.19, 179 n.28, 190, 192, 244, 247–9, 251, 256

Bachelard 78–80, 82–4
  problematic Idea (Deleuze) 13 n.4, 82, 84
Proust, M. 152, 173–4, 178 n.26
  Proust and Signs 25, 98 n.1, 172
psychiatry 40–1
psychology 6, 15, 17–23, 25–8, 48, 54, 59, 62, 107, 169, 216
psychotherapy, psychoanalysis 5, 7–8, 17, 20, 36, 38–43, 45 n.1, 47–9, 59, 61–4, 66–7, 86, 114–15, 161, 172, 207 n.34, 208 n.35, 210 n.60, 243. *See also* schizoanalysis

real, realism 134, 143, 163, 206 n.10
real, symbolic, imaginary (Lacan) 62, 68 n.14
recognition 76, 82–4, 123, 154, 163, 169, 172
Renaissance 136, 139, 150, 155 n.11
repetition 10, 29, 64–5, 69 n.25, 85, 124, 133–5, 137–43, 145, 151–2, 154 n.2, 157 n.28, 172
representation 2, 55, 61, 65, 68 n.15, 110, 119–20, 128 n.29, 132–3, 138, 141–4, 148, 163, 165, 167–70, 173–5, 182, 184, 191, 193, 199, 208 n.48, 209 n.50, 217–18, 229, 231 n.3, 238, 244
  antirepresentational, nonrepresentational 9, 115–16
research 3–4, 6–8, 17, 35–6, 38–40, 43–5, 73–4, 77–80, 86, 88–9, 92, 97, 98 n.1, 98 n.2, 106–9, 115, 123, 126 n.10, 126 n.12, 127 n.21, 128 n.24, 144, 259
resemblance 117, 123, 128 n.28, 133–4, 137, 142–3, 188
rhizome 5, 12, 44, 75, 111, 120, 127 n.20, 137, 202, 214, 217–24, 228–9, 232 n.7, 232 n.11, 232 n.12, 233 n.20, 240–1, 246, 249–51, 259 n.4
Ruyer, R. 75, 183, 205 n.8

Sartre, J.-P. 13, 20–2, 27, 31 n.7, 41, 176 n.5, 196, 246
Saussure, F. de 7–8, 48, 50–1, 53–4, 62–4, 66, 68 n.10, 69 n.21, 70 n.34
schizoanalysis 37, 47, 64, 115–16. *See also* institutional analysis; schizophrenic process

schizophrenic process 63, 66, 69 n.20, 111, 137, 146. *See also* schizoanalysis
science 5, 8, 12, 13 n.5, 15–16, 18, 20, 30, 35, 39, 47, 49, 57, 75–6, 79–88, 90–8, 99 n.14, 100 n.18, 106, 112, 121, 125 n.2, 126 n.10, 175, 185, 187, 193, 225, 227–8, 230, 231 n.2, 234 n.24, 235 n.27, 237, 242, 248–9, 251–2, 254–5, 257
  applied 88, 95
  functions, functives 15, 37, 93–4, 112–14, 121, 128 n.23, 185, 194, 225, 227–8, 230, 231 n.2, 234 n.22, 248–9, 251–3, 255–7
  laboratory 74–6, 79, 82, 84, 88, 95–7
  scientific mind (Bachelard) 79–83, 85, 96
  modern 81–2, 89, 91–2, 226
  nomad (Deleuze and Guattari) 94–5, 235 n.27
  scientific object (Bachelard) 80–1, 97
  royal (Deleuze and Guattari) 94–5, 235 n.27
Second World War 6, 16, 18
semiology 48, 50–1, 53, 63, 66
semiotics 5, 7, 36, 44, 48–59, 63–5, 67, 75, 107, 115–16, 123, 127 n.15, 183–4, 205 n.4
semiosis 7, 48, 50–1, 53, 55–8, 68 n.7, 139
sensation 9, 81, 94, 97, 113–14, 117, 119–21, 123, 129 n.31, 176 n.3, 186–7, 201, 204, 206 n.21, 217, 228, 252–3, 256
sense 13 n.4, 51–2, 69 n.21, 82–3, 189–93, 198–9, 207 n.34, 207 n.35, 209 n.55, 210 n.60, 239–40, 242, 250, 252
  common sense 83, 161, 163–5, 169–70, 172, 175
  nonsense 41, 61, 69 n.21
sensible, sensibility 120–3, 128 n.28, 164, 167, 172, 175, 188, 242, 244
signs 123, 128 n.29, 133, 139, 173, 194–5, 197, 199, 209 n.56, 218, 237
  asignifying 9, 55, 115–19, 121, 123, 221–2
  overcoded 49, 64, 116, 123
  "power signs" (Guattari) 64–6
signifier 4, 50, 55, 61, 63–6, 68 n.7, 69 n.21, 69 n.22, 70 n.32, 70 n.35

Simondon, G. 75, 84–5, 98 n.3
social sciences 3, 6, 16–17, 39, 97, 107, 111, 123, 127 n.14. *See also* human sciences; sociology
sociology 16–20, 23, 25, 28, 77, 96, 107, 125 n.2, 125 n.4, 125 n.8. *See also* social sciences
Sorbonne (University) 17–19, 21, 27, 163
Spinoza, B. 11, 24–5, 30, 132, 142, 148, 153–4, 156 n.25, 182, 184, 188–200, 205 n.2, 206 n.27, 207 n.29, 207 n.32, 208 n.39, 208 n.40, 208 n.43, 209 n.50, 209 n.54, 209 n.55. *See also* affects, affections; common notions (Spinoza)
   Ethics 30, 148, 188–9, 191–2, 194–5, 197–8, 200, 206 n.27, 207 n.31, 207 n.32, 208 n.39
   god or nature 191
   knowledge 194–9
   more geometrico 148, 194
   parallelism 192–4, 198–9, 209 n.53
Stein, G. 140–2, 145, 152, 155 n.13, 156 n.14, 156 n.16
Stengers, I. 23, 37–8, 76, 93–4, 153, 238
structuralism 4, 7–8, 13 n.4, 13 n.9, 36, 40–1, 47–59, 61–7, 67 n.2, 68 n.7, 68 n.10, 68 n.14, 69 n.16, 69 n.22, 69 n.27, 70 n.35, 84, 96, 99 n.13, 100 n.15, 114–19, 151, 207 n.34, 208 n.35, 210 n.60
style 26, 111, 135–6, 144–9, 151–4, 155 n.5, 156 n.21, 161, 175, 252
subject, subjectivity 2, 23, 35–6, 38, 41–2, 62, 66, 69 n.16, 69 n.17, 79–83, 90–1, 117, 119, 121–2, 136–40, 145–6, 151, 154 n.2, 169–70, 174–5, 176 n.5, 178 n.19, 183, 186–7, 191, 195, 197, 199, 206 n.23, 208 n.38, 208 n.48, 210 n.66, 211 n.70, 227, 235 n.29, 241. *See also* assemblage (*agencement*)
   Peirce 48, 50, 53–8, 68 n.12
   subject group, subjugated group (Guattari) 41
subjectivation 174, 202, 204, 211 n.78
substance 2, 53, 55–6, 68 n.12, 79, 116, 142, 182, 184, 189–94, 196, 198, 205 n.2, 211 n.70, 239–40, 248

technocracy 8, 73, 79, 112. *See also* bureaucracy
technology 5, 8, 26, 45, 82, 88–9, 95, 97, 100 n.20, 143
thing-presentation 59–61, 66. *See also* word-presentation
Tournier, M. 20–1, 27–8, 173
transcendence 3–4, 7, 23, 25, 47, 55, 120, 143, 148, 182, 184, 186, 188, 191, 197, 203–4, 211 n.70, 219, 240, 243, 245–7, 252
transcendental 8–10, 23, 25, 36, 76, 120, 128 n.31, 163–5, 168–9, 174, 176 n.4, 176 n.5, 177 n.7, 177 n.12, 178 n.19, 182–3, 208 n.47, 233 n.17, 239, 242, 256, 259. *See also* Kant
   a priori 12, 18, 120, 133, 162–4, 173, 177 n.6, 215–17, 226, 231 n.2
   conditions 76, 128 n.31, 132, 134, 145, 163–4, 166, 168–9, 173–5, 176 n.5, 177 n.14, 177 n.15, 182, 191, 225, 227, 239, 242, 245, 248–9, 256, 259
transcendental empiricism 10, 120, 123, 132, 162–3, 167–8, 170–5, 176 n.3, 176 n.5, 177 n.7, 178 n.21
transdisciplinarity 1–5, 9, 11–13, 13 n.7, 73–6, 80, 85, 94, 98 n.1, 110–14, 120, 122–4, 126 n.13, 127 n.17, 128 n.22, 128 n.25, 147, 154, 187, 238, 255–6, 259
   diagram 11, 116, 123, 201–3, 205
   experimentation 36, 73–4, 77, 96, 98
   Guattari 6–8, 35–6, 38–40, 42–5, 47–8, 115
   practice 38, 92–3, 97, 98 n.1, 122, 187, 202–3, 205
   technocratic model 4–5, 67 n.2, 73, 108, 112, 126 n.10, 126 n.11, 126 n.12
   transcendental 12, 214, 217, 223, 226, 228–30, 259
   transversality 3, 5, 39–40, 43–4, 67 n.2
transversality 3, 7, 9, 36, 38–45, 47, 49, 67 n.1, 67 n.2, 85, 98 n.1, 113–17, 140, 210 n.66, 224, 233 n.20

unconscious 8, 10, 37–44, 49, 53, 55, 58–63, 65–6, 67 n.1, 68 n.15, 69 n.17, 69 n.22, 70 n.28, 70 n.31, 70 n.35, 115, 209 n.52
   preconscious 59–61, 66, 70 n.31

univocity 183–5, 187–9, 191–3, 198, 207 n.32, 207 n.35, 209 n.53, 209 n.54, 239–40, 242
urbanism 38, 42, 44–5

virtual 2, 45, 47, 79, 91, 145, 150–1, 157 n.29, 223, 225, 227, 233 n.15, 234 n.22, 238, 240, 249–52, 259 n.4
visual culture 107–8, 118, 127 n.15
vitalism 29, 49, 56, 140, 142, 145, 147–8, 152, 183, 186, 196, 199, 205 n.4, 219. *See also* life

What is Philosophy? 1–2, 4–6, 8, 10, 12, 13 n.5, 15, 28, 76, 85–6, 92–8, 111–13, 119–20, 123, 133, 153, 183, 189–90, 192–3, 200, 202, 204, 206 n.13, 207 n.32, 207 n.34, 208 n.35, 208 n.49, 209 n.57, 210 n.60, 210 n.61, 211 n.69, 211 n.73, 214, 223, 225–7, 229–30, 233 n.17, 250, 255
word-presentation 60–3, 66, 69 n.17. *See also* thing-presentation